School Money Trials

School Money Trials

The Legal Pursuit of
Educational Adequacy

Martin R. West
Paul E. Peterson

editors

BROOKINGS INSTITUTION PRESS
Washington, D.C.

Copyright © 2007
THE BROOKINGS INSTITUTION
1775 Massachusetts Avenue, N.W., Washington, D.C. 20036
www.brookings.edu

Library of Congress Cataloging-in-Publication data
School money trials: the legal pursuit of educational adequacy / Martin R. West, Paul E. Peterson, editors.

    p.   cm.
    Includes bibliographical references and index.
    ISBN-13: 978-0-8157-7030-5 (cloth: alk. paper)
    ISBN-10: 0-8157-7030-8 (cloth: alk. paper)
    ISBN-13: 978-0-8157-7031-2 (pbk.: alk. paper)
    ISBN-10: 0-8157-7031-6 (pbk.: alk. paper)
    1. Educational equalization—Law and legislation—United States. 2. Educational accountability—Law and legislation—United States. 3. Discrimination in education—Law and legislation—United States. 4. Education—Finance—Law and legislation—United States—States. 5. Education—United States—Finance. I. West, Martin R. II. Peterson, Paul E. III. Title.

KF4155.S36 2007
344.73'076—dc22   2006037273

9 8 7 6 5 4 3 2 1

Typeset in Adobe Garamond

Composition by R. Lynn Rivenbark
Macon, Georgia

Printed by R. R. Donnelley
Harrisonburg, Virginia

Contents

v

PART FIVE
Reflections

Acknowledgments

A LL BUT ONE of the chapters in this volume were originally presented in October 2005 at a conference entitled "The Adequacy Lawsuit," which was held by the Kennedy School of Government's Program on Education Policy and Governance. The exception, chapter 5, by Matthew Springer and James Guthrie, is based on Guthrie's remarks as a discussant at the event. Partial funding for the conference and this volume was provided by the Lynde and Harry Bradley Foundation, the John M. Olin Foundation, the Rappaport Institute for Greater Boston, and the Taubman Center on State and Local Government. We are grateful for their support.

In addition to the authors and those acknowledged in specific chapters, we would like to thank the following scholars who participated in the conference as presenters, discussants, and panel chairs: Clint Bolick, Rajashri Chakrabarti, John Dinan, David Ellwood, Ron Ferguson, Chester E. Finn Jr., Caroline Hoxby, Molly Hunter, Morton Keller, Al Lindseth, Shep Melnick, Terry Moe, Deirdre Roney, Andrew Rotherham, Peter Schrag, Rocco Testani, John Coons, David Danning, Paul Gazzerro, Ed Glaeser, James Peyser, Michael Rebell, Robert Reich, Paul Reville, Joseph Viteritti, and Kenneth Wong. Their insightful criticism of draft papers helped to make this a stronger work.

Antonio Wendland and Mark Linnen at the Program on Education Policy and Governance provided outstanding logistical and administrative support before, during, and after the conference. We owe special thanks to Elena

Llaudet, whose diligent work on the volume's appendix represents an act of service to the entire scholarly community for years to come.

Tom Loveless at the Brookings Institution offered valuable feedback on the draft manuscript, as did three anonymous reviewers. Eileen Hughes and Elizabeth Forsyth improved the chapters immensely through the editorial process, while Susan Woollen handled the cover design with her usual skillfulness and care. Finally, we are especially grateful to Robert Faherty, director of the Brookings Institution Press, and Christopher Kelaher, acquisitions editor, for their continued commitment to readable and relevant academic books.

1 MARTIN R. WEST
PAUL E. PETERSON

The Adequacy Lawsuit: A Critical Appraisal

Public education has long been a core government function in the United States—"perhaps the most important function," according to Chief Justice Earl Warren's landmark 1954 opinion in *Brown* v. *Board of Education*. Writing for a unanimous Supreme Court, Warren noted that "compulsory school attendance laws and the great expenditures for education both demonstrate our recognition of the importance of education to our democratic society."[1] The depth of the nation's educational commitment is evident also in its state constitutions, forty-nine of which mention the government's responsibility in this area.[2]

Yet it is increasingly clear that the American school system is ill-equipped to meet the challenges of the twenty-first century. Although per-pupil spending, adjusted for inflation, has more than doubled since 1970, high school graduation rates and the test scores of seventeen-year-olds have hardly budged from levels attained years ago.[3] The performance of American students in mathematics and science continues to lag far behind that of their peers abroad.[4] A half-century after *Brown* put an end to legally sanctioned segregation in the schools, gaps in basic skills along lines of ethnicity and income remain scandalously wide.[5]

Policymakers seeking to enhance the school system's flagging productivity have proposed everything from new accountability systems to more parental choice, from data-driven instruction to a return to traditional teaching methods, and from handing schools over to mayoral direction to altering how teachers are paid. While all these reforms have gained widespread attention, their implementation has been haphazard and idiosyncratic. Pressures to generate sustained improvement, especially in troubled urban districts, have only grown.

Meanwhile, almost unnoticed, an alternative reform strategy—the adequacy lawsuit—has made rapid headway within the nation's judicial system (see figure 1-1). Advocates for increased school spending have gone to court in at least thirty-nine states to date. Armed with photographs of rundown school buildings, data revealing large numbers of uncertified teachers, and evidence of abysmal and unequal student performance, teams of lawyers allege that schools lack sufficient funding to provide children with the quality of education guaranteed by the state's constitution. As a remedy, they ask the courts to mandate large increases in state aid for public schools.

Often the proposed dollar amounts are staggering. A March 2006 ruling in New York, for example, ordered the state's elected officials to increase operating aid for schools in New York City alone by between $4.7 billion and $5.63 billion a year (roughly $5,000 per student), in addition to $9.2 billion over five years for capital improvements. If acted on by the governor and legislature, the increment for operations would by itself lift spending by more than one-third over current levels.[6]

Nor is it only in the Democratic "blue" states where courts have been impressed by plaintiff claims. Adequacy lawsuits have been decided in favor of plaintiffs in states as Republican-red as Kansas, Montana, and North Carolina. Meanwhile, the federal No Child Left Behind (NCLB) law, enacted in 2002, has given adequacy advocates new fuel for their claims by requiring states to collect detailed information on student performance. With victories in hand and fresh evidence to bolster the advocates' case, it is no wonder that at the end of 2005 adequacy claims were pending in at least fourteen states (see the appendix).

Is adequacy litigation a promising avenue for education reform? If success in the courtroom were the appropriate metric, the matter would be settled. Adequacy plaintiffs have won victories in twenty-five states, including ten of the fourteen cases decided between 2003 and 2005. Responding to complaints and court rulings in school finance cases has become a consuming concern of governors and legislators, who must balance educational spending against revenue constraints and other fiscal obligations. If court orders to improve educational outcomes could reliably do so, the story to be reported in the pages that follow would be as happy as the stories of the families that Tolstoy excluded from his canon as too dull to be worth the telling.

Figure 1-1. *Number of States Having Faced a Final Judgment on Equity Grounds and Adequacy Grounds, 1971–2005*[a]

Number

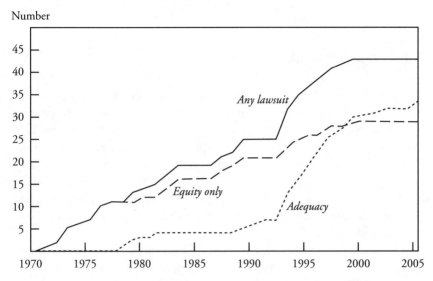

Source: Authors' tabulation of judgments listed in the appendix table.

a. Some decisions coded as adequacy judgments include rulings on equity grounds. Delaware, Hawaii, Mississippi, Nevada, and Utah have not faced a school finance lawsuit. Lawsuits in Indiana and Iowa were withdrawn and settled, respectively.

The path from courtroom to classroom is long and uncertain, however. Legislatures may opt not to comply with mandated spending increases, causing the lawsuits to fail on their own terms. Even when additional money reaches the schoolhouse door, there is no guarantee that it will benefit students, and courts may lack the capacity to ensure that new funds are put to good use. Indeed, it may be that these judgments are an instance of judicial overreaching that will do little to rectify the undeniable inadequacies and inequities in American education. The story, if not quite *Anna Karenina*, may not be so boring after all.

Those helping to tell the tale in this volume, all leading scholars in their fields, shed light on the nature and consequences of the adequacy lawsuit with fresh analyses of its legal, political, fiscal, and educational implications. In this chapter, we summarize their findings and offer our own interpretation of the lessons to be drawn. Adequacy litigation, we ultimately conclude, is unlikely to make educational opportunities more adequate or more equitable, and, by inviting ongoing judicial supervision of school spending, it threatens the separation of powers within state governments. Before reaching that conclusion, however, let's trace the origins of this remarkable development in American education policymaking.

The Origins of Adequacy Litigation

Adequacy lawsuits evolved from a prior legal innovation, the equity lawsuit, in which plaintiffs charged that wealth-related disparities in per-pupil spending among school districts violated students' rights to equal protection under the law. The precise point at which equity arguments morphed into claims rooted in the concept of adequacy is murky, and even the most recent adequacy judgments continue to reflect more than vestigial equity considerations. But the change, if not clear cut, has had significant consequences. A fairly transparent, if debatable, standard gave way to an abstruse concept open to an endless variety of interpretations.

The equity concept was first embraced in *Serrano* v. *Priest*, the celebrated decision handed down by the California Supreme Court in 1971 and reaffirmed in 1976.[7] "[Q]uality is money," members of the plaintiff's legal team had argued, and the court ultimately agreed that the state's school finance system would be constitutional if it were to eliminate wealth-related disparities in per-pupil spending across the state's school districts.[8]

The equity claim advanced in *Serrano* had one distinct advantage: the clarity of the legal principle requiring equal treatment for each school district, regardless of its wealth. To be sure, the principle did not give comprehensive guidance. Should state aid be adjusted for local differences in the cost of living? Should districts receive extra funds for students with special needs? But while these and other issues left ample room for debate and deliberation, the remedy could nonetheless be guided by a readily discernible principle that resonated with the concept of equal opportunity set forth in the nation's founding documents and powerfully reiterated in *Brown*.

Perhaps for this reason, the *Serrano* plaintiffs were victorious in court. Yet the case set off a series of developments within California that proved ominous for the equity movement's long-term prospects. By forcing the reallocation of funds from wealthy districts to districts with a smaller property tax base, the decisions provoked a backlash among many of the public schools' strongest supporters and led some families to seek out places in private schools.[9] Resentment over the legislature's response to *Serrano* also contributed to California's property tax revolt and to the passage of Proposition 13, approved in 1978, which prevents increases in taxes on residential property unless it is sold.[10] In subsequent years, as the burden of school funding shifted from local to state taxpayers, California's per-pupil spending on education fell dramatically, from among the top-ten states in the 1960s to the bottom ten just three decades later.[11]

Nor did the equity claim fare well in federal court, when plaintiffs in San Antonio, Texas, invoked the equal protection clause of the Fourteenth Amendment to the U.S. Constitution to challenge disparities in state per-pupil spending. Although they won at trial, on appeal a divided Supreme Court rejected the plaintiffs' claims, ruling in its 1973 decision in *San Antonio I.S.D.* v. *Rodriguez* that education was not a fundamental right requiring the highest level of judicial scrutiny.[12]

Rebuffed at the federal level, equity advocates redoubled their efforts in the states. If educational equity was not a fundamental federal right, they claimed, it was certainly guaranteed by those state constitutions that explicitly ordered the legislature to provide for the education of the citizenry. Yet many state judges proved hesitant to interpret their own states' equal protection clauses in a way that differed from the Supreme Court's reading of the U.S. Constitution. Others worried about the implications for other policy domains in which spending also varied from one part of the state to another.[13] When by 1990 the dust had more or less settled, courts had rejected plaintiffs' claims in well over half of the equity cases filed (see figure 1-2, panel A).

Even when plaintiffs in state-level equity litigation were successful—New Jersey's 1973 *Robinson* case being the most celebrated example—the implementation of court orders proved to be a political challenge. Remedies typically pitted the interests of high-spending districts against lower-spending ones, and the shifting of resources from one jurisdiction to another inevitably caused consternation among legislators asked to vote against their constituents' particular interests. Many of the equalization policies that legislatures adopted in response to equity judgments led overall spending on education to fall, much as it had in California. Intended to level school spending up, equity-based reforms, as often as not, leveled it down.[14]

Under the weight of these and other unintended consequences, enthusiasm for the equity movement gradually faltered. But advocates for poor districts soon inserted another, more robust arrow into their legal quiver. Rather than simply asking for fiscal equity, they argued that spending on education must be *adequate* to provide all students with an education of the quality guaranteed by their state's constitution. This new demand promised to halt cuts in educational spending, but it did so at a price. Having set aside the simple, readily justifiable standard of fiscal equity, plaintiffs now had to give specificity to educational adequacy, a much more ambiguous concept.

Figure 1-2. *Final Judgments on Equity and Adequacy Cases by Outcome,
1971–2005*[a]

Panel A

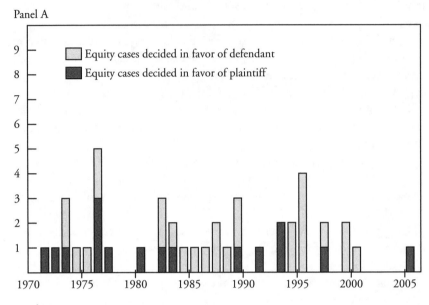

Panel B

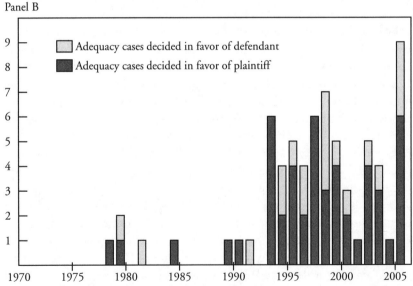

Source: Authors' tabulation of judgments listed in the appendix table.

a. Some decisions coded as adequacy judgments include rulings on equity grounds. Final judgments include all decisions by the state court of last resort and unappealed decisions by lower courts.

To do so, proponents turned to the education clauses in state constitutions. The wording of these provisions varies from one state to the next. Georgia's constitution, for example, says that "an adequate public education for the citizens shall be a primary obligation of the State."[15] Florida's constitution also refers specifically to an "adequate" education.[16] But the most common formulation reads quite differently, calling for the establishment of a school system that is "thorough and efficient"—a phrase found in the constitutions of Maryland, Minnesota, New Jersey, Ohio, Pennsylvania, and West Virginia.[17] Wyoming's constitution has it both ways, requiring the state to provide an education system that is at once "thorough and efficient" and "adequate to the proper instruction of all youth."[18]

Education clauses had figured in equity lawsuits only as evidence that citizens had an enforceable right to equal educational opportunity under state constitutions, even if not (after *Rodriguez*) a federal one. By incorporating adequacy claims into the litigation, plaintiffs infused the clauses with new meaning, arguing that they obligated legislatures to provide all students with an education of a specific quality. As early as 1979, the West Virginia Supreme Court of Appeals defined a "thorough and efficient" education as one that "develops, as best the state of education expertise allows, the minds, bodies and social morality of its charges to prepare them for useful and happy occupations, recreation and citizenship, and does so economically." It then articulated eight content areas ranging from "literacy" and "the ability to add, subtract, multiply, and divide" to "interests in all creative arts" and even "social ethics," deeming them all to be legally enforceable elements of such an education. The West Virginia court, however, allowed the legislature to determine how best to achieve these goals; it did not explicitly mention funding levels.[19]

It was left to a Kentucky case, *Rose v. Council for Better Education*, filed in 1985 and decided in 1989, to become the first case in which the courts mandated fiscal action to achieve an adequate education. When that lawsuit appeared to bear promise—and especially after a favorable decision was reached—plaintiffs incorporated adequacy claims into virtually all subsequent school finance lawsuits. In Kentucky itself, the highest court declared the state's entire public education system unconstitutional and ordered the legislature to provide, along with other reforms, "funding sufficient to provide every child in Kentucky with an adequate education."[20] Since that time, courts throughout the country have based their decisions at least partially on adequacy grounds in the vast majority of cases won by the plaintiffs (see figure 1-2, panel B).[21]

The early success of adequacy complaints reflected plaintiffs' skill in highlighting the deplorable conditions that have long existed in far too many

American schools. Dilapidated buildings, outdoor toilets, and other graphic evidence of substandard conditions, which plaintiffs attributed to a lack of funding rather than managerial incompetence, proved capable of spurring judicial action in states where discussions of equity indexes and property tax burdens had failed to do so.[22]

Adequacy advocates also drew support from a concurrent, if quite separate, reform effort, the national push for educational standards and accountability. The standards-based reform movement was jump-started in 1983 when the U.S. Department of Education issued a report, *A Nation at Risk*, warning the public of a "rising tide of mediocrity" afflicting America's schools.[23] In the wake of this widely publicized document, numerous governors called for schools and students to be held accountable for their academic performance.[24] Several states moved quickly on their own to establish proficiency standards and regular assessments of the performance of their students. In 1994, Congress, at the behest of the Clinton administration, enacted legislation urging other states to do the same. Plaintiffs in adequacy cases soon began citing newly collected data on student proficiency, which routinely revealed student performance to be lagging well below state targets.

When 2000 came and went with few states in full compliance with the 1994 accountability law and student achievement still stagnant, Congress acted again. The No Child Left Behind Act (NCLB), the much stronger accountability law enacted in 2002, requires that virtually all students achieve a state-determined level of proficiency in mathematics and reading by the year 2014. Schools not making sufficient progress toward that goal are to be identified as needing improvement and eventually subjected to a range of sanctions.[25]

At the time that NCLB became law, few realized its potential impact on adequacy lawsuits. But now that states, to receive federal funds, had to insist that schools meet statewide performance targets, plaintiffs were provided with a clearer definition of adequacy—one based on proficiency standards adopted by the legislature itself. Without additional fiscal support, they said, schools cannot provide the services necessary for students to achieve state-determined targets. Attorneys have turned classroom failure into courtroom success.

Exactly how this happened—and with what consequences—is explained in the chapters that follow. They cover five topics: the legal rationale for adequacy lawsuits; the character of the evidence presented before the courts; the impact of adequacy decisions on spending and other state policies; the future of adequacy litigation; and the meaning and significance of this far-reaching legal development.

Part 1: Legal Rationale

On one matter there is no disagreement: there is little in the text of state constitutions to guide courts on the amount of money that it takes to provide an
"adequate education." When courts have ruled in favor of plaintiffs, they seldom have justified their decision with reference to the original meaning of the
phrase as indicated by the convention debates at which state constitutions were
written.[26] Nor do judges ordinarily make even a token effort to unpack the language of the particular clause upon which their decision rests. Adequacy, like
beauty, is in the eye of the beholder, having more to do with each court's particular understanding of educational opportunity than the specific wording of
a state constitution.

For those that believe that judges have a duty to interpret a state constitution according to either the "original intent" of those who wrote it or the "plain
meaning" of the document itself, there is little basis for judicial determinations
requiring legislatures to spend more for education.[27] But for those who see
state constitutions as living documents that acquire new meaning over time,
the original meaning of the clause is merely a point of departure. In the aftermath of *Brown*, contemporary beliefs and values have, for many judges,
endowed the education clauses of state constitutions with a new meaning that
has powerful implications for what states must do.

Court rulings asserting a constitutional right to an adequate education are
not all of one piece. Richard Briffault, who provides in chapter 2 a comprehensive survey of state rulings in school finance cases, says that courts use the
adequacy concept in three distinct ways. Initially, some courts employed the
concept defensively to hold that inequitable school finance systems do not violate state constitutional requirements. Although they conceded the existence of
the right to an adequate education, the equity-based plea for more resources
for lower-spending schools failed. Other courts invoked the concept to compel states to spend more on lower-spending districts, but they interpreted adequacy narrowly, as requiring something less than full fiscal equity.

In recent years, however, these more limited notions of adequacy have given
way to a third, more expansive interpretation. Adequacy judgments now typically require that states increase overall spending, that they spend more on districts with student populations considered more expensive to educate, or that
they do both. In its pathbreaking 1989 ruling in *Rose*, for example, the Kentucky
Supreme Court concluded that school spending statewide was inadequate by
regional and national standards. Similarly, in 1990 the New Jersey Supreme
Court ruled in its second *Abbott* decision that the special disadvantages facing

students in poor, urban districts entitled them to educational programs and services "over and above those found in suburban districts."[28]

It is this third formulation that has given advocates for increased spending the greatest cause for optimism. Adequacy as "equity plus" avoids many of the perceived shortcomings of pure equity remedies, which, in addition to leaving states room to level down spending, ignore the fact that it may cost more to educate students from disadvantaged backgrounds or those with special needs. It also reflects a broader trend in education policymaking toward establishing minimum standards for student outcomes. Indeed, several courts have acknowledged that an adequate education cannot be achieved simply through fiscal measures and have asked legislatures to undertake specific interventions, such as increasing administrative oversight, defining performance standards, and creating accountability systems to ensure that those standards are met. Meanwhile, they have asserted the judiciary's role as the final arbiter of whether legislative efforts are sufficient.

This is a novel concept. As John Eastman shows in chapter 3, most of the early state constitutional provisions with respect to education, adopted in the eighteenth and nineteenth centuries, were hortatory rather than prescriptive, and courts treated them as such. A few states amended their constitutions in the twentieth century to include stronger language, but even these intended only that all students be provided with an education of a quality to be determined by the legislature. Not until the 1970s—an era marked by growing judicial willingness to discover new rights in constitutional texts—did courts begin to interpret these clauses as conferring a judicially enforceable right to an education of a particular quality that required a specific level of fiscal support.

Part 2: Evidence

Connecting educational quality to the amount of money spent on schools has proven to be the greatest challenge for adequacy plaintiffs. Their task has been simplified, to be sure, by the fact that all states have now established test-based accountability systems.[29] But documenting inadequate outcomes is only the first step; they must also demonstrate that the deficiencies can be remedied by additional expenditures.

The enormity of the challenge has given new impetus to what was once an obscure backwater of the academy, the study of school finance. Consulting firms, think tanks, and university-based academics have devised rival schemes to "cost out" the precise amount needed to provide students with an adequate education. Yet a quest for an objective, scientific solution to a legal question cannot succeed if available knowledge and tools are not up to the task. A close look at the analytic methods underlying costing out studies shows that they are hardly a reliable source of information for judges seeking guidance on necessary funding levels.

School finance analysts have relied on four main approaches when advising courts and legislatures on appropriate remedies. "Professional judgment" studies rely primarily on a panel of educators to determine the level of resources needed to ensure high achievement, while the "state-of the-art" model is based on the analysts' own reading of the research literature on the effects of various educational interventions. The "successful schools" approach uses as the governing standard the spending levels at a set of high-performing schools within the state, the assumption being that average expenditure levels in these schools can help indicate what is needed elsewhere. Finally, analysts using "cost function" techniques make extrapolations based on the overall relationship between expenditures and student achievement within the state—a relationship so slight that this method typically provides the most extravagant cost estimates.

In chapter 4, Eric Hanushek, who has testified for the defense in several adequacy cases, argues that each of these methods has been devised to deal with the simple fact that researchers have yet to determine how much spending is needed to bring students up to a given level of proficiency. As a disclaimer included in one such study puts it, "no existing research demonstrates a straightforward relationship between how much is spent to provide education services and performance, whether of student, school, or school district."[30] That being the case, it would seem to be impossible to use data on existing school operations to identify the amount of money needed to produce an adequate education. No approach currently applied—and none, it seems safe to say, that can currently be devised—can provide scientific evidence on how much to spend to get all students to the achievement level that a state wants them to attain.

In chapter 5, Matthew Springer and James Guthrie show how the unreliability of the available methods of costing out has led to the politicization of the legal process. Guthrie has testified as an expert witness for plaintiffs in both equity and adequacy cases. He and Springer argue that the issues raised by the early equity cases involved distributional issues suitable for judicial intervention, amenable to technical measurement, and within the capacity of courts to correct. Contemporary "adequacy" claims, on the other hand, increasingly reflect the agendas of narrow special interests—either the individual plaintiffs in the case at hand or the teacher unions and advocacy organizations allied with them.

Perhaps the greatest deficiency of most costing out studies is the failure to consider that education might be improved not by increasing resources but by improving the efficiency with which they are used. Nowhere is this more apparent than in the case of teacher pay, which, as the largest line item in most school district budgets, typically receives considerable attention in adequacy trials. With new federal mandates requiring all classroom teachers to be highly qualified, shortfalls in the number of teachers holding appropriate credentials have rhetorical weight. To remedy the problem, plaintiffs typically have proposed across-the-board increases in teacher pay.

The rationale for such proposals is scrutinized in chapter 6 by Michael Podgursky. Using data from the Bureau of Labor Statistics to compare the weekly pay and benefits of teachers with those of other professionals, Podgursky finds little evidence that teachers on average are poorly compensated. Nor does he find that teachers in the private sector earn more than their public school counterparts, an indication that average teacher pay is not out of line with market forces. For courts inclined to use the percentage of teachers lacking formal credentials as a measure of pay adequacy, he offers the helpful reminder that the complexity of current certification systems makes a modest percentage of uncertified teachers all but inevitable for most school districts.

With little evidence that teacher pay on average is too low, Podgursky offers a quite different strategy for recruiting and retaining effective teachers. He proposes the deregulation of teacher credentialing so that school principals have more leeway in determining who might be effective. He also calls for flexible salary schedules that reward teachers according to the scarcity of their skills, the difficulty of their assignments, and their effectiveness in the classroom, rather than simply according to credentials and experience. While these proposals are politically controversial, the documented importance of teacher quality for student achievement makes them worth taking seriously, and several states and districts are now considering proposals along these lines.[31] Existing costing out techniques, however, ignore the potential efficiency gains from such reforms and others like them.

Part 3: Impacts

Earlier courts may have been reluctant to charge into the political thicket of school finance in part for fear of revealing their own institutional incapacities. As Alexander Hamilton argued two centuries ago in *Federalist* 78, "the judiciary will always be the least dangerous branch." It has no influence over either the sword or the purse. It may truly be said to have neither force nor will, but merely judgment; and must ultimately depend on the aid of the executive arm even for the efficacy of its judgments.[32]

Indeed, when a court orders other branches of government to act, there is always the risk that they will refuse to do so, forcing the court to beat a retreat. Andrew Jackson, when ordered by Chief Justice John Marshall to protect the Cherokees from Georgia's efforts to expel them from their ancestral lands, is said to have replied: "John Marshall has made his decision, now let him enforce it."[33] Apocryphal or not, the statement conveys an important truth: the horrific forced exodus from Georgia took place nonetheless.

Presidents, governors, and legislatures now tend to show more respect for courts than in Jackson's time, and, as a result, judges are more willing to intrude on their affairs. But the more sophisticated state judges, many of whom must stand for election at regular intervals, can be expected to assess the political winds carefully before ordering the legislature to allocate substantial new sums for the state's schools.

So concludes Frederick Hess in his analysis of the political response to adequacy judgments in four states—Kentucky, Maryland, Ohio, and New Jersey—presented in chapter 7. Indeed, when the Kentucky Supreme Court ruled in *Rose* that the state's school system was inadequate and urged an elaborate set of remedies upon the legislature, it did so only after business leaders, elected officials, and influential educators had agreed on a plan for reform. The court decision was not so much an order as an attempt to provide cover for a set of consensus reforms that the state's political elites already planned to undertake. Likewise, a 1994 Maryland lawsuit filed on behalf of "at-risk" students in Baltimore produced a settlement that gave more state money not only to Baltimore but also to wealthier jurisdictions around the state, probably because only by doing so could a political consensus be realized.

When courts either fail to anticipate or choose to ignore entrenched opposition to increasing spending, the ensuing political fireworks can be impressive. The New Jersey Supreme Court's expansive rulings in *Abbott* v. *Burke* induced Governor James Florio to push through the legislature a measure to increase taxes by $1.3 billion. Florio soon found himself replaced by a fiscally conservative Republican, Christine Todd Whitman. Twenty-five years after the case was first filed and more than fifteen years since the state's high court handed down its first mandate, spending in the property-poor *Abbott* districts now exceeds spending elsewhere in the state. But the case continues to move from the courts to the legislature and back again, with advocates repeatedly challenging the legislature's response as insufficient.

A long-running adequacy case in Ohio, initially filed in 1991, has had no apparent impact on school spending. After the case slowly made its way through the state's courts, in 1997 the Ohio Supreme Court ruled, by a 4-3 vote, that the state's funding system was unconstitutional. But when the legislature continued to flout the court-ordered directive, the court withdrew from direct involvement in the case in 2005 with the Delphic proclamation that "the duty now lies with the General Assembly to remedy an education system . . . found . . . to still be unconstitutional." The court's change of heart took place after the election of several new judges, making transparent the issue's obvious politicization.

Nor do Hess's case studies give any reason to think that the quality of the educational system in these four states was dramatically altered simply because judges ruled in favor of the plaintiffs. The management and governance reforms pursued in the wake of the judgments were all quite modest, and student achievement in Baltimore and in New Jersey's *Abbott* districts continues to be dismal. Even in Kentucky, the lodestar of the adequacy firmament, school spending advocates remain disappointed. In 2005, they filed a new lawsuit alleging that court intervention is again required.

Perhaps no case better illustrates the limitations on the courts' ability to spur prompt legislative action than that of *Campaign for Fiscal Equity* v. *State*. As Joe Williams relates in chapter 8, in June 2003 New York's highest court affirmed the trial court's finding that students in New York City were not being given the "sound basic education" that the court had established as the constitutional standard in its 1982 *Levittown* decision. Ironically, the phrase was originally coined in a decision that denied claims for equal funding. But the court endowed "sound basic education" with new meaning in *Campaign for Fiscal Equity* v. *State* and ordered the state to come up with a fiscal remedy by July 30, 2004. When the state failed to meet the deadline, the trial court appointed a panel of special masters to devise a specific compliance plan for the state to follow. The eye-popping order for billions of additional dollars for New York City schools was the end result.

Although the judgment appears at first to be an overwhelming victory for the plaintiffs, it also illustrates the challenges that they face. The suit was initially filed in 1993, yet by 2006 no state action had yet been taken. In April 2006, the state agreed to increase spending on facilities but appealed the order to increase annual spending on school operations to the state's highest court. It remains to be seen what action, if any, the court will be willing to take in response to the legislature's recalcitrance. Meanwhile, state and local officials argue among themselves about who should foot the bill, an issue that the trial court left to the political process. The special masters and the trial court judge also left it to the legislature to devise any policy measures intended to ensure that the new money going to city schools was put to good use, setting aside the detailed accountability plans that the plaintiffs and the state had each submitted at trial.

Some may argue that the cases that Hess and Williams examined are exceptions, not the rule. But Christopher Berry's quantitative analysis of the effects of school finance judgments in chapter 9 suggests otherwise. Using information from all fifty states, Berry compares fiscal policies in states where courts have ruled school funding systems unconstitutional with policies in states where courts have not. He finds that school finance judgments tend to shift spending from the local property tax to statewide taxes, such as the sales and income tax. But a significant share of the increase in spending from state budgets is offset by spending cuts at the local level, making the aggregate impact of the court order on education spending statistically insignificant. Although many of the judgments included in his analysis were issued in equity cases, which were not explicitly intended to boost aggregate spending, Berry finds no evidence that adequacy and equity judgments differ in their effects.

It is important to note that Berry's results indicate that on average, school finance judgments have led to a 16 percent decrease in the inequality of spending between high- and low-spending districts within a state. And even where cases have not been filed, the threat of litigation may have led legislatures to be more aggressive in addressing fiscal inequities. School finance litigation thus seems to have contributed notably to the steady equalization of district resources that has proceeded in recent decades. Even a relatively small impact on spending inequality would be no small matter—if spending increases translated well into improved student outcomes. Unfortunately, the overall relationship between spending and achievement is notoriously weak, and most studies of the effect of court-induced equalization in specific states have found little or no impact of the new spending on student achievement.[34]

In sum, Berry's findings concerning the impact of past school finance judgments suggest that both the fiscal and the educational significance of adequacy lawsuits have been exaggerated. One can easily understand how this might occur. Plaintiffs are tempted to take pride in and credit for their legal accomplishments. Meanwhile, defendants have just as much reason to dramatize the harsh tax increases that the same remedies entail.

Yet for all the heated rhetoric, there is good reason to expect the fiscal impacts of these decisions to be modest. Complex legal cases usually take years to resolve, and the remedies finally fashioned may be only a distant relative of those initially proposed. Moreover, implementation of the remedy can be delayed so long that dollar amounts lose their original value, overtaken by both inflation and the steady growth in educational spending even in the absence of a court order. In the end, the adequacy lawsuit seems to have accomplished much less to date than advocates had hoped—or defendants had feared.

Part 4: Future Directions

Yet it may be too soon to dismiss adequacy lawsuits as having only limited impact. There have been only a handful of "equity plus" rulings—perhaps too few to reliably gauge their impact. And the movement's momentum has only increased in recent years, sustained by sizable grants from the Rockefeller and Ford foundations, by the heavy involvement of teacher unions and high-profile advocacy organizations, and by heightened attention to achievement disparities—attributable, at least in part, to the ongoing implementation of No Child Left Behind.

As Andrew Rudalevige explains in chapter 10, NCLB gives statutory recognition to the adequacy movement's argument that states have a duty to educate all students to proficiency. Just as important, it seems to offer justiciable standards to determine whether that duty has been fulfilled. There are no doubt tensions in the NCLB-adequacy alliance: many of the law's supporters see test-based accountability primarily as a way to ensure that schools use existing resources more effectively, and many adequacy sympathizers doubt the validity of standardized test results as a measure of educational quality. Even so, Michael Rebell, the lead attorney for the plaintiffs in *Campaign for Fiscal Equity* v. *State* and a professor of law and educational practice at Teachers College, Columbia University, contends that the passage of NCLB was "enormously helpful to us from a litigation point of view."[35]

If the new federal law has influenced the adequacy movement, the reverse is no less true. School officials in a growing number of states now contend that more federal aid is needed if they are to raise student achievement to mandated levels. They argue that the law, in violation of its own wording, places an unfunded mandate on the states. To press the argument, Connecticut filed a federal lawsuit, as did the National Education Association, in collaboration with various school districts. Ironically, in 2005 a task force convened by the National Conference of State Legislatures issued a report that estimated the costs of raising student proficiency levels under NCLB using the same techniques that Hanushek, Guthrie, and even many of the conference's member states have criticized as an unreliable gauge of a state's fiscal obligations.[36]

Indeed, the adequacy argument may ultimately bring about an enhanced federal role in education finance. As a grant in aid of state activity, NCLB does not meet the definition of a federal mandate, so any federal increment is more likely to result from congressional action than from judicial fiat.[37] But in the current era of budgetary constraint, additional funding may be less likely than an outcome that neither plaintiffs nor defendants would openly embrace—the dumbing down of state educational standards simply to avoid an adverse judicial decision.

As Michael Heise points out in chapter 11, there is nothing in NCLB that requires any particular level of proficiency by the students of any state. Even now, definitions of appropriate levels of proficiency vary widely from one state to the next.[38] States that were leaders in the standards movement set the proficiency bar for their students considerably higher than those states that established standards only in the wake of NCLB, and pressures to lower standards are intensifying as more schools are identified as needing improvement.

Yet there also are hints of a new judicial realism emerging that could shift the adequacy movement in a quite different direction. Heise reports that some courts have recently refused to impose large fiscal obligations on state legislatures. In Illinois and Rhode Island, for example, courts have declined to take up school finance claims on the grounds that the matter is a political question or lacks judicially manageable standards. And a few courts that had previously issued rulings declaring a constitutional violation have, in the context of subsequent litigation, declined to pursue the matter further. In 2005 the Ohio Supreme Court, after several failed attempts to win compliance with a mandated spending increase, left the matter to the legislature to resolve. Its counterpart in Alabama stated explicitly in a 2002 decision that "it is the Legislature, not the courts, from which any further redress should be sought."[39]

Perhaps the most telling adequacy case of recent vintage is *Hancock* v. *Commissioner of Education*, which was decided in 2005 by the Supreme Judicial Court in Massachusetts. The trial court in *Hancock* affirmed the plaintiffs' claims that schools needed more money. But when the case reached the state's highest court, a political consensus supporting the trial court's opinion was noticeably absent. On the contrary, the state education department, the Republican governor's office, and the Democratic attorney general's office worked together to fight the lawsuit vigorously. A group of about fifty state legislators filed an *amicus* brief on behalf of the plaintiffs, but the leaders in the state legislature gave the case no apparent support. Perhaps wary of the controversy that could follow an adverse ruling, the justices gave the adequacy movement one of its most stinging defeats to date.

The court's decision in *Hancock* is analyzed in chapter 12 by Robert Costrell, who served as an expert witness for the defense. The decision emphasized the state's steady educational progress, the closing of funding gaps between rich and poor districts, and its comprehensive accountability system—a system that includes high curricular standards, an intervention plan for failing schools, and a rigorous exit exam that all students must pass before graduating from high school. But even these signs of progress, Costrell explains, could not have sustained the court's decision if the justices still insisted on seeing strong educational outcomes in every school district. The larger lesson, perhaps, is that states can head off judicial intervention by adopting Massachusetts-style reforms.

Part 5: Reflections

Many of the Massachusetts reforms had little to do with spending levels, but the adequacy argument need not be limited to fiscal policy. Courts could just as easily interpret a less than "thorough and efficient" educational system as one that needs to make better use of existing funds. The courts, it would seem, could order changes in compensation schemes to recruit and retain effective teachers. Or they could order the creation of a student accountability system that would encourage schools and students to perform at higher levels. The case for such remedies is especially strong, given the fact that there is good reason to believe that, if implemented, they would prove more powerful than the fiscal remedies ordinarily attempted.[40]

Courts could even order, as requested by a New York City parent in an unsuccessful motion to intervene in *Campaign for Fiscal Equity* v. *State*, that students be given the immediate option of attending another school, public or private.[41] The argument for such a remedy appeals to common sense. After all, education reform is a long and arduous process, especially when courts are involved. If past experience is any indication, the students named as plaintiffs in adequacy suits are likely to have completed their scholastic careers before new resources are allocated or accompanying reforms are implemented. In July 2006, Clint Bolick, the chief litigator in the Supreme Court's landmark *Zelman* decision upholding the constitutionality of school vouchers for religious private schools, filed a class action lawsuit in New Jersey asking that children in those public schools where fewer than half of the students are proficient in math and reading be permitted to use the public funds spent on their education to attend public or private schools.[42] Few proposals are as controversial as the provision of school vouchers, however, and courts do not seem likely to order their adoption by a resistant political system.

In chapter 13, Kenneth Starr asks courts considering any remedy, fiscal or otherwise, to recall, with humility, the impact of court decisions on school segregation—an area where the constitutional principle was clear, the harm was obvious, and an appropriate remedy seemed readily apparent. *Brown* had established a principle that proved effective in eliminating de jure segregation in the South, even if reform proceeded at a more "deliberate speed" than re-formers hoped. But when courts tried to legislate the particulars of racial balance within jurisdictional boundaries, they entered into a political morass from which they could not easily extricate themselves without doing harm to their own prestige or to the very principle that they had set forth. As central city schools were desegregated, white families moved to the suburbs. In the end, schools remained almost as segregated at the beginning of the twenty-first century as they had been in 1970.[43]

Courts can enunciate principles to guide policymaking, as did state courts, to a certain extent at least, in the early equity cases that came before them. But they lack the information and institutional capacity to accomplish something as complicated as assessing the best way to achieve an adequate state education system. Effectively executing remedies with the most potential to enhance educational opportunities for all students, including the most disadvantaged, would require a political coalition to support their implementation. Yet the very same coalition would render the judicial mandate unnecessary. In sum, as Joshua Dunn and Martha Derthick point out in this volume's concluding chapter, "If money—and money alone—were all that is required to educate the nation's children and if courts alone could provide the money, then perhaps one would be willing to entertain, if only for a fleeting moment, [a] departure" from the normal constitutional processes to allow government by judicial decree. But after reading the pages that follow, few readers will be any more convinced than Dunn and Derthick that the adequacy lawsuit is a promising avenue for reform.

Notes

1. *Brown* v. *Board of Education*, 347 U.S. 493 (1954).

2. The exception is Mississippi. For one typology of education provisions in state constitutions, see William E. Thro, "To Render Them Safe: The Analysis of State Constitutional Provisions in Public School Finance Reform Litigation," *Virginia Law Review* 75, no. 8 (November 1989): 1639–79.

3. Eric A. Hanushek, "The Failure of Input-Based Schooling Policies," *Economic Journal* 115 (February 2003): F64-F98. Although observers often attribute the growth in school spending since 1970 to expanded special education programs, research indicates that special education spending accounts for only a small share of the overall increase; see Eric A. Hanushek and Steven G. Rivkin, "Understanding the Twentieth-Century Growth in U.S. School Spending," *Journal of Human Resources* 32, no. 1 (Winter 1997): 35–68. For evidence on high school graduation rates, see Jay P. Greene and Greg Forster, "Public High School Graduation and College Readiness Rates in the United States," Manhattan Institute Education Working Paper 3 (New York: Manhattan Institute, September 2003); Christopher B. Swanson, "Who Graduates? Who Doesn't? A Statistical Portrait of Public High School Graduation, Class of 2001" (Washington: Urban Institute, 2004).

4. Alan Ginsburg and others, "Reassessing U.S. International Mathematics Performance: New Findings from the 2003 TIMSS and PISA" (Washington: American Institutes for Research, November 2005).

5. James J. Heckman and Alan B. Krueger, *Inequality in America: What Role for Human Capital Policies?* (MIT Press, 2003).

6. See chapter 8 in this volume, p. 195.

7. *Serrano* v. *Priest*, 5 Cal.3d 584, 487 P2d 1241 (1971); *Serrano* v. *Priest*, 18 Cal.3d 728 (1976). Although the 1971 *Serrano* decision did not rule on the merits of the plaintiffs' claims, by declaring education to be a fundamental constitutional right it provided the legal basis for the superior court's later finding that the state's school finance system was in fact unconstitutional.

8. John E. Coons, William D. Clune, and Stephen D. Sugarman, *Private Wealth and Public Education* (Harvard University Press, 1970), p. 25; *Serrano* v. *Priest*, 18 Cal.3d 728 (1976).

9. The percentage of California students attending private schools rose by about 50 percent as the *Serrano* decisions were implemented. Thomas Downes and David Schoeman, "School Finance Reform and Private School Enrollment: Evidence from California," *Journal of Urban Economics* 43, no. 3 (May 1998): 418–43.

10. William A. Fischel, "Did *Serrano* Cause Proposition 13?" *National Tax Journal* 42, no. 4 (December 1989): 465–74; and William A. Fischel, "How *Serrano* Caused Proposition 13," *Journal of Law and Politics* 12, no. 4 (Fall 1996): 607–36.

11. Jon Sonstelie, Eric Brunner, and Kenneth Ardon, "For Better or for Worse: School Finance Reform in California" (San Francisco: Public Policy Institute of California, February 2000).

12. *San Antonio Independent School District* v. *Rodriguez* 411 U.S. 1 (1973).

13. Molly McUsic, "The Use of Education Clauses in School Reform Litigation," *Harvard Journal of Legislation* 28, no. 2 (1991): 307–41.

14. Caroline M. Hoxby, "All School Finance Equalizations Are Not Created Equal," *Quarterly Journal of Economics* 66, no. 4 (2001): 1189–1232.

15. Georgia Constitution, art. VIII, sec. 1.

16. Florida Constitution, art. IX, sec. 1.

17. Colorado, Idaho, and Montana require "thorough" systems, while Arkansas, Delaware, Illinois, Kentucky, and Texas require "efficient" systems. Thro, "To Render Them Safe."

18. Wyoming Constitution, art. VII, sec. 9.

19. *Pauley* v. *Kelly*, 162 W.Va. 672, 705-06, 255 S.E.2d 859, 875 (1979).

20. *Rose* v. *Council for Better Education*, 790 S.W.2d 186 (Ky. 1989).

21. For an analysis by an early observer of this transition, see William H. Clune, "The Shift from Equity to Adequacy in School Finance," *Educational Policy* 8, no. 4 (1993): 376–94.

22. Michael A. Rebell, "Adequacy Litigations: A New Path to Equity?" in *Bringing Equity Back: Research for a New Era in American Educational Policy,* edited by Janice Petrovich and Amy Stuart Wells (Teachers College Press, 2005), pp. 291–323.

23. National Commission on Excellence in Education, *A Nation at Risk* (U.S. Department of Education, 1983).

24. Diane Ravitch, "A Historic Document," in *Our Schools and Our Future . . . Are We Still at Risk?* edited by Paul E. Peterson (Hoover Institution Press, 2003).

25. Andrew Rudalevige, "No Child Left Behind: Forging a Congressional Compromise," in *No Child Left Behind? The Politics and Practice of School Accountability,* edited by Paul E. Peterson and Martin R. West (Brookings, 2003), pp. 23–54.

26. One exception is the Supreme Court of Ohio, which wrote in its 1997 decision in *DeRolph* v. *State of Ohio* that debates at the state's 1850–51 constitutional convention revealed the delegates' "strong belief that it is the state's obligation, through the General Assembly, to provide for the full education of all children within the state." Quoted in Rebell, "Adequacy Litigations: A New Path to Equity?" in *Bringing Equity Back,* edited by Petrovich and Wells, p. 300.

27. John Dinan, "The Meaning of the Education Clauses in American State Constitutions," paper presented at the annual meeting of the American Political Science Association, Philadelphia, August 31–September 3, 2006.

28. *Abbott* v. *Burke,* 575 A.2d 359 (N.J. 1990), 403.

29. Eric A. Hanushek and Margaret Raymond, "Lessons from State Accountability Systems," in *No Child Left Behind,* edited by Peterson and West, pp. 127–51.

30. See chapter 4 in this volume, p. 77.

31. Steven G. Rivkin, Eric A. Hanushek, and John F. Kain, "Teachers, Schools, and Academic Achievement," *Econometrica* 73, no. 2 (March 2005): 417–58; Jonah E. Rockoff, "The Impact of Individual Teachers on Student Achievement: Evidence from Panel Data," *American Economic Review* 94, no. 2 (2004): 247–52.

32. Clinton Rossiter, ed., *The Federalist Papers* (Mentor, 1961), p. 465.

33. C. Herman Pritchett, *The American Constitution* (McGraw-Hill, 1959), p. 99.

34. Thomas A. Downes, "Evaluating the Impact of School Finance Reform on the Provision of Public Education: The California Case," *National Tax Journal,* 45, no. 4 (December 1992): 405–19; William Duncombe and Jocelyn M. Johnston, "The Impacts of School Finance Reform in Kansas: Equity Is in the Eye of the Beholder"; Ann E. Flanagan and Sheila E. Murray, "A Decade of Reform: The Impact of School Reform in Kentucky"; Julie B. Cullen and Susanna Loeb, "School Finance Reform in Michigan: Evaluating Proposal A"; and Thomas A. Downes, "School Finance Reform and School Quality: Lessons from Vermont," all in *Helping Children Left Behind: State Aid and the Pursuit of Educational Equity,* edited by John Yinger (MIT Press, 2004), pp. 148–93, 195–214, 215–49, 284–314.

35. See chapter 10 in this volume, p. 243.

36. National Conference of State Legislatures, *Task Force on No Child Left Behind: Final Report* (Washington: 2005).

37. It is worth noting, however, that at least one prominent legal scholar has advanced a new constitutional argument rooted in the Fourteenth Amendment's citizenship clause: Goodwin Liu, "Education, Equality, and National Citizenship," *Yale Law Journal* 116, no. 2 (November 2006): 330–411.

38. Jennifer Sloan McCombs and Stephen J. Carroll. "Ultimate Test: Who Is Accountable for Education if Everybody Fails?" *RAND Review* 29, no. 1 (Spring 2005): 10–15.

39. *Ex parte James*, 836 So.2d 813, 815 (Ala. 2002). The decision was unusual in that the court chose of its own volition to reopen the case, which it had previously reaffirmed four times.

40. Hanushek, "The Failure of Input-Based Schooling Policies."

41. David J. Hoff, "N.Y. Parent Seeks Tuition from Judge in Aid Case," *Education Week*, January 25, 2006.

42. Clint Bolick, "Remedial Education," *Wall Street Journal,* July 12, 2006.

43. Charles Clotfelter, *After Brown: The Rise and Retreat of School Desegregation* (Princeton University Press, 2004).

PART I

Rationale

2 RICHARD BRIFFAULT

Adding Adequacy to Equity

T HE LAW OF school finance reform is conventionally described as consisting of three "waves," each associated with a distinctive legal theory.[1] In the first wave, which began in the late 1960s, plaintiffs relied on the equal protection clause of the U.S. Constitution to challenge the disparities in per-pupil expenditures among school districts within a state attributable to the state's reliance on the local property tax to fund elementary and secondary education. That wave ebbed abruptly in 1973 when, in *San Antonio Independent School District* v. *Rodriguez,* the U.S. Supreme Court rejected the equal protection theory.[2] It was, however, immediately followed by a second wave, in which plaintiffs continued to focus on the interdistrict spending inequities resulting from the property tax–based system of school funding but grounded their legal attack on the equal protection provisions of state constitutions. Plaintiffs won a number of notable state cases based on those provisions in the 1970s and 1980s. By the mid-1980s, however, that wave, too, receded, as more state courts rebuffed equal protection challenges.

The third wave arose in 1989 with decisions by the state supreme courts of Kentucky, Montana, and Texas that assertedly shifted the basis of litigation and adjudication from state equal protection clauses to state constitutional provisions directing state governments to provide public elementary and secondary education. Accordingly, the constitutional case for reform shifted from the theory of equity to the theory of adequacy. Under the adequacy theory, the constitutional violation is not that school districts depend on drastically unequal property tax bases or that per-pupil expenditures vary across districts largely according to local wealth, but that the state government has failed to ensure that all public school children in the state receive an adequate education. Concomitantly, the appropriate remedy shifts from equalizing tax bases or per-pupil spending to ensuring that an adequate education is provided to all school children. The shift from equity to adequacy has been credited with the greater success that school finance reform plaintiffs have enjoyed in the last fifteen years.

The Limits of the Wave Theory of School Finance Reform

The wave metaphor—and especially the differences between the second and third waves—has been sharply overstated, temporally, textually, in terms of litigation success, and as a matter of legal theory. Temporally, some pre-1989 cases also addressed the financing question in terms of adequacy and, more broadly, raised the question of whether state governments were doing enough to discharge their state constitutional education mandates. Indeed, in the late 1970s and early 1980s, courts in Washington and West Virginia awarded victories to plaintiffs on what could be called adequacy grounds.[3] By the same token, even after 1989 school finance litigants continued to bring equity cases, and during the 1990s courts in several states—including Tennessee, Wyoming, Vermont, and New Hampshire—awarded victories to litigants on what are best recognized as equity grounds.[4] Indeed, even in the *annus mirabilis* of 1989, at least two plaintiffs' victories—in Montana and Texas—were at least as much about equity as adequacy.[5]

Textually, many of the pre-1989 equity decisions relied to a significant degree on the articles in state constitutions dealing with education. The presence of constitutional provisions requiring state legislatures to create and maintain public school systems enabled some state supreme courts to find that education is a fundamental interest for state equal protection purposes, thus leading to the application of strict judicial scrutiny to interdistrict funding disparities. Indeed, that is precisely what occurred in the decision that ushered in the "second wave," *Robinson* v. *Cahill*.[6] Handed down by the New Jersey Supreme Court just days after the U.S. Supreme Court's *Rodriguez* decision, *Robinson* was textually grounded in the New Jersey constitution's "thorough and efficient" education clause but embraced an equity theory.[7]

Conversely, many recent adequacy cases rely on education provisions in state constitutions that explicitly incorporate equity concerns. Very few state constitutions explicitly use the term "adequate" education[8]—and the supreme courts of two of those states (Georgia and Florida) rejected school finance reform claims predicated on the adequacy theory.[9] Typically, the state constitutional text creating the duty to provide public schools refers to a "thorough and efficient" or "general and uniform" educational system. A number of courts that have focused on the education articles of state constitutions have found an egalitarian principle, rather than or in addition to the principle of adequacy, implicit in the "thorough" or "uniform" requirements.[10] Indeed, some constitutional texts appear to fuse the adequacy and equity concepts, as in the Montana provision that announces "It is the goal of the people to establish a system of education which will develop the full educational potential of each person. Equality of educational opportunity is guaranteed to each person of the state."[11]

With respect to litigation success, although the emergence of the adequacy theory was accompanied by a number of significant plaintiff victories, adequacy has by no means been a panacea for school finance reform. Since 1989, state supreme courts have rejected adequacy challenges to school finance systems in Florida, Illinois, Minnesota, North Dakota, Oregon, Pennsylvania, Rhode Island, Virginia, and Wisconsin.[12] Even when inadequacy has been found, courts have been uncertain of just how far they can push their state legislatures to adopt a remedy, as indicated by recent decisions by the Alabama and Ohio supreme courts terminating judicial proceedings and leaving the matter of remedies entirely to the legislature.[13]

The Blurring of Adequacy and Equity

What is more important for understanding the relationship between adequacy and equity in legal theory is that courts have repeatedly recognized the interconnectedness of the adequacy and equality concepts, even as they have struggled to separate the two.[14] In many cases, judicial analysis of adequacy is heavily suffused with equity concerns. A judicial determination of educational inadequacy in a particular school district is almost always predicated on some finding of inequity. Typically, the court compares the quality of the education provided in the plaintiff district with that provided in other, usually more affluent, districts. Quality may be measured in terms of inputs like class size, teacher qualifications, curricular scope, physical plant, or textbooks and other educational materials or in terms of educational outputs such as performance on standardized tests, graduation and dropout rates, and need for remedial education.[15] Significant inequalities are treated as powerful evidence of inadequacy.

Moreover, some adequacy courts have also been concerned about the gap between low and high spenders, even though a basic theoretical distinction between adequacy and equity is that while equity might insist on eliminating interdistrict differences, adequacy permits some districts to spend above an adequate level. The Montana Supreme Court, for example, assumed that "the wealthier school districts are not funding frills or unnecessary education expenses."[16] Other courts have noted that when a significant number of districts spend above the adequacy level, the resulting inequality can lead to a redefinition of what is needed to achieve adequacy as "today's supplementation tomorrow become[s] necessary to satisfy the constitutional mandate" of what is needed to provide an adequate education.[17]

Not only is proof of inadequacy sometimes grounded on evidence of inequality, but the judicial definition of adequacy may also incorporate equality concerns. Several state supreme courts have emphasized that a central purpose of the state constitution's education mandate is to enable children to compete successfully after graduation.[18] Competitiveness looms large in the most widely noted judicial definition of an adequate education—the seven capacities identified by the Kentucky Supreme Court in *Rose* v. *Council for Better Education*.[19] Specifically, the court required that in order to satisfy the state constitution, the state legislature must create an education system that gives every child "sufficient levels of academic or vocational skills to enable public school students to *compete favorably* with their counterparts in surrounding states, in academics, or in the job market [emphasis added]."[20] The New Jersey Supreme Court in the *Abbott* litigation repeatedly emphasized that an adequate education must enable disadvantaged children to compete against children who hail from affluent suburban districts.[21] Adequacy defined in terms of competitiveness necessarily has a comparative and egalitarian component. In order to vie with their future competitors in higher education or the labor market, students in plaintiff districts will need an education that is at least as good as that their competitors receive. In other words, when an adequate education is a competitive one, it must also be (at least) an equal one.

Because courts frequently blur adequacy and equity concerns, it may be difficult to determine whether a case is premised on equity or adequacy theory, let alone what either equity or adequacy means. This blurring of the two concepts can occur as a court's analysis unfolds over a succession of cases, and it can be seen even as a court grapples with the school finance problem in a single case.

A nice example of how a court's school finance theory can morph over time is the New Hampshire Supreme Court's decisions in the *Claremont* litigation. In *Claremont I*, decided in 1993, the New Hampshire court determined that the state constitution's education clause—which makes it "the duty of the legislators and magistrates . . . to cherish the interest of literature and the sciences, and all seminaries and public schools"—provided a constitutional basis for an attack by five property-poor districts on the state's local property tax–based school finance system. The court determined that the constitution imposed on the state a duty "to provide a constitutionally adequate education to every educable child . . . and to guarantee adequate funding."[22] However, the court gestured toward an egalitarian theory of what adequacy requires when it indicated that an adequate education is one that prepares "citizens for their role as participants and as potential competitors" in the marketplace.[23]

When *Claremont* returned to the court four years later—following a remand to the lower court, a lower court trial, and an appeal—the court shifted gears and determined that the state education system was unconstitutional because it violated the state constitutional requirement that taxes be "proportional and reasonable."[24] Because different local districts taxed at different rates, reflecting, in significant part, disparate local property tax bases, the school finance system violated the constitutional tax uniformity requirement—a kind of equality theory, albeit one that emphasized the equal treatment of taxpayers, not of students. The next three New Hampshire Supreme Court school finance decisions over the next three years all dealt with the tax uniformity provision and considered whether various state legislative reforms of the school tax system satisfied its requirements.[25] To be sure, the taxpayer equity decisions were linked to the education clause and the adequacy requirement. Because the state constitution's education clause makes an adequate education a state responsibility, the court ruled that the property tax for education must be treated as a state tax and thus must be uniform statewide rather than merely within a district.[26] Moreover, the court reiterated the need for the state to fund education at a level sufficient to achieve adequacy. Even in discussing funding rather than taxing, the court combined the adequacy and equity concepts, reiterating its earlier concern that an adequate education be one that enables students to compete[27] and that "comparable funding must be assured in order that every school district will have the funds necessary to provide such education."[28] Finally, in 2002, the *Claremont* court added a new concept to the mix when it held that the state's "duty to provide a constitutionally adequate education includes accountability," that is, measures designed to ensure that even adequately funded local districts actually provide an adequate education.[29] Thus, over the course of a decade of doctrinal shape-shifting, the court fused notions of adequacy, taxpayer equity, spending equity, and accountability in its evolving approach to public education.[30]

A striking instance of the simultaneous separation and blurring of adequacy and equity concerns in a single case is the 1994 decision of the Arizona

Supreme Court in *Roosevelt Elementary School District. No. 66* v. *Bishop.*[31] That case challenged the state's reliance on local school taxes to fund capital facilities, although the court expanded its analysis to include the entire educational financing scheme.[32] The court focused its analysis on the state's education article—which contains a "general and uniform" clause—at least in part to avoid reopening an earlier, second-wave decision in which it rejected a state equal protection challenge to the school financing system.[33] The court repeatedly sought to separate the concepts of adequacy and equity, noting that they present separate issues, and yet it repeatedly combined the two.[34] Thus, the court observed that the state constitution did not require all school districts to offer a program that was "exactly the same, identical, or equal. Funding mechanisms that provide sufficient funds to educate children on substantially equal terms tend to satisfy the general and uniform requirement."[35] It went on to find that the education article did "not require perfect equality and identity"[36] and did not limit the ability of more affluent districts to devote more resources to their schools. Indeed, the court stressed that "it is . . . not the existence of disparities between or among districts that results in a constitutional violation." But the court also said that the "critical issue is whether those disparities are the result of the financing scheme the state chooses" and described the state's financing system as characterized by "heavy reliance on local property taxation, arbitrary school district boundaries, and only partial attempts at equalization"—supporting the inference that, indeed, unequalized disparities violate the "general and uniform" requirement.[37] It is difficult to tell from the Arizona court's opinion whether it was relying on adequacy, equity, or some hybrid of the two.[38]

Three Versions of the Adequacy-Equity Relationship

Although courts often have blended adequacy and equity concerns, in many cases, adequacy theory does add something new to the legal analysis. Some courts treat claims based on state constitutions' equal protection and education clauses as involving distinct legal arguments and analyze them separately. Moreover, a significant number of courts have reached different results based on equality and adequacy theories. Courts in Arizona, Idaho, Kansas, New Jersey, New York, and Ohio rejected equality challenges to school financing systems but found for the plaintiffs on an education clause–based adequacy theory.[39] On the other hand, many state supreme courts resolved adequacy and equality claims the same way: the Arkansas, Tennessee, and Wyoming courts found for plaintiffs on both adequacy and equality grounds, while state supreme courts in ten other states rejected both adequacy and equity claims.[40] Nonetheless, although some state supreme courts found for plaintiffs on equal protection grounds without considering an adequacy claim (or found for plaintiffs on adequacy grounds without considering equality), there do not appear to be any courts that combined rejection of an adequacy attack with validation of an equality challenge. In other words, no court has found that a state was providing an education that was adequate but also unconstitutionally unequal. Thus the adequacy theory adds to the arsenal of plaintiffs' legal weapons, although it is by no means certain of leading to victory in court.

Although equity and adequacy are distinct legal theories, judicial approaches to adequacy clearly have been shaped by equity concerns. That is true partly as a matter of history, as earlier court decisions that focused primarily on equity informed later cases in which adequacy took center stage. It is also, as previously suggested, a matter of theory, as ideas about equity have influenced judicial approaches to the meaning of adequacy. However, finding that a state is failing to provide an adequate education and finding that a system is unequal can lead to different remedies. Affirmative decisions in equity cases have, not surprisingly, sought to equalize tax bases or per-pupil spending. Affirmative decisions in adequacy cases, by contrast, have not focused on equity—although greater equity in funding typically results—but on ensuring an "adequate education" in all districts. That has often proven to be a complex task, requiring judicial attention to the structure of the state-local educational system and the content of the education provided, in addition to how that education is financed.

In a fifty-state legal system—with at least one state supreme court decision concerning school financing reform in three-quarters of the states and multiple decisions in several states—it is difficult to find a consistent relationship between adequacy and equity in the law. Judicial decisions in this area often are far from models of clarity, and doctrines within a state can and do change over time. Very roughly, however, state judicial decisions concerning the adequacy-equity relationship can be grouped into three categories, which may be labeled "inequity excused," "equity minus," and "equity plus."

In the first category, adequacy and equity are separate concerns, but adequacy is invoked to excuse or mitigate a court's determination that an education system does not violate constitutional equality norms. Adequacy is treated as a relatively minimal requirement, easily satisfied by the state education system subject to challenge.

In the "equity minus" cases, the main significance of adequacy is to compel states to devote more resources to the schools in their poorest districts, without requiring the poorest districts to be made fully equal to the rich. In other words, adequacy operates to "level up" the poor to some middle, acceptable level of spending or achievement but does not require the poor to be brought up to the top—or the top to be brought down to a lower level—in the name of equality.

In the "equity plus" decisions, courts have held that adequacy requires *more* than equity. That "more" can be more resources, either for the state as a whole or for the poorest districts in the state, so that their harder-to-educate students can reach the same level of educational attainment as students in more affluent areas. The "more" can also mean state government activity beyond financing, such as more precise state definition of the components of an adequate education or the creation of a monitoring and oversight structure that ensures that students throughout the state in fact receive the state-defined adequate education. In these cases, courts focus on educational outputs—such as student performance on tests designed to measure academic achievement—as well as on inputs. There is still a strong egalitarian component, as the purpose of "equity plus" requirements often is to ensure that the children in the poorest areas actually receive the same education as more affluent children. But some of these cases also indicate a state judicial intention to upgrade the state educational system overall.

Adequacy as Inequality Excused or Mitigated

The origins of adequacy as an excuse for or mitigation of inequality can be seen in the Supreme Court's *Rodriguez* decision. In holding that interdistrict spending inequalities in Texas, which were linked to disparities in local tax bases, did not violate the Constitution's equal protection clause, the Court noted that "no charge fairly could be made that the basic system fails to provide each child with an opportunity to acquire the basic minimal skills necessary" to constitute an education.[41] In other words, although the right to an adequate education was not strictly speaking before the Court, *Rodriguez* did appear to take some comfort from the fact that even though the Texas school system was marked by spending inequalities, the system at least provided all schoolchildren with "basic minimal skills."

The New York Court of Appeals took a similar approach to adequacy in its 1982 *Levittown* decision, although in *Levittown*, unlike *Rodriguez*, plaintiffs had stated a cause of action under the state's education article as well as its equal protection clause, so educational adequacy theory was actually before the court.[42] Having rejected plaintiffs' equal protection claim, the court acknowledged that the education article—which requires the legislature to "provide for the maintenance and support of a system of free common schools"—in theory could support a constitutional challenge to the state's school financing system, but it then rejected the claim on the merits by simply declaring that "a sound basic education" with "minimally acceptable facilities and services" was being provided throughout New York.[43] The only evidence the court cited to bolster its claim that a constitutionally adequate education was being provided was the fact that compared with other states, New York—which was the third-highest of the fifty states in expenditures per pupil—was devoting a significant amount of resources to public schools.[44] At about the same time, the Georgia Supreme Court in *McDaniel* v. *Thomas* also took comfort in the presumed adequacy of the education its state was providing. The Georgia court rejected an equity claim, took up an adequacy claim—the Georgia constitution is one of the rare ones that actually uses the term "adequate" in establishing the duty to provide education[45]—denied that adequacy included any egalitarian component,[46] and then found, on the basis of the "massive" level of state support for education, that the adequacy requirement had been satisfied.[47] Courts in Colorado, Idaho, Maryland, Ohio, Oklahoma, and Pennsylvania reached similar conclusions during the second wave in the 1970s and 1980s.[48]

Even in the 1990s, courts in Maine, Minnesota, and Nebraska continued to mitigate the sting of their rejection of equality challenges by asserting the adequacy of the state school systems, although in each case the court found that the plaintiffs had failed to make or support an adequacy argument and so the court could assume the adequacy of the state systems.[49] In another decision in the early 1990s, the Kansas Supreme Court acknowledged that some districts were underfunded relative to others but concluded that such underfunding did not make the financing system "unsuitable" within the meaning of the Kansas constitutional provision requiring "suitable provision for financing of the educational interest of the state."[50] The Wisconsin Supreme Court has been clearest in linking a rejection of an equity claim to a presumption of adequacy, in a case in which adequacy was at least implicitly put at issue by plaintiffs' invocation of the Wisconsin education article. Moreover, the Wisconsin court's conception of adequacy was strikingly limited. It held that adequacy requires no more than that the state offer students the "opportunity to be proficient" in core subjects; "adequacy" did not require that students attain proficiency: "This means that poor student performance on proficiency tests in school districts is not, without much more, an indicia of the unconstitutionality [on adequacy grounds] of the state school finance system."[51]

Three factors seem to characterize this first set of adequacy cases. First, as exemplified by the Wisconsin decision, they typically adopt a fairly limited definition of what constitutes an adequate education. These courts refer to "minimally acceptable facilities and services" or to a "basic adequate education," rather than to the high-quality version of adequacy that has become more common in recent cases.[52] Second, they may restrict the scope of the constitutional adequacy requirement. In a number of the states where the education article refers to a "uniform" education, courts have found that uniformity does not require equal spending but concerns only matters like the length of the school year or the content of the curriculum.[53] Third, these cases rarely involve a full judicial investigation of the adequacy of the education actually offered. Adequacy is generally inferred from the amount of state money devoted to education or from the existence of state standards, or adequacy is deemed to be conceded by the plaintiffs. It is in the last set of cases—in which adequacy has not even been at issue—that it is clearest that the courts are turning to adequacy to excuse or mitigate inequality rather than to consider what "adequacy" means. But in all these cases, it is implicit that adequacy has little to do with equity and imposes no more than a modest burden on the state, which the state can easily satisfy.

In these cases, of course, the adequacy argument failed—or was not even tried. Educational adequacy, while nominally required for state school systems, was not taken all that seriously by the courts.

However, judicial minimization of the content and significance of adequacy appears to be on the wane. Most of the adequacy-as-excuse cases predate the contemporary dominance of the adequacy theory. The more recent judicial statements occurred in disputes in which plaintiffs did not even bring an adequacy claim. In most recent cases in which constitutional inadequacy has been alleged, courts have either taken the issue seriously and required a full-scale fact-finding study, or they have rejected it on justiciability grounds—that is, they have treated adequacy as a matter for the political process, not for litigation. Still, in taking the full measure of the impact of the adequacy theory on school finance reform, it is worth noting the significant set of cases in which adequacy had little impact at all, except perhaps to excuse or mitigate judicial acquiescence in an unequal school funding system.

Adequacy as "Equity Minus"

In the adequacy as "equity minus" cases, the thrust of the adequacy theory is to ensure greater parity in the funds available to and in the education supplied by local school districts but not to require complete equalization across the board. This version of adequacy responds to some of the practical and political shortcomings of equity as a legal theory of school finance reform. As some scholars have suggested, state courts might have found it awkward to use state equal protection provisions in school financing cases because that would involve adopting an interpretation of equal protection sharply at variance with that of the U.S. Supreme Court in *Rodriguez*. As a matter of legal doctrine, state judges are free to construe state constitutional provisions differently from even identically worded provisions of the U.S. Constitution, but such divergence might still seem arbitrary and subject a state court to criticism. By relying on a state constitutional provision that has no federal counterpart, adequacy avoids this problem.[54]

More significant is that the "equity minus" version of adequacy responds to one of the flaws identified early on in the equity theory, which is that due to the drastic disparity in local property wealth per pupil across districts—as demonstrated by the record of nearly every school finance reform case—it is likely to be extremely costly for a state to ensure that all districts have access to the same resources that the wealthiest districts enjoy. In theory, equality would require raising all districts to the level of the wealthiest district or reducing the expenditures of the wealthiest in order to achieve equity at a lower level of spending. The former course of action is likely to be prohibitively expensive, but the latter is a direct challenge both to the widespread practice of decentralized school district decisionmaking and to the political power of the wealthiest districts. Although some states have moved to cap local spending, courts may well be reluctant to force such a dramatic and politically difficult action. Moreover, at a time when the quality of the public schools seems increasingly uncertain and many have stressed the need for paying greater attention to achieving excellence in education, some judges have doubted the wisdom of limiting spending on public education, even by affluent districts.[55] Adequacy as "equity minus" eliminates this problem by requiring an infusion of resources into less affluent districts while accepting higher levels of spending by more affluent districts. Courts that adhere to this view treat adequacy as a means for improving the quality of the education provided by the poorest school districts—and thus securing a greater measure of equality—without requiring that the poor districts be made fully equal to the rich.

Probably the first state court to embrace adequacy as "equity minus" was the New Jersey Supreme Court in the *Robinson* saga. In *Robinson V,* the New Jersey Supreme Court upheld the Public School Education Act of 1975—the state legislature's response to earlier court decisions holding that the state school financing system violated the "thorough and efficient" education provision of the state constitution. The act provided for a significant increase in state support for education that would effectively equalize spending in roughly two-thirds of the school districts of the state and guarantee each district an effective tax base that was somewhat higher than the statewide average per-pupil tax base.[56] Although that fell well short of full equalization, the act was such a significant improvement in equity that combined with other improvements in the state educational system, including greater state oversight of local district performance, the state supreme court held that it would satisfy the state constitutional requirement if it was fully funded.[57]

In *Robinson* the court's treatment of adequacy as "equity minus" came late in the litigation story as the court assessed the state's response to its earlier mandates. In other states, the judicial distinction between adequacy and equity—and the determination that adequacy requires more money for poorer districts but not necessarily as much money as is available to the more affluent—came earlier on, as courts set out the criteria for determining whether state school finance measures satisfied constitutional adequacy requirements.

Thus, in the first *DeRolph* decision in Ohio, the state supreme court, which had previously rejected an equal protection challenge, held that plaintiff school districts had proven that the current school finance system violated the state constitution's "thorough and efficient" requirement because those districts "were starved for funds" and therefore lacked teachers, buildings, and equipment and were compelled to offer educational programs that were inferior to those of other districts.[58] Insufficient funding and the resulting unequal educational offerings made a case for inadequacy, but full equalization of funding or programs would not be required: "We recognize that disparities between school districts will always exist. . . . We are not stating that a new financing system must provide equal educational opportunity for all."[59] Indeed, the court insisted that state satisfaction of the "thorough and efficient" requirement was consistent with both higher spending and more expansive programs in more affluent districts.[60] But the court insisted that all districts must have enough money to offer an adequate educational program.

Similarly, the South Carolina Supreme Court in *Abbeville County* found that a claim that education in forty less-wealthy school districts was underfunded and therefore inadequate could go forward under the state constitution's education article—despite the court's earlier determination that interlocal school revenue disparities are not unconstitutional—because requiring adequacy would not require equity.[61] And in the *McDuffy* decision, the Massachusetts Supreme Judicial Court walked the line between adequacy and equity by holding on one hand that the state constitution's education provision did not mandate equal expenditures per pupil but, on the other hand, that "fiscal support, or the lack of it, has a significant impact on the quality of education each child may receive."[62]

Finally, in a decision handed down in 2005, the Kansas Supreme Court, which had made adequacy—in the words of the state constitution, "suitable provision" for education—a judicially enforceable mandate only in 2003, again illustrated the idea of adequacy as partial, but not full, equality.[63] The court held that a state school finance law permitting "local option budgets," which enabled districts to spend beyond the basic state definition of an adequate education, was consistent with the constitution since adequacy did not require equality and instead permitted local "enhancements" above the adequacy level. But it invalidated the law anyway because it found the state's aid formula to be too low, making local districts too heavily dependent on property taxes to fund an adequate education and thereby resulting in "wealth-based disparity."[64] In other words, ensuring suitability or adequacy required some amelioration of wealth-based differences, but the principle was not offended by the ability of wealthier districts to spend above the suitable or adequate level.

Adequacy as "equity minus" seems a pragmatic tempering of the potentially radical thrust of a pure equity theory. In fact, it is not so clear that equity and adequacy as "equity minus" are all that different in practice. Even in states in which courts embraced an equity approach and invalidated the school finance system under the state equal protection clause, courts were sometimes willing to accept legislative remedies that brought up the bottom and leveled spending up to the middle or upper-middle tier without fully equalizing spending or revenue-raising capacity by all districts.

In Connecticut, for example, the state supreme court, which invalidated its state school finance system on equal protection grounds, ultimately accepted a state legislative response that significantly increased the state's share of total education expenditures (although the state's share was still below the local share) and provided all districts with "significant equalizing state support" but also left "significant disparities in the funds that local communities spend on basic public education."[65] As the reform measure created "substantially equal educational opportunities," the "remaining disparities do not undermine the basic policy of equalizing state support for education."[66]

Similarly, in Texas, the *Edgewood* saga began with the state supreme court determining that the "efficient system" of education mandated by the state constitution requires all school districts to have "substantially equal access to similar revenue per pupil at similar levels of tax effort"—in essence adopting the fiscal neutrality version of equity found in the early school finance reform cases.[67] Six years later, the Texas court concluded that "an efficient system does not require equality of access to revenue at all levels."[68] The court sustained a school financing scheme in which most money for schools was still raised by local taxation and still allowed the wealthiest school districts to raise and spend more money than their less affluent peers. As the court subsequently observed, legislation that significantly reduced without eliminating wealth-based disparities was constitutionally sufficient "only when viewed through the prism of history. In other words, it was better than it had been."[69]

Adequacy as "equity minus" may have emboldened some otherwise reluctant state courts to enter the school finance reform arena, and the concept may also have provided courts with a principled rationale for making peace with their legislatures by accepting finance reform measures that were less than fully equalizing. Adequacy as "equity minus" is more modest than full equity, costs less, and makes space for a significant continuing local financing role. It achieves equity's leveling-up goal for the poorest districts of a state without threatening the school financing system as a whole. Yet, as noted, it may not be all that different from equity in practice.

Relatively few state courts have embraced adequacy as "equity minus"—or rather, few have limited their understanding of adequacy to just leveling up the bottom. Most state courts that adopted the adequacy theory either moved over time from "equity minus" to "equity plus" or came to add aspects of "equity plus" to the limited equalization of "equity minus." Despite its pragmatic appeal, adequacy as "equity minus" appears increasingly to be giving way to adequacy as "equity plus."

Adequacy as "Equity Plus"

Probably the most significant development in school finance litigation has been the rise of the theory of adequacy as "equity plus." Although aspects of "equity plus" can be seen as far back as the original New Jersey *Robinson* decision and West Virginia's *Pauley* decision, adequacy as "equity plus" really emerged only in 1989–90 with the Kentucky *Rose* decision and the New Jersey Supreme Court's *Abbott* line of cases. Adequacy as "equity plus" draws on three related strands of thinking that address some of the shortcomings of the pure equity theory of school finance reform.

In the first strand, adequacy as "equity plus" has focused on the need for school financing systems to provide more than equal funding to certain groups of schoolchildren, particularly the urban poor, in order for those children to receive a truly adequate education. One problem with equity as equalization of either tax bases or per-pupil spending—the two dominant versions of equity in the case law of the first and second waves—is that neither fits well with the needs of the urban poor. As the Supreme Court noted in *Rodriguez*, many urban areas are not property poor but, due to the presence of industrial and commercial property, are close to if not above the average property wealth of the state. Moreover, due to competing demands for urban services, many urban areas often are unable to devote as high a fraction of their tax dollars to education as suburban and rural districts can. Many of these districts would benefit little from tax-base equalization.[70] Furthermore, these districts often have high concentrations of children who are poor and harder to educate, and so they incur considerably higher per-pupil education costs. Equity theory did not provide much affirmative support for additional state assistance to such districts, although most courts that embraced the equity theory rejected the idea that strict equality of per-child educational expenditures was constitutionally mandated and agreed that higher needs and higher costs could justify greater state aid.[71] The adequacy as "equity plus" theory, by contrast, provides a basis for arguing that if more state funds are needed in some districts than in others in order to provide an adequate education, then those additional funds must be provided. This could also be described as adequacy as "vertical equity," in which differently situated children require different amounts of public school dollars in light of their differing educational needs, in contrast to the traditional "horizontal equity" approach, which sought to provide different school districts with a relatively equal number of dollars per child.[72]

The prime instance of adequacy as "equity plus" for the educationally needy is the New Jersey Supreme Court's second *Abbott* decision in 1990.[73] In that case, the court concluded that the children in the vast majority of the state's school districts were receiving the "thorough and efficient" education required by the state constitution but that "based both on the absolute level of education in those districts and the comparison with the education in affluent suburban districts," such an education was not being provided in twenty-eight poor urban districts.[74] Noting that due to social, economic, and demographic factors the "educational needs of students in poorer, urban districts vastly exceed those of others, especially those from richer districts,"[75] the court held that the educational offerings in what subsequently became known as "special needs districts" (SNDs) "must contain elements over and above those found in the affluent suburban districts. . . . [I]n poor urban districts, something more must be added to the regular education in order to achieve the command of the Constitution."[76] The court specifically required that per-pupil educational expenditures in the SNDs must equal the current average per-pupil expenditures of the state's top school districts, with the SNDs' budgets rising as the budgets of the top districts rise, and that "in addition, their special disadvantages must be addressed."[77] Four years later, the court invalidated one state legislative response to its holding because, although the law reduced the spending gap between the SNDs and the top districts, some disparities remained. Moreover, the state failed to provide "special funds and services targeted to the needs of those disadvantaged students."[78] Three years later the court held unconstitutional the funding provisions of another state legislative response because once again the state's financial assistance to the SNDs was "incapable of providing the remediation that will overcome that constitutional deprivation."[79] Ultimately, in order to provide the extra support to which the SNDs were deemed constitutionally entitled under the "equity plus" theory, the court ordered adoption of a special master's report that called for the implementation of "whole-school reform" for elementary schools, full-day kindergarten for five-year-olds, half-day pre-kindergarten for three- and four-year-olds, provision of health and social services, additional school security measures, and other special programs for the SNDs.[80] In other words, adequacy required not merely that the neediest districts receive funding equal to that of the most affluent but that they actually provide extra programs and receive the funding necessary to pay for them in order to overcome the educational disadvantages that children in these districts face.

The North Carolina Supreme Court embraced a similar "equity plus" approach in its 2004 decision in *Hoke County*, when it held that the state constitution's education provisions were violated in the poor rural districts that brought suit.[81] Following the trial court, the state supreme court found that the "bulk of the core" of the state's "educational delivery system" was sound and passed constitutional muster but that the state's failure to provide an effective mechanism to deal with the educational needs of "at-risk children"— defined by a complex of social, economic, and demographic factors[82]—meant that the state was failing to secure the education guaranteed by the state constitution.[83] The state was directed to assess the special needs of at-risk children and to develop a plan to address them, including the redeployment of state education aid. But the court drew back from the lower court's determination to mandate pre-kindergarten programs for at-risk four-year-olds, finding that it unduly trenched on the authority of the executive and legislative branches.[84]

The second strand of adequacy as "equity plus" can be seen in the state court decisions requiring state governments to devote more money to education statewide, not just in the property-poorest districts. The prime exemplar of this version of adequacy as "equity plus" is the Kentucky Supreme Court's *Rose* decision. Although *Rose* discussed inequalities within the Kentucky school system that meant that "students in property-poor districts receive inadequate and inferior educational opportunities as compared to those offered to those students in the more affluent districts,"[85] the court concluded that the level of support for education in Kentucky was inadequate in all districts.[86] The court found that education in Kentucky overall was marked by low effort and low achievement—in per-pupil expenditures, teacher salaries, graduation rates, and scores on achievement tests. Rather than just compare inputs and outputs across districts within the state, the court also compared Kentucky with other states within the region and nation in terms of the resources devoted to education and the measures of educational attainment, and it found that Kentucky fell short. Adequacy required an increase in resources for education throughout the state.

Other state courts, such as those in Alabama and Arkansas, have followed Kentucky's lead in assessing adequacy in terms of the state's dedication of resources to education and the performance of the state's school districts compared with that of districts in other states. Like Kentucky, they found their school systems inadequate in an absolute sense—although that inadequacy was evidenced by comparing their states to other states. In these states, adequacy would require not just bringing up the poorest districts to some undefined middle but increasing the resources devoted to education in the state as a whole.[87]

This aspect of adequacy as "equity plus" also derives from some of the perceived shortcomings of early equity cases. First, in the fiscal neutrality aspect of equity embraced by the California Supreme Court in *Serrano,* the equity problem was often tax-base inequity. Taxpayers in low-wealth districts had higher tax rates but generated less revenue per pupil than taxpayers in high-wealth districts. Power equalization could remedy that by ensuring that each district had an equivalent tax base and thus equal revenue for equal effort. But that did nothing to ensure that low-wealth districts would devote their equalization aid to education rather than cut their tax rates. Second and relatedly, even if equalization were achieved by a general state takeover of school funding, that would not ensure improvement of the education provided in the poorest districts. Although equalization often leads to an increase in per-pupil spending, California provides evidence that equalization can be accomplished by leveling down as well as by leveling up.[88] Adequacy defined as increasing the resources for education in the course of reducing inequalities within a state is clearly about improving education funding, not taxpayer equity, and it is unlikely to permit equality to be achieved at lower levels of spending.

Adequacy as "equity plus" also clearly reflects the growing public concern about the uncertain quality of public education. In the aftermath of the publication of *A Nation at Risk* in the early 1980s, excellence (or its lack) replaced equity as the public's "top concern" about education.[89] "Equity plus" unites equity and excellence in a court order, rooted in the state constitution, to devote greater resources to education.

Rose's vision of adequacy as more than just equalizing spending within a state has not been limited to court decisions based solely on an adequacy theory. In both the Alabama and Arkansas decisions, the courts combined equal protection and education provisions as well as equity and adequacy reasoning in finding that their state constitutions required the devotion of additional funding to education. The Wyoming Supreme Court, relying on both equal protection and education provisions, found that the state constitution required both "financial parity" and sufficient funding statewide to provide all students with the "best educational system." In the Wyoming court's view, equity involves not merely serving equal slices of the funding pie, in addition, "the pie must be large enough to fund [educational] need" statewide.[90] Similarly, the Montana Supreme Court, which in 1989 had relied on the "equality of educational opportunity" guarantee of the state constitution to invalidate a school funding system marked by substantial interdistrict disparity in per-pupil spending, held in 2005 that even though a legislative school financing reform had eliminated most interdistrict spending differences, the state's education funding legislation failed to meet the state constitutional requirement for a "basic system of free quality public elementary and secondary schools" because the state was not providing enough money overall.[91]

The third strand in "equity plus" goes beyond financing. The adequacy courts have required their state governments to spell out the elements of a constitutionally adequate education, determine the inputs—including curriculum, staffing, facilities, and educational materials—necessary to provide it, and more effectively oversee whether local school districts are providing an adequate education. That may involve state measures for assessing students' academic attainment, greater state monitoring of local school district performance, and state intervention when local districts fall short. This aspect of adequacy dates back to the initial reliance on state education articles during the so-called second wave. Both the New Jersey court in *Robinson* and the West Virginia court in *Pauley* v. *Kelley* called on their states to define the "thorough and efficient education" that their state constitutions required, with attention to the necessary facilities, instructional materials, personnel, performance standards, and administrative oversight.[92] State definition of educational content and greater state monitoring of and responsibility for local school district performance was also central to the Kentucky court's decision in *Rose*. In recent years, courts in Kansas, New Hampshire, Ohio, and Texas have focused their interpretation of their states' education clauses on educational content definition, the monitoring of local performance, and state and local accountability for performance shortfalls.[93] Indeed, as with the enhanced funding aspect of "equity plus," this increasing judicial attention to state satisfaction of content-definition and oversight requirements has not been limited to adequacy states. Courts in Arkansas, Montana, Tennessee, and Wyoming all have looked to whether states have set curricular requirements, adopted accountability standards, and put in place means of measuring pupil performance in their analysis of school finance reform claims.[94]

In these cases, educational content issues are not separate from financing issues. Rather, courts increasingly are treating state specification of educational content and state provision of adequate financing as closely connected. An important new development is the adequate education cost study. In just the years since the turn of the millennium state courts in Arkansas, Kansas, Montana, New York, Ohio, Tennessee, and Wyoming have required their legislatures or state education departments to determine the components of an adequate education, specify the inputs necessary to achieve adequacy, and then cost out those inputs in order to determine the amount of funding that must be devoted to education, either statewide or in the plaintiff school districts.[95] When states have failed to justify their funding decisions in terms of such a cost-of-adequacy study or a state legislature has departed from the study's conclusion when it enacted a state aid formula, the state supreme court may be sharply critical and even invalidate the state financing measure.[96] Moreover, as the list of state courts that have looked to cost-of-adequacy studies in making their decisions indicates, as with other aspects of adequacy such as "equity plus," the requirement that state funding decisions be closely justified in terms of the funds needed to pay for an adequate education is not limited to state courts that have premised their interventions on adequacy requirements. Rather, such cost-justified decisionmaking is a theme in many recent school finance reform cases.

The three strands of adequacy as "equity plus" clearly demonstrate equity concerns—to make sure that poor districts get the funding that, in light of their special needs, they must have in order to be truly equal with more affluent districts; to bring up to the regional or national level the funding of education in states that have provided limited support for education; and to adopt administrative measures and cost studies that ensure that funding is sufficient to provide truly equal educational opportunities within a state. From this perspective adequacy as "equity plus" reflects a maturation of the equity idea from one of simple equalization of interdistrict tax-base or per-pupil spending to a more sophisticated understanding of the additional resources, structural reforms, enhanced oversight, and cost-justified spending that may be necessary in order to actually equalize educational opportunities. Indeed, this evolution in the idea of what equity requires can also be seen in contemporary cases that rely on equity, or a combination of equity and adequacy, rather than adequacy alone.

On the other hand, in many state courts adequacy as "equity plus" also goes beyond even the most sophisticated definition of fiscal equity to encompass an overall assessment of the state's role in discharging the constitutional mandate to provide public education. It involves education *governance* reform rather than education *finance* reform. Indeed, as noted, this version of adequacy incorporates into school finance reform the public concern about improving school quality and educational outcomes that first became politically salient in the 1980s and can also be seen in the No Child Left Behind law. Under adequacy as "equity plus," courts are requiring legislatures to do more than equalize school funding; they are requiring them to create stronger, more accountable educational systems.

Adequacy, Equity, and the Judicial Role in Education Finance Reform

Early in the third-wave period some academic advocates of the adequacy approach asserted, pragmatically, that adequacy is the better approach for reformers to take because courts will see it as both more legitimate and less challenging to the political branches than arguments from equity.[97] Adequacy is arguably more legitimate because it builds on the special state constitutional commitment to education, thus providing a judicial theory with more constitutional purchase than the equality requirement that the U.S. Supreme Court rejected in this very context. And arguments from adequacy are less challenging to the political branches than arguments from equity since adequacy leaves some inequalities in place and, in particular, does not threaten the ability of politically powerful affluent districts to spend more on their schoolchildren. These arguments for an adequacy approach are best reflected in the "equity minus" form of adequacy. However, the adequacy theory tends to stretch the limits of the institutional competence and power of courts that define adequacy as "equity plus" by embroiling them in efforts to define an "adequate" education, to appraise the sufficiency of state measures to oversee and finance local provision of such an education, and to force state legislatures to give a greater priority to education than the legislators themselves would prefer. With courts increasingly viewing adequacy as "equity plus," the question of the judicial role in defining and enforcing adequacy becomes more difficult.

The very concept of an "adequate" education is inherently fraught with uncertainty. State constitutions say virtually nothing about what constitutes an adequate education. By comparison with adequacy, equality is a relatively determinate idea. Equality requires that all districts be treated alike. In theory, equity can be attained without any decision about what an education ought to achieve or how much money ought to be devoted to education. Equity can base the standard on existing levels of education spending. Adequacy, on the other hand, is totally free-floating. It requires difficult and deeply contestable determinations about the purposes of education, how to achieve it, and what resources are necessary to do so. As opposed to equity, adequacy would appear to lack "judicially manageable standards" and therefore be a poor candidate for judicial enforcement.

Indeed, a number of state supreme courts—in Florida, Illinois, Pennsylvania, Rhode Island, and Virginia—have taken that position.[98] When school finance reform plaintiffs have pressed arguments based on the education requirements of their state constitutions, these courts determined not that their states satisfied the adequate education mandated by the constitution but that educational quality is a matter to be resolved through the political, not the judicial, process. Most of these decisions were issued in the mid- and late 1990s. Although it is not clear that they were driven by the rise of the "equity plus" idea, it is not surprising that some courts would be concerned about the scope of the judicial role at a time when adequacy was increasingly turning into a vehicle for judicial oversight of entire state school systems.

On the other hand, many state courts have determined that challenges to school financing systems based on the state constitution's education article are justiciable, and these courts have found ways of making the definition of an adequate education judicially manageable. Most commonly, that has involved a combination of judicial articulation of some unexceptionable general principles of the purpose of education coupled with a directive to the state legislature or state education department or both to develop more specific standards, including standards regarding the components of an adequate education, and the educational inputs and performance measures necessary to ensure that an adequate education is actually provided. The general criteria listed by the West Virginia court in *Pauley* and the Kentucky court in *Rose* have been repeatedly cited, sometimes with modifications, by other state courts. State legislatures typically have acceded to such court decisions by adopting laws that define educational requirements and call for monitoring local school districts and testing student performance. The definition of a "general and uniform" or "thorough and efficient" education, then, has been determined in a surprisingly cooperative and interactive process, with courts initially forcing the legislatures to take the necessary steps and then generally accepting the results.[99]

The greater difficulty for many adequacy courts, as for equity courts, has been getting state legislatures to fully fund the adequate education that the legislature has been willing to define and test. State supreme court orders requiring additional school funding to meet adequacy requirements have frequently encountered legislative resistance, necessitating multiple trips to the courthouse and numerous follow-up court decisions and orders. In states like Arizona, Kansas, New Jersey, and Ohio, school financing and administrative reforms have ping-ponged between the legislatures and the courts, as the legislatures have adopted measures to respond to court declarations of unconstitutional inadequacy and the courts have found the state enactments wanting.[100]

At least three state supreme courts—in Arkansas, Massachusetts, and Ohio—adopted "equity plus" requirements but then backed down and accepted state actions (and inactions) that arguably fell short of both adequacy and equity.[101] These courts decided to declare victory, in spite of the opposition of dissenters and in the face of evidence that the state reform measures fell short of fully addressing the issues that triggered the initial finding of a state constitutional violation. In the Massachusetts case, a plurality of the court found that the state's Education Reform Act provided a "long-term measurable, orderly and comprehensive process of reform," with greater state articulation of educational requirements, new additional financial assistance to poorer schools, and significant performance and accountability standards.[102] To be sure, "significant shortcomings" also remained in the plaintiff school districts, but they did not constitute an "egregious" departure from the adequacy goal previously articulated by the court. Moreover, the plurality emphasized the primacy of the governor and legislature in "educational policymaking."[103]

The Ohio Supreme Court was, if anything, even more candid in describing its action as a compromise. After generally praising the latest legislative reform, the court indicated that certain modifications would be necessary in order for the law to pass constitutional muster and that adequacy would also depend on full funding; however, the court held that it was willing to assume the "good faith" of the legislature and terminated the case.[104] The Arkansas court also praised the "progress" that the legislature had made in standardizing the curriculum, increasing state oversight, and improving funding, and the court then released jurisdiction of the case.[105] Within a year, however, both the Arkansas and Ohio supreme courts recanted, found that their legislatures had not sufficiently funded their reform measures, and issued new orders requiring further legislative action[106]—although the Ohio court thereafter changed its mind again, declared an end to further judicial involvement, and announced that it was leaving the question of remedies to the legislature.[107]

However, not all adequacy decisions have encountered such stubborn resistance. Some state courts have been relatively successful at forcing dramatic state-level legislative or administrative action with respect to the definition of an adequate education, the financing of school districts, and the monitoring of school reforms without protracted legislative-judicial conflicts. Kentucky and Vermont, for example, seem to present examples of fairly radical court orders followed by substantial political compliance. Moreover, it is not clear that adequacy decisions create more difficulties for political implementation and judicial enforcement than equality decisions. In the face of legislative noncompliance with its orders, the Alabama Supreme Court declared that judicial involvement in school finance reform was over and directed plaintiffs "to seek further redress from the legislature, not the courts."[108] Yet the judicial invalidation of the school finance system in Alabama was based as much on equality as on adequacy. More generally, "equity plus" concerns with governance, monitoring, performance measures, and accountability have spread to courts relying on state equal protection clauses or on equal protection and education provisions together, rather than on equality alone.[109]

In practice, then, as in theory, there does not appear to be a significant difference between the equity and adequacy approaches to school finance reform. As plaintiffs combine claims based on equal protection and education provisions and as courts track developments in other jurisdictions, equity ideas have come to play an important role in adequacy thinking much as adequacy concerns about the definition of education, governance, monitoring, and performance have come to affect courts initially concerned primarily with the equalization of tax bases or spending. So, too, even though adequacy claims and judicial adequacy rulings have become more ambitious—folding in, among other things, accountability mandates and requirements that states justify education spending in terms of an expert-determined cost of an adequate education—and thereby have made it hard to argue that adequacy is a less interventionist theory than equity, it is not clear that adequacy holdings have become less judicially enforceable—or, at least, that they are less so than rulings premised on equity. To be sure, a significant number of courts have stressed justiciability concerns in declining to enter the thicket of court-ordered school finance reform. But once courts have entered the adequacy battle, it does not seem that they are any less successful overall than courts that have endorsed the equity theory.

As a matter of legal theory, the general blurring of adequacy and equity concerns appears to have led those courts willing to engage with school finance reform to converge on a common set of goals, including greater state definition of educational requirements; state adoption of performance standards; state monitoring of and accountability for local educational outcomes; requirements that states cost out the price of an adequate education and then ensure provision of the necessary funds; partial equalization of financing, aimed more at bringing up the bottom than holding down the top; and a special concern with the needs of educationally at-risk students or the poorest districts. The success of this judicial program is uncertain, and results vary considerably across states. But that is mostly a matter of differences in state politics and in the judiciary's stomach for conflict with the political branches, not the legal theory—equity or adequacy—on which judicial intervention is based.

Notes

1. See, for example, William E. Thro, "The Third Wave: The Impact of the Montana, Kentucky, and Texas Decisions on the Future of Public School Finance Reform Litigation," *Journal of Law and Education* 19 (Spring 1990): 219, 239–42; Deborah A. Verstegen, "The New Wave of School Finance Litigation," *Phi Delta Kappan* 76 (December 1994): 243, 244.

2. *San Antonio Independent School District* v. *Rodriguez,* 411 U.S. 1 (1973).

3. *Seattle School District No. 1* v. *State,* 585 P.2d 71, 102 (Wash. 1978) (the state failed to fund a basic program of education sufficiently); *Pauley* v. *Kelley,* 255 S.E.2d 859 (W.Va. 1979) (the state was required to define and ensure the funding of a "thorough and efficient system" of public education).

4. *Tennessee Small School Systems* v. *McWherter,* 851 S.W.2d 139, 156 (Tenn. 1993) (the state was required to provide "substantially equal educational opportunities"); *Campbell County School District* v. *State,* 907 P.2d 1238, 1276 (Wyo. 1995) (any interdistrict funding disparity that was not based on cost was "constitutionally infirm"); *Brigham* v. *State,* 692 A.2d 384 (Vt. 1997) (the "state must ensure substantial equality of educational opportunity throughout Vermont"); *Claremont School District* v. *Governor,* 703 A2d 1353, 1354-56 (N.H. 1997) (the New Hampshire school finance system violated the tax uniformity provision of the state constitution because different districts had different tax rates).

5. See *Helena Elementary School District No. 1* v. *State,* 769 P.2d 684 (Mont. 1989) (the funding system failed to provide equal educational opportunity); *Edgewood I.S.D.* v. *Kirby,* 777 S.W.2d 391, 397 (Tex. 1989) (the state financing system was unconstitutional because it failed to ensure that districts "have substantially equal access to similar revenues per pupil at similar levels of tax effort").

6. *Robinson* v. *Cahill,* 303 A.2d 273 (N.J. 1973).

7. Ibid. at 283 (rejecting the state equal protection clause as "unmanageable" and turning to the "thorough and efficient" clause); ibid. at 294 (in interpreting the thorough and efficient clause, "we do not doubt that an equal educational opportunity for children was precisely in mind").

8. See, for example, *McDuffy* v. *Secretary of the Executive Office of Education,* 615 N.E.2d 516, 519 n. 8 (Mass. 1993).

9. See *McDaniel* v. *Thomas,* 285 S.E.2d 156 (Ga. 1981); *Coalition for Adequacy and Fairness in School Funding* v. *Chiles,* 680 So.2d 400 (Fla. 1996).

10. See, for example, *Roosevelt Elementary School District No. 66* v. *Bishop,* 877 P.2d 806 (Ariz. 1994) (interpreting "general and uniform"); *Lake View School District No. 25* v. *Huckabee,* 91 S.W.3d 472 (Ark. 2002) ("general, suitable, and efficient" requires both adequacy and equality); *Tennessee Small School Systems* v. *McWherter,* 851 S.W.2d 139 (Tenn. 1993) ("maintenance and support" requires "substantially equal educational opportunities"); *Campbell County School District* v. *State,* 907 P.2d 1238 (Wyo. 1995) ("complete and uniform" and "thorough and efficient" provisions mandate equality).

11. Montana Constitution, art. X, sec. 1.

12. *Coalition for Adequacy and Fairness in School Funding* v. *Chiles*, 680 So.2d 400 (Fla. 1996); *Committee for Education Rights* v. *Edgar*, 672 N.E.2d 1178 (Ill. 1996); *Skeen* v. *State* 505 N.W.2d 299 (Minn. 1993); *Bismarck Public School District No. 1* v. *State*, 511 N.W.2d 247 (N.D. 1994); *Coalition for Equitable School Funding, Inc.* v. *State*, 811 P.2d 116 (Ore. 1991); *Marrero* v. *Commonwealth*, 739 A.2d 110 (Pa. 1999); *City of Pawtucket* v. *Sundlun*, 662 A.2d 40 (R.I. 1995); *Scott* v. *Commonwealth*, 443 S.E.2d 138 (Va. 1994); *Kukor* v. *Grover*, 436 N.W.2d 568 (Wis. 1989); *Vincent* v. *Voight*, 614 N.W.2d 388 (Wis. 2000). In *Bismarck Public School District No. 1* v. *State*, three of the five members of the North Dakota Supreme Court determined that the state's school financing system violated the education article of the state constitution. However, the North Dakota constitution requires four votes on the court to invalidate a state law, so despite winning a favorable majority opinion, the plaintiffs lost the case.

13. See, for example, *Ex parte James*, 836 So.2d 813 (Ala. 2002) (terminating proceedings in the Alabama school finance reform case); *State ex rel. State* v. *Lewis*, 789 N.E.2d 195 (Ohio 2003) (issuing writ prohibiting further litigation in Ohio school finance reform case).

14. As the Arkansas Supreme Court put it, "There is no doubt in our minds that there is a considerable overlap between the issue of whether a school funding system is inadequate and whether is it inequitable." *Lake View School District No. 25* v. *Huckabee*, 496.

15. See, for example, Opinion of the Justices, 624 So.2d 107, 155 (Ala. 1993); *Lake View School District No. 25* v. *Huckabee*; *Rose* v. *Council for Better Education, Inc.*, 790 S.W.2d 186, 198 (Ky. 1989); *McDuffy* v. *Secretary of the Executive Office of Education*, 519; *Helena Elementary School District No. 1* v. *State*, 690; *Abbott* v. *Burke I*, 495 A.2d 376, 390 (N.J. 1985) (both "thorough and efficient" and equal protection claims "turn on proof that plaintiffs suffer educational inequities and that these inequities derive in significant part from the funding provisions" of state law).

16. *Helena Elementary School District No. 1* v. *State*, 690.

17. *Edgewood Ind. School District* v. *Meno*, 917 S.W.2d 717, 732 (Tex. 1995).

18. Professor Enrich has emphasized the pivotal role of competitiveness in adequacy and how the focus on competitiveness embeds equality concerns in the adequacy theory. See Peter Enrich, "Leaving Equality Behind: New Directions in School Finance Reform," *Vanderbilt Law Review* 48 (January 1995):101, 134.

19. *Rose* v. *Council for Better Education*.

20. Ibid. at 212.

21. *Abbott* v. *Burke I*, 390; *Abbott* v. *Burke II*, 575 A.2d 359, 372 (N.J. 1990).

22. *Claremont School District* v. *Governor*, 635 A.2d, 1375, 1376 (N.H. 1993).

23. Ibid.

24. *Claremont School District* v. *Governor*, 703 A.2d 1353 (N.H. 1997).

25. See Opinion of the Justices (School Financing), 712 A.2d 1080 (N.H. 1998); *Claremont School District* v. *Governor*, 744 A.2d 1107 (N.H. 1999); Opinion of the Justices (Reformed Public School Financing System) 765 A.2d 673 (N.H. 2000).

26. Tax issues loomed large in the most recent Texas school finance decision, but from the opposite perspective. The Texas Supreme Court held that Texas was providing a constitutionally adequate education but that state law effectively required many school districts to tax at the statutory property tax ceiling, thus effectively converting the local property tax into a state tax in violation of the state constitution's prohibition of a state property tax. See *Neeley* v. *West Orange-Cove Consolidated Independent School District*, 176 S.W.2d 746, 794–98 (Tex. 2005).

27. *Claremont School District* v. *Governor*, 703 A.2d 1353,1359 (N.H. 1997).

28. Ibid. at 1360.

29. *Claremont School District* v. *Governor*, 794 A.2d 744 (N.H. 2002).

30. Some of these concerns are reflected in the most recent New Hampshire judicial action, the March 2006 decision of the superior court holding unconstitutional the legislature's response to the state supreme court's mandate because the legislature failed to provide an accountability mechanism for ensuring that underperforming schools complied with state standards and also failed to provide for a uniform statewide property tax rate to fund education. See *Londonderry School District SAU No. 12* v. *State*, N.H., 2006 WL 563120 (N.H. Super. Mar. 3, 2006).

31. *Roosevelt Elementary School District No. 66* v. *Bishop* 877 P.2d 806 (Ariz. 1994).

32. Ibid. at 810, n. 3.

33. *Shofstall* v. *Hollins*, 515 P.2d 590 (Ariz. 1973).

34. See, for example, *Roosevelt Elementary School District No. 66* v. *Bishop,* 877 P.2d 806, 814, n. 7 (Ariz. 1994) ("Satisfaction of the substantive education requirement does not necessarily satisfy the uniformity requirement, just as satisfaction of the uniformity requirement does not necessarily satisfy the substantive education requirement").

35. Ibid. at 814.

36. Ibid. at 816.

37. Ibid. at 815.

38. In a later decision, a lower Arizona appellate court determined that inequality of funding alone was not enough to support a determination that the state's building renewal fund violates the "general and uniform" clause, holding that there could be no constitutional violation unless plaintiffs could show that a cutback in state aid had an impact on students' academic achievement. See *Roosevelt Elementary School District No. 66* v. *State*, 74 P.3d 258 (Ariz. Ct. App. 2003).

39. *Roosevelt Elementary School District No. 66* v. *Bishop*, 877 P.2d 806 (Ariz. 1994); *Idaho Schools for Equal Educational Opportunity* v. *Evans*, 850 P.2d 724 (Idaho 1993) (dismissing equity theories based on equal protection and the term "uniform" in the state's "general, uniform, and thorough system" of education clause, but permitting an adequacy case to go forward based on violation of the "thorough" requirement); *Montoy* v. *State*, 102 P.3d 1160 (Kan. 2003); *Robinson* v. *Cahill,* 303 A.2d 273 (N.J. 1973); Compare *R.E.F.I.T.* v. *Cuomo*, 86 N.Y.2d 279 (N.Y. 1995) with *Campaign for Fiscal Equity* v. *State*, 86 N.Y.2d 307 (N.Y. 1995); and *DeRolph* v. *State*, 677 N.E.2d 733 (Ohio 1997) (upholding adequacy claim and distinguishing earlier *Walter* decision rejecting equity claim).

40. See, for example, *Lujan* v. *Colorado State Board of Education*, 649 P.2d 1005 (Colo. 1982); *McDaniel* v. *Thomas; Committee for Educ. Rights* v. *Edgar*, 710 N.E.2d 798 (Ill. 1996); *Hornbeck* v. *Somerset County Board of Education*, 458 A.2d 758 (Md. 1983); *Skeen* v. *State*, 505 N.W.2d 299 (Minn. 1993); *Fair School Finance Council of Oklahoma, Inc.* v. *State*, 746 P.2d 1135 (Ok. 1987); *Olsen* v. *State*, 554 P.2d 139 (Ore. 1976); *Marrero* v. *Commonwealth*, 739 A.2d 110 (Pa. 1999); *City of Pawtucket* v. *Sundlun*, 662 A.2d 40 (R.I. 1995); *Vincent* v. *Voight.*

41. *San Antonio Independent School District* v. *Rodriguez*, 37.

42. *Board of Education, Levittown Union Free School District* v. *Nyquist,* 57 N.Y.2d 27 (1982).

43. Id. at 47–48.

44. Id. at 48.

45. See Georgia Constitution, art. VIII, sec. 1, para. 1.

46. *McDaniel* v. *Thomas.*

47. Ibid.

48. See *Lujan* v. *Colorado State Board of Education; Thompson* v. *Engelking,* 537 P.2d 635 (Idaho 1975); *Hornbeck* v. *Somerset County Board of Education; Board of Education of City School District of City of Cincinnati* v. *Walter,* 390 N.E.2d 813 (Ohio 1979); *Fair School Finance Council of Oklahoma, Inc.* v. *State,* 746 P.2d 1135 (Ok. 1987); *Danson* v. *Casey,* 399 A.2d 360 (Pa. 1979).

49. See *School Admin. District No. 1* v. *Comm'r, Department of Education,* 659 A.2d 854, 856–57 (Me. 1995); *Skeen* v. *State,* 505 N.W.2d 299, 302, 312 (Minn. 1993); *Gould* v. *Orr,* 506 N.W.2d 349, 353 (Neb. 1993).

50. *Unified School District No. 229* v. *State* (Kan. 1994).

51. *Vincent* v. *Voight.*

52. *Fair School Finance Council of Oklahoma, Inc.* v. *State.*

53. *Idaho Schools for Equal Educational Opportunity* v. *Evans,* 850 P.2d 724, 730–31 (Ida. 1993); *Withers* v. *State,* 891 P.2d 675 (Ore. App. 1995); *Kukor* v. *Grover,* 577; *Vincent* v. *Voight,* 402.

54. See, for example, Molly McUsic, "The Use of Education Clauses in School Reform Litigation," *Harvard Journal on Legislation* 28 (Summer 1991): 307, 312–15. Similarly, some state courts may have been concerned that the equity argument cannot be limited to education but would have to be extended to other public services. Rooted as it is in state education articles, adequacy eliminates that concern. Ibid.

55. See, for example, *Roosevelt Elementary School District No. 66.* v. *Bishop,* 815 (arguing that it is important to let some districts "go above and beyond the state financed system"; otherwise "public education statewide might suffer" because "those who could might opt out of the system for private education" and thus reduce public support for education funding).

56. *Robinson* v. *Cahill V,* 355 A.2d 129, 137 n. 4. (N.J. 1976).

57. Ibid. at 139.

58. *DeRolph* v. *State,* 677 N.E.2d 733, 742–44 (Ohio 1997).

59. Ibid. at 746.

60. Ibid.

61. *Abbeville County School District* v. *State,* 515 S.E.2d 535 (S.C. 1999).

62. *McDuffy* v. *Secretary of the Executive Office of Education.*

63. *Montoy* v. *State,* 62 P.3d 228 (Kan. 2003).

64. *Montoy* v. *Kansas,* 112 P.3d 923, 937 (Kan. 2005).

65. *Horton* v. *Meskill,* 486 A.2d 1099, 1107 (Conn. 1985).

66. Ibid. at 1108.

67. *Edgewood I.S.D.* v. *Kirby,* 777 S.W.2d 391, 397 (Tex. 1989).

68. *Edgewood I.S.D.* v. *Meno,* 917 S.W.2d 717, 729–30 (Tex. 1995).

69. *West Orange-Cove Consolidated Independent School District* v. *Alanis,* 107 S.W.3d 558, 572 (Tex. 2003). In its most recent school finance decision, the Texas Supreme Court again held that funding disparities between the richest and poorest districts are constitutionally acceptable. *Neeley* v. *West Orange-Cove Consolidated Independent School District,* 176 S.W.2d 746, 790–93 (Tex. 2005).

70. As the California court of appeal noted, "Some of the state's most urban districts, with large concentrations of poor and minority students, are high-revenue districts," including San Francisco, Oakland, and Berkeley. *Serrano* v. *Priest,* 220 Cal. Rptr. 584, 619 (Cal. Ct. App.2d 1986). The school finance reform adopted by the California legislature in the aftermath of

Serrano (and Proposition 13) made these districts worse off financially than before. See ibid. at 618.

71. See, for example, Paul A. Minorini and Stephen D. Sugarman, "Educational Adequacy and the Courts: The Promise and Problems of Moving to a New Paradigm," in *Equity and Adequacy in Education Finance: Issues and Perspectives,* edited by Helen F. Ladd, Rosemary Chalk, and Janet S. Hansen (Washington: National Academy Press, 1999), p. 183.

72. See, for example, Robert Berne and Leanna Stiefel, "Concepts of School Finance Equity: 1970 to the Present," in Ladd, Chalk, and Hansen, *Equity and Adequacy in Education Finance*, pp. 18–21.

73. *Abbott* v. *Burke II*, 575 A.2d 359 (N.J. 1990).

74. Ibid. at 394.

75. Ibid. at 400.

76. Ibid. at 403.

77. Ibid. at 408.

78. *Abbott* v. *Burke III*, 643 A.2d 575, 580 (N.J. 1994).

79. *Abbott* v. *Burke IV*, 693 A.2d 417, 432 (N.J. 1997).

80. *Abbott* v. *Burke V*, 710 A.2d 450 (N.J. 1998).

81. *Hoke County Board of Education* v. *State*, 599 S.E.2d 365 (N.C. 2004).

82. These included belonging to a low-income family, participating in a free or reduced-cost lunch program, having parents with a low-level education, showing limited proficiency in English, being a member of a racial or ethnic minority group, and living in a home headed by a single parent or guardian. Ibid. at 389, n. 16.

83. Ibid. at 387.

84. Ibid. at 393–95.

85. *Rose* v. *Council for Better Education, Inc.*, 197.

86. Ibid. at 198.

87. See Opinion of the Justices, 624 So.2d 107 (Ala. 1993); *Lake View School District No. 25* v. *Huckabee*, 91 S.W.3d 472, 488 (Ark. 2002).

88. Minorini and Sugarman, "Educational Adequacy and the Courts: The Promise and Problems of Moving to a New Paradigm," p. 186.

89. See, for example, Melissa C. Carr and Susan H. Fuhrman, "The Politics of School Finance in the 1990s," in *Equity and Adequacy in Education Finance,* edited by Ladd, Chalk, and Hansen, p. 146.

90. *Campbell County School District* v. *State*, 907 P.2d 1239, 1279 (Wyo. 1995).

91. *Columbia Falls Elementary School District No. 6* v. *State*, 109 P.3d 257 (Mont. 2005).

92. *Robinson* v. *Cahill*, 303 A.2d at 295–97; *Pauley* v. *Kelley*, 255 S.E.2d 859, 877 (W.Va. 1979).

93. See *Montoy* v. *State*, 102 P.3d 1160 (Kan. 2005); *Claremont School District* v. *Governor*, 794 A.2d 744 (N.H. 2002); *DeRolph* v. *State*, 728 N.E.2d 993 (Ohio 2000); *Edgewood Ind. School District* v. *Meno*, 917 S.W.2d 717 (Tex. 1995).

94. See, for example, *Lake View School District No. 25* v. *Huckabee*, 2004 WL 1406270 (Ark. 2004); *Columbia Falls Elementary School District No. 6* v. *State*, 109 P.3d 257 (Mont. 2005); *Tennessee Small School Systems, Inc.* v. *McWherter*, 91 S.W.2d 232 (Tenn. 2002); *State* v. *Campbell County School District*, 19 P.3d 518 (Wyo. 2001).

95. See, for example, *Lake View School District No. 25* v. *Huckabee*, 2004 WL 1406270 (Ark. 2004); *Montoy* v. *State*, 102 P.3d 1160 (Kan. 2005); *Columbia Falls Elementary School*

District No. 6 v. *State*, 109 P.3d 257 (Mont. 2005); *Campaign for Fiscal Equity* v. *State*, 100 N.Y.2d 893 (2003); *DeRolph* v. *State*, 728 N.E.2d 993 (Ohio 2000); *Tennessee Small School Systems, Inc.* v. *McWherter*, 91 S.W.2d 232 (Tenn. 2002); *State* v. *Campbell County School District*, 19 P.3d 518 (Wyo. 2001).

96. See *Lake View School District No. 25* v. *Huckabee*, S.W.3d, 2005 WL 3436660 (Ark. 2005) (adopting special master's report and finding the public school funding system constitutionally inadequate because the state legislature failed to undertake the required study of the cost of an adequate education); *Londonderry School District SAU No. 12* v. *State*, 2006 WL 563120 (N.H. Super. 2006) (holding New Hampshire education finance law unconstitutional for failure to define and determine the cost of a constitutionally adequate education). See also *Campaign for Fiscal Equity, Inc.* v. *State*, 814 N.Y.S.2d 1, 2006 WL 724551 (N.Y., App. Div., 1st Dept. 2006) (reviewing and adopting, with modifications, report of referees concerning the cost of providing a constitutionally adequate education in New York City schools).

97. See McUsic, "The Use of Education Clauses in School Reform Litigation"; Michael Heise, "State Constitutions, School Finance Litigation, and the 'Third Wave': From Equity to Adequacy," *Temple Law Review* 68 (Fall 1995): 1151.

98. *Coalition for Adequacy and Fairness in School Funding, Inc.* v. *Chiles*, 680 So.2d 400 (Fla. 1996); *Committee for Education Rights* v. *Edgar*, 710 N.E.2d 798 (Ill. 1996); *Marrero* v. *Commonwealth*, 739 A.2d 110 (Pa. 1999); *City of Pawtucket* v. *Sundlun*, 662 A.2d 40 (R.I. 1995); and *Scott* v. *Commonwealth*, 443 S.E.2d 138 (Va. 1994).

99. Indeed, the Texas Supreme Court recently concluded that *progress* toward meeting state standards—even when actual achievement levels are low—is enough to satisfy the state's constitutional requirements. See *Neeley* v. *West Orange-Cove Consolidated Independent School District*, 176 S.W.2d 746, 787-90 (Tex. 2005).

100. See *Hull* v. *Albrecht*, 950 P.2d 1141 (Ariz. 1997); *Hull* v. *Albrecht*, 960 P.2d 634 (Ariz. 1998); *Montoy* v. *State*, 62 P.3d 228 (Kan. 2003); *Montoy* v. *State*, 102 P.3d 1160 (Kan. 2005); *Montoy* v. *Kansas*, 112 P.3d 923 (Kan. 2005); *Abbott v. Burke*, 643 A.2d 575 (N.J. 1994) (*Abbott III*); *Abbott* v. *Burke*, 693 A.2d 417 (N.J. 1997) (*Abbott IV*); *DeRolph* v. *State*, 728 N.E. 2d 993 (Ohio 2000); *DeRolph* v. *State*, 754 N.E.2d 1184 (Ohio 2001); *De Rolph* v. *State*, 780 N.E.2d 529 (Ohio 2002).

101. *Lake View School District No. 25* v. *Huckabee*, 189 S.W. 3d 1, 2004 WL 1406270 (Ark. 2004); *Hancock* v. *Commissioner of Education*, 822 N.E.2d 1134 (Mass. 2004); *DeRolph* v. *Ohio*, 754 N.E.2d 1184 (Ohio 2001). The Texas Supreme Court has also been relatively deferential in accepting the state's definition of a proper educational curriculum, state accreditation standards, and state accountability mechanisms. It has held that in reviewing education legislation to see whether the state has met the state's constitutional requirements, it will apply the extremely deferential "arbitrariness" standard—for example, it will uphold the law unless its provisions are arbitrary (*Neeley* v. *West Orange–Cove Consolidated Independent School District*, 783–85), and it has concluded that given the improvements in the Texas schools, the state's education system cannot be called "arbitrary" even though many students fall short of state standards. Id. at 789–90.

102. *Hancock* v. *Commissioner of Education*, 822 N.E.2d at 1140.

103. Ibid. at 1152–53.

104. *DeRolph* v. *State*, 754 N.E.2d 1184,1201 (Ohio 2001).

105. *Lake View School District No. 25* v. *Huckabee*, 2004 WL 1406270 (Ark. 2004).

106. *Lake View School District No. 25* v. *Huckabee*, 2005 WL 1041144 (Ark. 2005), *Lake View School District No. 25* v. *Huckabee*, 2005 WL 3436660 (Ark. 2005); *DeRolph* v. *State*, 780 N.E.2d 529 (Ohio 2002).

107. *State ex rel. State* v. *Lewis*, 780 N.E.2d 529 (Ohio 2003).

108. *Ex parte James*, 836 So.2d 813 (Ala. 2002).

109. See, for example, *Tennessee Small School Systems, Inc.* v. *McWherter*, 91 S.W.3d 232 (Tenn. 2002); *State* v. *Campbell County School District*, 19 P.3d 518 (Wyo. 2001).

3 JOHN C. EASTMAN

Reinterpreting the Education Clauses in State Constitutions

I N THE PAST decade, a number of state courts have found a new "fundamental right" to education in centuries-old provisions in state constitutions.
Those courts have then used that fundamental right determination to establish
the level of educational funding that, from their particular point of view, is
required to be constitutionally "adequate" and even to mandate the content of
the curriculum itself. In the process they have ignored considered legislative
judgments to the contrary. In this chapter, I explore the historical understanding of the actual language of the state constitutional provisions on which the
new state court decisions rest, concluding that in almost every instance the original provisions were designed to set only hortatory goals for the legislature, not
to confer a judicially enforceable individual right to a certain level of financial
support for—or quality of—public education. I next consider some recent constitutional amendments that might be read as supporting the fundamental right
holdings and conclude that in most cases those amendments, too, fall short of
conferring a judicially enforceable right to a constitutionally mandated "adequate" public education. Finally, I take issue with judicial holdings that have,
through the use of fundamental right determinations, injected themselves into

The author wishes to thank Chapman University law student Kristi Collins for her stel-
lar contribution to the research for this article and also former Chapman law students Monica Edwards and Cecilia Aguayo, who collected much of the research in an earlier phase of
this project.

what is inherently a policy issue, reserved by the state constitutions to the political branches of government. I conclude with a cautionary note about the threat to participatory democracy that those holdings might pose.

A Constitutional Puzzle

In 1998, I published a somewhat provocative article in the *American Journal of Legal History* entitled "When Did Education Become a Civil Right? An Assessment of State Constitutional Provisions for Education, 1776–1900."[1] Starting with the Supreme Court's doctrinaire, positive-law holding in *San Antonio Independent School District* v. *Rodriguez* that education was not a fundamental right for purposes of federal constitutional analysis because there was no mandate for education to be found, either directly or indirectly, in the U.S. Constitution, I undertook a comprehensive review of education provisions in the constitutions of the several states.[2] At first glance, one might have concluded that under the *Rodriguez* formulation, the states would be treating education—by which I mean state-financed education—as a fundamental right. After all, from the outset state constitutions contained pretty significant provisions addressing education.

My review of the first century and a quarter of U.S. history, however, led me to draw the opposite conclusion. As described more fully below, most of the education provisions in state constitutions adopted during the eighteenth and nineteenth centuries were only hortatory, and even those that contained apparently obligatory language were in most cases not interpreted as imposing any specific mandate on the legislature and certainly not as conferring a judicially enforceable right to education.

The "hortatory" story from the eighteenth and nineteenth centuries holds true through the first three-quarters of the twentieth century. Even states that adopted somewhat obligatory language continued to treat that language as setting legislative goals, not as imposing judicially enforceable mandates. Not until the 1970s, following the "rights revolution" of the Warren Court, does one find courts actually starting to hold that the education provisions in state constitutions afforded fundamental right status to public education, conferring a judicially enforceable individual right not just to an education but to a certain level of financing for—and even a certain quality of—education. In most cases, those court decisions were rendered without much focus on the actual language of the particular education provision at issue and without much consideration of the inherent policy judgments that underlie a determination of funding level and quality. Far from enforcing a constitutional mandate, therefore, those decisions have effected a fundamental shift of policy-making power away from legislatures and to the courts, posing a serious threat to the principle of separation of powers and ultimately to government by consent itself.

Eighteenth- and Nineteenth-Century Recap

Most of the state constitutional provisions adopted during the nation's founding period contained language that was clearly only hortatory, describing goals that the legislatures "ought"[3] to pursue "as soon as conveniently may be,"[4] but most assuredly not providing a judicially enforceable right to any particular level or quality of education. The constitutions of a few early states flirted with obligatory language, but those provisions obligated the legislature to establish schools,[5] not to provide an individual right to education, and even those nominally obligatory provisions were quickly repealed or entirely unfulfilled. Georgia, for example, did not establish a common school system until 1873, despite language in the Georgia Constitution of 1777 mandating that "schools *shall be erected* in each county, and supported at the general expense of the State, as the legislature shall hereafter point out."[6]

New state constitutions adopted in the early part of the nineteenth century almost uniformly followed the hortatory model if they made provision for education at all. Two states did open the door to a claim of a right to education, but the door was quickly closed by judicial interpretation in one of them, and the mandate in the other seems not to have been enforced for a century and a half. The constitutions of Indiana and Connecticut, in 1816 and 1818, respectively, both required the state's schools to be open to "all" the children of the state. Indiana's provision was mitigated somewhat by the caveat "as soon as circumstances will permit," but even more by a decision of the state supreme court holding that the constitutional mandate that the state's schools be "equally open to all" meant "all the white children resident within the district."[7] Oddly, the Indiana court relied on an Ohio court interpretation of the Ohio Constitution, which contained only hortatory language, quite unlike the obligatory language of the Indiana Constitution.

Of the nearly two dozen new or amended constitutions that were adopted between 1835 and 1860, more than half followed the hortatory model. Several contained obligatory language, typically requiring the legislature to establish a "system" of schools, even a "thorough and efficient system," rather than conferring an individual right to public education, enforceable in the courts of law.[8] Three—New Jersey in 1844, Wisconsin in 1848, and Iowa in 1857—

contained requirements that their "system" be free and open to "all."[9] But Iowa's mandate was gutted by another clause allowing the legislature to void the mandate any time after 1863, which it promptly did in 1864. Wisconsin's mandate was gutted by judicial interpretation in the 1886 decision of *The State ex rel. Comstock* v. *Joint School District No. 1 of Arcadia*,[10] holding that a child residing in a district without a school had no constitutional right to attend school in a neighboring district free of charge. And New Jersey's mandate, held to provide a "legal right" for children to attend the school in their district, was nevertheless interpreted as not applicable if "the schools . . . were full."[11] In other words, the constitutional provision conveyed a right to access whatever educational system was available, but left it to the legislature to determine the scope of the educational opportunity that would be provided.

Following the Civil War, a number of states adopted new constitutional language specifying that the legislature create a "thorough and efficient system" of education open to "all children" in the state. Louisiana in 1864, Missouri in 1865 and 1875, Pennsylvania in 1873, Nebraska in 1875, and Colorado in 1876 all contained that apparent mandate,[12] as did the "reconstruction" constitutions in Alabama in 1867 and in Arkansas, Florida, Georgia, Louisiana, Mississippi, North Carolina, South Carolina, and Texas in 1868.[13] The Illinois Constitution of 1870 added the mandate that a "good" common school education be provided to all children, the first state to include such an obviously qualitative component.[14]

After reconstruction, most of these states continued to have constitutional provisions apparently mandating the creation of a "system" of education open to "all" children in the state. In none of the states, however, had those clauses been interpreted as conferring a judicially enforceable right to education at all, much less a judicially enforceable right to a certain level of spending on education or a certain quality of educational opportunity. Whatever the state legislature chose to provide had to be available equally to all the children of the state, but that requirement was imposed as much by the equal protection clause of the U.S. Constitution as by state provisions requiring that whatever education systems were established be open to all children.[15]

Twentieth-Century Constitutional Amendments

Most of the new state constitutional provisions for education adopted in the twentieth century continued to track the language of provisions that were adopted in the late nineteenth century and that were not interpreted at the time to confer a judicially enforceable right. Those provisions fell into two principal groups—one requiring the state legislature to establish a *system* of schools, and the other requiring that education in the system be equally open (and free) to *all* children. The latter arguably provided stronger grounds for the "individual right" arguments, or at least for the claimed right of equal access to whatever educational system was provided. In the former category, Arkansas in 1968 retreated from the 1874 language extending free education to "all" children between the ages of six and twenty-one, providing instead for a "suitable and efficient system of free public schools" "to secure to the people the advantages and opportunities of education," a provision that has not been found to provide a fundamental right to education.[16] Florida added a provision to its constitution in 1968 that "[a]dequate provision shall be made by law for a uniform system of free public schools," and shortly thereafter the Florida Supreme Court found this "system" clause to confer an individual "right"; however, that holding was effectively overturned by a 1998 amendment to the Florida Constitution declaring education a "fundamental value" rather than a fundamental right, expressly to avoid the consequences of the interpretation that had been given by the Florida courts.[17] Georgia wanted its system of free common schools to provide "an adequate education for the citizens." The Georgia Supreme Court first interpreted the clause in 1979 as creating a right, but then in 1981 held the right not to be "fundamental."[18] Hawaii provided for a "system of public schools,"[19] and Louisiana directed the legislature to establish a "public educational system,"[20] but neither provision has been held to confer an individual or fundamental right.

Indeed, more than half the states have thus far adhered to the view, universally accepted through the end of the nineteenth century, that the provision of public education is inherently a policy judgment best left to the discretion of the political branches, primarily the legislature.[21] Idaho, which provided for a "general, uniform and thorough system of public, free common schools," adhered to the earlier, original understanding of its 1890 constitutional clause.[22] In 1975 the Idaho Supreme Court held that "[o]n its face, [section 1] mandates action by the Legislature. It does not establish education as a basic fundamental right. Nor does it dictate a central state system of equal expenditures per student."[23] Even after other states interpreted similar state constitutional language as creating a fundamental right to publicly financed education, the Idaho Supreme Court reiterated in 1993 that "education is not a fundamental right because it is not a right directly guaranteed by the state constitution. Rather, art. 9, §1 imposes [a duty upon the legislature]."[24]

Illinois, too, resisted the trend, amending its constitution in 1970 to designate education in its "system" of free public schools to be a "fundamental goal" rather than a "right," a decision that the Illinois Supreme Court respected in the 1996 decision in *Committee for Education Rights* v. *Edgar*.[25] Maine retained its 1820 provision making it the duty of its towns "to make suitable provision" for the support of public schools,[26] and it has not interpreted that provision as creating a fundamental right. Maryland mandated that a "thorough and efficient System of Free Public Schools" be established at the first legislative session after adoption of its 1867 constitution,[27] yet its supreme court held in 1983 that that provision—standing alone or in conjunction with a related budgetary provision—did not create a fundamental right:

> The directive contained in Article VIII of the Maryland Constitution for the establishment and maintenance of a thorough and efficient statewide system of free public schools is not alone sufficient to elevate education to fundamental status. Nor do the budgetary provisions of §52 of Article III of the Constitution require that we declare that the right to education is fundamental. The right to an adequate education in Maryland is no more fundamental than the right to personal security, to fire protection, to welfare subsidies, to health care or like vital governmental services; accordingly, strict scrutiny is not the proper standard of review of the Maryland system of financing its public schools.[28]

The Michigan appellate courts, after first holding that Michigan's "system" provision[29] clearly bestowed on Michigan citizens a "fundamental right to a free public education,"[30] ultimately rejected that position, holding in a series of cases that "education is not a fundamental right under Michigan's Constitution of 1963"[31] and concluding that "although a free public education is a vitally important service provided by this state, there is no fundamental right to such an education under our constitution."[32] New Mexico held in 1987 that its mandate for a "uniform system of free public schools sufficient for the education of, and open to, all the children" did not give rise to a contractual relationship that would permit suits for breach of contract.[33] The supreme courts of Ohio and Oregon both declined to find a constitutional right in their century-old provisions providing for, respectively, a "thorough and efficient" and a "uniform, and general" system of common schools.[34]

In contrast, Connecticut in 1977 found that a 1965 amendment to its constitution that required the legislature to "implement . . . by appropriate legislation" the principle that "there shall always be free public . . . schools in the state" conferred a judicially enforceable "fundamental right" to education that subjected legislative financing judgments to "strict judicial scrutiny."[35] And the initial reticence of the Pennsylvania courts in the 1970s to find a "fundamental right" in the state's "thorough and efficient" constitutional provision was reversed in 1995 when the state supreme court squarely held that "public education in Pennsylvania is a fundamental right."[36]

The second category of provisions shifted the focus from "system" of schools to the provision of education to "all children." Alaska's new constitution of 1959 required the legislature to establish a "system of public schools open to *all* children of the state."[37] Nebraska required its legislature to provide free instruction in the common schools to "all" children.[38] New Jersey mandated a "thorough and efficient system" of education for "all" children.[39] And New York mandated a "system of free common schools, wherein all the children of the state may be educated."[40] Of these, the courts in both New Jersey and New York, in 1975 and 1976, respectively, found their respective clauses to create fundamental rights,[41] and the Alaska Supreme Court held in 1972 that the provision in its state constitution conferred "a right to public education."[42]

Some states adopting provisions for "all" children included caveats that had undercut any claim of right in parallel provisions that were adopted in the nineteenth century. Arizona, for example, required the legislature to provide for the establishment of a "general and uniform public school system," which "*shall be as nearly free as possible*" and which shall consist of a free school "in every school district for at least six months in each year" and "open to all pupils between the ages of six and twenty-one years."[43] Colorado continued to require the establishment "*as soon as practicable*" of a "thorough and uniform system of free public schools" for "all" the children of the state.[44] The Arizona Supreme Court nevertheless found its clause to confer a "fundamental right,"[45] while the Colorado Supreme Court expressly "refuse[d] . . . to venture into the realm of social policy under the guise that there is a fundamental right to education."[46]

The initial forays by Alaska, Arizona, New Jersey, New York, and Connecticut into "discovering" a fundamental right to education based on relatively recent, twentieth-century amendments to their state constitutions were followed in several other states despite the fact that the other states were still operating under constitutions or constitutional provisions adopted in the nineteenth century (or earlier) without any notion that the provisions created a judicially enforceable right or fundamental right to education at the time that they were drafted and ratified. The Delaware Supreme Court, for example, in 1980 found a constitutional right to education in its 1897 constitutional provision providing for a "system of free public schools."[47] The Kentucky high court in 1989 found a "fundamental right" in its 1891 constitutional directive to the state legislature to provide "by appropriate legislation" for an "efficient system of common schools."[48] The Supreme Judicial Court of Massachusetts and the Supreme Court of New Hampshire held in 1993 and 1997, respectively, that the parallel provisions of their respective constitutions (the 1780 Massachusetts Constitution and the 1784 New Hampshire Constitution) that made it the "duty" of the legislature "to cherish the interests of literature and the sciences, and all seminaries of them" conferred the right to an "adequate" education despite explicit acknowledgement that the word "adequate" was not to be found in the constitutions at all.[49] The Minnesota Supreme Court in 1993 found a "fundamental right" to education in the state's 1857 constitutional provision describing the duty of the legislature "to establish a general and uniform system of public schools."[50] The North Dakota Supreme Court found in 1992 and 1994 first a "right" and then a "fundamental right" in its 1889 provision for a "uniform system" "open to all children of the state."[51] The South Carolina Supreme Court likewise waited more than a century to find in 1999 that its 1895 provision providing for a "system of free public schools open to all children" conferred the right "for each child to receive a minimally adequate education," which it then proceeded to define *ex nihilo*.[52] Tennessee's high court found in 1993 that the "right to a free public education" was guaranteed to the children of the state in an 1870 provision "encourag[ing] support" of a "system" of education. It did so after discussing the opinions of other state courts that had found a "fundamental right" to education in their own, typically much stronger, constitutional provisions.[53] A Texas appellate court found in 1987 a "fundamental right" in its 1876 provision to create an "efficient system of public free schools."[54] Washington's 1889 "ample provision for the education of all children" through a "general and uniform system" was held in 1975 to be a "fundamental constitutional right."[55] West Virginia's 1872 requirement that "the legislature shall provide, by general law, for a thorough and efficient system of free schools" was interpreted in 1979 as conferring a "fundamental constitutional right," obligating the legislature to develop "certain high-quality statewide educational standards."[56] Wisconsin's 1848 provision for "as nearly uniform as possible" district schools, free to "all children," was held in 1976 to create a "fundamental right."[57]

Perhaps most stark of all was the 1997 decision of the Vermont Supreme Court in *Brigham* v. *Vermont*,[58] interpreting a more than 200-year-old constitutional provision in the Vermont Constitution of 1793:

> Laws for the encouragement of virtue and prevention of vice and immorality ought to be constantly kept in force, and duly executed; and a competent number of schools ought to be maintained in each town unless the general assembly permits other provisions for the convenient instruction of youth.[59]

Despite the clearly hortatory nature of this provision, the Vermont Supreme Court in 1997 effectively treated the provision as creating a judicially enforceable fundamental right, going so far as to state that "[t]he contention that the framers intended these fundamental freedoms to be mere aspirational ideals rather than binding and enforceable obligations upon the state cannot be seriously maintained."[60]

An even odder story comes out of Alabama. The Alabama Constitution of 1901 contained an education provision virtually identical in relevant respects to the provision in its 1875 constitution: "The legislature shall establish, organize, and maintain a *liberal* system of public schools throughout the state for the benefit of the children thereof between the ages of seven and twenty-one years."[61] Only the word "liberal" was added. As was clear with countless other provisions adopted during the nineteenth century, the mandate to establish a "system" of schools did not confer a judicially enforceable right on *individuals*. Nevertheless, to confirm that understanding in the wake of *Brown* v. *Board of Education*[62] and to delete a requirement for segregated education (though retaining permissive segregation), the people of Alabama in 1956 amended their constitution to provide:

> It is the policy of the state of Alabama to foster and promote the education of its citizens in a manner and extent consistent with available resources, and the willingness and ability of the individual student, but nothing in this Constitution shall be construed as creating or recognizing any right to education or training at public expense, nor as limiting the authority and duty of the legislature, in furthering or providing for education, to require or impose conditions or procedures deemed necessary to the preservation of peace and order. . . .
>
> To avoid confusion and disorder and to promote effective and economical planning for education, the legislature may authorize the parents or guardians of minors, who desire that such minors shall attend schools provided for their own race, to make election to that end, such election to be effective for such period and to such extent as the legislature may provide.[63]

Shortly after the 1956 amendment was adopted, the Alabama Supreme Court held in *Mitchell* v. *McCall* that "the State of Alabama is under no constitutional obligation to provide public schools" under section 256 of the Alabama Constitution of 1901, as amended.[64] But the amendment was held to be unconstitutional by a state trial court in the 1990 case of *Alabama Coalition for Equity* v. *Hunt* because of its obvious racially discriminatory purpose.[65] Then, in a magnificent feat of logic, the state supreme court subsequently reinterpreted the 1901 version of section 256 as leaving no doubt "that Alabama schoolchildren have an enforceable constitutional right to an education."[66] Because the 1956 amendment "modified the original provision to eliminate any implication that there is a constitutional right to public education in Alabama,"[67] noted the court, the *unamended* version of section 256 must have conferred a constitutional right to education if the 1956 amendment was not to be deemed a "futile act."[68]

The route to finding a fundamental right in these states, through judicial interpretation (one might say judicial fiat), stands in stark contrast to the route pursued in North Carolina, which in 1970 amended its constitution to provide that "the people have a right to the privilege of education, and it is the duty of the State to guard and maintain that right."[69] Yet even in North Carolina, the courts have gone beyond the constitutional mandate, holding in 1997 that the long-standing constitutional requirement for a "general and uniform system of free public schools"[70] gave to "every child a fundamental right to a *sound* basic education."[71]

Consequences of the 1970s "Rights" Trend

The full import of the trend toward treating education as a judicially enforceable fundamental right is only now beginning to come into view. Recent cases in Nevada and Kansas, for example, demonstrate just how great a threat to citizen self-government the fundamental right formulation is. Before turning to those cases, it is important to define just what is meant by the new treatment of education as a fundamental right.

At one level, the right to pursue an education has always been viewed as fundamental in this country. The Wyoming Constitution of 1890 accurately conveys the prevailing sentiment: "The right of the citizens to opportunities for education should have practical recognition."[72] And the Supreme Court's recognition in *Pierce* v. *Society of Sisters*[73] and *Meyer* v. *Nebraska*[74] of a right of parents to direct the education of their children marks the beginning of the era of substantive due process in the noneconomic arena. State court decisions treating education as a fundamental right would therefore seem to be entirely unobjectionable.

Yet the recent state court holdings have understood the fundamental right to education at an entirely different level—not just the right to pursue the education of one's choice, but the "right" to have someone else—the government, which is to say taxpayers—pay for that education. But how much education, at what cost, and for what purpose? Even states that have constitutional provisions which, on their face, appear to impose qualitative mandates—"adequate,"[75] "suitable,"[76] "good,"[77] "quality" or "high-quality"[78]—hardly provide judicially manageable criteria for answering such questions. Any answers are inherently policy judgments, not matters that can be determined by the courts as if there were some scientifically correct standard to be applied.[79]

It should come as no surprise, therefore, that courts that begin with finding a constitutionally protected fundamental right to education quickly progress to making policy judgments about funding levels and even curricular design. In *Rose* v. *Council for Better Education, Inc.*, for example, the Kentucky Supreme Court set out the contours of a curriculum necessary for a constitutionally adequate education.[80] Such a curriculum should, according to the Kentucky court, foster oral and written communication skills; provide knowledge of different economic, political, and social systems; foster mental and physical health; develop an appreciation for the arts; and prepare students for higher education or vocational training and ultimately employment. The West Virginia Supreme Court adopted a similar approach, determining in *Pauley* v. *Kelly* that a curriculum fostering literacy, mathematical ability, knowledge of government, knowledge of one's self, preparation for a career or further education, recreational activities, the arts, and social ethics, was constitutionally mandated.[81]

The Maryland Supreme Court seems to have understood that such judicial policymaking is a necessary consequence of court decisions converting aspirational goals into fundamental rights. "The right to an adequate education in Maryland," it held in *Hornbeck* v. *Somerset County Board of Education*, "is no more fundamental than the right to personal security, to fire protection, to welfare subsidies, to health care or like vital governmental services."[82] Yet when only one of those fundamentally important government services is deemed a fundamental right, courts claim the ability to vindicate that right even at the expense of other government services (or, conversely, by ordering the imposition of taxes not approved by the people's representatives). This was the scenario that came to pass in Nevada in 2003 and Kansas in 2005.

In 1994 and again in 1996,[83] Nevada voters overwhelmingly approved an amendment to their state constitution that prohibited the state legislature from imposing new or increased taxes without the concurrence of two-thirds of the members of each house of the legislature.[84] In 2003, the Nevada Supreme Court found in *Guinn* v. *Legislature of State of Nevada* that this core structural restriction on the taxing power of the state legislature was interfering with the legislature's ability to fund fully the state's $1.6 billion education budget, which the court found to be mandated by the state constitution (even though the only requirement in the state constitution was that the state establish a school in each district for at least six months a year—a mandate that would be fulfilled at significantly less than the $1.6 billion budgeted for education).[85] The court then issued a truly extraordinary opinion and writ of mandamus directing the Nevada legislature to consider tax-increase legislation by "simple majority rule" rather than by the two-thirds vote required by the state constitution. The court found the structural limitation imposed by Nevada voters on their legislature to be a mere "procedural and general constitutional requirement" that had to "give way to the substantive and specific constitutional mandate to fund public education."[86]

Similarly, the Kansas Supreme Court in *Montoy* v. *Kansas*[87] found that the largest education budget in that state's history was not constitutionally adequate and so issued an order directing the legislature to appropriate additional funds to meet the court's view of what would constitute the "suitable" funding mandated by the state constitution.[88] It did so despite the fact that in Kansas, as elsewhere, the power to tax and spend the fiscal resources of the state is assigned to the legislature, not to the courts, and despite the fact that the constitutional mandate that the "legislature shall provide for intellectual, educational, vocational and scientific improvement by establishing and maintaining public schools" was expressly subject to the discretionary caveat "which may be organized and changed in such manner as may be provided by law."[89]

Both courts expressly rested their rulings on *Marbury* v. *Madison* and the Supreme Court's view in that case that it is the role of the courts to interpret the constitution and enforce its provisions against contrary legislation.[90] Yet, truth be told, both reflect a significant expansion of the holding in *Marbury* itself, especially considering the indefinite nature of the constitutional text at issue in these cases.

It is important to remember the precise claim that Chief Justice Marshall staked out in *Marbury* v. *Madison*. As I have noted elsewhere,[91] it was not that the courts are the *only* arbiter of constitutional questions (the Kansas Supreme Court went so far as to claim in *Montoy* "that the final decision as to the constitutionality of legislation rests *exclusively* with the courts").[92] Nor was it even that the Supreme Court is the *final* arbiter of all constitutional questions, not just for the judicial branch but for all three branches of government, though that claim certainly was urged by Marbury's counsel.[93]

Rather, Marshall made the much more limited, commonsense claim that, in a regime operating under a constitution by which only certain limited, enumerated powers were granted to the government, laws made in excess of that delegated authority could not be applied by judges bound by oath to uphold the Constitution.[94] The courts, then, were not only authorized to refuse to give unlawful statutes any effect in the cases before them but were in fact obligated to take that course.

Marshall was not the first to make such a claim, of course. Alexander Hamilton made it explicitly in *Federalist* 78:

> The complete independence of the courts of justice is peculiarly essential in a limited Constitution. By a limited Constitution, I understand one which contains certain specified exceptions to the legislative authority; such, for instance, as that it shall pass no bills of attainder, no *ex post facto* laws, and the like. Limitations of this kind can be preserved in practice no other way than through the medium of courts of justice, whose duty it must be to declare all acts contrary to the manifest tenor of the Constitution void. Without this, all the reservations of particular rights or privileges would amount to nothing.[95]

Oliver Ellsworth likewise contended during the Connecticut ratifying convention that judicial review would also be available to enforce the limits of the powers granted to the national government.[96] Indeed, the idea that judicial review would be used to ensure conformity with *all* the Constitution's provisions—the limits of enumerated powers as well as the express prohibitions—seems to have been assumed by the delegates to the Constitutional Convention, even during a debate in which the convention rejected efforts to have the Supreme Court justices serve as a council of revision that would have a share in the president's veto power. George Mason noted, for example, that judges "could declare an unconstitutional law void."[97] Luther Martin, who opposed including Supreme Court justices in a council of revision, and James Wilson, who supported such a council, both agreed that judges, in their judicial capacity, would already have "a negative on the laws."[98] The debate over the council of revision was thus about whether the justices should *also* have the power to negate laws on policy grounds before they took effect, not whether they would be obliged, when asked to enforce an unconstitutional law in a case or controversy before them, to give effect to the unconstitutional law, the Constitution itself notwithstanding.

The line between a court properly invalidating unconstitutional legislation, on one hand, and interjecting itself into the policy judgments of the elected branches of government, on the other, has been well established ever since the Constitutional Convention rejected a policymaking role for the courts that would have been established had the council of revision task been added to the judiciary's constitutional duties. The former is designed to uphold constitutionalism and "government by consent of the people," the foundation upon which it rests, while the latter undermines government by consent by permitting an unelected (or at least less accountable) judiciary to make fundamental policy choices that ought to be made by the people or their direct representatives.

Admittedly, precisely defining that constitutional line may be a difficult task, but some state educational provisions provide a model of judicially enforceable clauses. Florida's Constitution was amended in 2002 to specify maximum class sizes, for example;[99] Pennsylvania's 1874 constitution contained a requirement that the legislature appropriate "at least one million dollars each year" "for the maintenance and support of a thorough and efficient system of public schools";[100] and Nevada's 1864 constitution contained a mandate (still in effect) that the "legislature shall provide for a uniform system of common schools, by which a school shall be established and maintained in each school district at least six months in every year."[101] All of those provisions are specific enough to lend themselves quite readily to judicial enforcement and also to the argument that, by enforcing such provisions, the courts are merely giving voice to the higher mandate that the people have imposed through their state constitution. The several state constitutional mandates that public schools be open to "all" the children of the state are of a similar nature, easily and properly enforceable by the courts.

Indeterminate provisions that mandate a "thorough and efficient system" of public schools[102] and even those that call for "suitable"[103] or "adequate"[104] education systems are not as susceptible to judicial enforcement, and the clearly hortatory clauses are not susceptible to judicial enforcement at all, at least not on any theory of constitutional interpretation remotely resembling the holding of *Marbury* v. *Madison,* which is based on the authority of the people.[105] Yet the recent spate of state court "adequacy" holdings purport to enforce such clauses.

Whether decisions such as those recently issued by the supreme courts of Kansas and Nevada, made possible by fundamental right determinations, result in the reallocation of state resources or the imposition of additional taxes, the fact remains that considered policy judgments of state legislatures are being altered by the courts on the basis of expansive interpretations of what is, in most cases, clearly hortatory constitutional language. Quite apart from the threat to separation of powers, such decisions also threaten the very essence of government by consent and, collaterally, the benefits to be gained from participatory democracy.

In contrast, Thomas Jefferson's own plans for public education in Virginia were developed to foster participatory democracy. Jefferson proposed the establishment of a school in each community, managed by the citizens of that community. The plan appears to have been designed not just to educate the community's children in the basic common school subjects, but also to educate the local citizenry in the habits of self-government. That plan, or something quite like it, was common in New England towns and was adopted in the western territories of the United States as well, with early federal educational land grants to townships made directly to the people of the township. This aspect of "civic education" is quite salutary though largely overlooked in current debates over educational policy. Its import was somewhat impaired with the advent of the centralization plans of the early nineteenth century, by which the setting of educational policy was largely transferred from the local township to the state. But even at the state level, determinations of educational policy were still part of the political process, with ultimate responsibility resting with the people themselves.

The initial round of "equity" litigation ensured that the people did not use their responsibility and power to allocate educational resources in an inequitable fashion—a salutary judicial check on majority tyranny. The new "adequacy" litigation, however, removes educational policymaking from the political process altogether, permitting the courts to countermand the educational decisions that the people (or their direct representatives) make for themselves. Quite apart from the fact that the courts have no particular expertise that would suggest that they are more capable of making such policy judgments than the legislature, the demise of citizen participation that will most certainly follow cannot be a good thing, even for the success of the education programs themselves.

Notes

1. John C. Eastman, "When Did Education Become a Civil Right? An Assessment of State Constitutional Provisions for Education, 1776–1900," *American Journal of Legal History* 62 (1998): 1–33.

2. *San Antonio Independent School District* v. *Rodriguez,* 411 U.S. 1 (1973).

3. See, for example, Vermont Constitution of 1786, ch. II, sec. 38; Vermont Constitution of 1793, ch. II, sec. 41.

4. See, for example, Pennsylvania Constitution of 1790, art. VII, sec. 1; Georgia Constitution of 1798, art. IV, sec. 13.

5. See, for example, North Carolina Constitution of 1776, art. XLI; Pennsylvania Constitution of 1776, sec. 44; Vermont Constitution of 1777, sec. 40.

6. Georgia Constitution of 1777, art. LIV (emphasis added).

7. *Lewis* v. *Henry,* 2 Ind. (2 Cart.) 332, 334 (1850).

8. See, for example, Michigan Constitution of 1835, art. X, sec. 2; Iowa Constitution of 1846, art. IX, sec. 3; California Constitution of 1849, art. IX, sec. 3; Ohio Constitution of 1851, art. VI, sec. 2; Minnesota Constitution of 1857, art. VIII, sec. 3.

9. New Jersey Constitution of 1844, art. IV, sec. 7, pt. 6; Wisconsin Constitution of 1848, art. X, sec. 3; Iowa Constitution of 1857, art. IX (1st), sec. 12.

10. 65 Wis. 631 (1886).

11. *Pierce* v. *Union District School Trustees*, 46 N.J. Law (17 Vroom) 76, 78 (1884).

12. Louisiana Constitution of 1864, Title XI, art. 141; Missouri Constitution of 1865, art. VIII, sec. 1; Pennsylvania Constitution of 1873, art. X, sec. 1; Nebraska Constitution of 1875, art. VIII, sec. 6; Colorado Constitution of 1876, art. IX, sec. 2.

13. Alabama Constitution of 1867, art. XI, sec. 6; Arkansas Constitution of 1868, art. IX, sec. 1; Florida Constitution of 1868, art. IX, secs.1–2; Georgia Constitution of 1868, art. VI, sec. 1; Louisiana Constitution of 1868, title VII, art. 135; Mississippi Constitution of 1868, art. VIII, sec. 1; North Carolina Constitution of 1868, art. IX, sec. 2; South Carolina Constitution of 1868, art. X, secs. 3 and 10; Texas Constitution of 1868, art. IX, sec. 1.

14. Illinois Constitution of 1870, art. VIII, sec. 1. Despite this apparent qualitative mandate, I have located no case interpreting the clause as conferring a judicially enforceable right to a certain qualitative level of education, although there are cases holding that the "thorough and efficient" clause, immediately preceding, required that school districts be compact and contiguous. See, for example, *People ex rel. Community Unit School District No. 1* v. *Decatur School District No. 61*, 194 N.E.2d 659, 661-62 (Ill. App. 1963) (citing *People ex rel. Tudor* v. *Vance*, 29 N.E.2d 673 (Ill. 1940); *People ex rel. Bartlett* v. *Vass*, 155 N.E. 854 (Ill. 1927); *People ex rel. Beedy* v. *Regnier*, 37 N.E.2d 186 (Ill. 1941)). In any event, the qualitative language was dropped from the education provision in the Illinois Constitution of 1970.

15. See *Ward* v. *Flood*, 48 Cal. 36 (1874).

16. Arkansas Constitution of 1874, art. XIV, sec. 1 (as amended by Amendment 53, adopted 1968). The requirement that the state maintain "a general, *suitable* and efficient system of free public schools" might be read to import a qualitative component, but thus far the Arkansas courts have not interpreted the clause in that manner, and the final clause of the provision—that the amendment was intended to authorize the provision of educational services to children under six and to adults over twenty-one years of age and that "no other interpretation shall be given to it"—strongly counsels against any such interpretation.

17. Florida Constitution of 1868, art. IX, sec. 1; *Scavella* v. *School Board of Dade County*, 363 So.2d 1095 (Fla. 1978). The Florida Constitution was amended again in 2002 to provide specific mandates regarding class size. See Florida Constitution of 1968, art. IX, sec.1, as amended.

18. Georgia Constitution of 1976, art. VIII, sec. 1, par. 1; *Crim* v. *McWhorter*, 252 S.E.2d 421 (Ga. 1979); *McDaniel* v. *Thomas*, 285 S.E.2d 156, 167 (Ga. 1981).

19. Hawaii Constitution of 1978, art. X, sec. 1.

20. Louisiana Constitution of 1974, art. VIII, sec. 1.

21. For an example of the earlier understanding, which prevailed even through the first three-quarters of the twentieth century, see *Logan City School District* v. *Kowallis*, 77 P.2d 348, 351 (Utah 1938): "The provision for being open does not apply to matters financial; it does not mean they must be free. It simply means that all children must have equal rights and opportunity to attend the grade or class of school for which such child is suited by previous training or development"; Utah Constitution of 1895, art. X, sec. 1 (providing for "system" "which shall be open to children of the state").

22. Idaho Constitution of 1890, art. IX, sec. 1.

23. *Thompson* v. *Engelking*, 537 P.2d 635, 648 (Idaho 1975).

24. *Idaho Schools for Equal Educational Opportunity* v. *Evans*, 850 P.2d 724, 733 (Idaho 1993).

25. *Committee for Educational Rights* v. *Edgar*, 672 N.E.2d 1178, 1194-95 (Ill. 1996).

26. Maine Constitution of 1820, art. VIII, sec. 1.

27. Maryland Constitution of 1867, art. VII, sec. 1.

28. *Hornbeck* v. *Somerset County Board of Education*, 458 A.2d 758, 786 (Md. 1983).

29. See Michigan Constitution of 1963, art. VIII, sec. 2.

30. *Lintz* v. *Alpena Public Schools of Alpena and Presque Isle Counties*, 325 N.W.2d 803, 805 (Mich. Ct. App. 1982).

31. See, for example, *East Jackson Public Schools* v. *State*, 348 N.W.2d 303, 305-06 (Mich. Ct. App. 1984); *Palmer* v. *Bloomfield Hills Board of Education*, 417 N.W.2d 505, 506 (Mich. Ct. App. 1987).

32. *Feaster* v. *Portage Public Schools*, 534 N.W.2d 242, 246 (Mich. Ct. App. 1995).

33. *Rubio by and through Rubio* v. *Carlsbad Municipal School District*, 744 P.2d 919, 921 (N.M. Ct. App. 1987).

34. *Board of Education of Cincinnati* v. *Walter*, 390 N.E.2d 813 (Ohio 1979); Ohio Constitution of 1851, art. VI, sec. 2; *Olsen* v. *State*, 554 P.2d 139, 144 (Ore. 1976); Oregon Constitution of 1857, art. VIII, sec. 3.

35. *Horton* v. *Meskill*, 376 A.2d 359, 374 (Connecticut 1977); Connecticut Constitution of 1965, Article Eighth, sec. 1.

36. *School District of Wilkinsburg* v. *Wilkinsburg Education Association*, 667 A.2d 5, 9 (Pa. 1995); Pennsylvania Constitution of 1967, art. III, sec.14; compare *O'Leary* v. *Wisecup*, 364 A.2d 770, 773 (Pa. Commw. Ct. 1976): "A public education . . . is not a fundamental right"; *Lisa H.* v. *State Board of Education*, 447 A.2d 669, 673 (Pa. Commw. Ct. 1982): same as finding in *O'Leary* v. *Wisecup*, 364 A.2d 770 (Pa. Commw. Ct. 1976).

37. Alaska Constitution of 1959, art. VII, sec. 1 (emphasis added).

38. Nebraska Constitution of 1920, art. VII, sec. 1.

39. New Jersey Constitution of 1947, art. VIII, sec. 4.

40. New York Constitution of 1938, art. XI, sec. 1.

41. *Robinson* v. *Cahill*, 351 A.2d 713, 720 (N.J. 1975); *Matter of Wagner*, 383 N.Y.S.2d 849 (N.Y. Fam. Ct. 1976).

42. *Breese* v. *Smith*, 501 P.2d 159, 167 (Alaska 1972).

43. Arizona Constitution of 1912, art. XI, sec. 6 (emphasis added).

44. Colorado Constitution of 1876, art. IX, sec. 2 (emphasis added).

45. *Shofstall* v. *Hollins*, 515 P.2d 590, 592 (Ariz. 1973).

46. *Lujan* v. *Colorado State Board of Education*, 649 P.2d 1005, 1017-18 (Colo. 1982).

47. *Plitt* v. *Madden*, 413 A.2d 867 (Del. 1980); Delaware Constitution of 1897, art. X, sec. 1.

48. *Rose* v. *Council for Better Education, Inc.*, 790 S.W.2d 186, 206 (Ky. 1989); Kentucky Constitution of 1891, sec. 183.

49. *McDuffy* v. *Secretary of Executive Office of Education*, 615 N.E.2d 516 (Mass. 1993); Massachusetts Constitution of 1780, part the second, ch. V, sec. 2; *Claremont School District* v. *Governor*, 703 A.2d 1353, 1359 (N.H. 1997); New Hampshire Constitution of 1784, art. 83.

50. *Skeen* v. *State*, 505 N.W.2d 299, 313 (Minn. 1993); Minnesota Constitution of 1857, art. XIII, sec.1.

51. *Lapp* v. *Reeder Public School District No. 3*, 491 N.W.2d 65, 67 (N.D. 1992); *Bismarck Public School District No. 1* v. *State*, 511 N.W.2d 247 (N.D. 1994); North Dakota Constitution of 1889, art. VIII, sec. 1.

52. *Abbeville County School District* v. *South Carolina*, 515 S.E.2d 535, 540 (S.C. 1999); South Carolina Constitution of 1895, art. XI, sec. 3.

53. *Tennessee-Small School District* v. *McWherter*, 851 S.W.2d 139, 151 (Tenn. 1993); Tennessee Constitution of 1870, art. XI, sec. 12.

54. *Stout* v. *Grand Prairie Independent School District*, 733 S.W.2d 290, 294 (Tex. App. 1987); Texas Constitution of 1876, art. VII, sec. 1.

55. *Darrin* v. *Gould*, 540 P.2d 882, 888 (Wash. 1975); Washington Constitution of 1889, art. IX, sec.1.

56. *Pauley* v. *Kelly*, 255 S.E.2d 859, 878 (W. Va. 1979); West Virginia Constitution of 1872, art. XII, sec. 1.

57. *Buse* v. *Smith*, 247 N.W.2d 141, 149 (Wis. 1976); Wisconsin Constitution of 1848, art. X, sec. 3.

58. *Brigham* v. *Vermont*, 692 A.2d 384 (Vt. 1997).

59. Vermont Constitution of 1793, ch. 2, sec. 68.

60. *Brigham*, 692 A.2d, at 394.

61. Alabama Constitution of 1901, art. XIV, sec. 256 (emphasis added).

62. *Brown* v. *Board of Education*, 347 U.S. 483 (1954).

63. Alabama Constitution of 1901, art. XIV, sec. 256, as amended by Amendment 111 (ratified September 7, 1956).

64. *Mitchell* v. *McCall*, 273 Ala. 604, 606, 143 So.2d 629, 631 (Ala. 1962). The federal district court for the southern district of Alabama apparently did not share this view or the traditional understanding that the state supreme court was the final arbiter of state constitutional law, holding in *Smith* v. *Dallas County Board of Education*, 480 F.Supp. 1324, 1337 (S.D. Ala. 1979), that "the state constitution provides all children with an entitlement to public education."

65. *Alabama Coalition for Equity, Inc.* v. *Hunt*, CV-90-833 (Mont. Cty. Cir. Ct., 1993), cited in Opinion of the Justices, No. 338, 624 So.2d 107 (1993).

66. Opinion of the Justices, No. 338, 624 So.2d 107, 147 (Ala. 1993).

67. Ibid., quoting *Mobile, Alabama–Pensacola, Florida Building and Construction Trades Council* v. *Williams*, 331 So.2d 647, 649 (Ala. 1976).

68. Ibid.

69. North Carolina Constitution of 1970, art. I, sec. 15. A similar change occurred in Florida in 2002, when the people of Florida added a specific mandate for class-size reduction to the state constitution. See Florida Constitution of 1868, art. IX, sec. 1 (as amended 2002).

70. Ibid., art. IX, sec. 2 (reiterating provision of 1868 constitution).

71. *Leandro* v. *State*, 488 S.E.2d 249, 255–56 (N.C. 1997).

72. Wyoming Constitution of 1890, art. I, sec. 23.

73. *Pierce* v. *Society of Sisters*, 268 U.S. 510 (1925).

74. *Meyer* v. *Nebraska*, 262 U.S. 390 (1923).

75. Georgia Constitution of 1968, art. VIII, sec. 1; Florida Constitution of 1968, art. IX, sec. 1.

76. Arkansas Constitution of 1874, art. XIV, sec. 1; Kansas Constitution of 1859, art. VI, sec. 6(b) (added by amendment 1966).

77. Illinois Constitution of 1870, art. VIII, sec. 1.

78. Montana Constitution of 1972, art. X, sec. 1; Illinois Constitution of 1970, art. X, sec. 1; Virginia Constitution of 1971, art. VII, sec. 1.

79. A couple of state constitutions have provided judicially manageable standards. As noted above, Florida's Constitution was amended in 2002 to require specific class-size reductions, for example. Florida Constitution of 1868, art. IX, sec. 1, as amended. And Pennsylvania's 1874 Constitution contained a requirement that the legislature appropriate "at least one million dollars each year" "for the maintenance and support of a thorough and efficient system of public schools." Pennsylvania Constitution of 1874, art. X, sec. 1, *repealed* 1967.

80. *Rose* v. *Council for Better Education, Inc.,* 790 S.W.2d 186, 215 (Ky. 1989).

81. *Pauley* v. *Kelly,* 255 S.E.2d 859, 877 (W. Va. 1989).

82. *Hornbeck* v. *Somerset County Board of Education,* 458 A.2d 758, 786 (Md. 1983).

83. Nevada Constitution, art. 19, sec. 2(4) provides that a constitutional amendment requires the approval of a majority of the voters at two general elections. The two-thirds-vote tax initiative at issue here, also known as the Gibbons Tax Restraint Initiative, after its chief sponsor, Jim Gibbons (now a member of the U.S. House of Representatives from Nevada's 2nd District), was supported by more than 70 percent of the voters in each of the two elections.

84. Nevada Constitution, art. IV, sec. 18(2).

85. *Guinn* v. *Legislature of State of Nevada,* 71 P.3d 1269, 1275 (Nev. 2003), *clarified on denial of rehearing,* 76 P.3d 22 (Nev. 2003).

86. Ibid., at 1272.

87. *Montoy* v. *Kansas,* 120 P.3d 306 (Kan. 2005).

88. Kansas Constitution, art. VI, sec.6(b), dealing with school finance, provides: "The legislature shall make suitable provision for finance of the educational interests of the state."

89. Kansas Constitution, art. VI, sec. 1.

90. *Marbury* v. *Madison* 5 U.S. (1 Cranch) 137 (1803); *Guinn,* 71 P.3d at 1272; *Montoy* v. *State,* 112 P.3d 923, 930 (Kan. 2005 ("Montoy II").

91. John C. Eastman, "Judicial Review of Unenumerated Rights: Does *Marbury's* Holding Apply in a Post-Warren Court World?" *Harvard Journal of Law and Public Policy* 28 (Summer 2005): 713–40.

92. *Montoy II,* 112 P.3d at 930 (emphasis added).

93. Philip Kurland and Gerhard Casper, eds., *Landmark Briefs and Arguments of the Supreme Court of the United States,* vol. 1 (Arlington, Va.: University Publications of America, 1978), p. 145 n. 3.

94. *Marbury* v. *Madison,* 5 U.S. (1 Cranch) 137, 177–79 (1803); see also R. Kent Newmyer, *John Marshall and the Heroic Age of the Supreme Court* (Louisiana State University Press, 2001), p. 174 (describing Marshall as holding that "only the people, acting in specially called constitutional conventions, could create a written constitution that limited and defined government and was 'permanent' and supreme over ordinary law"); compare *Ware* v. *Hylton,* 3 U.S. (3 Dall.) 199 (1796) (holding that contrary state laws must yield to the U.S. Constitution, laws, and treaties).

95. Clinton Rossiter, ed., *The Federalist Papers* (*Federalist* 78, Alexander Hamilton) (Signet, 1961), p. 466.

96. Oliver Ellsworth, Speech in the Connecticut Ratifying Convention (January 7, 1788), reprinted in Jonathan Elliot, *The Debates in the Several State Conventions on the Adoption of the Federal Constitution,* vol. 2 (J.B. Lippincott, 1859), p. 196; see also Randy E. Barnett, "The Original Meaning of the Judicial Power," *Supreme Court Economic Review* 12 (2004): 115, 115–16 (quoting Ellsworth).

97. Max Farrand, ed., *The Records of the Federal Convention*, vol. 2 (Yale University Press, 1911), p. 78.

98. Ibid., p. 76 (noting that "the Judges, as expositors of the Laws would have an opportunity of defending their constitutional rights").

99. Florida Constitution of 1868, art. IX, sec. 1, as amended.

100. Pennsylvania Constitution of 1874, art. X, sec. 1, repealed 1967.

101. Nevada Constitution of 1864, art. XI, sec. 2.

102. See, for example, New Jersey Constitution of 1947, art. VIII, sec. 4, cl. 1; Ohio Constitution of 1851, art. VI, sec. 2; Pennsylvania Constitution of 1874, art. III, sec. 14 (as amended 1967); West Virginia Constitution of 1872, art. XII, sec. 1.

103. Arkansas Constitution of 1874, art. XIV, sec.1 (as amended 1968); California Constitution of 1879, art. IX, sec. 1; Indiana Constitution of 1851, art. VIII, sec. 1; Maine Constitution of 1820, art. VIII, sec. 1; Nevada Constitution of 1864, art. XI, sec.1; South Dakota Constitution of 1889, art. VIII, sec. 1; Texas Constitution of 1876, art. VII, sec. 1; Wyoming Constitution of 1977, art. I, sec. 23.

104. Florida Constitution of 1968, art. IX, sec.1; Georgia Constitution of 1976, art. VIII, sec. 1, para. 1.

105. See, for example, Alabama Constitution of 1901 (as amended in 1956), art. XIV, sec. 256 ("It is the policy of the state of Alabama to foster and promote the education of its citizens in a manner and extent consistent with its available resources"); Kansas Constitution of 1859, art. VI, sec. 1 ("The legislature shall provide for intellectual, educational, vocational and scientific improvement by establishing and maintaining public schools, educational institutions and related activities which may be organized and changed in such manner as may be provided by law"); Massachusetts Constitution of 1780, Part the Second, ch. V, sec. 2 ("It shall be the duty of legislatures and magistrates, in all future periods of this commonwealth, to cherish the interests of literature and the sciences, and all seminaries of them"); Michigan Constitution of 1963, art. VIII, sec. 1 ("Schools and the means of education shall forever be encouraged"); Nevada Constitution of 1864, art. XI, sec. 1 ("The legislature shall encourage by all suitable means the promotion of intellectual, literary, scientific, mining, mechanical, agricultural, and moral improvements"); New Hampshire Constitution of 1784, art. 83 ("It shall be the duty of the legislators and magistrates, in all future periods of this government, to cherish the interest of literature and the sciences, and all seminaries and public schools, to encourage private and public institutions"); Vermont Constitution of 1793, ch. 2, sec. 68 ("A competent number of schools ought to be maintained in each town unless the general assembly permits other provisions for the convenient instruction of youth").

PART II

Evidence

4

ERIC A. HANUSHEK

The Alchemy of "Costing Out" an Adequate Education

HOLDING SCHOOLS ACCOUNTABLE for student performance has high-lighted a simple fact: many students are not achieving at desired levels. Significant achievement gaps by race and income persist, and concerns abound about whether most schools are on the path to improving the achievement of all students. While people of diverse perspectives have offered reform plans and solutions, a prevailing argument is that the schools lack sufficient resources to support academic success, and a variety of parties have sued states to compel them to provide greater funding for education. A key question in those lawsuits—"What will it cost to improve student achievement?"—has led courts and legislatures to seek out a scientific determination of the amount of spending required by schools. And there has been no shortage of consultants offering to provide one.

Consultants have developed four distinct methods for "costing out"—that is, estimating—the additional spending necessary to secure an adequate education. They are generally referred to as the "professional judgment," "state-of-the-art" (or "evidence-based"), "successful schools," and "cost function" methods. Costing out studies are frequently contracted for by plaintiffs or other

This analysis benefited from the research assistance of Brent Faville and the editorial acumen of the editors. This is a companion piece to "Science Violated: Spending Projections and the 'Costing Out' of an Adequate Education," in *Courting Failure: How School Finance Lawsuits Exploit Judges' Good Intentions and Harm Our Children*, edited by Eric A. Hanushek (Education Next Books, 2006), pp. 258–311.

interested parties who desire increased levels of spending for education, although defendants may commission one in an attempt to neutralize a rival study. This chapter describes the main features of each method and explains why they all fall short of scientific standards of inquiry and validity.

The Origin of School Finance Lawsuits

The judiciary's involvement in the evaluation of education funding schemes has prompted a significant shift in policy discussions about school finance. All state constitutions mandate a statewide educational system and prescribe a legislative process for determining state and local government funding for public elementary and secondary education (and for the many other public services that these governments provide). Nationwide, less than 10 percent of spending on education comes from the federal government, with the balance split roughly equally between state and local governments. The exact distribution of fiscal responsibility differs significantly from one state to the next, but in almost all states, local governments, usually independent school districts, raise their share mainly through the local property tax. States generally distribute their funds so as to compensate, at least partially, for differences in local property values that affect the ability of local school districts to raise funds.

Following the California court case *Serrano* v. *Priest*, initially decided in 1971, a majority of states saw legal actions designed to equalize funding across districts. The plaintiffs in those cases argued that some school districts—by virtue of a low property tax base or unwillingness to support school funding—spent significantly less than other, often more advantaged, districts. That disparity created an equity concern because children growing up in a low-spending jurisdiction might thereby receive an inferior education.

The outcomes of the suits, argued under separate state constitutions, were mixed, with some state courts finding such disparities to be constitutional and others not.[1] Whether or not they were successful, the lawsuits tended to increase the state share of funding and brought about more equalized funding within states, with many state legislatures acting without being pressured to do so by a court judgment.[2] Interestingly, although school funding suits were based on the assumption that an inferior education put students at a disadvantage, until recently virtually no scholars had examined whether student test scores or other educational outcomes tended to be more equal after spending was equalized. In fact, the few investigations of this issue that have been conducted show that the spending increases produced by equity lawsuits have had little or no effect on student achievement.[3]

Adequacy Litigation

Beginning in the 1980s, some plaintiffs argued that children might not be getting a constitutionally acceptable level of education even when spending across a state was more or less equal. Alabama, the target of a 1993 case, *ACE* v. *Hunt*, epitomized this situation: spending across districts was quite equal but student achievement levels were near the bottom for the nation. The juxtaposition of an equitable system and poor performance led to a new legal and policy goal, described as "adequacy." The plaintiffs in adequacy lawsuits argue that students' low achievement stems from insufficient public funding and ask the courts to correct that fiscal inadequacy.

The new focus on adequacy dovetailed with the accountability and standards movement, which has asked states to track student educational proficiency relative to state standards or goals. The federal No Child Left Behind Act of 2001 (NCLB) has reinforced and extended this movement, requiring testing in grades three through eight and once in high school to give the public detailed information on how well students are performing in school. Plaintiffs engaged in adequacy litigation have been able to use that information to assert that a state has failed to meet its constitutional obligations as described in the educational clause of its constitution. They then find it easy to argue that the state is not investing the necessary resources to ensure that students are reaching the proficiency standards the state itself has set. Costing out studies purport to show what it will cost for students to reach proficiency.

Costing Out Approaches

In court, adequacy litigants present such costing out studies as "scientific" evidence of the amount of money needed to obtain an adequate education. Such studies have been conducted or are in progress in a vast majority of states, and the demand for new ones has only continued to rise as adequacy lawsuits proliferate.[4] Plaintiffs have discovered that there is great value in presenting to the court and the public a specific "number" for total "required" state spending, which they want to be treated as the amount that is both necessary and sufficient.[5] Courts have clearly been influenced by this strategy, as judges have been willing to write that specific number, derived from costing out studies, into the remedies that they order.[6] Legislatures also consistently use the studies to guide their appropriations.

Before describing and assessing the various costing out methods, it is worthwhile to discuss some of the terminology that they use and a fundamental problem common to them all. School finance discussions are punctuated by certain terms, whose meaning in this context often differs greatly from its generally accepted meaning. Most notably, the concepts of *cost* and *efficiency* have been redefined to suit the argument at hand. Ordinarily, ensuring "efficiency" (sometimes called "cost efficiency") requires finding the least expensive way of achieving one's objective, but adequacy consultants have not only ignored this definition but also refashioned it to support their case that more money—indeed, as much money as is politically feasible—should be spent on education.

The overarching problem stems from the nonexistence of empirical evidence on which to base estimates of the costs of adequate student proficiency. The consultants' work would be simple if scholars could show, repeatedly, something like the following: an additional expenditure of $1,000 per pupil will translate, on average, into a 15 percent gain in student proficiency. Unfortunately, such studies do not exist. Research has not shown a clear causal relationship between the amount that schools spend and student achievement.[7] After hundreds of studies, it is now generally recognized that *how* money is spent is much more important than *how much* is spent. This finding is particularly important in considering judicially ordered changes in school finances, because such alterations offer little control over how any new moneys are spent.

A simplistic view of this argument—conveniently raised by spending advocates as a straw man to be beaten down—is that "money never matters."[8] The research, of course, does not say that. Nor does it say that "money cannot matter." It simply underscores the fact that historically a set of decisions and incentives existing in schools have blunted any impacts of added funds, leading to inconsistent outcomes. That is, more spending on schools has not led reliably to substantially better results on the tests that states use to determine whether students are proficient—the same tests that plaintiffs use to document inadequacy in a state's educational system.

The absence of a systematic positive relationship between spending and achievement also underscores the challenge facing the consultants who purport to describe the spending necessary to achieve adequate levels of student achievement. Because looking at a state's schools—where spending a lot shows little relationship to the desired performance—is fraught with embarrassment, they must find some way around current reality. Each of the costing out methods takes a different approach for dealing with this dilemma. As might be guessed, these methods fall far short of standards for scientific validity, even if they demonstrate some considerable ingenuity in crafting arguments with surface plausibility.

Professional Judgment Approach

Perhaps the most commonly applied approach is the "professional judgment" method.[9] With a few nuances, the approach involves asking a chosen panel of educators—teachers, principals, superintendents, and other education personnel—to develop an educational program that would produce certain specified outcomes. Their efforts typically produce "model schools," defined in terms of class size, guidance and support personnel, and other programs that might be necessary. The analysts undertaking the study then provide missing elements (for example, central administration costs or computers and materials) and employ externally derived cost factors (for example, average teacher or principal salaries) to determine the total cost of the model schools. The panel may or may not provide guidance on extra resources needed for disadvantaged children, special education, or the like.

Professional judgment panels generally are instructed not to consider where revenues would come from or any other restrictions on spending. In other words, they are allowed to "dream big," unfettered by any sense of reality or thought of trade-offs. Indeed, one motivation for filing adequacy lawsuits is to resolve financial questions in an arena other than that provided by state legislatures or local school boards, which are not single-issue oriented and of necessity take such practicalities into account. If courts can be induced to ignore practical constraints, more money for education might well be obtained. A 2003 study by Augenblick, Palaich, and Associates not only illustrates the issue but also shows the kind of interplay that occurs between consultants and professional judgment panels (this time in North Dakota): "We worked hard to push people to identify resources they thought were needed to help students meet state and federal standards in spite of their natural tendency to exclude items because local voters might not approve of them or schools could 'get by' without them."[10]

Admonitions to professional judgment panels to dream big amount to a fundamental redefinition of the term *cost*. Whether one is discussing the purchase of a car, home, or service, the term *cost* is usually understood to mean the *minimum* expenditure necessary to achieve a given outcome.[11] The idea is to establish the desired level of quality and determine the least amount of money required to obtain it. By contrast, professional judgment panels are effectively encouraged to identify the maximum expenditure imaginable, in the hope that the amount will be enough to produce adequately proficient students. A 2004 New York study conducted by a consortium of researchers from two groups— the American Institutes for Research and Management Analysis and Planning, Inc. (AIR/MAP)—even used a two-stage process in which a superpanel was given the results from separate subpanels that had each estimated the desirability of some educational component. The superpanel then aggregated the results, input by input, from each of the subpanels. This design effectively maximized expenditure estimates by ensuring that any trade-offs between programs and resources made by the individual subpanels were ignored and that the resulting recommendation would be the maximum possible. The very design of the study, though couched in scientific terms, reflected the underlying policy goal of increasing spending on education.

Courts relying on professional judgment studies to mandate spending levels assume that the panelists' model school will produce the desired results just because that was the panel's objective. None of the reports ever test that assumption. In fact, the reports often admit that there is little reason to expect that students will achieve at the desired levels. The AIR/MAP team's November 2002 proposal to conduct its costing out study promised that the consultants would answer the question "What does it actually cost to provide the resources that each school needs to allow its students to meet the achievement levels specified in the Regents Learning Standards?" Yet the 2004 study based on that proposal includes a disclaimer that the courts apparently overlooked:

> It must be recognized that the success of schools also depends on other individuals and institutions to provide the health, intellectual stimulus, and family support upon which public school systems can build. Schools cannot and do not perform their role in a vacuum, and this is an important qualification of conclusions reached in any study of adequacy in education. Also, success of schools depends on effective allocation of resources and implementation of programs in school districts.[12]

The 2003 study conducted by Augenblick, Palaich, and Associates with data from North Dakota illustrates the extent to which costing out studies using the professional judgment method ignore empirical evidence.[13] The authors of this study prescribe the necessary spending level for each of the K–12 districts in North Dakota in 2002. Two points are important: first, there is wide variation in the calculated needs of districts. Second, a number of districts were spending *more* in 2002 than the consultants (through their professional judgment panels) thought necessary to achieve the full 2014 performance goals.

Because information is available on students' actual performance in North Dakota for 2002, the relationship between performance and the fiscal deficits and surpluses that were calculated by the professional judgment (PJ) model can be seen. (Here, spending less than the study found necessary is termed a

"PJ deficit"; spending more is termed a "PJ surplus.") It seems natural to expect that student performance within districts with PJ surpluses would exceed their panel's achievement goals. It is also plausible to expect that districts with larger PJ fiscal deficits would be further from achieving their goals than those with smaller PJ fiscal deficits. Such expectations are appropriate, since the methodology was designed to adjust for needs that arise from the concentration within a district of a disadvantaged population, variation in school size, and the like.

Yet what is observed is exactly the opposite of what might reasonably be expected. A regression of reading or math proficiency percentages of North Dakota districts on the PJ deficits indicates a *positive* relationship between a PJ deficit and student achievement. In other words, the larger the PJ deficit, the higher the students' performance. The positive relationship between deficits and achievement results remains the same even after trimming off all surpluses and deficits greater than $2,000 to ensure that the analysis is not distorted by outliers (figure 4-1). Moreover, in terms of simple averages, student achievement in districts with a PJ surplus was significantly lower than that found in districts with a PJ deficit. In other words, the information given by PJ deficits is worse than no information, because the deficits are inversely related to "needs" as indicated by student performance.

Incredibly, the Augenblick, Palaich, and Associates 2003 study actually discusses the lack of empirical validation of the professional judgment approach in North Dakota: "The advantages of the approach are that it reflects the views of actual service providers and its results are easy to understand; the disadvantages are that resource allocation tends to reflect current practice and there is *only an assumption, with little evidence, that the provision of money at the designated level will produce the anticipated outcomes* [emphasis added]."[14]

In sum, the professional judgment model lacks all empirical grounding. The professional educators called on for their judgment generally lack expertise in designing programs to meet objectives that are outside of their experience. While they may have experience making trade-offs within current budgets, they do not have the research knowledge or personal experience to know how resource needs will change if they design a program for higher student outcomes or for different student body compositions. Most important, the direct conflicts of interest are palpable: the outcomes may directly affect participants' compensation and working conditions, creating an incentive for them to distort whatever judgments they might otherwise make. The professional judgment approach could be more accurately described as the *educators' wish list* model.

Figure 4-1. *North Dakota Professional Judgment Results*[a]

Panel A. Reading achievement and PJ spending deficits

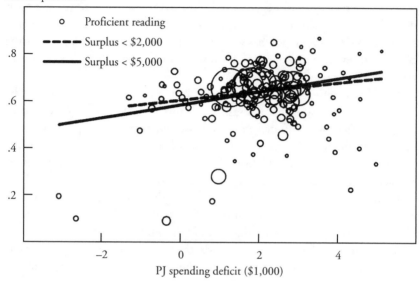

Percent proficient

PJ spending deficit ($1,000)

Panel B. Math achievement and PJ spending deficits

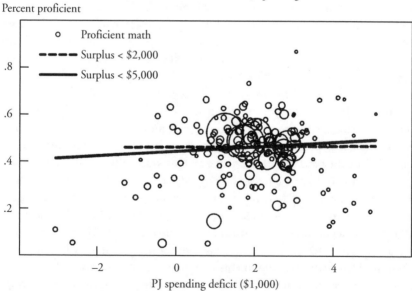

Percent proficient

PJ spending deficit ($1,000)

a. Size of circle indicates student population in district. PJ = professional judgment.

State-of-the-Art or Evidence-Based Approach

If the professional judgment model relies on self-interested experts, the second costing out approach relies on the judgments of the analysts involved. This approach has been immodestly called "state-of-the-art" by the major firms using it.[15] Seeking to give their study scientific cachet, they also refer to it in more recent applications as the "evidence-based" method. The consultants involved sort through available research, select specific studies that relate to elements of a model school, and translate those studies into precise estimates for resource needs. A set of model schools are subsequently costed out in the same manner as the professional judgment model schools.

The state-of-the-art approach relies on the consultants' conclusions about the best evidence on the effectiveness of different policies. The early studies simply listed findings of research they found that showed some program or resource that was related in a statistically significant way to achievement.[16] The more recent versions of the evidence-based model quantify their assessments of the effectiveness of components that they include in their model school.[17] This new information thoroughly impeaches the evidence and vividly shows its selective and biased nature. It also shows why the consultants do not use their own evidence to make any projections of achievement.

One way of seeing the problems with their work is simply to take their analysis at face value. They design a school around a series of programs that have surface plausibility: smaller class size, full-day kindergarten, expanded summer school, more professional development for teachers, and the like. They report what they believe to be the best evidence about how much achievement would be improved with each component. They then advocate including all of the components.

Looking at their evidence, however, it is easy to see why these consultants never provide an explicit projection of how achievement would improve with their model school. The programs that they advocate would, by their reporting of the evidence, lift the achievement of the average student beyond that of today's best-performing student.[18] By looking at past policy outcomes, it is obvious that the consultants' programs—which are simply repackaged versions of preexisting programs—will not have any such results. The easiest interpretation of this summary of their work is that the evidence is not reliable. The consultants have either selected a particularly biased set of program evaluations or the program evaluations in the area are deeply flawed.

The simplest conclusion is that the evidentiary base on which the evidence-based analyses are built is insufficient to provide policy guidance. The usual response when confronted with such evidence is simply to say that "while the evidence may not be perfect, it is the best we have." If it is that bad, however, it should never be used for policymaking.

This methodology again specifically eschews taking costs into account or attempting to calculate the minimum costs of achieving any level of achievement. In fact, their analysis shows more of the spirit of maximizing expenditures, which can be seen through in their programmatic recommendations. The specific programs (repeatedly recommended across states) include ones that, according to their evidence, have widely varying effectiveness and costs. Yet, instead of recommending programs that yield high achievement per dollar invested, the consultants recommend doing everything. Some parts of their programs, however, would purportedly produce ten times the achievement of others for each dollar spent. Rational government decisionmaking would never make programmatic decisions in this manner (unless one really believed that cost efficiency was irrelevant).

The only empirical bases for state-of-the-art analyses come from a small number of selected research studies that do not necessarily reflect the experience in the individual state being sued. And, most important, because those studies have been selected from the research base to suit the consultant's own purposes, there is no reason to believe that they provide an unbiased estimate of the empirical reality more generally. Indeed, given the consultants' selectiveness, the state-of-the-art model would more appropriately be termed the *consultants' choice* model.

Successful Schools Approach

The "successful schools" approach begins by identifying schools—or districts—in a state that are effective at meeting established educational goals. Various methods may be used to identify successful schools. Typically, the process concentrates on student achievement, occasionally with some allowance for student background.[19] Spending on special programs—say, remedial education or special education—is stripped out of budgets in order to obtain a "base cost" figure for each district. Typically, then, exceptionally high- or low-spending schools are excluded, and the base costs for the remaining schools are averaged to arrive at a level of spending that can feasibly be expected to yield high performance. To get the full costs of the school, expenditures on special programs are then added back in, based on the distribution for each school of students with such special needs.

The method used for selecting successful schools is obviously important. The typical method is to take the highest-performing schools in the state, defined by student test scores and other educational outcomes. While that may seem appropriate, it ignores the many non-school factors that affect student performance, such as family background, peer relationships, and previous schooling experiences. When the consultants ignore such considerations, they can hardly conclude that the high performance in successful schools is driven by the amount of spending on those schools. There is no reliable evidence that equivalent spending in other social contexts would yield similar levels of student performance. Indeed, there is powerful evidence to the contrary.

Quite apart from such considerations, the successful schools approach attempts to predict the future from what is known about the present. The consultants are asked to project the future levels of student proficiency that would occur if spending were increased. Yet the methodology is rooted in a school's current operations. Therefore, it can say something about meeting the performance goals that states have established under NCLB *only if* some subset of schools is currently achieving at the level that NCLB requires. However, no district has yet reached the standards that NCLB has set forth. Because the approach relies on observations about one set of schools with a given level of success, it has no way to project those observations to any higher performance level. Assume, for illustration, that in the set of schools identified as successful, 70 to 80 percent of students perform at the proficiency level. There is no way to extrapolate those results to a 95 percent level.[20]

Policy decisions should be based on the joint consideration of program effectiveness and costs. Although most analyses of public decisionmaking take for granted that *efficiency*—achieving a given outcome, such as a given amount of learning, at the minimum cost—is a desirable goal, efficiency often has a bad name in education discussions. In part this results from its being taken, wrongly, to mean least cost without regard to outcome.[21] When it comes to consideration of school achievement, however, it is simply not possible to ignore efficiency.

Using an efficiency standard in education requires acknowledging that different schools operate at different levels of efficiency. Presumably, a court would want to compel only additional expenditures that can and will be used efficiently. Yet the very range of expenditure levels found among "successful" schools (those meeting a prescribed student output standard) implies that not all school systems are using their funds as effectively as others. Should the starting point of discussion be current spending, accepting whatever is being done, or should there be some attempt to deal with the efficiency issue?

The panel of referees appointed by the trial court judge in the landmark New York case *Campaign for Fiscal Equity (CFE)* v. *State* addressed the idea of efficiency, but their approach was only a little less than bizarre. The plaintiffs presented to the referees the professional judgment cost estimates of the

AIR/MAP team discussed above. The state, which used much lower estimates provided by Standard & Poor's School Evaluation Service, had suggested that it was reasonable to concentrate on the spending patterns of the most efficient of the successful schools—those with high levels of student performance at lower levels of expenditure. In making their calculations, the S&P analysts therefore excluded the top half of the spending distribution for the successful districts. But to reconcile the state's recommendation of $1.9 billion with the AIR/MAP estimate of more than $5 billion, the referees insisted on adding back in the higher-spending successful districts, even when those districts did not produce better academic outcomes. After all, the referees reasoned, "there was no evidence whatsoever indicating that the higher spending districts . . . were in fact inefficient."[22] In other words, spending more to achieve the same outcome should not be construed as being inefficient. One might then ask what, if anything, would indicate inefficiency. The significance of their reasoning is clear: if spending must be sufficient to bring up achievement regardless of how efficiently resources are used, the amount is likely to be a very large number.

The successful schools approach calculates costs for a unique subset of successful schools. The chosen subset of schools conflates the various reasons why achievement may be high, including the family background of those attending the schools. This approach is better labeled the *successful students* model, because it does not separate the effects of school expenditures from other, external factors that are probably much more important.

Cost Function

The "cost function" approach, sometimes also referred to as the "econometric" approach, relies on current spending and achievement patterns across the full set of schools in a state. In economics and other quantitative sciences, one variable is said to be a function of another if its level is shown to vary, whether positively or negatively, in response to changes in another variable—for example, when the price of gas increases, demand for gas goes down; demand for gas is therefore a function of price. The cost function label reflects the assumption made in these studies that the level of required spending in a district varies predictably along with various observable characteristics of its students and the desired achievement level.

The methodology is similar to that of the successful schools approach in its attempt to characterize districts that are meeting desired achievement standards. Consultants use statistical methods to estimate the relationships statewide between spending levels and different combinations of student achievement levels and student characteristics. They then use the results of the analysis to derive appropriate spending levels for each district. Cost function studies may or may not attempt to distinguish between efficient and inefficient producers of outcomes—that is, between districts that spend more for some given level of achievement and those that spend less.[23]

For all their scientific pretensions, however, all cost function studies fail to adequately identify the causal relationship between student performance and spending. As noted above, there is a large body of statistical research examining how various measures of the resources available influence student achievement, taking into account differences in a range of background characteristics. This research has generally found little in the way of a consistent relationship between spending and student outcomes. Among just the estimates that do suggest a positive spending-achievement relationship, the estimates typically show only a very small effect of spending on student outcomes.[24] The obvious implication of this literature is that, absent other reforms that would make the education system more efficient, large spending increases are required to obtain a noticeable achievement gain.

Consultants conducting cost function studies turn that analysis on its head. They begin by estimating a statistical relationship between spending (as the dependent variable) and achievement and characteristics of the student population (as the explanatory variables).[25] That is, they reverse the usual relation of spending and achievement in standard evaluations of education policy, which typically predict achievement based on spending and various other student characteristics.[26] Although consultants refer to these results as the "cost function," they actually just describe the existing spending patterns across districts with different achievement levels.[27] Unless one can assume that all districts are spending money wisely—an assumption broadly contradicted by existing research—their studies cannot be interpreted as finding minimum costs.[28] They can simply indicate that the current pattern of spending is not very productive.

Yet this is just the most obvious of the problems plaguing these studies. Cost function analyses have to deal with the fact that frequently there are no districts that achieve at the performance levels defined as adequate. In such cases, the consultants typically assume that the relationship between spending and achievement remains the same regardless of achievement level. That is, if they observe proficiency levels to be increasing by 10 percentage points for every additional $1,000 per pupil spent in a set of districts with a maximum proficiency rate of 60 percent, they assume that the relationship remains unchanged as districts near the target of 100 percent proficiency. There is, of course, no way to know whether that is true.

Finally, cost function analyses also have to make analogous assumptions about the way in which various factors based on student characteristics, such as the percentage of low-income students in a district, affect required costs. The cost function studies' apparent strength—the fact that they draw on all the available data on performance and spending in a state—here becomes a weakness. It is unclear whether the evidence from Westchester County is at all informative about how to improve student achievement in the Bronx or about precisely what adjustments would have to be made to account for the many differences in the two locations. Yet that is exactly the kind of analytic leap of faith that cost function studies conducted in New York State are forced to make. Indeed, taking this leap leads William Duncombe and John Yinger to suggest, apparently seriously, that New York City should spend 3.5 times as much per student to obtain the same level of achievement as other districts in New York state.[29]

The cost function approach cannot identify the costs of an adequate education, as they do not even attempt to trace out the necessary cost of a given performance level. Instead, their name should reflect the fact that they simply capture the *expenditure function* for education—how much schools now spend to achieve at current levels.

Additional Causes for Concern

The four approaches to determining the costs of an adequate education each have some superficial appeal, but the methodological flaws outlined above render their conclusions unreliable. Several additional issues—the process for choosing a method, the definition of an outcome standard, the assumptions used in developing cost estimates, and the lack of evidence that greater funding brings its intended results—raise further questions about the validity of their calculations.

Choosing a Method

The costing out approach to be used is generally chosen by the party requesting the analysis. It appears that the choice made might be quite purposeful, given that many costing out studies are funded by parties with an interest in the outcome.[30] For example, a review of analyses by Augenblick and his colleagues in four states where they applied both professional judgment and successful schools methods found that the professional judgment method yielded systematically higher estimates of "adequate" expenditure.[31] That finding apparently has influenced the choice of methodology by clients, who almost uniformly prefer to begin with the professional judgment approach.[32]

A recent compilation of estimates of necessary per-pupil expenditures for an adequate education across states and studies underscores the arbitrariness of these estimates.[33] Even after one adjusts for geographic cost differences across states and puts the estimates in real (inflation-adjusted) dollars for 2004, they differ by more than a factor of three. If the methods systematically produce very different results when addressing the same question, they obviously cannot be taken as a reliable and unbiased estimate of the resources required. It is difficult to imagine what true underlying differences could drive such disparities, given the many similarities in the school systems of different states. A more plausible explanation for the differences is that methods are chosen in order to provide politically palatable estimates for different state deliberations.

Defining an Outcome Standard

Organizations that commission costing out studies appear to recognize the importance of the outcome standard chosen. The courts, in contrast, seldom focus on the standard employed by the consultant and instead tend to concentrate on the cost figures. Yet the outcome standards that are embedded in adequacy calculations clearly should have a significant impact on the cost analysis. For example, the state of New York's goal of ensuring that all New York State public school students graduate with an elite "regents diploma" is one of the loftiest goals of any state in the nation.[34] This standard is substantively different from the constitutional requirement of a "sound basic education." Each of the methods for costing out adequacy explicitly or implicitly bases its calculations on a particular definition of desired outcomes, yet the political judgments involved in defining those outcomes are seldom admitted.

NCLB has only complicated matters. It is now popular to link costing out studies to achieving the goals of NCLB, even though NCLB achievement goals have no obvious relationship to the language or intent of state constitutions that provides the legal basis for adequacy lawsuits. By declaring proficiency the goal nationwide, the law would seem to have set in place a universal outcome standard. Yet although NCLB requires all states to ensure that every student is "proficient" by 2014, it leaves the task of defining proficiency to the states. As a result, proficiency in one state differs markedly from proficiency in another.

Before NCLB, some states chose to establish very high achievement standards—what might be termed aspirational goals. Others chose modest standards that did not exceed by much the standards that many students already were meeting. Deciding what level of achievement constitutes "proficiency" is, then, a political choice that almost certainly changes over time. Thus, when adequacy suits are pinned to a state proficiency level, it is important to consider where the standard came from and how it should be interpreted.

The plaintiff in the New York City adequacy suit, the Campaign for Fiscal Equity, hired two consulting firms, AIR and MAP, to cost out an adequate education in New York City under the New York state constitutional requirement for providing a "sound basic education."[35] The consultants chose instead to evaluate the costs of meeting the regents learning standards. The governor's commission adopted a lower standard in its estimation of costs, conducted for it by Standard & Poor's School Evaluation Service. The judicial referees, who were appointed by the court to advise it on the appropriate decision, were pleased by the consistency of the two estimates (after they made adjustments for their own disregard of "efficiency"), even though the estimates used different outcome standards and should not have been the same according to the logic of costing out.[36] The referees even went on to recognize that the highest court said that the regents learning standards were inappropriate, even as they ignored that statement in reviewing the cost estimates.[37]

In Kentucky, three separate studies were conducted in 2003 by two firms: Verstagen and Associates and Picus and Associates, which conducted parallel studies using a professional judgment and a state-of-the-art approach. Picus and Associates let the professional judgment panels interpret the seven constitutional requirements of education laid down by the Kentucky Supreme Court.[38] Verstegen and Associates added to those seven an extensive set of input and process requirements included in the current Kentucky school regulations.[39] These are simply arbitrary choices made by the consultants.

An analysis by Augenblick and others that was written into the judgment of the Kansas State Supreme Court provides insight into the consultant's role in establishing an outcome standard:

A&M worked with the LEPC [Legislative Education Planning Committee] to develop a more specific definition of a suitable education. We suggested using a combination of both input and output measures. For the input measures, it was decided that the current QPA [Quality Performance Accreditation] requirements would be used, along with some added language provided by the LEPC. This additional language included vocational education as a required course offering, and identified other programs and services that might be provided as part of a suitable education. Next we set the performance measures that would be used. Again, A&M worked with the LEPC. Together we determined which content areas and grade levels would be used. The math and reading tests are given in the same grade levels every year[;] the writing, science, and social studies tests are given in alternating years. A&M felt that the reading and math tests, which are given every year, gave us the most flexibility in setting the output measures.[40]

Perhaps more interestingly, the definition of adequacy is not always related to outcomes. In North Dakota, Augenblick, Palaich, and Associates, the successor firm to Augenblick and Myers, noted that the state did not have explicit outcome standards but instead had input requirements. For their analysis, they simply added a set of outcomes that were related to state goals under the No Child Left Behind Act.[41]

Duncombe, Lukemeyer, and Yinger analyzed the impacts of different goals on the estimated costs under alternative estimation approaches. They demonstrated that reasonable differences in the loftiness of educational goals can lead to a 25 percent difference in estimated costs within their cost function analysis and to a 50 percent difference across alternative approaches to costing out, including the professional judgment approach.[42]

No matter how one judges the analytical capabilities of the consultants, their expertise does not extend to deciding the educational requirements of the state constitution. The plaintiffs and other interested parties can, of course, argue these matters in court, but they invariably attempt to submerge the centrality of the choice of output standards and goals in the costing out studies.

Assumptions Used in Developing Cost Estimates

All approaches use information about current spending of schools—generally with important modifications—to estimate what resources are needed to bring students up to the desired level of proficiency. But using existing spending, within existing structures and under existing incentive systems, is a dubious way to begin. That is never more evident than it is when one estimates the cost of obtaining higher-quality teachers.

If one wished to hire teachers of higher quality than those currently employed, what would it cost? The answer depends markedly on whether one reproduces the current single-salary schedule—which pays teachers the same salary, except for differences in education and experience, and does not recognize differences in teachers' effectiveness in the classroom—or whether one introduces a different pay and incentive scheme.

The same holds for often-noted shortages, say in mathematics and science or language teachers. The "cost" of addressing these issues depends crucially on whether a district pays all teachers higher salaries in the hope of attracting those in shortage areas or whether it just pays bonuses or higher salaries to fill the demand in the shortage areas.

The calculation of salaries is a particularly interesting point of comparison across different studies. Sometimes the consultants simply use the average salaries for existing teachers[43] or increase them by some amount (for example, 10 percent in North Dakota in one study and 18 percent in Arkansas in another),[44] arguing vaguely in terms of what other states spend. They then imagine that such increments will improve teacher quality. In other cases, the consultants dream up a bonus for teachers.

While the widely varying teacher salary factor has obvious and powerful effects on any cost estimates, none of the various costing out studies provides any evidence about the current quality of teachers as measured by their impact on the achievement gains of individual students. Nor is there *any* research that shows that teacher salaries are related to the ability to raise student achievement. So any salary adjustment is a whimsical act based on the consultant's personal sense of whether average salaries are high enough for some unspecified quality level. If consultants want to improve teacher quality, they simply increase the average salary by some arbitrary percentage.

Lack of Evidence of Higher Achievement

As previously noted, virtually none of the reports actually says that it has calculated the level of resources necessary to yield desired outcomes. When it comes time to write the reports—and to produce a document by which the consultants might be judged—the language generally changes to providing an "opportunity" to achieve a standard, not actually achieving it.

The motive for undertaking a costing out analysis is that children are not learning at a putative constitutional level (or an NCLB level or a state standards level), but the reports essentially never say explicitly that the resources identified in the study are either necessary or sufficient to achieve that level. Instead, they say that the resources will provide an opportunity to meet the standard established.

That change of language means that the consultants are not predicting any level of achievement if the stated resources are provided. In fact, none of the reports states that the added resources will yield achievement that is any higher than currently observed. The reports provide no predictions about outcomes, and thus they are *completely unverifiable*. Put differently, there is no scientific basis for deciding among alternative estimates, because data on student outcomes are not informative.

Interestingly, this is true for the consultants' choice model, even though the consultants purport to know how achievement will change under the components of their program. Presumably they realize that their selective reporting of evidence yields results that are not credible, and they make sure that the research evidence is never linked with any prediction of results on their part.

The same failing is seen in all of the methods used and in all of the currently available reports. A possible exception is some of the successful student or expenditure projection studies, in which the authors might suggest that a given school could achieve a given level of performance *if it could figure out why some other school achieved that level and if it could reproduce it in another setting.* Yet no guidance on either the source of achievement or the way to reproduce it is ever given.

If the costing out studies do not provide any clear view of the outcome expected, they become just the whim of the consultant—even when based on a methodology that has previously been applied or has a "scientific" air to it. There is no way to judge among alternative spending projections based on any evidence about outcomes, thus putting each in the category of personal opinion and not science. There is no obvious reason for giving deference to the personal opinion of consultants hired by interested parties in the debate.

Such studies also do not help the political and legislative debate on school finance. They are designed to give a spending number; they do not indicate how achievement is likely to be different from the current level if such an amount is spent. Neither do they suggest how achievement—or even opportunity—would differ if a state spent 25 percent more or 25 percent less than the consultant's personal recommendation about how much to spend.

Returning to the courts' dilemma, the terms of the "Does money matter?" debate are central. Simply stating that money can be effective if it is spent in the right way is tautological. Without a proven strategy for using money wisely, the existing evidence overwhelmingly indicates that just adding money is likely to be broadly ineffective. The historical record indicates that left to their own devices, districts have not ensured that added money is spent wisely. Moreover, with the possible exception of the consultant's choice model (which, as described above, is not credible), none of the approaches even attempts to offer any guidance about setting up effective programs or policies that would provide for enhanced achievement when broadly employed.

Conclusions

Early school funding lawsuits centered on equity, defined simply as equal per-pupil funding across school districts.[45] That has given way to an emphasis on adequacy, as measured by student performance and other educational outcomes, moving the courts into areas in which they are completely unprepared to go. They cannot simply mandate a given level of student achievement. Instead, the courts must define their remedy in terms of instruments that are expected to lead to desired outcomes, instruments that can be monitored by the court. The easiest thing to monitor is the amount that states are spending, which has led to an inevitable focus on the financial resources committed to education. But how much money is enough? To answer that question, the courts have come to rely on outside consultants, who frequently are hired by interested parties. Those consultants, and the people who hire them, suggest that "costing out" exercises provide a scientific answer to a simple question: "How much does it cost to provide an adequate education?"

The methodologies that have been developed lack all semblance of a scientific determination of what a court needs to know—how much is needed to reach a desired level of proficiency. They do not provide reliable and unbiased estimates of the costs necessary to achieve desired goals. Nor do they provide any reason to expect that once the financial remedy is ordered the desired educational goal will be achieved. In many studies, especially those that use the popular professional judgment model, the results cannot be readily replicated by others. And they obfuscate the fact that they are unlikely to provide a path to the desired outcome. Even the consultants themselves admit the weakness of such studies' underlying premise:

> The effort to develop these approaches stems from the fact that no existing research demonstrates a straightforward relationship between how much is spent to provide education services and performance, whether of student, school, or school district.[46]

All of the methods rely crucially on existing educational approaches, existing incentive structures, and existing teacher hiring and retention policies. Each calls for doing more of the same—reducing pupil-teacher ratios, paying existing teachers more, retaining the same administrative structure and expense. Thus, they reinforce and solidify the existing structure, which is arguably incapable of bringing about the kinds of improvements that they purport to cost out.

As the courts typically have no expertise in the institutions, funding, and incentives of schools, they generally are quite eager to have somebody tell them the answer; they jump on "the number," even while recognizing it may not be correct. Costing out studies do not and cannot provide rational support for such judicial decisionmaking.

Those who wish the courts to be more deeply involved in the appropriations process—faced with evidence that the existing costing out methods lack credibility—frequently push for an alternative. After all, they note, it is necessary to have some method of determining how much should be spent on schools. But, in fact, historically there has been a method. Duly elected legislatures, local school boards, and other officials are charged with resolving differences of opinion on education issues, including those regarding education funding. Certainly, the outcome of even a democratic decisionmaking process will not satisfy everyone, but, as currently conducted, costing out studies do not provide a scientific alternative.

There simply is not any reliable, objective, and scientific method to answer the question of how much it would cost to obtain achievement that is noticeably better than that currently seen. The courts can judge the constitutionality of legal provisions relating to the schools, but they should show some humility in their attempts to change the outcomes radically. Judging by the historical record, their chosen instrument—the level of funding for schools—simply is not the key to solving the current achievement problem.

Notes

1. An early suit in federal court, *Rodriguez* v. *San Antonio*, was brought under the Fourteenth Amendment to the U.S. Constitution, but the U.S. Supreme Court ruled in 1973 that state funding arrangements in Texas did not violate the U.S. Constitution. The nature of the ruling implied that the result would generally hold for other states also, leading to the emphasis on state constitutions.

2. Sheila E. Murray, William N. Evans, and Robert M. Schwab, "Education Finance Reform and the Distribution of Education Resources," *American Economic Review* 88, no. 4 (September 1998): 789–812.

3. See, for example, Thomas A. Downes, "Evaluating the Impact of School Finance Reform on the Provision of Public Education: The California Case," *National Tax Journal* 45, no. 4 (December 1992): 405–19; Eric A. Hanushek and Julie A. Somers, "Schooling, Inequality, and the Impact of Government," in *The Causes and Consequences of Increasing Inequality*, edited by Finis Welch (University of Chicago Press, 2001), pp. 169–99; and William Duncombe and Jocelyn M. Johnston, "The Impacts of School Finance Reform in Kansas: Equity Is in the Eye of the Beholder"; Ann E. Flanagan and Sheila E. Murray, "A

Decade of Reform: The Impact of School Reform in Kentucky"; Julie B. Cullen and Susanna Loeb, "School Finance Reform in Michigan: Evaluating Proposal A"; and Thomas A. Downes, "School Finance Reform and School Quality: Lessons from Vermont," in *Helping Children Left Behind: State Aid and the Pursuit of Educational Equity,* edited by John Yinger (MIT Press, 2004), pp. 148–93, 195–214, 215–49, 284–314.

4. A review of past costing out studies can be found in *Education Week*'s annual report for 2005: "Quality Counts 2005: No Small Change: Targeting Money toward Student Performance," *Education Week*, January 6, 2005. See also the ACCESS Project website (www. schoolfunding.info), a project of the Campaign for Fiscal Equity (CFE), the plaintiffs in the New York City adequacy case *Campaign for Fiscal Equity v. State*. CFE states that its primary mission is to "promote better education by conducting research, developing effective strategies for litigation and remedies (including cost studies), and providing tools for public engagement." The count of prior costing out studies came from the ACCESS Project website (September 13, 2006).

5. This explains why the websites for advocacy organizations give top billing to costing out studies. For an example, see the ACCESS Project website.

6. See, for example, *Campaign for Fiscal Equity v. State* and *Montoy v. State of Kansas*.

7. Eric A. Hanushek, "The Failure of Input-Based Schooling Policies," *Economic Journal* 113, no. 485 (February 2003): F64–F98.

8. Outside the courtroom, most discussion of the "money never matters" debate, a controversy of a decade ago, has subsided. For the historical framing of the question, see the following exchange: Larry V. Hedges, Richard D. Laine, and Rob Greenwald, "Does Money Matter? A Meta-Analysis of Studies of the Effects of Differential School Inputs on Student Outcomes," *Educational Researcher* 23, no. 3 (April 1994): 5–14, and Eric A. Hanushek, "Money Might Matter Somewhere: A Response to Hedges, Laine, and Greenwald," *Educational Researcher* 23, no. 4 (May 1994): 5–8.

9. Examples of this include Augenblick and Myers, Inc., *Calculation of the Cost of an Adequate Education in Indiana in 2001–2002 Using the Professional Judgment Approach, Prepared for Indiana State Teachers Association,* 2002; John Augenblick and others, *Calculation of the Cost of a Suitable Education in Kansas in 2000–2001 Using Two Different Analytical Approaches, prepared for Legislative Coordinating Council,* Augenblick and Myers, Inc., 2002; Augenblick, Palaich, and Associates, Inc., *Calculation of the Cost of an Adequate Education in North Dakota in 2002–2003 Using the Professional Judgment Approach* (North Dakota Department of Public Instruction, 2003); American Institutes for Research and Management Analysis and Planning (AIR/MAP), *The New York Adequacy Study: Determining the Cost of Providing All Children in New York an Adequate Education,* 2004; Lawrence O. Picus, Allan Odden, and Mark Fermanich, *A Professional Judgment Approach to School Finance Adequacy in Kentucky,* Lawrence O. Picus and Associates, 2003; and Verstegen and Associates, *Calculation of the Cost of an Adequate Education in Kentucky, prepared for the Council for Better Education,* 2003. A majority of these reports are available from the websites of the relevant states.

10. Augenblick, Palaich, and Associates, *Calculation of the Cost of an Adequate Education in North Dakota in 2002–2003 Using the Professional Judgment Approach.*

11. The terms *cost, cost efficiency,* and *efficiency* often are used interchangeably to indicate the minimum spending required to achieve a given outcome. For example, in comparing different programs that are designed to achieve the same outcome, the most cost-efficient program would be the one requiring the least spending. It is important, however, to understand that the "most cost-efficient" description applies only to one of various alternative ways of achieving the same

objective. If one wished to compare programs that yielded different outcomes, the most efficient one would not necessarily be the one requiring the smallest expenditure.

12. AIR/MAP, *The New York Adequacy Study.*

13. Augenblick, Palaich, and Associates, *Calculation of the Cost of an Adequate Education in North Dakota in 2002–2003 Using the Professional Judgment Approach*

14. Ibid., pp. II–3.

15. See Allan Odden, Mark Fermanich, and Lawrence O. Picus, *A State-of-the-Art Approach to School Finance Adequacy in Kentucky,* Lawrence O. Picus and Associates, 2003.

16. Eric A. Hanushek, "The Evidence on Class Size," in *Earning and Learning: How Schools Matter,* edited by Susan E. Mayer and Paul E. Peterson (Brookings, 1999), pp. 131–68.

17. See Allan Odden and others, *An Evidence-Based Approach to School Finance Adequacy in Washington,* Lawrence O. Picus and Associates, June 30, 2006. This repeats the analysis of an earlier study for Wyoming: Allan Odden and others, *An Evidence-Based Approach to Recalibrating Wyoming's Block Grant School Funding Formula,* Lawrence O. Picus and Associates, November 30, 2005.

18. The technical basis for this conclusion comes from their assessment of the "effect sizes," or the predicted standard deviations of improvement in achievement. (An effect size of 1.0 means that achievement would improve by one standard deviation; an improvement of one standard deviation would move the average student to the 84th percentile.) Their model school is reported to have a total effect size of 3.0 to 6.0 standard deviations, a completely implausible outcome that would place the average beyond the 99.9th percentile of the prior distribution.

19. See, for example, Augenblick and Myers, Inc., *Recommendations for a Base Figure and Pupil-Weighted Adjustments to the Base Figure for Use in a New School Finance System in Ohio,* 1997; John L. Myers and Justin Silverstein, *Successful School Districts Study for North Dakota,* Augenblick, Palaich, and Associates, Inc., 2005; and Standard & Poor's School Evaluation Service, *Resource Adequacy Study for the New York State Commission on Education Reform,* 2004.

20. A second extrapolation problem frequently occurs. Schools identified as successful just on the basis of student proficiency levels on state tests tend to have students whose parents are of higher socioeconomic status (SES). These parents have provided considerable education to their children that, although it is reflected in student scores, is not appropriately attributed to the school. The methodology concentrates on base spending for a typical successful school but then must indicate how much remedial spending would be necessary to bring schools with students of lower-SES backgrounds up to the proficiency of the higher-SES schools. The appropriate way to do this is entirely unclear within this methodology, because again the impact of SES is mostly outside of the successful schools analysis.

21. The classic misstatement of efficiency in education is found in Raymond E. Callahan, *Education and the Cult of Efficiency* (University of Chicago Press, 1962). Callahan failed to hold outcomes constant but instead looked at pure minimization of spending.

22. John D. Feerick, E. Leo Milonas, and William C. Thompson, *Report and Recommendations of the Judicial Referees* (Supreme Court of the State of New York, 2004).

23. Gronberg and others explicitly analyzed the efficiency of districts, but their analysis was not well received in the courtroom; see the decision of Judge John Dietz in *West Orange–Cove Consolidated Independent School District et al.* v. *Neeley et al.,* November 30, 2004. Timothy J. Gronberg and others, *School Outcomes and School Costs: The Cost Function Approach* (Texas A&M University, 2004).

24. Hanushek, "The Failure of Input-Based Schooling Policies."

25. Note that these estimates bear little relationship to classic cost functions in microeconomic theory, which uses an underlying assumption of optimal firm behavior to translate the production function (achievement related to various inputs) into a cost function that describes how cost relates to the price of inputs. None of the work in education observes any variations in input prices (for example, teacher wages, textbook costs, and the like). The empirical work in education described here relates spending to outputs and inputs such as the number or type of teachers and the poverty rate.

26. Some approaches to cost estimation are not done in this way but instead use various optimization methods to obtain the minimum cost of achieving some outcomes. They are nonetheless subject to the same interpretative questions about causation.

27. There are some serious statistical complications in this work. The econometric methodology places requirements on the modeling that are almost certainly violated in this estimation. The cost function estimation essentially assumes that districts first specify the outputs that they will obtain and that those desired outputs and the characteristics of the student body determine the spending that would be required (that is, achievement is exogenous, in statistical parlance). This approach, while summarizing the average spending patterns of different districts, is inconsistent with the interpretation that the level of resources available to a district determines student outcomes. The specific data and modeling also are very important. As Gronberg and others state, "The measurement of efficiency in producing a set of outcomes is directly linked to the particular set of performance measures that are included in the cost model and the particular set of input measures." Gronberg and others, *School Outcomes and School Costs: The Cost Function Approach.*

28. Other techniques found in the scholarly literature have been developed to consider cost minimization. See Eric A. Hanushek, "Publicly Provided Education," in *Handbook of Public Economics,* edited by Alan J. Auerbach and Martin Feldstein (Amsterdam: Elsevier, 2002), pp. 2045–141. Even when considered, it is generally impossible to describe how efficiency is achieved. See Gronberg and others, *School Outcomes and School Costs: The Cost Function Approach.*

29. William Duncombe and John Yinger, "Financing Higher Standards in Public Education: The Importance of Accounting for Educational Costs," CPR Policy Brief 10/1998 (Center for Policy Research, Syracuse University, 1998). Their subsequent estimates of adequacy for New York City are lower but still far above those of the other costing out studies for New York. See, for example, William Duncombe, Anna Lukemeyer, and John Yinger, "Financing an Adequate Education: A Case Study of New York," in *Developments in School Finance: 2001–02,* edited by William J. Fowler (Washington: National Center for Education Statistics, 2003), pp. 129–53.

30. See, for example, Eric A. Hanushek, "Pseudo-Science and a Sound Basic Education: Voodoo Statistics in New York, " *Education Next* 5, no. 4 (Fall 2005): 67–73.

31. *Education Week,* "Quality Counts 2005," p. 36.

32. For example, Thomas Decker describes the choice of the professional judgment model for the costing out study to be commissioned by the North Dakota Department of Public Instruction: "The professional judgment approach we were aware would probably produce a higher cost estimate for achieving adequacy than [the] successful schools [approach]." Transcript of Deposition of Thomas G. Decker in *Williston* v. *State of North Dakota,* August 17–18, 2005, p. 312.

33. *Education Week,* "Quality Counts 2005."

34. New York state traditionally granted two different diplomas with different requirements. In 1996, the New York Regents determined that all students would have to qualify for a regents diploma (the previously optional high-standard diploma sought by roughly half of the public school students in the state). This requirement has seen a very long phase-in period with altered testing requirements.

35. Details of the costing out exercises in the CFE case can be found in Hanushek, "Pseudo-Science and a Sound Basic Education."

36. Ibid. The referees made $1.9 billion equal $5 billion by adding back all high-spending schools that the Standard and Poor's analysis excluded on efficiency grounds.

37. Feerick, Milonas, and Thompson, *Report and Recommendations of the Judicial Referees.*

38. Instructions regarding what was needed were given to the panelists: sufficient oral and written communication skills to enable students to function in a complex and rapidly changing society; sufficient knowledge of economic, social, and political systems to enable students to make informed choices; sufficient understanding of government processes to enable students to understand the issues that affect their community, state, and nation; sufficient self-knowledge, including knowledge of students' own mental and physical health; sufficient grounding in the arts to enable each student to appreciate his or her cultural and historical heritage; sufficient training or preparation for advanced training in either academic or vocational fields to enable each student to choose and pursue life work intelligently; and sufficient level of academic or vocational skills to enable public school students to compete favorably with their counterparts in surrounding states, in academics or in the job market. Picus, Odden, and Fermanich, *A Professional Judgment Approach to School Finance Aadequacy in Kentucky.*

39. Verstegen and Associates, *Calculation of the Cost of an Adequate Education in Kentucky.*

40. Augenblick and others, *Calculation of the Cost of a Suitable Education in Kansas in 2000–2001 Using Two Different Analytical Approaches.*

41. Augenblick, Palaich, and Associates, *Calculation of the Cost of an Adequate Education in North Dakota in 2002-2003 Using the Professional Judgment Approach.*

42. William Duncombe, Anna Lukemeyer, and John Yinger, "Education Finance Reform in New York: Calculating the Cost of a 'Sound Basic Education' in New York City," CPR Policy Brief 28/2004 (Center for Policy Research, Syracuse University, 2004).

43. See Odden, Fermanich, and Picus, *A State-of-the-Art Approach to School Finance Adequacy in Kentucky.*

44. See Augenblick, Palaich, and Associates, *Calculation of the Cost of an Adequate Education in North Dakota in 2002–2003 Using the Professional Judgment Approach*, and Odden, Fermanich, and Picus, *A State-of-the-Art Approach to School Finance Adequacy in Kentucky.*

45. In most cases, it is not truly equal spending but equal spending after adjusting for extra needs such as special education, disadvantaged background, language deficiencies, and the like. It might also include adjustments for other circumstances such as diseconomies of scale in small urban districts.

46. Augenblick and Myers, Inc., *Calculation of the Cost of an Adequate Education in Indiana in 2001–2002 Using the Professional Judgment Approach.*

5

MATTHEW G. SPRINGER
JAMES W. GUTHRIE

The Politicization of the School Finance Legal Process

CONTEMPORARY NOTIONS OF educational finance adequacy have not sprung *ab initio* from the brow of Zeus, nor do they appear to be simply the latest incremental phase in an evolutionary sequence of technical developments in public finance. Rather, twenty-first-century legal and public finance concerns regarding the adequacy of education finance have roots reaching far back into the dynamics of the twentieth-century distribution of education finance.

Education finance practices, at least early- to mid-twentieth-century versions, were the province of a few green-eyeshade technical experts. Generally, these accounting experts were consigned to remote alcoves of state education departments and were invisible except when responding to regulatory questions from business managers of local school districts. Their moments of maximum visibility likely came during annual or biannual legislative budget hearings, when they were called on to construct the formulas that would be used to allocate increments in annual revenue to local districts. The usual legislative and gubernatorial strategy was first to determine politically acceptable tax rates

The authors wish to express their appreciation to David Frisvold, Eric Houck, Paul Peterson, James Smith, and Martin West for helpful comments. Although the topic has been approached in a balanced and scholarly manner, it is important to disclose that the authors have testified as expert witnesses or served as consultants or performed both roles in many of the examples provided in this chapter.

and then to permit educational revenues to be distributed according to a formula. Education was routinely expected to fit, à la Cinderella, into whatever public revenue slipper was politically determined for it.

Under this paradigm, the challenge to academic and technical experts such as Elwood Patterson Cubberley and H. Thomas James of Stanford University, George D. Strayer, Robert Murray Haig, and Paul R. Mort of Teachers College, Roe L. Johns of the University of Florida, Henry C. Morrison and J. Alan Thomas of the University of Chicago, and Edgar L. Morphet and Charles Scott Benson of the University of California was not to decide how much funding was to be distributed, but to generate a rational basis for distributing the predetermined quantity of revenue. While matters of distributional equity entered into their calculations, the organizational base of education and statutory arrangements for directing state-supported subsidies (called flat grants) were their primary concerns. As a result, their distributional formulas did not strive for resource parity.

Take, for example, the twentieth-century disparities delineated in *Edgewood Independent School District* v. *Kirby*, a 1989 school finance equity case in which the Supreme Court of Texas declared the state's system of funding public education to be unconstitutional.[1] Property wealth in Texas then ranged from approximately $14 million per student in the highest-wealth districts to $20,000 per student in the lowest-wealth districts. In light of the fact that approximately half of school districts' revenue was generated from local taxation, Supreme Court Justice Oscar H. Mauzy translated Texas's property wealth disparities into substantive terms such that "the 300,000 students in the lowest-wealth schools have less than 3 percent of the state's property to support their education, while the 300,000 students in the highest-wealth schools have over 25 percent of the state's property."[2] That is, Texas's funding scheme enabled the 100 wealthiest districts to spend, on average, 2.43 times more per pupil at about two-thirds the tax rate of the 100 poorest districts ($7,233 per student versus $2,978 per student).[3]

Education funding mechanisms that enabled variations in local wealth to penetrate a finance system once a district reached a so-called "foundation level" in per-pupil revenue and produced sizable distributional disparities were not unique to the Lone Star State.[4] Many states labored under similar distributional arrangements as recently as the third quarter of the twentieth century. For example, figure 5-1, which displays the ratio of district spending per pupil at the ninety-fifth and fifth percentiles by state for fiscal 1977, illustrates that the highest-spending school districts in nearly half of all states spent at least 1.6 times more than the lowest-spending school districts in the same state.[5] To put it another way, if district spending at the fifth percentile were $5,000 in

Figure 5-1. *Ratio of District Spending per Pupil at the Ninety-Fifth and Fifth Percentile, by State, Fiscal 1977*

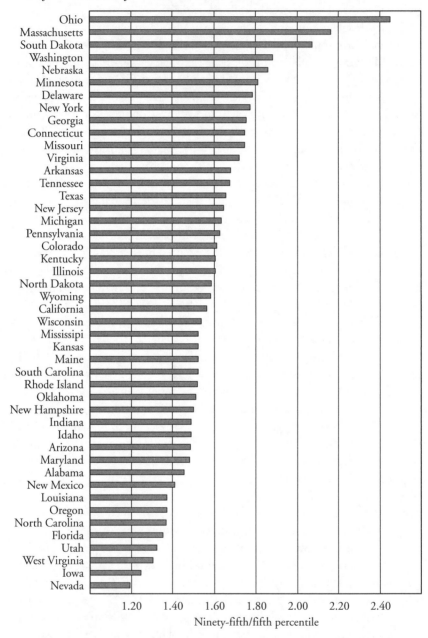

Ninety-fifth/fifth percentile

Source: Authors' calculations using *Census of Governments*, School District Finances File (F-33).

South Dakota, Massachusetts, and Ohio, then districts at the ninety-fifth percentile of per-pupil spending in these states would be spending $5,361,
$5,817, and $7,257 more per pupil, respectively.

It was not until the legal theories constructed in *Private Wealth and Public
Education,* by Coons, Clune, and Sugarman, and in *Rich Schools, Poor Schools,*
by Wise, took hold that educators and policymakers began to see a reduction
in wealth and spending disparities.[6] Initially written in isolation from one
another, each of these books targeted property-related resource disparities
within states as an injustice and constructed a constitutional argument, based
on the Fourteenth Amendment's equal protection clause, by which resource
disparities could become a productive province for adjudication.[7]

The artful legal reasoning constructed by Wise and the team of Coons,
Clune, and Sugarman also contributed to education finance's Proposition
One: *The quality of a child's schooling should not be a function of wealth, other
than the wealth of the state as a whole.* It is this formulation that provided state
judicial systems with a purchase on remedy, a criterion by which to judge
equity reforms. Proposition One does not specify what spending should be.
Rather, it ingeniously places the issue in the obverse. That is, it specifies what
the pattern of finance distribution should not be and that, whatever it should
be (presumably a legislative option), it should not be a function of local or
personal wealth. Prior to the formulation of Proposition One, courts avoided
education finance litigation for fear that there were no judicially manageable
solutions.[8]

Twenty-first-century questions of how much money is adequate for students to achieve state constitutional guarantees and how districts can be induced to spend resources more wisely to generate academic achievement were
seldom part of mid- to late-twentieth-century discussions. Indeed, it was not
until nearly two decades of state-promulgated achievement standards and standardized statewide examinations—a movement recently reinforced by the
2001 enactment of the No Child Left Behind Act—that policymakers set out
to determine how much money is enough.

This quest has been compounded by the clever construction of arguments by
advocacy organizations that rely on state learning standards as a means for pro-
pelling questions of financial adequacy before courts as a constitutional issue.[9]
This legal strategy has had substantial success in placing the issue of funding adequacy on the policy agenda. As of 2006, thirty-nine states had the constitutionality of their funding mechanism challenged on adequacy grounds; of these challenges, twenty-four were ruled unconstitutional.[10] Moreover, in 2005 alone,
high-court decisions were handed down in Kansas and Texas, a decision with
national implication was awaiting appeal in South Carolina, and states such as

Kentucky, Missouri, and Nebraska were moving closer to the trial phase, as new cases were filed in Alaska, Connecticut, Georgia, Nebraska, and Washington.

Ensuring that sufficient resources are available to all students to meet state-specified learning standards is a laudable policy objective. Unfortunately, contemporary legal laments regarding resource adequacy have extended beyond the analytic capacity of present-day social science to construct credible answers. Old style, conventional equal protection education finance issues were successful in the latter portion of the twentieth century because they were amenable to reasonably accurate technical appraisals achieved through widely accepted statistical measures.[11]

However, the evolving modern concept of financial adequacy, in addition to measuring the equity of revenue distribution, requires researchers to ascertain far more elusive relationships among education inputs, processes, throughputs, and outcomes. Researchers simply have not yet discovered answers to many of the questions regarding these relationships. For example, the amount of money or configuration of schooling resources needed to compensate educationally for childhood conditions of impoverishment, disability, or language deficiency is simply not known. Similarly, other than sensing that there assuredly are diseconomies of size in the operation of schools with varying enrollments, researchers are unable to specify these diseconomies in a manner sufficiently precise as to justify inclusion in state funding mechanisms.[12]

In the presence of this evidentiary void, a combination of ill-conceived and heavily biased advocacy testimony and pseudo-scientific analyses thinly disguised as social science research, for which courts frequently seem to be receptacles, has rendered the status of education finance adequacy alarming and triggered a trajectory that ultimately may prove inimical to the public's long-run interests.

Still, education finance adequacy cost studies and court cases proceed, even proliferate. According to the Advocacy Center for Children's Educational Success with Standards (ACCESS), a project of the Campaign for Fiscal Equity, a total of fifty-eight cost studies had been conducted in thirty-nine states as of January 2006.[13] Of these cost studies, state courts initiated seven, a state government agency initiated thirty-four, and independent groups initiated seventeen. At least twenty cost studies in fourteen states were undertaken between January 2004 and December 2005, with a potential for at least five additional studies in 2006.

Against this backdrop of growing judicial and legislative interest in educational adequacy, the remainder of this chapter explores the state of evidence. The first section identifies the principal strategies for modeling the cost of education finance adequacy that have dominated policy and legal decisionmaking and provides a case illustrating how each modeling strategy is deficient in practical utility. The second illustrates the way in which self-interested testimony is increasingly plaguing litigation, as advocacy groups are concocting education funding scenarios that reflect personal predilections rather than operational realities. The third section provides three recommendations for salvaging education finance adequacy as a legitimate consideration of public policy.

Inadequate State of Adequacy Cost Modeling Strategies

There are four generally recognized analytic means by which the costs of education programs and services are approximated when an attempt is made to specify an adequate educational opportunity: the econometric or cost function approach, the successful schools or "empirical" approach, the state-of-the-art or research-based approach, and professional judgment models.[14] While some may argue that cost modeling strategies are better than guesses and better than uninformed political judgment alone, the following analyses and anecdotes indicate that the current scientific state of cost modeling strategies severely undermines the credibility of financial extrapolations. At best, the results of existing cost modeling might be considered as information for legislative deliberation. The scientific state of these methods is presently so primitive that they deserve no place in the machinations of a court.

Econometric or Cost Function Approach

In the recently decided *Neeley* v. *West Orange-Cove Consolidated Independent School District* case in Texas,[15] plaintiff and intervening districts claimed that newly elevated state learning standards imposed far higher revenue needs on the Texas education system than the previously specified performance expectations. They claimed that revenues were insufficient to provide an adequate opportunity for students to achieve what was now expected. The evidence marshaled on behalf of all parties involved in the lawsuit effectively illustrates weaknesses associated with using the cost function approach to cost out adequacy.

Generally speaking, researchers employing the cost function strategy engage in the duel of the traditional education production function.[16] They specify a desired level of student performance and then seek school variables or components of the student condition such as household and community characteristics and school service levels (for example, teacher qualifications) that are statistically associated with that outcome.[17] Once conditions associated with a specified student or school performance outcome are known—even if these conditions are remote from actual education production processes—the cost function model approximates spending associated with achieving the desired outcome or condition. There are even means for determining the lowest costs at which the highest correlated mix of resources associated with a preferred outcome can be produced (for example, reliance on data envelopment analysis, stochastic frontier estimation, and the Herfindahl index).

The heart of the evidence regarding adequacy in *West Orange-Cove* was provided by two cost function studies, one conducted by Jennifer Imazeki and Andrew Reschovsky (hereinafter referred to as plaintiff experts) and a second conducted by Timothy Gronberg, Dennis Jansen, Lori Taylor, and Kevin Booker (hereinafter referred to as defense experts) at the request of the Texas Joint Select Committee on Public School Finance.[18] Table 5-1 identifies several similarities and differences between the plaintiff and defense studies.[19] Both studies, for example, relied on similar econometric models, data, and proficiency standards. Differences existed in the treatment of value-added measures, tests (SAT/ACT variables), and school district efficiency controls.

While the plaintiff and defense cost functions initially appeared quite similar, subtle differences resulted in drastically different conclusions. The defense's cost function estimated that $226 million to $408 million in additional state or local funding was needed for the entire state's student enrollment to achieve a 55 percent passing standard, whereas the plaintiffs' cost function estimated that $1.7 billion to $5.4 billion more in public funding was needed. At the very least, this translates into a difference of nearly $1.3 billion if one compares the defense's upper-bound estimate to the plaintiffs' lower-bound estimate. At the widest bounds, there is a discrepancy of $5 billion, or 12.5 percent of the total amount of public education revenues and receipts that were available for spending in Texas K–12 schools during the 2002–03 school year.

Such radically different estimates stem from the fact that the current state of cost function analysis is so tightly tied to institutional production unknowns, technical assumptions, elastic model specifications, and data deficiencies that the analyses necessarily lack precision, robustness, and objectivity. Defense and plaintiff models lack any recognition of educationally relevant production components. Without taking into consideration elements that can be reasonably presumed or empirically proved to enhance the development of students' skill, knowledge, and capacity, their results can only identify the resource levels that may be associated with acceptable achievement (with inefficient practices removed, to the extent known), not the resource levels that would be necessary, if used efficiently, to achieve a specified outcome.[20]

Table 5-1. *Comparison of Select Characteristics from Two Texas Cost Function Studies*

Dimension	Similarities and differences	
	Similarities	
Cost strategy	Cost function	
Dependent variable	2001–02 average district operating expenditures	
Independent variable	2001–02 TAAS (Texas Assessment of Academic Skills) district passing rates converted to 2005 TAKS (Texas Assessment of Knowledge and Skills, with a 55 percent passing rate threshold)	
Control variables	District-level percent free or reduced-price lunch status; percent limited English proficiency; percent enrolled in high school	
Cost index	Teacher cost index	
Special education	Percent high incidence/low cost; percent low incidence/ high cost	
	Differences	
	GJTB	*IR*
Value-added measure	Two-year lag	One-year lag
Efficiency measure	Does not employ Herfindahl Index	Employs Herfindahl Index
Cost comparison	Total operating revenues	Total operating expenditures
Inflation adjustment	Bureau of Labor Statistics estimate of 7.4	Bureau of Labor Statistics estimate of 7.9
Proxy for geographic isolation	Employs distance to closest large city	Does not employ an isolation measure
Race and ethnicity	Does not include black and Hispanic	Includes percent black and Hispanic
Free and reduced-price lunch status and limited English proficiency	Elementary school percentages	Total district percentages

Source: GJTB: Timothy Gronberg and others, "School Outcomes and School Costs" (2004); IR: Jennifer Imazeki and Andrew Reschovsky, "Estimating the Costs of Meeting Texas Education Accountability Standards" (2004).

This rendering is not intended as a criticism of the defense's or plaintiffs' research. To the contrary, they have addressed a significant policy issue, and their cost functions are advancing the state of cost modeling strategies. Moreover, deficiencies diluting the research validity and policy utility of their findings are not of their making and probably not to their liking. Indeed, these two research teams and others who ply this particular analytic trade to a high standard might eventually suggest useful answers to policymakers starved for guidance regarding education spending. Nevertheless, one must realize that seemingly innocent assumptions made by each research team—none of which can be proven to be technically "wrong"—yield radically different results and, as a result, speak to why the current state of cost function analyses is inappropriate for guiding alterations in the system of state education finance policy.

Successful Schools or Empirical Approach

The successful schools approach was first employed in 1995 by John Augenblick, Kern Alexander, and James Guthrie and subsequently advanced in 1997 by Augenblick for the state of Ohio.[21] Based on a spectrum of desired student outcomes (that is, standardized test scores and graduation rates) identified by districts as vital criteria for an adequate education system, the successful schools approach identifies schools or districts that effectively meet these criteria. These schools or districts are then used as models to construct base funding levels for target schools or districts. In effect, the successful schools approach is an unsophisticated adaptation of the econometric or cost function approach.

The successful schools approach is often appealing to public policy interest groups and education advocates because it is relatively easy to identify schools meeting specified outcomes and then to determine how much those schools are spending. The basis for setting base funding levels also tends to be transparent to the public. However, the successful schools approach leaves results vulnerable to data dredging and strategic manipulation. Moreover, as the following example of a successful schools study undertaken for a recent adequacy trial in Alaska illustrates, the successful schools approach can produce internal contradictions that undermine its credibility. In the Alaska case for which more detail is provided below, a successful schools model enables the plaintiff expert to construct a means by which to conclude that per-pupil state and local revenue needs to be increased by nearly one-third. Yet when descriptive statistics are entered into the diagnostic models used to construct a prototype district, one can see the obverse; the plaintiff expert's analyses could also conclude that a reduction in per-pupil state and local revenue would increase the percentage of students who are considered proficient or advanced.[22]

To cost out a baseline revenue figure for Alaska's public school system, using the successful schools approach, the plaintiff's expert witness obtained district-level data from the state Department of Education and identified thirty-four potentially "relevant" fiscal and nonfiscal input and output variables. These variables were then entered into a commonly available statistical software package to extract characteristics deemed to be the best predictors of the chosen outcome of interest. The plaintiff expert then used these derived characteristics to construct a prototype school district that ultimately provided scaffolding for a per-pupil state and local revenue cost estimate recommending a 32 percent increase to achieve education financial adequacy in Alaska.

While one could spend considerable time dissecting the individual steps that composed this haphazard data-dredging endeavor, we skip such an exercise to concentrate on the most telling issue. That is, the plaintiff expert's reliance on a standardized statistical software program to identify a set of "relevant" variables rendered his search for more money devoid of any theoretical or logical connection to education finance and econometric principles and practices. The following equation, in a simplified form, was included in the plaintiff's evidentiary submission and used to advocate higher spending:

$$\% \, proficient_i = 144.579 - 0.419(\%FRPL_i) - 55.994(\%minority_i)$$
$$+ \, 49.003(dropout \, rate_i) - 0.008(state \, and \, local \, revenue_i).$$

The dependent variable is the percentage of students considered proficient or advanced in sixth grade for school district i in Alaska and includes the percentage of free or reduced-price lunch-status students, percent of minority students, and dropout rate in a school district. State and local revenue in fiscal 2001 is the variable of interest.

When the mean value for each independent variable is input into the equation reported above, on average, 56.8 percent of sixth-grade students are considered proficient or advanced.[23] If state and local revenue is increased by one standard deviation, then 47.7 percent of sixth-grade students are considered proficient or advanced according to the plaintiff expert's report. Conversely, if the average state and local revenue value reported by the plaintiff expert is reduced by one standard deviation, then 65.8 percent of sixth-grade students are determined to be proficient or advanced. Ironically, results from the plaintiff expert's "analytic" strategy can also be used to argue for a reduction in state and local revenue.

Does this seem logical? The interpretation presented in the previous paragraph is natural to expect if Alaska's education funding formula is redistributed (that is, any mechanism in the formula that strives to distribute educational dollars more proportionately in order to make the financing system more just). The absurd implications resulting from the plaintiff expert's successful schools model, however, speak to why estimating the cost of an adequate educational opportunity may ultimately prove inimical to the public's long-run interest.

The problem is that unsubstantiated claims and ridiculous requests eventually erode public interest in and support of K–12 education policy.

State-of-the-Art or Research-Based Approach

The state-of-the-art approach specifies research-based programs and interventions for which verified successful outcomes have been claimed. The underlying rationale of this approach is that any level of school-provided resources specified to operate these programs and interventions should have the capacity to produce the desired student outcomes. The research-based approach was first used to estimate the costs of implementing models of whole-school, systemic reform that address student needs as a collective unit rather than as part of compartmentalized instructional programs. More recently, the approach has been extended to include programs and interventions as varied as preschool, full-day kindergarten, smaller schools, a principal for every school, instructional facilitators, school-based coaches or mentors, smaller class size, planning and preparation time or collaborative professional development, extra-help strategies for struggling students, student support or family outreach, extended school day, ongoing professional development and training, and technology.[24]

The research-based approach suffers from a severe shortage of valid research on which to base its cost estimates. Take, for example, optimal class size. Tennessee's Student Teacher Achievement Ratio (STAR) study, after approval from the Tennessee state legislature, conducted a randomized field trial that provided additional appropriations to kindergarten through third-grade classes to create smaller class sizes. Although several analyses of the STAR data indicated that smaller class size significantly enhanced student achievement in primary school, subsequent papers have argued that the results do not fully withstand scientific scrutiny.[25]

Does this mean that results from STAR were wrong? No one knows for sure. The only certainty is that highly contentious debate rages on nearly every front of social science research (for example, potential program elements such as teacher training or certification level, professional development, teacher aides, instructional technology, and use of guidance counselors). Without the backing of definitive empirical research, state-of-the-art techniques, no matter how useful and perhaps desirable, should not serve to compel substantive changes in state funding mechanisms. Nevertheless, uncertainty about the potential efficacy of programs and interventions has not precluded courts from mandating reform based on the so-called state-of-the-art cost modeling strategy. Indeed, this cost modeling strategy has recently served as a basis for school finance judgments in both Arkansas and Wyoming.

Professional Judgment Approach

The modern introduction of the professional judgment approach into education finance began in Wyoming as a consequence of *Campbell County School District v. State of Wyoming* in 1995.[26] The challenge resulting from *Campbell* was to provide the legislature, not the court, with an estimate of what it would cost to achieve a "visionary" school system, mandated by the court to be the best in the world. The absence of a statewide student achievement test limited the means by which the cost to Wyoming of such a high-performing school system could be determined.[27] As such, finance experts retained by the state turned to and modeled their practices after the professional judgment panels constructed by the Food and Drug Administration, Air Traffic Control Administration, and Veterans Administration, all of which have relied for years on professional judgment panels when faced with informational deficiencies.

Generally speaking, a professional judgment approach to costing out adequacy relies on experienced professional educators to identify resources deemed necessary to produce desired outcomes. This presumes the ability of professional educators to design instructional programs and auxiliary services to ensure an adequate opportunity for students of all capacities to satisfy state-promulgated expectations of knowledge and skills. Once a panel has designed the instructional program, economic and finance experts take steps to impute current market prices (for example, salaries, fringe benefits, and supplies) to create a final per-pupil block grant.

In its early days, circa 1995, the professional judgment approach was favored because it provided the best "analytic" strategy for costing out adequacy given informational and data constraints. Researchers employing the approach were careful to ensure that everything regarding the professional judgment endeavor was transparent and met as rigorous a standard as possible. For example, panel participants were selected carefully to be as representative and objective as possible and not to represent any particular group of education stakeholders. Furthermore, for those engaged in what was openly acknowledged as a porous means of determining costs, solace flowed from knowing that recommendations were being provided to an executive branch agency or a legislature, a deliberative body whose participants could take into account evidentiary frailties.

The professional judgment approach proliferated in education finance litigation following *Campbell*. Approximately eighteen professional judgment studies, conducted by at least seven different research groups, were tendered as evidence in education finance adequacy litigation from 1996 to 2003. Yet, even though some of these studies were conducted because of informational deficiencies similar to those in *Campbell* and may have followed best practices for generating objective cost estimates, an increasing number of contemporary professional judgment studies are devoid of methodological rigor and have been infected with self-serving biases hardly worthy of legislative, executive, and judicial consideration.

Take, for example, a recent professional judgment study prepared by Verstegen and Associates for *Young et al.* v. *Williams et al.*, an education finance adequacy trial pending in Kentucky.[28] Verstegen and Associates' evidentiary submission relied principally on two organizations to select teachers, curriculum specialists, and administrators to serve on professional judgment panels that constructed the resource ingredients that would ultimately help to determine the cost of an adequate education in Kentucky. The first organization was the Council for Better Education (CBE), a coalition of school districts that brought an adequacy suit against the Commonwealth of Kentucky first in the late 1980s and then for a second time in 2003. The second organization was the Kentucky Education Association (KEA), the state's National Education Association (NEA) affiliate, whose mission targets "improved" education funding and which further identifies "enhancing" compensation and benefits as a principal reason for educators to join the union. To the extent that panel participants knew that their work product was likely to be used to advocate for additional funding for the state's public schools (or that panel participants were disposed to share CBE's or KEA's mission and values) and that additional funding for public schools would likely result in improved working conditions and higher salaries for participants, there was a patently obvious bias in the Verstegen and Associates study from its inception. For that reason, it is not surprising that the report concluded that an additional $892 million to $1.2 billion was needed to achieve an adequate education and that raising teacher salaries was one of three "key resource requirements" for attaining educational adequacy.[29]

To examine further whether professional judgment studies are subject to human inconsistencies (and potentially self-serving inclinations), we reviewed results from eight professional judgment studies in eight states, released between 2001 and 2003.[30] All studies were conducted by Augenblick and Myers (hereinafter referred to as A&M) or Augenblick, Palaich, and Associates (hereinafter referred to as APA). This review was limited to studies by these two groups for three main reasons. First, professional judgment exercises organized by A&M and APA impose similar constraints on panel participants across studies and, in most instances, relied on similarly trained staff members to facilitate panel deliberations, thus making cross-state and cross-study comparisons more reasonable. Second, they report the number of instructional personnel required per 1,000 "regular" students in nearly every professional judgment study conducted. This provides a common metric for comparison. Finally, they have conducted the most professional judgment studies of any single group of consultants, thus providing the largest possible sample with a common metric for comparison purposes.

Table 5-2 reports values for instructional personnel per 1,000 "regular" students for elementary schools, middle schools, and high schools nested in a hypothetical K–12 school district identified as moderate or average in size.[31] Across the board, the projected number of instructional personnel varies significantly, even when contextual constraints are intended to be similar.[32] For example, professional judgment panels in Maryland estimated, on average, that elementary schools need 30.0 instructional aides per 1,000 "regular" students to meet state standards, while average panel estimates in Indiana, Kansas, and North Dakota recommended 0.0, 6.5, and 8.0 instructional aides per 1,000 "regular" students, respectively. Furthermore, Nebraska middle schools require 98.8 instructional personnel per 1,000 "regular" students, whereas Montana only needs 51.7 instructors.

Differing pedagogical climates, geographic composition, organizational conditions, and governance structures might explain some variance across professional judgment estimates. However, in the A&M and APA studies, the magnitude of resource variance across professional judgment studies is much more likely a result of human inconsistency and potentially self-serving behavior than contextual uniqueness.

As a whole, the present state of the art of education finance adequacy cost modeling is highly vulnerable to assumptions made by researchers in attempting to calculate the cost of an adequate educational opportunity. Even within studies, one can find great disparities. For example, the team providing advice to New York plaintiffs in the *Campaign for Fiscal Equity* v. *State of New York* remedy phase, a joint venture of the American Institutes for Research (AIR) and Management Analysis and Planning (MAP), had contrasting approaches for adjusting differences between cost estimates generated by multiple professional judgment panels.[33] The differences, distilled to their essence, were as follows. AIR aggregated cost estimates across multiple panels, essentially taking a higher recommended level for each category. MAP averaged the cost estimates from different panel submissions. The different approaches resulted in estimates of billions of dollars in additional funding needed to achieve adequacy. Such palpable inconsistencies provide testament to why the contemporary state-of-the-art cost modeling is deficient in practical utility for adjudicating "adequacy of what" and "how much is adequate."[34]

Table 5-2. *Descriptive Statistics for Teacher Aides, Other Teachers, and All Instructional Personnel Required per 1,000 "Regular" Students for Elementary, Middle, and High Schools in Moderate-Size K–12 Districts to Meet State Standards in Select States as Determined by Professional Judgment Panels*

Type of personnel and level of school	Indiana	Kansas	Maryland[a]	Missouri	Montana	Nebraska	North Dakota	Tennessee
Teacher aides								
Elementary	0.00	6.50	30.00	10.90	10.00	27.70	8.00	18.80
Middle	0.00	5.00	12.50	10.90	8.60	2.50	N/A	12.50
High school	0.00	2.50	4.00	9.50	10.80	6.50	0.00	3.80
Other teachers								
Elementary	6.40	12.50	6.00	14.50	10.00	12.90	8.00	9.40
Middle	0.00	16.70	3.65	18.90	8.60	23.80	N/A	16.30
High school	16.20	13.80	6.00	29.90	29.10	15.00	0.00	24.40
All instructional personnel								
Elementary	62.80	74.00	116.00	89.90	75.00	90.00	72.00	87.60
Middle	59.20	73.40	72.50	78.90	51.70	98.80	73.00	78.80
High school	59.90	83.80	79.00	88.30	84.10	79.00	58.00	66.30

Source: Compiled by authors from values reported in professional judgment studies conducted by Augenblick and Myers and by Augenblick, Palaich, and Associates.

a. Studies reviewed typically reported values for teachers, teacher aides, and other teachers. The Maryland study reported values for teachers, teacher aides, and all instructional personnel. We assume that (All instructional personnel) – (Teachers + Teacher aides) = (Other teachers).

How Advocacy Is Hijacking Adequacy Litigation and Reform

Juxtaposing twentieth-century equity analysis and litigation with recent research and court proceedings under the guise of adequacy reveals the widespread and increasingly transparent political self-interest characterizing today's educational adequacy finance litigation and reform. Where initially, in the equity-based litigation of the 1970s and 1980s, researchers investigated and courts intervened in deep-seated education finance issues of public policy significance, contemporary adequacy research and lawsuits are increasingly guided by narrowly self-interested plaintiffs seeking to bypass the conventional competitive political process and procure private gain at public expense. Furthermore, it is typically these very same "we need more money" groups that ardently oppose experimentation with alternative governance and operational innovations, such as competition and performance pay, that are designed specifically to increase efficiency and productivity and to ensure that all children are provided the opportunity for an excellent education. Moreover, adequacy advocates seldom open the door to alternative public policy solutions, such as income maintenance, housing subsidies, or health and nutrition improvement, for aiding the educational problems of the disadvantaged.[35]

Selfishness is not new to jurisprudence. Certainly, other parties at interest have pursued the protected calm and rational patois provided by the judicial process in place of subjecting themselves to the bare-knuckle pummeling of political debate. If this alone were all that was taking place, there would be little or no news here. However, a deeper and more sinister dynamic is at play in modern research and litigation regarding education finance adequacy. Self-interested advocacy has become a primary driver of adequacy research and, as the following examples illustrate, now plagues the contemporary adequacy reform movement.

Adequacy Research as Advocacy

In August 2003 a nineteen-member task force commissioned by Minnesota Governor Tim Pawlenty convened the first of nine monthly meetings to examine and make recommendations for revamping Minnesota's K–12 education finance system. In addition to including prominent Minnesota superintendents, a former state finance director, a state board of education president, and local community leaders, the School Funding Task Force engaged MAP, a Davis, California–based consulting firm specializing in education finance and litigation support.[36] The principal recommendations, as delineated in the task force's report, included linking education funding to student learning, elevating school accountability, fostering community engagement, encouraging educator creativity, continuing to value school choice, and sustaining progress toward funding equity.[37]

In September 2005, approximately eighteen months after the School Funding Task Force released its report, the Association of Metropolitan School Districts, the Minnesota Rural Education Association, and Schools for Equity in Education contracted the services of APA to "examine the Task Force results and, using widely accepted methodologies, determine the costs necessary to ensure that each public school student is educated to meet the state's academic standards."[38] APA's "continuation" of the School Funding Task Force's report resulted in an estimate that would have required $8 billion to realize educational adequacy for the 2003–04 school year, which implied that Minnesota's public school system was underfunded by approximately $952.9 million during the 2003–04 school year.

There is considerable evidence that APA's reexamination of the Minnesota School Funding Task Force's report was a product of advocacy and not an objective evaluation of Minnesota's mechanism for funding public education. An econometric model predicting relationships between per-pupil expenditures and free and reduced-price lunch status is informative because it estimates the degree to which a state's education finance system raises spending in districts serving low-socioeconomic-status students relative to all other districts.[39] That is, it helps to answer the following questions: Does Minnesota's funding mechanism target districts with a high proportion of low-socioeconomic-status students (that is, students who may require additional resources to meet state-specified learning standards)? To what extent are funds allocated to these districts? How does Minnesota's funding mechanism compare to that of the United States? And how does Minnesota's funding mechanism rank relative to the funding mechanisms of other states?

Results from this new analysis indicate that, on average, the association between per-pupil expenditure and percent free and reduced-price lunch status grew stronger in Minnesota from 1990 to 2000. In 2000, for example, a 1 percent increase in free and reduced-price lunch-status students was associated with a $45.18 increase in pupil spending. In substantive terms, this equates to a district with 75 percent of its students qualifying for free and reduced-price lunch status spending, on average, $2,259 more per pupil than a district with only 25 percent of its students qualifying for free and reduced-price lunch status.

The econometric model further indicates that, on average, the association between per-pupil expenditure and percent free and reduced-price lunch status situates Minnesota well above the U.S. average. Minnesota spent $25.71 more per unit increase of free and reduced-price lunch-status students compared to the United States. This means that a district in Minnesota with 75 percent of its students qualifying for free and reduced-price lunch status spent, on average, $1,928 more per pupil than the average district in the United States with 75 percent of its students qualifying for free and reduced-price lunch status. In fact, only three states allocated more to low-socioeconomic districts in 2000 (Wyoming, Utah, and North Dakota).

A similar analysis of U.S. public education finance was recently conducted by Kevin Carey of the Education Trust.[40] Carey's analyses are informative because they rely on revenue and not expenditure data, contain more recent education finance and district demographic data, use a different coding scheme and methodological strategy from the one explained above, and, most important, were conducted independently from the discussion at hand. According to Carey, the gap in spending between the highest- and lowest-poverty district in Minnesota increased by more than $500 per pupil from 1997 to 2002 (in favor of low-poverty districts), so that disadvantaged districts received approximately $650 more per pupil in 2002 than in 1997.

Perhaps even more informative is the fact that Carey's estimates include a 40 percent cost adjustment for low-income students, as "recommended" by No Child Left Behind.[41] "By accounting for the fact that high-poverty school districts face stiffer challenges," according to Carey, such an analysis arrives "at a more complete picture of whether states are really providing equitable resources to all children."[42] However, when APA researchers used their self-proclaimed "widely accepted methodologies" to advance the work of the School Funding Task Force, they found that Minnesota would need to raise average per-pupil revenue to around $11,000, or about $2,000 more than the U.S. average.

Recognizing that these examples only illustrate input dimensions of Minnesota's public school system, it is worth noting that student outcomes measured by the National Assessment of Educational Progress (NAEP) are equally favorable. For example, in 2005 only Massachusetts had a greater percentage of students than Minnesota at or above proficiency in mathematics in fourth grade, while no state had a greater percentage of students than Minnesota at or above proficiency in mathematics in eighth grade. Moreover, charting the average mathematics score and percentage of students eligible for free and reduced-price lunch in the fourth and eighth grades shows that only nine or fewer states had a smaller percentage of students than Minnesota below "basic" proficiency.[43] While areas in need of improvement surely exist, it is difficult to believe that an "inadequate" state is among the national leaders in student achievement, as indicated by a widely accepted measure.

The notion of tweaking prior analyses by adding an unverified factor for historically "disadvantaged" students requiring 20 percent additional revenue per pupil to meet state-specified learning standards indicates the state of the art of adequacy analysis. The problem is that strategies for modeling the cost of education finance adequacy are presently neither analytic nor art. Increasingly, adequacy research has simply become advocacy, and this advocacy has hijacked a once legitimate effort to reform public schooling.

Overtly Politicized Nature of the Plaintiffs' Position

The senior author of this chapter first came to understand the overtly politicized nature of the plaintiffs' position many years ago when he was contacted by an associate state supreme court justice. The justice inquired of Guthrie's willingness to serve as a special master[44] for an adequacy case and informed him that he was the state's top choice. Guthrie stated that he believed himself to possess the technical expertise that would prove useful to the court and confirmed his willingness and availability to serve as special master. The associate justice, in return, expressed his gratitude and concluded the call by informing Guthrie that he would be back in touch in the near future with contractual details and the like.

The "near future" had passed when Guthrie encountered the associate justice while traveling on unrelated business. In jest, Guthrie let the associate justice know that he was still waiting for the call, knowing full well that somebody else had been named special master a month or so prior. It turned out that the state had been unable to get clearance for Guthrie to serve as the special master. A teacher union that was not a party, at least not an ostensible party, to the case had found a way to veto his nomination. Even more peculiar was the fact that the teacher union was not even in the same state as the school finance adequacy litigation. Yet this special interest group was able to exert a significant level of control and influence through informal networks, resulting in Guthrie's exclusion.

While one may never know the extent of the teacher association's influence beyond this candid exchange between Guthrie and the associate justice, an increasingly greater number of other such politicizations are contaminating the legal process of school finance adequacy. Regrettably, it might be impossible for the school finance profession to restore the credibility of adequacy research in the eyes of the public and obtain the full potential from adequacy-driven reform unless such politicization is decontaminated.

Salvaging Adequacy as Legitimate Public Policy

While we have lamented the rate at which deficient cost modeling, pseudo-scientific research practices, and advocacy testimony are tainting litigation regarding education finance adequacy, we are not calling for an end to the adequacy reform movement. The principled cause of adequacy is noble in character, and America's public schools surely would be enhanced if assured the optimal mix of resources, incentives, practices, and structures. Consequently, we set forth three recommendations by which adequacy-driven reform and cost modeling strategies could become more effective. These recommendations assume not only that a significant set of cost modeling research deficiencies could, over time, be ameliorated but also that the role of cost studies should be restricted until the underlying science is rendered more rigorous and evidentiary standards are objectified.

Relocating the Education Finance Adequacy Venue

If notions of educational adequacy currently influencing contemporary educational policy are to have even a minimally useful role, then the venue for applying adequacy should bypass the courthouse and be concentrated in the statehouse. The judicial system is generally restricted to considering solutions for issues brought before the court. Take, for instance, a recent education finance decision in Kansas in which the judge acknowledged that ineptly derived evidence was provided to the court but proceeded to state that, in the absence of any research evidence, the court had no alternative but to acquiesce to the available findings.[45] Legislative and executive branch deliberations are better adapted to accommodating uncertainty, deconstructing complexity, and considering trade-offs since their operational arrangements permit a far wider opportunity for constructive criticism and successive approximation to take place.

Perhaps a more appropriate response to allegations of resource inadequacy, and a key advantage found in moving adequacy deliberations to legislative and executive bodies in such instances, is to consider resource investments alongside interventions aimed at using those resources more effectively. Take, for example, the fact that the United States now expends approximately $3 billion per operating day in support of K–12 public schools. For more than a half-century, two-thirds of this total has been disbursed for salaries and fringe benefits of professional educators, an aggregate figure that has increased annually at rates well in excess of general price inflation. Yet there is little evidence that schools have achieved the remarkable productivity gains that have characterized other sectors of the U.S. and world economies by addressing the instructional effectiveness of teachers, a facet of schooling most widely identified as influencing a child's education.[46]

Recognizing that more than 96 percent of U.S. public schoolteachers are presently paid on a uniform schedule, with salary increments based on years of employment and post–bachelor's degree college course credits—two conditions correlated marginally, at best, to student achievement and teacher effectiveness—interventions aimed at compensating teachers who routinely instruct effectively or who possess skills in high demand may be a more appropriate means of ensuring that all students are provided an adequate educational opportunity.[47] Accordingly, decisions regarding whether a sufficient level of resources is presently available to all students and designing means by which all students have an opportunity to reach at least a level of proficiency defined by state standards should reside with state legislative and executive branch officials.

Research Investment to Advance Cost Modeling Strategies

If adequacy research and cost studies are eventually to have a useful role, then steps must be taken to elevate their scientific sophistication. The policy system thirsts for more precise information regarding the manner in which education resources can be deployed to improve student performance and how much money is needed to give students an opportunity to learn what is expected. With a new generation of reform-minded philanthropists targeting high-profile efforts that will influence educational politics and policy, the time is ripe for a project that targets methodological advancements and improvements in cost modeling strategies.[48] Ultimately, of course, even improved cost modeling strategies are enslaved to data availability. Whereas the United States and various individual states have made progress in improving their data systems, the principal deficiency is an inability, presently, to link data on spending with information on student achievement. Whereas the building of such linkages in federal and state data systems is a sine qua non for better analyses, it is not expensive, relative to the overall costs of the nation's K–12 endeavor.

A modest expenditure, in the range of $10 million to $20 million, could have a dramatic effect if expended on convening the nation's top-flight statisticians and economists to construct a research and methodological task force to buttress cost modeling strategies. The impact of such an endeavor could be expanded even further by engaging both plaintiff and defense attorneys, and perhaps jurists, in an effort to understand the methods and limitations of cost modeling strategies. Moreover, integrating these efforts with programs designed to train education finance scholars would provide a further foundation for understanding the means to provide all students with an adequate educational opportunity.

In the 1970s the Ford Foundation made a significant investment in constructing a base of interdisciplinary scholarship for studying the financing and economics of public education. Conferences and seminars convened economists, political scientists, legal scholars, social scientists, legislators, and education experts, graduate research and training programs were established and subsidized at the University of California, Berkeley, the University of Chicago, Stanford University, and Teachers College to train the next generation of education finance experts, and scholarly publications were initiated to solidify a new base of research. The result was the formation of a storehouse of intellectual capital that served the education finance and education policy field for four decades.[49] A similar investment now could make the difference for adequacy research and policy analysis.

Review Standards

If adequacy research and cost studies are to have a useful role, then steps must be taken to construct higher evidentiary standards. An independent organization such as the National Research Council, the Council of Chief State School Officers, or the Education Commission of the States should convene a panel of finance experts to construct adequacy research, cost study standards, and screening criteria. A clear set of standards for evidence and criteria for screening would be useful to legislative and executive bodies when appraising the objectivity and scientific reliability of cost studies and determining the adequacy of state funding mechanisms.

Conclusion: Await Science, Avoid Science Fiction

The chain of education changes that has transpired in the United States, beginning with the 1983 publication of *A Nation at Risk* and continuing through today with the complicated policy challenges surrounding implementation of the No Child Left Behind Act, has provoked a parallel evolution of education financing issues. What was once, at least in retrospect, a relatively simple set of technical matters regarding revenue and taxation equity has evolved into a complicated matrix of interconnected econometric and psychometric measurements. On many fronts, the complexity of issues surrounding resource adequacy has outstripped the capacity of social science research to supply valid answers. This evidentiary void has facilitated the manipulation of strategies for modeling the costs of education finance adequacy to advocate for greater resources for education and for educators. Accordingly, this chapter has illustrated the deficiencies of existing cost modeling strategies and called for a more deliberative, objective, and scientific process for realizing adequacy. Moving toward a more scientific base, and away from what today is often science fiction, could dampen fiscal waste and mitigate policy mistakes likely resulting from today's unalloyed advocacy.

Failure to move cautiously toward a scientific base likely will produce a negative outcome. California as a state found that strict financial equality could be achieved in more than one way. Proponents of equity had long assumed that funding fairness would stem from leveling up expenditures. After Proposition 13, officially known as the People's Initiative to Limit Property Taxation, it became evident that equality could be achieved by holding down spending.

There is an analog for adequacy. If higher student achievement goals are said, almost always, to necessitate more and more money for educators, then policymakers have the option, unfortunately, of depreciating specified standards for student achievement. In this way, money might be saved, but the nation's well-being, and that of individual students, sacrificed.

Notes

1. *Edgewood Independent School District* v. *Kirby*, 777 S.W.2d 391 (Tex. 1989).
2. Ibid., at 2.
3. Ibid., at 3.
4. In this parlance, "foundation" implied an amount providing sufficient opportunity for students or an amount below which a state would not tolerate less per-pupil spending. It was also a foundation on which a local district could add more revenue from its own sources. Whatever the meaning, it seldom, if ever, was a rationally derived dollar amount sufficient to meet some state-determined standard of student achievement.
5. We removed outlier values in each state before identifying the value of current spending per pupil at the fifth and ninety-fifth percentiles and computing the ninety-fifth/fifth percentile inequality measure for each state. We also removed four states and the District of Columbia. Montana and Vermont were not included because they are composed predominantly of independent school districts. Hawaii and District of Columbia were deleted because each has a single school district. Alaska was deleted because it has a unique governance structure.
6. John E. Coons, William H. Clune, and Stephen D. Sugarman, *Private Wealth and Public Education* (Harvard University Press, 1970); Arthur E. Wise, *Rich Schools, Poor Schools: The Promise of Equal Educational Opportunity* (University of Chicago Press, 1969).
7. Even though the U.S. Supreme Court's 1973 decision in *San Antonio Independent School District* v. *Rodriguez*, 411 U.S. 1 (1973), neutered the issue, at least for a while, as a federal constitutional matter—the legal reasoning was based on state equal protection language

constructed by Wise and Coons—Clune and Sugarman prevailed. Various adequacy groups and scholars are revisiting the issue and providing means by which the 1973 *Rodriguez* decision might be overturned. See, for example, Goodwin Liu, "Education, Equality, and National Citizenship," Working Paper (University of California, Berkeley, 2005) for an explanation of the evolution of education finance equal protection from a U.S. constitutional issue to a state constitutionally based tactical legal pursuit.

8. For example, in an early Illinois case, *McInnis* v. *Shapiro*, 293 F. Supp. 327 (N.D. Ill. 1968), plaintiffs asked the court to remedy the situation by redistributing revenues in "keeping with the needs of children." The court refused to grant relief on grounds that there were no judicially manageable means for accurately determining the "needs of children." In a similar case, *Burrus* v. *Wilkerson*, 310 F. Supp. 572 (W.D. Va. 1969), aff'd per curium, 397 U.S. 44 (1970), a Virginia court concluded, "Courts have neither the knowledge, nor the means, nor the power to tailor the public moneys to fit the varying needs of these students throughout the State." See Paul A. Minorini and Stephen D. Sugarman, "School Finance Litigation in the Name of Educational Equity: Its Evolution, Impact, and Future," in *Equity and Adequacy in Education Finance: Issues and Perspectives*, edited by Helen F. Ladd, Rosemary Chalk, and Janet S. Hansen (Washington: National Academy Press, 1999).

9. Douglas S. Reed, *On Equal Terms: The Constitutional Politics of Educational Opportunity* (Princeton University Press, 2001); Michael A. Rebell and Robert L. Hughes, "Schools, Communities, and the Courts: A Dialogic Approach to Education Reform," *Yale Law and Policy Review* 14, no. 1 (1996): 99–168; Michael A. Rebell, "Education Adequacy, Democracy, and the Courts," in *Achieving High Educational Standards for All*, edited by Timothy Ready, Christopher Edley, and Catherine Snow (Washington: National Academy Press, 2000), pp. 218–67; Minorini and Sugarman, "School Finance Litigation in the Name of Educational Equity."

10. Matthew G. Springer, Keke Liu, and James W. Guthrie, "The Impact of Education Finance Litigation Reform on Resource Distribution: Is There Anything Special about Adequacy?" Peabody Center for Education Policy Working Paper (Peabody College of Vanderbilt University, 2005).

11. Distributional equity and taxpayer fairness can be measured by widely accepted statistical methods and long-standing public finance principles. For a comprehensive overview and assessment of these methods, see Robert Berne and Leanna Steifel, *The Measurement of Equity in School Finance* (Johns Hopkins University Press, 1984).

12. Research on economies of size and returns to size suggest mixed evidence. Some studies find constant returns; see, for example, Richard J. Butler and David H. Monk, "The Cost of Public Schooling in New York State: The Role of Scale and Efficiency in 1978–1979," *Journal of Human Resources* 20, no. 3 (1985): 3–38; D. N. Baum, "A Simultaneous Equations Model of the Demand for and Production of Local Public Services: The Case of Education," *Public Finance Quarterly* 14, no. 1 (1986): 157–78. Many studies find economies of size; see, for example, Thomas A. Downes and Thomas F. Pogue, "Adjusting School Aid Formulas for the Higher Cost of Educating Disadvantaged Students," *National Tax Journal* 47, no. 1 (1994): 89–110; Kerri Ratcliffe, Bruce Riddle, and John Yinger, "The Fiscal Condition of School Districts in Nebraska: Is Small Beautiful?" *Economics of Education Review* 9 (Winter 1990): 81–99. Some find increasing returns: Lawrence W. Kenny, "Economies of Scale in Schooling," *Economics of Education Review* 2, no. 1 (1982): 1–24. Still, studies suggest a U-shaped function; see, for example, William D. Duncombe, John Ruggiero, and John Yinger, "Potential Cost Savings from School District Consolidation: A Case Study of New York," *Economics of Education Review* 14, no. 3 (1995): 265–84.

13. Molly A. Hunter, "Status of Education Cost Studies in the 50 States" (New York: Campaign for Fiscal Equity, 2006).

14. For a more complete description of cost strategies, see James W. Guthrie, Matthew G. Springer, R. Anthony Rolle, and Eric A. Houck, *Modern Education Finance: Principles, Practices, and Policies* (Tappen, N.J.: Allyn and Bacon, forthcoming); Lori L. Taylor, Bruce D. Baker, and Arnold Vedlitz, "Measuring Educational Adequacy in Public Schools," Working Paper 580 (Texas A&M University, Bush School of Government and Public Service, September 2005); William Duncombe and Anna Lukemeyer, "Estimating the Cost of Educational Adequacy: A Comparison of Approaches" (Syracuse University, Center for Policy Research, March 2002); and James W. Guthrie and Richard Rothstein, "Enabling 'Adequacy' to Achieve Reality: Translating Adequacy into State School Finance Distribution Arrangements," in *Equity and Adequacy in Education Finance,* edited by Ladd, Chalk, and Hansen; Helen F. Ladd and Janet S. Hansen, *Making Money Matter: Financing America's Schools* (Washington: National Academy Press, 1999).

15. *Neeley* v. *West Orange-Cove Consolidated Independent School District,* 176 S.W.2d 746, 794–98 (Tex. 2005).

16. For formulaic details of cost modeling, see James M. Henderson and R. E. Quandt, *Microeconomic Theory: A Mathematical Approach,* 3rd ed. (Columbus, Ohio: McGraw-Hill, 1980); Elchanan Cohn and Terry G. Geske, *The Economics of Education* (Oxford, U.K.: Pergamon Press, 1990).

17. A general cost function equation can be written as $f(y; p,x) = C(y)$, where y represents an educational outcome (single-output cost function) or a vector of educational outcomes (multiple-output cost function), which is a function of school and nonschool inputs; p is a vector of price inputs; x is a vector of inputs used to produce y outputs; and f is a functional operator that specifies the shape of the production function.

18. Jennifer Imazeki and Andrew Reschovsky, "Estimating the Costs of Meeting Texas Education Accountability Standards," report submitted to the plaintiffs as evidence in *West Orange-Cove et al.* v. *Neeley et al.* (District Ct. of Travis County, Tex., rev'd, July 8, 2004); Timothy Gronberg, Dennis W. Jansen, Lori L. Taylor, and Kevin Brooker, "School Outcomes and School Costs: The Cost Function Approach" (Texas A&M University, March 2004).

19. For a more detailed comparison of the Texas studies, see Andrew Reschovsky and Jennifer Imazeki, "Assessing the Use of Econometric Analysis in Estimating the Costs of Meeting State Education Accountability Standards: Lessons from Texas," *Peabody Journal of Education* 80, no. 3 (2005): 96–125.

20. Guthrie and Rothstein, "Enabling 'Adequacy' to Achieve Reality."

21. John G. Augenblick, Kern Alexander, and James W. Guthrie, "Report of the Panel of Experts: Proposals for the Elimination of Wealth-Based Disparities in Education," report submitted by Ohio Chief State School Officer Theodore Sanders to the Ohio Legislature (1995); John G. Augenblick, "Recommendations for a Base Figure and Pupil-Weighted Adjustments to the Base Figure for Use in a New School Finance System in Ohio," report presented to the Governor's School Funding Task Force (July 1997).

22. The subsequent discussion does not disclose the author of the report because the relevant documents associated with the adequacy trial are not yet a matter of public record.

23. The estimated value of 56.8 percent is very similar to the mean sixth-grade proficiency value of 56.5 percent that was reported in the plaintiff expert's descriptive statistics.

24. Lawrence O. Picus and Associates, "A State-of-the-Art Approach to School Finance Adequacy in Kentucky" (North Hollywood, Calif., February 2003); Lawrence O. Picus and Associates, "An Evidence-Based Approach to School Finance Adequacy in Arkansas" (North Hollywood, Calif., September 2003); Lawrence O. Picus and Associates, "An Evidence-Based Approach to School Finance Adequacy in Arizona" (North Hollywood, Calif., 2004). Lawrence O. Picus and Associates, "An Evidence-Based Approach to Recalibrating Wyoming's Block Grant School Funding Formula," report prepared for the Wyoming Legislative Select Committee on Recalibration (North Hollywood, Calif., November 2005).

25. Frederick Mosteller, "The Tennessee Study of Class Size in the Early School Grades," *The Future of Children* 5, no. 2 (1995): 113–27; Eric A. Hanushek, "Some Findings from an Independent Investigation of the Tennessee STAR Experiment and from Other Investigations of Class Size Effects," *Educational Evaluation and Policy Analysis* 21, no. 2 (1999): 143–63; Alan B. Krueger and Diane Whitmore, "The Effect of Attending a Small Class in the Early Grades on College-Test Taking and Middle School Test Results: Evidence from Project STAR," Working Paper 427 (Princeton, N.J.: Princeton Industrial Relations Society, 1999); Barbara Nye, Larry V. Hedges, and Spyros Konstantopoulos, "The Long-Term Effects of Small Classes: A Five-Year Follow-up on the Tennessee Class Size Experiment," *Educational Evaluation and Policy Analysis* 21, no. 2 (1999): 127–42; Lawrence Mishel and Richard Rothstein, "The Class Size Debate" (Washington: Economic Policy Institute, 2002).

26. *Campbell County School District* v. *State of Wyoming (Campbell I)*, 907 P.2d 1238 (Wyo. 1995).

27. It was not until the 1998–99 school year that the Wyoming Department of Education began the annual administration of the Wyoming Comprehensive Assessment System (WyCAS). WyCAS is administered to all public school students in grades four, eight, and eleven. Wyoming has also recently developed Proficiency Assessments for Wyoming Students (PAWS), an assessment system focusing on the growth and performance of individual students.

28. Deborah A. Verstegen, "The Cost of an Adequacy Education in Kentucky," report submitted to the Council for Better Education (February 2003); Deborah A. Verstegen, "Calculation of the Cost of an Adequate Education in Kentucky: A Professional Judgment Approach," *Education Policy Analysis Archives* 12, no. 8 (2004) (epaa.asu.edu/epaa/v12n8 [October 2006]).

29. Verstegen, "Calculation of the Cost of an Adequate Education in Kentucky," p. 1.

30. Augenblick and Meyers, "Calculation of the Cost of an Adequate Education in Indiana in 2001–2002 Using the Professional Judgment Approach," report prepared for Indiana State Teachers Association (September 2002); John Augenblick and others, "Calculation of the Cost of a Suitable Education in Kansas in 2000–2001 Using Two Different Analytic Approaches," report prepared for the Legislative Coordinating Council (May 2002); Augenblick and Meyers, "Calculation of the Cost of an Adequate Education in Maryland in 1999–2000 Using Two Different Analytic Approaches," report prepared for Maryland Commission on Education Finance, Equity, and Excellence (Thornton Commission) (September 2001); Augenblick and Meyers, "Calculation of the Cost of an Adequate Education in Missouri Using the Professional Judgment and the Successful School District Approach," report prepared for the Missouri Education Coalition for Adequacy (February 2003); Augenblick and Meyers, "Calculation of the Cost of a Suitable Education in Montana in 2001–2002 Using the Professional Judgment Approach," report prepared for the Montana School Boards Association, Montana Quality Education Coalition, Montana Rural Education Association,

Montana Association of School Business Officials, and Montana Association of County School Superintendents (August 2002); Augenblick and Meyers, "Calculation of the Cost of an Adequate Education in Nebraska in 2002–2003 Using the Professional Judgment Approach," report prepared for Nebraska State Education Association, Greater Nebraska Schools Association, Lincoln Public Schools, Nebraska Association of School Boards, Nebraska Coalition for Educational Equity and Adequacy, Nebraska Council of School Administrators, Nebraska Rural Community Schools Association, Omaha Public Schools, and Westside Community Schools (n.d.); Augenblick, Palaich, and Associates, "Calculation of the Cost of an Adequate Education in Tennessee in 2001–02 Using the Professional Judgment Approach and the Successful School District Approach," report prepared for the Coalition for Tennessee's Future (December 2003).

31. Although many A&M studies report similar figures for districts considered very small, small, large, and very large, we only report on moderate-size K–12 school districts since this combination of constraints has only one missing data value (that is, North Dakota middle school).

32. A similar critique of professional judgment panels can be found in Thomas Downes, "What Is Adequate? Operationalizing the Concept of Adequacy for New York," paper prepared for the Education Finance Research Consortium (EFRC) symposium on School Finance and Organizational Structure in New York (February 2004).

33. *Campaign for Fiscal Equity, Inc.* v. *State of New York*, 100 N.Y.2d 893 (N.Y. 2003). For a more complete critique of adequacy cost studies in New York, see Eric A. Hanushek, "Pseudo-Science and a Sound Basic Education: Voodoo Statistics in New York," *Education Next* 5 (Fall 2005): 67–73, and the following rejoinder: James R. Smith and James W. Guthrie, "Correspondence: Checking NYC's Facts," *Education Next* 6 (Winter 2006): 8; Eric A. Hanushek, "Eric Hanushek Replies," *Education Next* 6 (Winter 2006): 8–9.

34. The phrases "adequacy of what" and "how much is adequate" are borrowed from Ladd and Hansen, "Making Money Matter," p. 104.

35. Richard Rothstein, *Class and Schools: Using Social, Economic, and Educational Reform to Close the Black-White Achievement Gap* (New York: Teachers College Press, 2006).

36. James W. Guthrie is the chairman of the board of directors of MAP and was engaged with Governor Pawlenty's School Finance Task Force.

37. School Funding Task Force, "Investing in Our Future: Seeking a Fair, Understandable, and Accountable 21st Century Education Finance System for Minnesota," report prepared for Governor Tim Pawlenty, Deputy Education Commissioner Chas Anderson, and Minnesota's Citizens (July 2004), p. 5.

38. Augenblick, Palaich, and Associates, "Determining the Cost of Education in Minnesota: Continuing the Work of the Governor's Education Funding Reform Task Force," executive summary prepared for Association of Metropolitan School Districts, Minnesota Rural Education Association, and Schools for Equity in Education (December 2005).

39. The model controls for state and year fixed effects and uses the percentage of students receiving free and reduced-price lunches as a proxy for students requiring additional resources. While one would typically prefer to use a more comprehensive set of school, student, and community characteristics, such as poverty status, limited English proficiency classification, high mobility, learning disability status, and property wealth, to model whether additional money is being allocated to districts based on student need, free and reduced-price lunch status provides an acceptable proxy.

40. Kevin Carey, "The Funding Gap: Low-Income and Minority Students Still Receive Fewer Dollars in Many States" (Education Trust, 2004).

41. Carey, "The Funding Gap," pp. 2–3. Carey deduces that No Child Left Behind recommends a 40 percent cost adjustment because the federal legislation rewards districts if they allocate additional dollars to high-poverty schools. For a more complete description of his reasoning, see Carey, "The Funding Gap," p. 6. Also refer to the Elementary and Secondary Education Act, sec. 1125 (A), Education Finance Incentive Grant Program.

42. Carey, "The Funding Gap," p. 4.

43. We focus on mathematics scores, and not reading, since mathematics scores are more likely to reflect schooling and not out-of-school influences such as home environment.

44. A special master is appointed by the court or chief justice to oversee either the planning for or the implementation of a court decree. A special master is assumed to be an expert in the area under consideration.

45. See *Ryan Montoy et al.* v. *State of Kansas et al. (Montoy III)*, 112 P.3d 923, WL 1316989 (Kans. 2005), wherein the court stated, "This case is extraordinary, but the imperative remains that we decide it on the record before us. The A&M study, and the testimony supporting it, appear in the record in this case. The state cites no cost study or evidence to rebut the A&M study, instead offering conclusory affidavits from legislative leaders. Thus the A&M study is the only analysis resembling a legitimate cost study before us. Accordingly, at this point in time, we accept it as a valid basis to determine the cost of a constitutionally adequate public education in kindergarten through the twelfth grade. The alternative is to await yet another study, which itself may be found legislatively or judicially unacceptable, and the schoolchildren of Kansas would be forced to further await a suitable education. We note that the present litigation was filed in 1999."

46. Eric A. Hanushek, John Kain, and Steven Rivkin, "Teachers, Schools, and Academic Achievement," NBER Working Paper 6691 (Cambridge, Mass.: National Bureau of Economic Research, 1998); Dan Goldhaber, "The Mystery of Good Teachers," *Education Next* 2, no. 1 (2002): 50–55.

47. Michael Podgursky, "Reforming Teacher Pay," *Texas Education Review* 2, no. 3 (Winter 2003–04); Dale Ballou and Michael Podgursky, "Let the Market Decide," *Education Next* 1, no. 1 (2001): 16–25.

48. For a comprehensive examination of how philanthropists are influencing contemporary educational policy and politics, see Frederick Hess, ed., *With the Best of Intentions: How Philanthropy Is Shaping K–12 Education* (Harvard Education Publishing Group, 2005).

49. Some notable publications produced directly or indirectly from such Ford Foundation efforts include Charles Benson and others, *Planning for Educational Reform: Financial and Social Alternatives* (New York: Dodd, Mead and Company, 1974); David Kirp and Mark Yudof, *Educational Policy and the Law: Cases and Materials* (Berkeley: McCutchan Publishing, 1974); John E. Coons and Stephen D. Sugarman, *Education by Choice: The Case for Family Control* (University of California Press, 1978); Walter I. Garms, James W. Guthrie, and Lawrence C. Pierce, *School Finance: The Economics and Politics of Public Education* (Upper Saddle River, N.J.: Prentice-Hall, 1978); John J. Callahan and William H. Wilken, *School Finance Reform: A Legislators' Handbook* (National Conference of State Legislators, 1976); Michael W. Kirst, *Governance of Elementary and Secondary Education* (New York: Aspen Foundation for Humanistic Studies, 1976); Michael W. Kirst and Joel Berke, *Federal Aid to Education: Who Benefits? Who Governs?* (Lexington, Mass.: D.C. Heath, 1972); Joel S. Berke,

"The Current Crisis in School Finance: Inadequacy and Inequity," *Phi Delta Kappan* (September 1971): 2–7; James W. Guthrie, George B. Kleindorfer, Henry M. Levin, and Robert T. Stout, eds., *Schools and Inequality* (MIT Press, 1971); Alan Rosenthal, "The Emerging Legislative Role in Education," *Compact* 5, no. 9 (Winter 1977): 2–4; Susan Fuhrman, *State Education Politics: The Case of School Finance Reform* (Denver, Colo.: Education Commission of the States, 1980); Allen Odden, John Augenblick, and Kent McGuire, *School Finance Reform in the States: 1980* (Denver, Colo.: Education Commission of the States, 1980).

6

MICHAEL PODGURSKY

Is Teacher Pay "Adequate"?

T EACHER PAY PLAYS a major role in school finance lawsuits. Total expenditures for public school K–12 instructional staff (primarily teachers) totaled $205 billion for the 2001–02 school year, or 56 percent of current school spending. Plaintiffs typically claim that these outlays are not sufficient to recruit teachers who can deliver constitutionally mandated levels of educational services. For example, in a recent case, *Campaign for Fiscal Equity* v. *State,* the plaintiffs successfully argued that because teacher pay schedules in New York City were well below those in the wealthier suburban counties such as Westchester or Nassau it was not possible to recruit or retain adequate numbers of qualified teachers. In Massachusetts (*Hancock* v. *Driscoll*), the plaintiffs in the focus districts complained that they lacked

The author wishes to thank Art Peng and Samantha Dalton for research assistance and Michael Wolkoff, Caroline Hoxby, and Rajashri Chakrabarti for helpful comments. The usual disclaimers apply. While I believe that I have approached this issue in a detached and scholarly manner, the reader should be aware that I have testified as an expert witness or served as a consultant in many of the school finance cases mentioned in this chapter. This chapter is a condensed version of a longer working paper presented at a Kennedy School of Government conference, "Adequacy Lawsuits: Their Growing Effect on American Education," October 13–14, 2005. The latter is available at the University of Arkansas, Education Working Paper Archive (www.uark.edu/ua/der/EWPA/).

resources to pay competitive salaries or provide adequate opportunities for professional development.

These school finance cases, and the more general policy debate about teacher quality, have raised concern about the "adequacy" of teacher pay. Are the resources provided to public schools adequate to recruit and retain a teaching workforce that can deliver educational services that pass constitutional muster? In this chapter I consider three common approaches to the question of teacher pay adequacy, each of which can in principle lend itself to measurement and statistical testing. All three have appeared in the claims of plaintiffs in school finance cases and in the more general policy debate about teacher quality.

The first considers the compensation of teachers vis-à-vis that in other professions. If it were found that teacher pay was substantially below that of workers in other professions with similar levels of education, then that would at least provide prima facie evidence of underpayment or inadequacy of teacher pay. In fact, plaintiffs' experts in adequacy cases routinely cite data on the pay of teachers relative to other professions. A second approach, which I term "regulatory compliance," focuses on school staffing. Given the per-pupil resources provided to districts, are schools able to fill vacancies with teachers qualified under state licensing or federal No Child Left Behind (NCLB) requirements? The high proportion of teachers with emergency or other substandard certification figured prominently in California (*Williams* v. *California*) and in the New York City case noted above, and the figure was taken by the court as evidence that the pay of teachers was too low.

A final approach, which I term "social underinvestment," views teacher qualifications as a continuum and asks whether public schools are buying enough teacher quality. In this view, teachers are "underpaid" if the social benefits from raising teacher pay exceed the costs—that is, if an additional dollar spent on teacher pay yields a discounted stream of student benefits that is worth more than one dollar. Thus, even if the current pay and benefits of teachers are adequate to staff classrooms with teachers who are qualified under state and federal regulations, pay may still be too low from a social investment point of view. This view is often implicit in the arguments of those who focus on the pay of teachers compared with that of nonteachers: higher relative pay will yield higher relative quality, and it is assumed that the improvement in quality will be large enough to make the investment worthwhile in cost-benefit terms. I consider each of these views in turn, beginning with the issue that seems, deceptively, most easily measured—relative teacher pay.

Relative Teacher Pay

How does the pay of teachers compare with that of nonteachers with similar levels of education?[1] Data from the U.S. Department of Labor show that in September 2004 the average annual full-time earnings of public elementary school teachers in the Chicago metropolitan area was $47,856. For computer systems analysts it was $72,206, or 51 percent more. Clearly, the two professions differ by many factors. The training required is very different; so, too, are working conditions. Systems analysts may have to work long, irregular hours on site when a system malfunctions and be on call to solve any problems that arise. Continual changes in technology require them to pursue ongoing training to keep up with the field.[2] Finally, as the dotcom "meltdown" illustrates, a systems analyst's risk of job loss is likely much greater than that for public elementary school teachers.

What matters from an economic point of view is the degree of substitution between the two professions. Does an increase in elementary school teacher pay relative to that of systems analysts lead some teachers who might have quit teaching to become computer systems analysts to remain teachers, or lead some computer science majors to switch to teaching in response? If there is little occupational mobility or crossover in response to relative pay changes, then from an economic point of view the earnings of computer analysts are irrelevant in a discussion of the adequacy of teacher pay. In fact, the pay of computer analysts is probably not relevant to the career decisions of most current or would-be elementary school teachers. However, it probably is relevant for high school computer or math teachers. That suggests that discussions of the adequacy of teacher pay should take a teacher's academic field into account.[3]

Studies of teacher mobility also find that teacher labor markets tend to be localized. Most teachers take jobs near the place where they grew up or went to college.[4] Thus, to extend the example, it is not the national earnings of computer analysts that matter, it is the earnings of computer analysts in the local labor market (particularly for the 80 percent of teachers who are women, most of whom are married; as second earners, married teachers tend to be less geographically mobile than unmarried women or men).

Another problem in comparing teacher to nonteacher earnings is differences in annual work hours. The standard approach in labor economics is to compare the pay of two jobs or professions for an identical period of work—hourly, weekly, or monthly. For professions the usual metric is annual pay, but that implicitly assumes that annual hours of work for the professions compared (for example, doctors and lawyers) are similar. The problem with comparing doctors or lawyers to K-12 teachers is that there is a very large difference in annual hours of work on site for the two jobs. Teacher contracts typically run for nine to ten months; twelve-month contracts are the rule for other professions.[5]

Teacher contracts are tied to the school year. Data from the 1999–2000 Schools and Staffing Surveys find that the median number of days for a school year is 181. Most teacher collective bargaining agreements add several additional work days for grading, parent-teacher meetings, and so forth. A representative national survey of 524 school districts by the Education Research Service found an average contract year of 186 days for teachers.[6] Over summer months, teachers are not employees of the public school system.

Thus, there are two ways to make an apples-to-apples comparison of teachers to nonteachers. One approach is to annualize teacher pay. If it is assumed that teachers have a thirty-eight-week contract, annual teacher pay can simply be multiplied by 1.37 (52/38) and compared with that of nonteachers. Alternatively, weekly pay can be compared for teachers and nonteachers while they are under contract.

How does overall teacher pay compare with nonteacher pay in local labor markets? Many employers, including the federal government, need reliable data that permit comparison of pay and benefits for similar jobs in the public and the private sector or across different metropolitan areas. That need led to the development of the National Compensation Survey (NCS) by the Bureau of Labor Statistics (BLS), the data-gathering arm of the U.S. Department of Labor. The NCS—a survey of employers concerning employee salaries, wages, and benefits—is designed to produce reliable earnings and benefit estimates at the local level, within a broad region, and across the nation. One attractive feature of the NCS is that it provides data on earnings by occupation in dozens of metropolitan areas (MSAs).

NCS data are available for dozens of MSAs; however, I limit this analysis to the fifteen largest.[7] These MSAs accounted for roughly one-third of the U.S. population in 2003; therefore it may be assumed that they represented roughly one-third of the public school teachers as well. For this comparison, I selected occupations for which a college degree (but generally not a postgraduate degree) is common or required and for which data are available for many of the MSAs. I do not claim that these occupations necessarily represent the relevant nonteaching earnings for all teachers. However, they probably are relevant for many. Moreover, earnings in these broad occupation groups probably reflect the general wage structure in the area labor market.[8]

Figure 6-1 reports the gap between teacher pay and that in other occupations within the largest MSAs. I report a population-weighted average over all the MSAs for which data are available. For each occupation there are two

Figure 6-1. *Weighted Average Percent Gap between Teacher Pay and Pay of Selected Other Professionals in the Fifteen Largest U.S. Metropolitan Statistical Areas*[a]

Percent gap

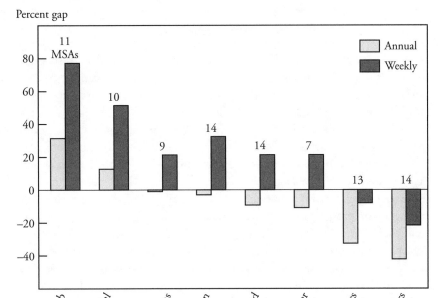

Source: U.S. Department of Labor, Bureau of Labor Statistics, National Compensation Survey, various MSA surveys.
a. Data are not available for all MSAs. The number of MSAs included is indicated above each bar.

"gap" bars; the first is the percentage gap in annual earnings and the second is the percentage gap in weekly earnings. A positive value means that teachers earn more; a negative value means that they earn less. I have sorted occupations from most to least favorable vis-à-vis teaching on the basis of annual earnings.

In comparison with clinical lab technicians and social workers, for example, teachers have a large premium in annual and weekly earnings. They have virtual parity in annual earnings but a 20 percent premium in weekly earnings with respect to librarians. Their annual pay is roughly 10 percent below that of computer programmers, but on a weekly basis it is 20 percent higher. Annual teacher pay is less favorable compared with that of architects, engineers, and managers; however, weekly pay is very similar. In sum, NCS data suggest that on a weekly basis, teacher pay is quite competitive with pay in many other professions, at least in major metropolitan areas.

Allegretto, Corcoran, and Mishel argue that the NCS data presented in figure 6-1 are unfair to teachers.[9] They make the following argument (I have rounded weeks for simplicity): Nonteachers work under fifty-two-week contracts; in computing their weekly pay, the BLS simply divides annual earnings by fifty-two weeks. For teachers, the BLS divides annual pay by thirty-eight weeks. However, if nonteachers have, say, four weeks of paid vacation, then the authors claim that the comparison is a biased measure of pay for weeks worked. In my simple example above, nonteachers' weekly earnings are underestimated by 8 percent (that is, 4/48 weeks). If teachers actually worked every day during their thirty-eight-week contracts, then this critique would have empirical significance. In fact, even under a thirty-eight-week contract, teachers have a good deal of paid leave.[10] According to NCS benefits data, paid leave, including vacations, amounted to 7.9 percent of total compensation for managers and professionals in the private sector compared with 5.1 percent for public school teachers (see table 6-2). Thus, in the example above, in order to compute a measure of pay per weeks actually worked (versus weeks under contract), weekly pay would be multiplied by $52 \times (1 - .079)$ for managers and professionals and by $38 \times (1 - .051)$ for public school teachers. This calculation suggests that a "weeks worked" comparison would result in roughly a 4 percent upward adjustment in relative weekly pay for nonteachers. While not trivial, that adjustment is much smaller than suggested by Allegretto, Corcoran, and Mishel and in no way changes my general conclusions based on the unadjusted data in figure 6-1.

Most economists would probably agree that employer-reported data on employee pay and benefits are much more reliable than household survey data, which is the other main source of data on workers in various professions. However, household survey data do have the virtue of permitting the researcher to control for individual worker demographics in making pay comparisons. For that reason, I also examined household survey data from the March Current Population Survey (CPS). In the March CPS household respondents (not necessarily the workers themselves) answer a series of questions about employment and earnings during the previous year. I used data from the 2003 survey to compare the full-time earnings of public school teachers with those of other full-time employees. Table 6-1 shows how the gap between the log of annual earnings for teachers and the log for nonteachers changes as various adjustments are made for demographic characteristics and place of residence.

The March CPS results reinforce the findings from the NCS. If teachers and non-teachers had identical weekly earnings but thirty-eight-week and

Table 6-1. *Difference in Log of Annual Earnings:*
Teachers versus Other College Graduates[a]

Subjects	Total earnings			
	OLS	OLS	OLS	Median regression
Females	−.048*	−.039*	−.026	−.053**
	(2.31)	(1.97)	(1.33)	(3.31)
Covariates[b]	N	Y	Y	Y
Regions (4)	N	Y	N	Y
States (50 plus Washington, D.C.)	N	N	Y	N
N	8,134	8,134	8,134	8,134
Males	−.343**	−.304**	−.281**	−.305**
	(10.14)	(9.63)	(14.88)	(10.04)
Covariates[b]	No	Yes	Yes	Yes
Regions (4)	No	Yes	No	Yes
States (50 plus Washington, D.C.)	No	No	Yes	No
N	10,437	10,437	10,437	10,437

Source: U.S. Bureau of Labor Statistics and U.S. Bureau of the Census, March 2003 Current Population Survey.

a. Sample consisted of college graduates eighteen to sixty-four years of age who worked full-time at least thirty-six weeks in 2002, with non-imputed earnings on longest job. Dependent variable equals total annual earnings. *T* values are in parentheses. OLS = ordinary least squares. * Significant at 5 percent. ** Significant at 1 percent.

b. Covariates include quartic in age, education dummies (M.A., Ph.D./Ed.D.), race/ethnicity, married, residence in metropolitan area.

fifty-two-week contracts respectively, then in an annual earnings regression the gap in their natural log of earnings would be -.314, indicating a 27 percent pay gap (38/52 − 1). The estimates in the first column of table 6-1 have no covariates, and I progressively added covariates along with variables controlling for the region and state in which a household was located. The estimates in column three, which absorb a state effect along with rural and urban residence effects, probably provide the most accurate estimate of the annual earnings gap. The log gap in earnings for women in this analysis is quite small, on the order of 4 percent. For males it is on the order of negative 30 percent. Thus, the March CPS earnings regressions suggest that on a weekly basis, on average, female teachers earned more than female nonteachers and that the small annual pay gap is entirely explained by fewer weeks of work.

These findings are consistent with those of Lori Taylor, who analyzed a very large national sample of workers from the 5 percent Individual Public Use Microdata Sample (IPUMS) from the 2000 Census of Population.[11] Taylor found that college-educated nonteachers were much less likely to live in rural areas than were teachers. Since earnings for all occupations tend to be lower in rural areas, failing to take account of the spatial distribution of teachers tends to substantially understate their earnings vis-à-vis those of other college-educated workers. Her estimates also combine public and private school teachers. If it is assumed that private school teachers on average earn 70 percent of public school pay, then her estimates suggest that the (self-reported) hours-adjusted gap in earnings between teachers and college-educated nonteachers is only 4 to 6 percent.[12] Thus both the employer-based NCS as well as household survey data suggest that, when teachers' shorter annual hours are taken into account, public school teachers and nonteachers have approximate parity in earnings.[13]

The Implicit Value of Having Summers Off

While the weekly earnings of teachers under contract may compare favorably with those of people in some other professions, it may be the case that individuals who choose nonteaching occupations prefer more weeks of paid work than teaching provides. For such individuals, annual rather than weekly earnings are the more relevant measure of remuneration. In fact, the majority of public school teachers do not work in the summer, and there has been no tendency for that finding to change over the last two decades. In the 1987–88 Schools and Staffing Surveys (SASS), 32.5 percent of teachers reported working for pay during the summer. In the 1999–2000 SASS (the most recent available) the percentage was virtually identical (34.5 percent). Unfortunately, the SASS data provide no information on the number of days worked by teachers during the summer, only whether they worked and their total summer earnings. The average earnings of the 34.5 percent of teachers who worked were roughly $3,500, but it is not known whether they earned that amount in two days or twenty days.

Clearly teaching tends to attract individuals who value short and predictable hours of work on site and long summer vacations—for example, women with children or who plan to have children. Data from the 1990 Census of Population show that college-educated women aged forty years and younger employed in teaching have a considerably higher number of children on average than do women in other occupations (2.1 versus 1.7).

The share of women in teaching is high and rising. From 1960 through the mid-1980s, women accounted for roughly 68 to 69 percent of public school teachers. However, the most recent national data available, for the period from the mid-1980s to 2001, show that the female share has increased to 79 percent.[14] Clearly, the modest gaps in annual pay estimated in the previous section for females would be easily offset by savings in daycare over the summer and during the work year. This type of benefit may be of less value to males, many of whom, as the primary earner in a family, may desire more hours of work. Not surprisingly, far more males than females move into administrative K–12 positions, suggesting that if the goal is to increase the number of male teachers, teacher pay may need to be increased.[15]

Earnings of Exiting Teachers

If public school teachers are underpaid, then earnings for teachers who quit teaching and move to nonteaching jobs could be expected to jump sharply. In another analysis, Monroe, Watson, and I analyzed new teachers who terminated initial teaching spells between 1990–91 and 1999–2000 and who did not subsequently return to public school teaching.[16] We matched records for the exiting teachers against the Missouri master unemployment insurance earnings files for the four quarters of the calendar year following their last year of teaching and compared their post-teaching earnings with the earnings that they would have had if they had stayed in their school district (using district salary schedule data). For males, average nonteaching earnings were slightly lower than teaching earnings, and only about 45 percent of male teachers earned more than they did when teaching. For women, however, nonteaching earnings were substantially below teaching earnings. These findings mirror those in Stinebrickner, Scafidi, and Sjoquist (2002), a similar study using Georgia unemployment insurance (UI) earnings data and findings from a study that I conducted with Michael Wolkoff using Wyoming UI data.[17]

Fringe Benefits

Anecdotal data suggest that the fringe benefits of public school teachers compare favorably with those of teachers in the private sector. However, systematic data on this point have only recently become available. One valuable feature of the NCS is that it also provides data on the costs of employee benefits and detailed data on the character of fringe benefits for public and private employees. Unfortunately, due to concerns about inadequate sample size, the BLS

Table 6-2. *Selected Fringe Benefit Costs as a Percent of Total Compensation: Public School Teachers versus Private Sector Professionals*
Percent

Subjects	*(1)* Insurance	*(2)* Retirement and savings	*(3)* Legally required benefits (Social Security, workers' unemployment insurance	Total *(1) – (3)*	Paid leave as a percent of total compensation
Public school teachers	9.1	5.9	5.2	20.2	5.1
Management, professional, and related private sector employees	6.0	3.8	7.2	17.0	7.9

Source: U.S. Department of Labor, Bureau of Labor Statistics, "Employer Costs for Employee Benefits: June 2004," tables 4 and 5 (www.bls.gov/ncs/ect/home.htm).

until recently did not disaggregate fringe benefit costs for public school teachers.[18] Public school teachers were grouped with college professors as well as preschool teachers. However, more recent reports have begun to present some limited data broken out for public school teachers. Table 6-2 presents data from the most recent BLS report. Here I report selected fringe benefits as a percent of total compensation. Insurance (primarily health insurance) and retirement contributions are a substantially larger percent of total compensation for teachers than for professional employees in private sector employment. However, most teachers are not covered by the federal social security system, so legally required contributions are somewhat smaller for teachers. Overall, these three components of benefits total 20.2 percent of payroll for teachers and 17.0 percent for private sector managers and professionals. Thus, fringe benefits are at least comparable to those of professionals in the private sector.

Why Spending per Student Rises Faster than Teacher Pay

Any discussion of teacher pay needs to be combined with a discussion of staffing. If revenues available for payroll rise by 5 percent, school districts face a trade-off. They can hold staffing ratios constant and raise pay by 5 percent, freeze pay and lower staffing ratios by 5 percent, or pursue some combination

Figure 6-2. *Public K-12 Full-Time Equivalent Teachers, Nonteachers, and Student Enrollment*[a]

Percent

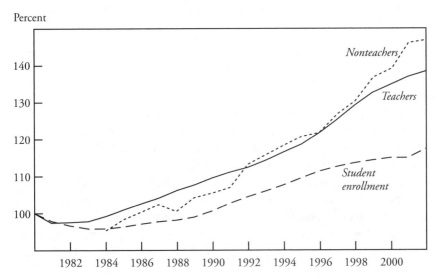

Source. U.S. Department of Education, National Center for Education Statistics, *Digest of Education Statistics* 2004, 2000.
a. Nonteacher = total FTE − teacher FTE; 1980 = 100 percent.

of the two strategies that totals 5 percent. Over the last two decades, public schools have absorbed professional and nonprofessional staff at rates well in excess of student enrollment growth. Figure 6-2 shows that since 1980 public school enrollment has grown by 17 percent while teacher employment has grown by 37 percent. By fall 2002, the overall student-teacher ratio had fallen from 18.7 in 1980 to 16.1. These statistics count teachers only. If teacher aides, librarians, counselors, and other instructional staff are included, the student-teacher ratio falls to 12. If all adults on the payroll (for example, administrators, secretaries, custodians) are counted, the ratio drops to 8.1. Again, it would be possible to raise the pay of teachers if other staff were trimmed. In fact, as seen in figure 6-2, since 1980 employment of nonteaching staff has grown faster than employment of teachers. Simply put, any school district could raise teacher pay with current revenues by increasing the student-teacher ratio or by lowering the ratio of nonteaching to teaching staff.[19]

In sum, when adjusted for annual hours of work, the pay of teachers is not obviously out of line with that of other college-educated workers. Indeed, when expressed on a weekly basis, teachers' pay compares favorably with that of many other professionals in metropolitan labor markets. Teacher benefits compare quite favorably as well. By allowing professional and nonprofessional employment to far outstrip enrollment growth over the last two decades, school districts have passed up major opportunities to make teacher pay even more competitive.

Regulatory Compliance

A second approach to the question of adequacy is to determine whether schools have resources sufficient to staff their classrooms with teachers who are qualified according to state and federal regulations. Clearly this criterion is related to the previous one regarding teacher pay. Presumably districts with higher relative pay will have lower turnover and thus fewer vacancies; they also will have larger applicant pools and hence more qualified applicants per vacancy. However, there is no reason to believe that the level of pay necessary to staff classrooms with qualified teachers will produce "parity," however defined, with earnings in other professions. It may be that the level of pay adequate to staff an elementary school classroom, for example, is only one-half of accountants' earnings. In addition, these benchmarks are likely to vary by teaching field and from one geographic labor market to another.

Teachers in all states must be licensed by the state to teach in public school classrooms, and in nearly all states licensing requires completion of a state-approved teacher training program that includes a period of supervised student teaching. In addition, thirty-seven states require teachers to pass a pre-professional test before entering a teacher training program; thirty-eight require a field-specific licensing exam; and sixteen require candidates to pass a performance evaluation one or two years after they have been on the job. Many states require ongoing professional training or evaluation for license renewal.[20]

The NCLB Act, which mandates having a "highly qualified" teacher in every classroom, adds further hoops for both new and incumbent teachers to jump through in qualifying to teach core academic subjects. All new teachers must hold at least a baccalaureate degree or higher, must be fully licensed, and must have demonstrated subject matter competence in the areas that they teach. Similarly, all incumbent teachers must meet a similar standard, although states are permitted to come up with their own methods (subject to federal approval) to demonstrate compliance. The latter are called HOUSSE standards (High Objective Uniform State Standard of Evaluation).

How well, then, are school districts able to meet these regulatory standards? As of this writing no national data have been published. That is due in part to that fact that licensing and HOUSSE standards vary from state to state, although the U.S. Department of Education is compiling compliance data. A widely used national data file, the Schools and Staffing Surveys, includes a teacher survey wherein roughly 42,000 public school teachers are asked about their educational background and teaching credentials. Tabulations from the most recent available survey (1999–2000) show that 90 percent of public school teachers report that they hold regular state certification in their primary teaching area. Administrative data from state or school district report cards tend to reinforce that finding. While I am aware of no systematic compilation of state data, a simple perusal of state and district report cards finds compliance figures on the order of 90 percent or higher.

Consider the example of California, which represents one of the most highly stressed public systems in the nation. The state has major fiscal difficulties, and its school age population is growing rapidly. Less well known is the fact that in 1996 voters statewide passed a class size reduction initiative that greatly exacerbated teacher shortages and led to an exodus of teachers from many urban classrooms as suburban jobs opened up.[21] In spite of such travails, in school year 2003–04, 89.4 percent of California public school teachers held full ("clear") teaching credentials in their teaching area. Another 5.3 percent were in supervised intern or pre-intern programs. Only 5.2 percent were teaching with substandard credentials (emergency or waiver). Data reported for Illinois for 2004 provide a more detailed portrait in that state. Ninety-eight percent of teachers statewide held regular certification, a figure that varied little between high- and low-poverty districts. The percent of core academic teachers who were "highly qualified" by NCLB standards was 98.2 percent statewide and 93.4 percent in high-poverty districts.[22]

While overall compliance rates are very high, detailed examination of district data show that virtually no school district is in full compliance with licensing laws and that their compliance rates have little relationship to school spending. In Missouri during the 2002–03 school year, in only two of 447 K–12 school districts were no courses taught by an inappropriately licensed teacher (the average was 9.5 percent of courses). Moreover, the incidence of teaching with an inappropriate license is not associated with low levels of per-pupil spending. In fact, the correlation between the rate of unlicensed teaching and spending per student was positive and statistically significant (.27). An analysis of New York state's 703 school districts yields a similar finding. Virtually no district was 100 percent compliant, and high-spending districts were as likely to be out of compliance as low-spending districts. A case in point is Scarsdale, which boasted a 2002–03 median teacher salary of $95,326 but where nonetheless 4.8 percent of teachers were teaching with inappropriate credentials in their primary teaching field.

Why are nearly all school districts to some degree out of compliance with these certification laws, and why is noncompliance unrelated to spending? I would argue that given the Byzantine complexity of state teacher licensing laws, bureaucratic delay, and the natural dynamics of the teacher labor market, full compliance is nearly impossible (or random). Teacher labor markets are likely have a "natural rate of noncompliance" that is above zero for many of the same reasons that the economy as a whole has a "natural rate of unemployment" that is above zero.

Missouri, like all other states with which I am familiar, issues a single license to practice medicine, law, dentistry, accounting, nursing, and veterinary medicine. However, the Missouri Department of Elementary and Secondary education currently issues 260 certificates and endorsements (171 vocational, 89 nonvocational) in the area of K–12 education. However, that is only part of the story. There are levels of certification (permanent, provisional) for all of them and a host of "grandmothered" codes besides. As a consequence, there are 781 valid certification codes in the master teacher certification file. And there is nothing unique about Missouri.

Combine such a complex licensing regime with the dynamics of the teacher labor market and the result is less than full compliance even under the best of conditions. At the district level, roughly 10 to 12 percent of teaching positions turn over each year, many because teachers take a temporary leave of absence to attend to child-rearing or other family matters. Roughly one-third of district level turnover is interdistrict mobility of teachers; as a consequence, roughly 80 percent of teaching vacancies at the district level are filled by experienced teachers.[23] Given this labor market flux, school administrators find themselves scrambling under short deadlines to fill classrooms with qualified teachers, and it is inevitable that some classrooms will be filled with teachers whose credentials are not entirely in order, for various reasons. Perhaps a teacher's license has expired and new approval is pending. An elementary teacher in Missouri with a valid license and many years of teaching experience in Florida may fall short of some requirements for a regular Missouri certificate. A science position may be held by a new liberal arts college graduate who lacks one or two education school courses for certification. A chemistry teacher in rural high school may need to cover biology and math courses as well, or he or she may be subbing for the math teacher, who is temporarily out on maternity leave. Maybe the state regulators have simply misplaced a teacher's certification paperwork. For these and myriad other reasons, the complex licensing systems that states have constructed virtually guarantee a steady-state compliance rate of less than 100 percent. It is thus unrealistic for courts to hold school districts to a standard that requires perfect compliance for "adequacy"; nonetheless, that is the position taken by many adequacy plaintiffs. "A qualified teacher in every classroom" is taken to mean a fully certified teacher in every class, every hour of the day.

In short, given current levels of spending, the vast majority of public school districts have staffed public school classrooms with teachers who meet state licensing standards.[24] Education researchers and commentators may argue about the rigor or efficacy of some of these standards, and the jury is clearly out regarding their long-run effects. However, it is clear that the states and the U.S. Department of Education are groping toward designing workable regulatory standards to raise the quality of the teaching workforce. While this process is under way, courts should defer to education regulators in defining "qualified" rather than accepting definitions from education advocacy groups.

The Structure of Teacher Pay

A fundamental problem in assessing the adequacy of teacher pay is the fact that it is not market based; because of that, the question arises of how much inefficiency and waste will be tolerated in deciding how much is adequate. Working conditions, training, and, in particular, nonteaching opportunities differ greatly by teaching field and by school. The training and alternative employment opportunities for a typical second-grade teacher are very different from those for the typical high school chemistry teacher, yet both are paid from the same salary schedule in nearly all school districts in the U.S. For example, in 2004 there were twenty-five applicants for every elementary school vacancy in Missouri but just five for each chemistry opening. The level of pay and number of steps and columns vary from district to district; however, the general practice of setting base pay according to seniority and graduate degree credits is the same in nearly every U.S. school district, large or small.[25]

If, as is commonplace, a single salary schedule for a school district yields a large surplus of qualified applicants for elementary education, social studies, and physical education but no qualified applicants in physics or speech pathology, is teacher pay in this district inadequate? Suppose that a 10 percent pay increase is necessary to staff a speech pathology position. Should every other teacher, counselor, and librarian in the district get a 10 percent raise as well? That is what the single salary schedule, backed by strong union support, requires.

Recent value-added studies of teacher effects find no effects of experience on teacher performance beyond the first year of teaching, yet school districts routinely use additional revenues to "backload" pay increases by adding steps on salary schedules or longevity bonuses at twenty-five or thirty years of employment.[26] Hoxby and Leigh conclude that wage compression associated with collective bargaining and salary schedules helped push high-ability women out of teaching. Single salary schedules impose identical salaries across dozens or even hundreds of district schools that often differ greatly in their attractiveness as places to work. Experienced teachers often use their seniority to transfer from high-poverty to low-poverty schools, resulting in intradistrict inequities in school spending.[27] In short, courts must give some consideration to the structure as well as the level of teacher pay in assessing the adequacy of resources.

Should Courts Push the Bar Higher?

A critic of the regulatory compliance approach might argue that state licensing and NCLB "highly qualified" teacher standards are not very high. No doubt there is some merit in that charge. However, if states move away from using federal and state regulatory standards to measure teacher quality, what standards do they use? For example, in *Campaign for Fiscal Equity* v. *State*, plaintiff's experts presented evidence purporting to show that teachers in New York City were inferior to teachers in the rest of the state. Indicators of inferiority included multiple failures on licensing exams and the lower selectivity of colleges attended by NYC teachers. In other cases, plaintiffs have claimed that teachers lacked adequate opportunities for professional development. Or that a smaller share of teachers in plaintiff districts had a master's degree. A common feature of all such claims is an appeal to the courts to set the adequacy bar higher than the state regulators set it in defining their standards.

Such claims assume that the teacher characteristics in question—master's degrees, professional development courses, college selectivity—have a demonstrable and strong relationship to student achievement. In fact, the evidence linking any type of teacher training, licensing, or testing to student achievement is mixed at best. Even estimated effects of the general academic skills of teachers, such as SAT scores, while usually statistically significant, are generally modest. Master's degrees are especially suspect. A recent research survey found that of 170 reported estimates of postgraduate education effects on student learning gains, 86 percent were statistically insignificant. Of the statistically significant estimates, 9 percent were positive and 5 percent negative.[28] Nonetheless, interdistrict gaps in the share of teachers with master's or higher degrees are routinely presented as evidence of resource inadequacy.

Does this mean that teachers do not matter? On the contrary. While the effect of measured teacher characteristics is small, one consistent finding is that there seems to be considerable variation in teacher effectiveness across classrooms. Thus, if one compares the effect on student learning of the top and bottom 20 percent of teachers (ranked by performance), the effect is often quite substantial. However, these teacher effects are largely unrelated to traditional measures of teacher quality, such as licensing exam test scores, certification credentials, experience, or graduate degrees, a result highlighted in a recent survey of this literature.[29]

A recent study of Chicago public school teachers illustrates this point well. Like other such studies, this is based on a large longitudinal file of linked student achievement scores. What makes this study unique is that the authors also have very extensive administrative data on teacher characteristics that are unavailable in other studies, including education, experience, types of teaching licenses, and selectivity of the teacher's undergraduate college. They find that more than 90 percent of teacher effects are not explained by any measured teacher characteristics.[30]

In sum, the growing "teacher effects" literature suggests that teacher quality, as measured by student achievement gains, is highly idiosyncratic. That does not mean that the factors contributing to teacher quality are random or unknowable It simply means that traditional measures of teacher quality explain virtually none of the variation in teacher effectiveness. However much courts may wish to raise student achievement through improving teacher quality, research to date provides few or no observable "buttons" to push. Indeed, if anything, the trend is in the opposite direction: as the rigor of the studies grows, the effectiveness of our traditional measurable buttons tends to diminish or vanish altogether.

Underinvestment in Teacher Quality

The regulatory compliance approach to teacher pay adequacy defines teacher pay as adequate if schools are able to staff their classrooms with qualified teachers, with "qualified" being understood to mean that the teachers have met state licensing and NCLB requirements. As the previous discussion indicates, this is a fairly simplistic approach to defining teacher quality. Many economists would treat quality as a continuous variable. In that view, higher relative pay for teachers would improve the quality of the applicant pool, thereby allowing schools to recruit and retain better teachers who, in turn, would raise student achievement. Even if state regulators do not know what buttons to push, presumably local administrators do, and they will take advantage of the larger applicant pools to pick out the better applicants.

Surveys of the early education production function literature find little evidence of a strong positive effect of teacher pay on student achievement. Of

118 estimates reported in the literature, 73 percent were statistically insignificant, 20 percent were positive and significant, and 7 percent were negative and significant.[31] A subset of studies considered (appropriately) "high-quality" (student-level data, value-added econometric model, single state) report seventeen estimates; of those, 82 percent were statistically insignificant and 18 percent were positive and significant. Two recent, sophisticated studies of teacher effects, while narrow in scope (a single district), raise further questions about the link between teacher pay and productivity. Jacob and Lefgren found no relationship between teacher pay and teacher performance in a large urban school district, and Hanushek and colleagues reported no relationship between teacher productivity and changes in teacher pay for teachers who left a large Texas school district. Earlier studies using census data or aggregated district data found positive effects of teacher pay on student test scores or student graduation rates.[32] However, research support for a positive teacher pay effect can only be called mixed at best. I see it trending negative. Moreover, even in studies finding a positive effect, I have seen no evidence presented that across-the-board pay increases are cost efficient or that they would pass a cost-benefit test.

In the absence of direct support in the education production function literature, it is interesting to consider some indirect evidence concerning teacher pay from the market for private school teachers. Suppose that the benefits of higher teacher pay did, in fact, outweigh the costs, and that public schools were setting teacher pay inefficiently low. If that were the case, private schools, which operate in a very competitive market, could be expected to pay teachers more. After all, private school parents should be willing to pay higher tuition to support higher teacher pay if it were worth it in terms of their children's achievement. Many of these same parents will be paying college tuition rates far in excess of those in grades K–12, reflecting in part the higher faculty salaries at private colleges and universities.

Of course, in areas other than K–12 education, personnel managers routinely use private pay and benefits as a benchmark in setting government pay. Indeed, one important function of the NCS compensation data collected by the Bureau of Labor Statistics is to provide private sector as well as state and local benchmark data for setting federal wages. In higher education, administrators (and faculty) are keenly aware of the level and structure of compensation in private institutions.

Since 12 percent of teachers are employed in private schools, one might expect private sector compensation data to play a larger role in policy discussions concerning the adequacy of public school teacher pay. The two sectors compete for teachers, and mobility between the two is extensive. Data from the 1999–2000 School and Staffing Survey show that 36 percent of full-time private and 13 percent of full-time public school teachers report some teaching experience in the other sector.

In fact, comparisons of pay and benefits between the two sectors play little role in discussions of public school teacher pay. That reflects in part the role that teacher unions play in shaping the policy discussion—neither the American Federation of Teachers nor the National Education Association mentions private schools in its reports on teacher pay. There are, however, legitimate objections to public-private comparisons. First, many private schools have a religious orientation and are staffed by teachers of the same religious denomination. To the extent that such schools are advancing a religious mission, they and their teachers are not comparable to public K–12 schools. Second, private schools are generally more selective in admissions than public schools and, on average, they enroll students of higher socioeconomic status. To the extent that their admission policies result in better behaved and more academically motivated students, private school classrooms make for a more attractive teaching environment.

Table 6-3 presents regression estimates based on NCS data comparing public and private teacher salaries in an attempt to address such concerns. First, I present earnings data only for private school teachers in nonreligious private schools. In addition, I exclude private schools that have a special emphasis (for example, special education, Montessori, Waldorf) and focus only on schools whose mission most closely resembles that of traditional public schools. The 0.136 gap in log pay between teachers in private schools and public schools implies that private school teachers, on average, earn only 87 percent of what public school teachers earn.

Even with the above adjustments, a critic might argue that private school teaching is not comparable to public school teaching because the socioeconomic status of private school students is higher. In order to make the public and private schools more comparable, I exclude more than 90 percent of the public school teacher sample and retain only public school teachers in low-poverty, suburban schools (in which less than 5 percent of students are eligible for free or reduced-price lunches). If only very low-poverty suburban schools are considered, private school teachers earn just 79 to 81 percent of what public school teachers earn. Not only are private school salaries lower, but the benefits are lower as well.[33] The fact that selective private schools pay lower teacher salaries suggests that whatever positive effects higher teacher pay may have on teacher quality, those effects do not produce commensurate benefits in terms of student achievement—or at least benefits of such magnitude that parents are willing pay for them.

Table 6-3. *Gap between Pay of Full-Time Teachers in Private Nonsectarian Schools and Pay of Public School Teachers*[a]

Independent variable	All public school teachers	Public school teachers in low-poverty suburban schools	Public school teachers in low-poverty suburban schools	Public school teachers in low-poverty suburban schools
Private-public pay gap in logs	−.136 (11.90)	−.315 (22.61)	−.210 (12.88)	−.236 (14.82)
Private teacher pay as percent of public teacher pay (regression adjusted)	87.2	73.0	81.1	79.0
Other covariates	No	Yes	Yes	Yes
State effects	No	No	Yes	No
MSA effects	No	No	No	Yes
N	39,024	2,958	2,958	2,958

Source: U.S. Department of Education, 1999–2000 Schools and Staffing Surveys.

a. Yes/no indicators show which independent variables are included in the results presented in each column. Other covariates include indicators of teaching in a central city school or a suburban school, gender, race, education, total teaching experience, and teaching experience within the same district. State effects model absorbs state. MSA effects absorbs the first three digits of the school zip code. *T* values in parentheses.

Conclusion

Plaintiffs in school finance adequacy lawsuits often claim that teacher pay levels are too low to recruit or retain teachers of sufficient quality to deliver the level of educational services mandated by a state constitution. These claims, and the more general policy debate about teacher quality, have raised concern about the adequacy of teacher pay. In this chapter I consider three notions of adequacy in teacher remuneration. The first concerns the relative pay of teachers. If teacher pay were substantially below that of workers in other professions who have a roughly similar education, that would at least provide prima facie evidence of underpayment or inadequacy of teacher pay. In fact, when adjusted for annual weeks of work, teacher pay and benefits compare favorably with those of other college-educated workers. A second approach focuses on school staffing. Given the per-pupil resources provided to schools, are they able to fill vacancies with qualified teachers? In fact, the vast majority of public school classrooms are staffed by teachers who meet state licensing and federal NCLB requirements. The fact that compliance is not 100 percent is largely due to the bureaucratic complexity of state licensing regimes combined with the dynamics of teacher labor markets and seems to have little relationship to district resources. A final approach to adequacy treats teacher qualifications as a continuum and asks whether public schools are underinvesting in teacher quality relative to other inputs. In this view, teachers are "underpaid" if the social benefits from increasing teacher pay exceed the costs. At present, scientifically valid education research simply cannot identify a reliable relationship between spending on teachers—whether in the form of pay, benefits, or professional training—and student performance. Indirect evidence from the market for private school teachers suggests that the costs of higher relative teacher pay exceed any educational benefits.

If courts are predisposed to intervene on this matter, the most reasonable standard for determining the adequacy of teacher pay is determining whether resources available to a district are adequate to meet current regulatory standards. In this regard, I would make two provisos. First, the standard should require that districts spend money efficiently. A district that insists that it must raise the pay of all teachers in the district because it cannot recruit a certified speech pathologist is not spending money wisely. Second, state licensing standards must have some flexibility. The large number of certifications and endorsements issued by states guarantees that virtually no district can ensure that every class will be taught by a teacher with the right certificate or endorsement. Indeed, most of the "out of field" teaching in public schools would disappear overnight if states issued a single license in K–12 teaching as they do in medicine, law, accounting, and other professions. Short of that, "alternative route" licensing programs that target existing vacancies hold considerable promise. Teachers in some small rural schools cannot be licensed in every field in which their teaching skills are required. Here, too, licensing standards must have some flexibility.

Finally, let me conclude by saying that I have focused on the general level of teacher pay. Although I find little convincing evidence of general underpayment of teachers, there are likely some school districts among the 14,000 in the United States where the case for underpayment can be made. However, an even more compelling argument is that *some* teachers are underpaid (and some overpaid) in virtually all school districts. The problem with teacher pay in traditional public schools is not its overall level, but its rigid structure. Relative pay increases may be in order for some particularly valuable teachers (and relative pay decreases for others). In large urban school districts, rigid salary schedules cover hundreds of schools and thousands of teachers, rewarding teacher characteristics with little demonstrated relationship to student performance and suppressing differentials for teacher characteristics that may really matter (for example, high levels of student performance, willingness to teach in low-performing schools, and scarce field skills). A much more productive discussion concerning teacher pay would focus on its inefficient structure and the benefits of a more market- and performance-based system. So far, the state courts involved in adequacy litigation have demonstrated little inclination or capacity to shift the conversation in that direction.

Notes

1. Unless otherwise indicated, "teachers" refers to public school teachers only. The pay and benefits of private school teachers, particularly those in religious schools, are far below those of teachers in public schools. Obviously, combining the two groups lowers average teacher pay. Although the relevant policy debate is about public school teachers, some commentators on teacher pay combine public and private school teachers in their statistical analyses. See, for example: Sylvia Allegretto, Sean Corcoran, and Lawrence Mishel, *How Does Teacher Pay Compare?* (Washington: Economic Policy Institute, 2004).

2. U.S. Department of Labor, Bureau of Labor Statistics, *Occupational Outlook Handbook* (2005): "Computer systems analysts, database administrators, and computer scientists must be able to think logically and have good communication skills. Because they often deal with a number of tasks simultaneously, the ability to concentrate and pay close attention to detail is important. Although these computer specialists sometimes work independently, they frequently work in teams on large projects. They must be able to communicate effectively with computer personnel, such as programmers and managers, as well as with users or other staff who may have no technical computer background. . . . Technological advances come so rapidly in the computer field that continuous study is necessary to keep one's skills up to date."

3. For a concise discussion of the economics of pay comparability, see John Wenders, "Full of Sound and Fury and Signifying Nothing: Metaphysical and Other Irrelevant Debates about Teachers' Comparable Pay," policy briefing, Education Excellence Idaho, September 2004 (www.edexidaho.org).

4. Donald Boyd and others, "The Draw of Home: How Teachers' Preferences for Proximity Disadvantage Urban Schools," State University of New York at Albany, December 2003. The authors found that 85 percent of New York teachers took their first teaching job within forty miles of their hometown. Similar high rates occur outside of NYC as well. Data for Missouri show that a large share of the teaching workforce comes from the nearest teacher training programs, which, in turn, are generally housed in four-year colleges that tend to attract students from the same or contiguous counties. See "Teacher Preparation Institution Profiles" (http://dese.mo.gov/divteachqual/teached/teacherprepprof/index.html).

5. U.S. Department of Labor, Bureau of Labor Statistics, "National Compensation Survey: Occupational Wages in the U.S., July 2003 Supplemental Tables" (August 2004) (www.bls.gov/ncs/ocs/sp/ncbl0636.pdf). Scheduled hours of work on site also are much shorter for teachers. For example, NCS data for elementary school teachers in the New York metropolitan area show an average of 34.7 hours of work per week. The analogous figures for physicians and lawyers are 45.4 and 37.4 hours per week, respectively.

6. *Education Week*, "Salaries and Wages in Public Schools," April 13, 2005, p. 14.

7. The level of disaggregation tends to vary with the size of the MSA. Less detailed occupational data are provided in smaller MSAs, hence my decision to focus on only the largest.

8. The NCS reports pay for elementary and secondary public school teachers separately in many MSAs. Figures 6-1 and 6-2 report values for elementary teachers. Since elementary and secondary teachers are paid from the same salary schedules in public school districts, their average salaries are very similar in the NCS surveys.

9. Allegretto, Corcoran, and Mishel, *How Does Teacher Pay Compare?*

10. Teacher collective bargaining agreements typically provide ten to fifteen days of sick or personal leave during the 185- to 190-day contract. These days can be taken not only for illness of the teacher but also for illness of family members, often broadly defined. For example, a recent Columbus, Ohio, teacher contract provides fifteen sick days annually and allows teachers to use them not only for themselves but for "immediate family," defined as "father, mother, brother, sister, son, daughter, wife, husband, grandmother, grandfather, grandson, granddaughter, father-in-law, mother-in-law, legal guardian, or foster or step-parents of said teacher; and all dependents as defined by IRS living in the home or any person living in the home to whom a teacher becomes the primary caregiver" (http://www.ceaohio.org/Contract/Master_Agreement_05_08.2.pdf).

11. Lori L. Taylor, "Comparing Teacher Salaries," Bush School of Public Policy, Texas A&M University, 2005.

12. Marigee Bacolod, "The Role of Female Labor Markets in the Decline of Teacher Quality," University of California–Irvine, 2003. Taking a different statistical approach, Bacolod also found that teacher pay compared favorably to nonteacher pay in census data.

13. These gaps take no account of lower commuting costs or daycare expenses from the shorter hours on site and the much shorter work year for teachers. These would easily exceed the estimated 4 to 6 percent gap.

14. U.S. Department of Education, National Center for Education Statistics, *Digest of Education Statistics 2004* (2005), table 69.

15. Michael Podgursky, "Fringe Benefits," *Education Next* 3, no. 3 (2003): 73–76. Alternatively, licensing entry barriers will need to be changed. Many states have enacted alternative certification or alternative route programs to recruit career changers or post-baccalaureate candidates to enter teaching in a way that minimizes pre-service training. The population of teachers who enter through such programs tends to include relatively more men as well as minorities.

16. Michael Podgursky, Ryan Monroe, and Donald Watson, "Academic Quality of Public School Teachers: An Analysis of Entry and Exit Behavior," *Economics of Education Review* 23 (2004): 507–18.

17. Michael Wolkoff and Michael Podgursky, *Wyoming School District Employee Compensation* (Sacramento, Calif.: Management Analysis and Planning, 2002). Survey data are consistent with these UI findings. They find that only 19 percent of teachers who were in classrooms in 1999–2000 and who quit teaching the subsequent year reported "better salary or benefits" as very important or extremely important in their decision to leave teaching. U.S. Department of Education, National Center for Education Statistics, *Teacher Attrition and Mobility: Results from the Teacher Follow-Up Survey 2000–01*, NCES 2004-301 (August 2004), table 7.

18. Because of sample size restrictions, the BLS still does not disaggregate data on employee benefits for public K-12 school teachers.

19. See Darius N. Lakdawalla, "The Declining Quality of Teachers," Working Paper 8263 (Cambridge, Mass.: National Bureau of Economic Research, 2001), for an analysis of why school districts favor lower class size over higher teacher pay. It is sometimes argued that staffing growth is driven by special education spending, but Missouri data suggest otherwise. Missouri's student teacher ratio in 2002–03 (13.9) was below the national average, and, like the overall national rate, declined substantially over the last two decades. Since the early 1990s, the additional growth in the number of special education teachers lowered the Missouri student teacher ratio by .4 students and accounted for 19.6 percent of the decline. Thus just over 80 percent of the decline was due to other factors.

20. "Quality Counts 2005: No Small Change," *Education Week,* January 6, 2005, pp. 92–93. National Association of State Directors of Teacher Education and Certification, *The NASDTEC Manual on the Preparation and Certification of Educational Personnel* (Dubuque, Iowa: Kendall/Hunt Publishing, 2003).

21. Christopher Jenson and Steven Rivkin, "Class Size Reduction, Teacher Quality, and Academic Achievement in California Public Elementary Schools" (San Francisco: Public Policy Institute of California, 2000).

22. Illinois Board of Education, "2004 State Report Card" (www.isbe.net/research/pdfs/2004_StateReport_E.pdf).

23. U.S. Department of Education, National Center for Education Statistics, *Teacher Supply in the U.S.: Sources of Newly Hired Teachers in Public and Private Schools 1987–88 to 1993–94,* NCES 2000-309 (2000).

24. Wenders, "Full of Sound and Fury and Signifying Nothing."

25. Dale Ballou and Michael Podgursky, "Returns to Seniority among Public School Teachers," *Journal of Human Resources* 37, no. 4 (Autumn 2002): pp. 892–912; Michael Podgursky, "Teacher Licensing in U.S. Public Schools: The Case for Simplicity and Flexibility," *Peabody Journal of Education* 80, no. 3 (2005): 15–43. Charter and private schools are much less likely than traditional public schools to use these types of salary schedules.

26. Steven G. Rivkin, Eric A. Hanushek, and John F. Kain, "Teachers, Schools, and Academic Achievement," *Econometrica* 73, no. 2 (March 2005). On the backloading of teacher pay see Ballou and Podgursky, "Returns to Seniority among Public School Teachers"; and Hamilton Lankford and James Wyckoff, "The Changing Structure of Teacher Compensation, 1970–94," *Economics of Education Review* 16, no. 4 (October 1997): 371–84.

27. Caroline Hoxby and Andrew Leigh, "Pulled Away or Pushed Out? Explaining the Decline in Teacher Aptitude in the United States," *American Economic Review* 94, no. 2 (May 2004): 236–40; Marguerite Roza and Paul T. Hill, "How Within-District Spending Inequalities Help Some Schools to Fail," *Brookings Papers on Education Policy 2004* (Brookings, 2004).

28. Eric A. Hanushek, "The Failure of Input-Based Schooling Policies," *Economic Journal* 113, no. 485 (2003): F64-F98.

29. Dan Goldhaber, "The Mystery of Good Teaching," *Education Next* 2 (Spring, 2002): 50–55; and Eric A. Hanushek and Steven G. Rivkin, "How to Improve the Supply of High-Quality Teachers," *Brookings Papers on Education Policy 2004* (Brookings, 2004). Summarizing their own and other research, they come to the same conclusion.

30. Daniel Aaronson, Lisa Barrow, and William Sander, "Teachers and Student Achievement in the Chicago Public High Schools," Working Paper (Research Department, Federal Reserve Bank of Chicago, 2003).

31. Hanushek and Rivkin, "How to Improve the Supply of High-Quality Teachers."

32. Brian A. Jacob and Lars Lefgren, "The Impact of Teacher Training on Student Achievement: Quasi-Experimental Evidence from School Reform Efforts in Chicago," Working Paper 8916 (Cambridge, Mass.: National Bureau of Economic Research, 2002); and Eric A. Hanushek and others, "The Market for Teacher Quality," Working Paper 11154 (Cambridge, Mass.: National Bureau of Economic Research, February 2005). Earlier studies based on grouped data are Ronald F. Ferguson, "Paying for Public Education: New Evidence on How and Why Money Matters," *Harvard Journal on Legislation* 28 (1991): 465–98; and Susannah Loeb and Marienne E. Page, "Examining the Link between Teacher Wages and Student Outcomes: The Importance of Alternative Labor Market Opportunities and Non-Pecuniary Variation," *Review of Economics and Statistics* 82, no. 3 (2000): 393–408.

33. Michael Podgursky, "Fringe Benefits," *Education Next*, vol. 3, no. 3 (2003), pp. 73–76. Including private teachers in religious schools would also significantly lower the ratio of private to public school teacher pay.

PART **III**

Impacts

7

FREDERICK M. HESS

Adequacy Judgments and School Reform

A DEQUACY CASES ARE not narrow, legal disputes. Rather, given how difficult it is to prove that a state's education system is legally "inadequate" or "inefficient" by a clear statutory standard, adequacy suits argue that a state's educational performance is offensive in light of its self-proclaimed constitutional commitments. The adequacy strategy presumes that most elected officials are comfortable with a status quo that provides reasonably effective schools for the suburban majority, while depriving politically weak, poor, and disproportionately minority populations of equal educational opportunity.

Adequacy suits seek to stop legislators from regarding K–12 education as one state service competing for limited funds and instead to regard its provision to a specified level as securing a fundamental, inalienable right. Asserting that circumstances leave the poor unable to win legislative relief, adequacy proponents believe that the courts are obliged to intervene and compel legislators to bring policies into accord with constitutional requirements. Given that adequacy suits unflinchingly seek to use the courts as a lever of social and political change, the most interesting questions may address the degree to which they trigger the hoped-for changes in educational politics and policy.

Adequacy champions have been straightforward about the scope of their ambition. In an *Education Week* editorial defending adequacy litigation,

The author would like to thank Morgan Goatley and Rosemary Kendrick for their invaluable research assistance.

Michael Rebell—now executive director of the Campaign for Educational Equity at Teachers College, Columbia University—declared that it had produced "sweeping educational improvements and important new approaches to accountability and efficiency . . . What [opponents] fail to grasp is that the education adequacy lawsuits have become the driving force for achieving the aims of the standards-based-reform movement."[1]

As noted in other chapters in this volume, adequacy lawsuits grew out of earlier efforts to use the courts to promote school finance reform. The generation of "equity" cases that began in the 1960s and 1970s was victorious only about one-third of the time, due mostly to fierce opposition from suburbanites. Consequently, litigators eventually developed the bolder and more politically viable "adequacy" strategy. By promising every single student an "adequate" education and vaguely pledging to "level everyone up," this tactic seeks to skirt the redistributive struggles of equity and sidestep the sticky question of imposing concentrated costs on politically potent, high-spending suburbs. This strategy is politically attractive in the short term, although its implied need for new revenue may eventually spark opposition from antitax groups and supporters of competing programs.

Adequacy's appeal was its potential to shift the debate from divvying up limited revenue to determining what "adequacy" implied, allowing proponents to call for policy decisions based on expert determinations of "student need" rather than on mere "political" considerations.[2] The presumption was that student needs could be identified and addressed in an "objective" fashion divorced from the vagaries, imprecision, and relative judgments of democratic decisionmaking. This approach may have rested on an exaggerated confidence in "objective" expertise,[3] but, politically, it was a brilliant stroke. The costs would still be borne by the state's taxpayers, but those costs would be diffuse and not concentrated on particular communities. Litigants further strengthened the allure of adequacy by linking demands for new spending to calls for broader "reforms." As Peter Schrag has argued in *Final Test*, "Inevitably, adequacy goes beyond money . . . Adequacy has major consequences at all levels, in the schools, in the districts and the states, and for the governors, school board members, legislators, superintendents, and principals who are supposed to run them."[4]

In practice, because courts lack direct control over spending and because the adequacy of an education is determined by more than the amount spent, policymaking and implementation are crucial to determining the meaning of these victories. Few state constitutions actually mandate that the state must provide an "adequate" education. The courts—unable to rely on clear doctrine or precise determinations—have been forced to define new state obligations, speak broadly of possible solutions, and then enjoin the elective branches to act.

When it comes to practical outcomes, we know little about the actual impact of adequacy suits on student achievement, education policy, education decisionmaking, or the shape of school reform. At best, proponents can document an increase in school spending in particular locales. Ultimately, the impact will turn on the legislative branch and how it chooses to implement rulings that find existing arrangements to be inadequate or unacceptable.

Adequacy decisions create a "policy window" for reform—an opportunity in which a public problem is defined, attention is focused, judicial cover is provided for legislative activity, and a variety of remedies are put forward.[5] It is not self-evident how elected officials will react to this opportunity in the short term or how their reaction may evolve over time. There are at least three ways in which legislators might regard adequacy decisions: as a challenge to institutional prerogatives and a reason for resistance, as an excuse to spend more and push difficult reforms, or as a charge to spend more in a fashion consistent with long-standing political imperatives.

In the first case, protective of institutional prerogatives, resistant to judicial intrusion, and reluctant to raise taxes, legislatures may resist court orders or comply with them only half-heartedly. Legislators generally like to do things that they can get credit for (like initiating new programs) but are not enthusiastic about measures that are difficult to take credit for (like voting for arcane changes in funding formulas) and resist taking steps that will anger constituents (like raising taxes).

Alternatively, the judicial rulings might lift the budget constraints that usually force legislators and governors to make difficult (and potentially unpopular) choices. Adequacy rulings may make legislators and governors more amenable to asking the voters to accept otherwise unpalatable tax increases. Br'er Rabbit, in Uncle Remus's classic tale, tricked his tormentor by pleading not to be thrown into the briar patch, while hoping to goad him into doing just that. In the same way, elected officials may welcome the opportunity to oppose taxes publicly, while "reluctantly" complying with court direction to collect and disburse new revenues. The new spending may serve as the sugar that helps reformers to convince educators and other constituencies to swallow disruptive, distasteful change.

Finally, even if courts prompt legislatures to spend more, such actions may result in little substantive reform. Courts may be able to compel legislators to address budgetary disparities, build new school facilities, provide preschool programs, or adopt new governing arrangements, but the influential, active constituencies, political realities, and organizational inertia that produced the problematic arrangements reflected in existing educational outcomes may not be addressed so readily. They may return, either slowly or in a furious rush, and ensure that, post-reform, districts and schools do little differently than they did before. Dramatic-sounding school reforms that prove more symbolic than substantive are not an unfamiliar phenomenon.[6]

It is useful when assessing legislative response to court-ordered change to think of three kinds of change: new spending, accommodative reforms, and disruptive reforms. These approaches imply very different directions and pose distinct challenges for implementation. Courts frequently offer clear direction as to necessary additional spending but give elected officials ample leeway for determining how funds ought to be spent. Merely requiring new K–12 spending is the easiest demand for courts to make, the one most attractive to a range of influential education constituencies, and the one most readily implemented and monitored. Civil rights groups, teacher unions, school boards, advocates for bilingual or special education programs, and urban officials can all support efforts to grow the "pie" of education funding, even if they may clash over how to allocate the spending.[7] Because litigation does not specify concentrated costs for any group, the calls for new spending may spark little short-term opposition. Later, when new taxes become necessary and some residents are asked to bear concentrated costs, the politics may change.

Accommodative reforms augment current practices but do not significantly disrupt accepted routines or habits of mind. Expanded preschool programs, additional counseling, or new resources for literacy do not require existing educators, local officials, or community members to accept wrenching changes or threaten jobs or the stability of working conditions. Because it is difficult for courts to determine whether specific measures comply with judicial wishes, legislators inevitably have significant freedom and incentive to favor such reforms and craft them in ways that provoke as little resistance as possible.

Disruptive reforms are those that alter the status quo by fundamentally changing the way schools or districts operate, by restructuring jobs, compensation, benefits, or working conditions, by overturning established understandings about adult responsibilities, incentives, and routines, or by otherwise disrupting the prevailing routines of a state's school system. Whereas new spending and accommodative change unify disparate education constituencies, disruptive change creates division by asking certain constituencies to bear concentrated costs. Such an approach may unravel a coalition, encouraging even those who are not threatened to steer away from controversial measures like creating charter schools, shuttering low-performing schools, removing ineffective educators, or linking pay to performance.

Ultimately, there are powerful political incentives for plaintiffs and judges to steer clear of divisive proposals and focus on unifying measures like new money, additional services, and mild and popular reforms. Moreover, while the public attention and window of opportunity occasioned by an adequacy victory may spark legislative activity, it is not clear whether the courts or plaintiffs can safeguard policy victories over time. Adequacy cases raise fundamental questions about the ability of courts to compel substantive policy change in the face of existing institutional arrangements and political forces. When court decisions alter legislative behavior and spending, do they entail substantial remaking of school provision, or do even the successes serve primarily to increase funding for otherwise unaltered systems? How effectively does litigation mobilize the constituents necessary for lasting reform?

Examining Four "Victories"

By February 2005, lawsuits challenging state methods of funding public schools had been filed in forty-four states; in thirty-two of the states, the cases were adequacy lawsuits. Courts had ruled fourteen times that the school funding system violated the state's constitution, in whole or in part.[8] This section sketches the suit, political response, and substantive outcomes in four states where adequacy plaintiffs won significant victories: Kentucky, New Jersey, Maryland, and Ohio. All four states represent early victories for adequacy plaintiffs, providing an opportunity to observe the consequences unfold. Michael Rebell has credited the pioneering Kentucky verdict with spawning "a range of significant accountability initiatives," New Jersey's litigation with yielding "significant school reforms," and the Maryland lawsuit with spurring "a new, comprehensive accountability scheme" that ensures that "revenues are effectively used to improve student achievement."[9] Meanwhile, in Ohio, the plaintiffs in 1997 won a state supreme court decision declaring the funding system to be unconstitutional. What does the record suggest has been the impact of these victories?

The research, conducted during 2005, draws on archival searches, journalistic and scholarly accounts, state and federal data, and interviews with more than thirty state-level participants and observers. While brief case studies cannot provide the nuance necessary to convey the full array of developments in a given state, they may illuminate aspects of the broader impact of litigation that more microscopic examinations overlook.

Kentucky: A Miracle?

Kentucky is often heralded as the best-case scenario for the potential of adequacy litigation to drive transformative school reform.[10] At the time, the state school chief declared, "To say that this decision is historic or far-reaching is an understatement . . . It's simple, it's brilliant, and it's no doubt revolutionary."[11] Scholars Melissa Carr and Susan Fuhrman explained in 1999 that Kentucky is a "somewhat miraculous" example of "school finance reform that accomplished equalization and comprehensive reform at the same time."[12] In light of such optimistic assessments, the lessons of Kentucky, particularly regarding the possible limitations of adequacy suits, are especially instructive.

In 1989, when the Kentucky Supreme Court issued its precedent-setting decision in *Rose* v. *Council for Better Education*, Kentucky was a poor state hobbled by a weak education system.[13] In 1990 just over half of Kentuckians had completed high school, and the percentage of citizens twenty-five years of age and older who had completed four years of college was third to last in the country.[14] In 1987 the Carnegie Foundation had calculated that one-fourth of Kentucky's teachers were "teaching subjects [they were] unqualified to teach."[15] Civic leaders characterized the school system as a "laughing stock"[16] and on "the bottom rung."[17] By the late 1980s, there was a consensus that schooling was a statewide embarrassment and retarding economic development. Civic and political leaders welcomed the *Rose* decision as a chance to launch reform.

The plaintiffs in Kentucky enjoyed significant advantages. During the 1980s, would-be reformers had created an organization, the Prichard Committee for Academic Excellence, that would spearhead the next two decades of reform. Formed in 1980 as a thirty-member advisory panel to the State Council on Higher Education and chaired by Edward Prichard, a prominent Kentuckian long involved in education reform, the committee in 1983 morphed into an independent association focused on statewide educational improvement. In 1985 it issued an influential report entitled *A Path to a Larger Life: Creating Kentucky's Educational Future*, which called for dramatic school reform. In the early 1980s veteran school administrator Arnold Guess organized district superintendents into a second organization, the Council for Better Education, in order to build the political backing for an eventual adequacy lawsuit.

Education reform had been on the agenda for much of the 1980s. Democratic governor Martha Layne Collins (a former Kentucky high school teacher) focused extensively on schooling after her 1984 election. Collins's successor, Democrat Wallace Wilkinson, made education a central issue in his campaign. Both governors, however, met legislative resistance to new taxes. Collins fought for a $300 million tax package to fund her proposed reforms but, on her first attempt to pass it in 1984, could not find the votes even in a legislature where fellow Democrats controlled three-quarters of the seats in the

House and the Senate. Wilkinson, in turn, found himself limited by his pledge to veto any tax increase and to fund any education needs with a lottery.

The Council for Better Education filed the adequacy suit in 1985. The plaintiffs included a coalition of sixty-six school districts, about one-third of all the state's districts. Seeking to minimize resistance from wealthy counties concerned that they would lose out to poor rural communities, the council consciously characterized the proposal as "anti–Robin Hood."[18] In the 1989 *Rose* decision, a 5-2 state supreme court majority endorsed the plaintiffs' claim that the state had failed to provide or adequately fund the "efficient system of common schools throughout the state" that was mandated by Kentucky's constitution. The court's ruling went far beyond those in earlier equity cases, claiming that the *entire* Kentucky education system was unconstitutional, declaring, "This decision applies to the entire sweep of the system—all its parts and parcels." The court outlined seven broader educational goals dictating which subject areas should be covered, including everything from science and technology to the humanities and the arts; urged the General Assembly "to launch the Commonwealth into a new era of educational opportunity"; and ordered taxes raised to fund the reforms.

Given the support of political and civic elites, the process of enacting the ruling was a smooth one. In July 1989 the General Assembly created the Task Force on Education Reform. The final task force report, proposing the Kentucky Education Reform Act (KERA), was adopted by the legislature in March 1990. The executive director of the Prichard Committee said, "I doubt that any legislature in the country has responded so strongly and forthrightly to a Supreme Court decision."[19] The legislation would be funded by new taxes, primarily a 1 percent increase in the corporate tax rate and a 1 cent increase in Kentucky's sales tax, which would generate $1.3 billion annually.

KERA met with little opposition. Although the Kentucky Education Association (KEA) generally supported the law—and was enthusiastic about the new spending—it criticized a provision barring school employees from campaigning for potential school board members. The bill also met scattered opposition from the Kentucky School Board Association, pockets of antitax citizens in central Kentucky, and organizations concerned about increased state involvement in local schools.[20] However, the criticism was muted and never threatened passage of the bill.

The rapidity and ease with which the state enacted KERA and raised taxes were rather remarkable and may suggest just how "primed" elected officials were to take advantage of the policy window that the court opened. One scholar credited KERA with seeking "to change everything at once—from teaching methods and what is taught, to how student achievement is defined and evaluated, to school governance at all levels, to the school finance system."[21]

In truth, KERA was less disruptive than the more breathless accounts suggest. The Kentucky Legislative Research Commission noted that KERA focused on questions of curriculum, governance, and finance and on adding programs for at-risk students, strengthening accountability measures, improving professional development, and promoting "a major commitment to technology."[22] Among these, only the accountability elements were disruptive, and (as we see momentarily) these were less significant than some have suggested.

KERA's actual import was uneven. The "finance" component was the easiest to measure and implement. To tackle funding inequities, the legislature established a new funding system—Support Educational Excellence in Kentucky (SEEK). Between 1989 and 1999, SEEK reduced the gap in per-pupil spending between the wealthiest and the poorest districts by 37 percent, from $1,199 to $757.[23] Meanwhile, by 1992, the Kentucky Education Association was already urging more spending and declaring that KERA would fail if additional funds were not forthcoming.[24] The KEA president ruefully noted in 1997, "We're finding that KERA doesn't work as well in our classrooms as it did in the law."[25]

The KERA "governance" component, which included structural reforms and accountability measures, had more ambiguous results. On the state level, the elected position of state superintendent was eliminated and replaced by a commissioner of education, and the Department of Education was completely reorganized, with employees required to reapply for their jobs. At the district level, KERA transferred significant authority to school-based "decisionmaking councils." Comprising teachers, parents, and principals, the councils enjoyed significant managerial authority on a wide range of issues, including the hiring of principals and the budgeting of school funds. The councils gained authority at the expense of district superintendents and school boards, which had been plagued by nepotism. The number of schools with councils increased from 125 in 1990 to 1,238 in 2000. A Kentucky Institute for Education Research poll found in 1999 that the councils enjoyed high and rising levels of support among teachers, principals, and parents, with the strongest support among educators.[26]

It was on accountability, however, that implementation strayed most dramatically from KERA's blueprint. As enacted, accountability was the "lynchpin" of a systemic reform effort that included "adequate resources, good teaching, preschool, technology, professional administrators, and leadership."[27] The accountability system rested on the Kentucky Instructional Results Information System (KIRIS). KIRIS tested achievement through assessments that included portfolios and writing samples. The proposed accountability system included a widely discussed and ambitious plan to link monetary rewards and sanctions to school performance (including measures such as firing or transferring teaching staff and allowing students to transfer to "successful" schools.) The KERA *Citizen's Handbook* promised, for instance, "an accountability system to reward schools improving their success with students and to intervene in schools failing to make progress."[28] Some claimed that the language and structure of the accountability reforms were flawed to begin with, as student performance improved much more rapidly on KIRIS than it did on national assessments like the NAEP.[29] But the most dramatic alterations to the intent of these measures seem to have occurred in their actual implementation.

In hindsight, it is clear that implementation of the accountability system was much less consequential than its supporters have generally acknowledged. The practical meaning of the sanctions, in particular, was unclear. The implementation of sanctions was delayed until 1996. The sanctions were then removed in 1998, after just two years, when the state switched to the Commonwealth Accountability Testing System (CATS). Today the department's website contains no mention of the more disruptive types of sanctions KERA originally promised. According to the site, "Schools falling short of their goal at the end of a particular cycle . . . receive a Scholastic Audit, receive the assistance of a Highly Skilled Educator, and are eligible to receive state funds to be targeted toward improvement."[30] A state Department of Education official, when asked how many teachers or principals had actually been removed due to sanctions during KERA's fifteen-year existence, reported that not one person had been terminated. Particularly strong resistance to sanctions by established constituents seems to have delayed and softened implementation of the accountability measures. One 2004 quote by a Kentucky union leader captures the hostility to uncomfortable reforms, even after more than a decade. The official explained, "Sanctions are the wrong approach . . . [Instead] we ought to be about recognizing and rewarding successful schools and assisting and making a priority of those schools that have not yet been successful."[31]

The reward system, which took effect in 1994 and was arguably less vulnerable to opposition, was also tempered and ultimately, in essence, discarded during its implementation. Even in its early stages, the KERA teacher bonuses were largely symbolic and rather small, amounting to between $1,300 and $2,600 when first adopted and just $300 to $900 by 2002. The president of the Kentucky Education Association noted, "Sticking a few-hundred-dollars carrot out there is not the way to motivate" and called on the legislature to raise "teacher salaries across the board," "reduce class size," and add more "professional development."[32] Controlled by the school-site councils, there is little evidence that bonuses were seen as a tool for rewarding initiative or excellence. For example, Eastern High School in Jefferson County, which received $106,000 in rewards in 2002, spent the money on bonuses for all staff, including lunch and office workers. The school principal explained, "Everybody shared it. Everyone contributed to the atmosphere and the climate that led to students feeling good about taking CATS."[33] In 2003 the legislature cut funding for the $21 million bonus pool for high-achieving schools. The only other sizable cut was the decision to delay a $22 million order of math textbooks for a year.[34] In 2004, after draining the last $7 million out of the fund that rewarded schools for high performance, the governor completely eliminated the funding for the bonuses. The cuts were little lamented. State education secretary Virginia Fox said, "At this point in time, in tight budget times, I'm more focused on driving money to the classroom for all schools than on rewards for a few."[35]

Significant in light of *Rose*'s exalted status is that, in 2005, plaintiffs were pursuing a new suit arguing that court intervention was again necessary. Citing concerns that the state no longer viewed education and the provisions of KERA as a priority, the Council for Better Education sued again. Robert Sexton, president of the Prichard Committee, said, "We've already taken a step backward. We're starting to gradually chip away at a much-improved system . . . It's happening piece by piece—little step by little step."[36] Education spending had declined from 47 percent of the Kentucky budget in 1990 to 43 percent in 2000.[37] Kentucky Education Association members rallied to support the new suit, explaining, "We have to have the funding in order to do the things we think are important. Kentucky is well known for the successes with KERA, and if they cut back, we will just be dead in the water."[38] By 2004, the degree to which KERA had unraveled could be seen as legislators rehashed talking points from the late 1980s. Republican state senator Lindy Casebier said of the new litigation, "If there is a court decision, maybe that would provide the political cover that some of the legislators feel that they need."[39]

Kentucky illustrates both the possibilities and the limits of the adequacy strategy. Backed by leading civic figures, the court decision provided elected officials with the cover to make decisions previously deemed untenable. By enabling legislators to pass a tax increase and alter governance, *Rose* created a window that allowed officials to refashion a corrupt, ineffective, cash-starved education system into one that was no longer an embarrassment. When it came to thornier questions of making disruptive reforms stick, continuing to boost spending, or transforming the provision of education, however, the outcome was less impressive.

New Jersey: "This Ridiculous Dance"

In 1973, in one of the early equity decisions, the New Jersey Supreme Court ruled that the spending gap between districts violated the state constitutional clause requiring the state to provide a "thorough and efficient" system of education. In response, Democratic governor Brendan Byrne proposed a package of remedies, only to see it voted down by the Democratic legislature. Legislators rejected a revision of the funding formula and a new state income tax, which would have been partially offset by reductions in local property taxes.

Byrne responded by joining the plaintiffs in appealing to the courts for assistance. In 1975, prompted by a new order from the court, the legislature grudgingly enacted the Public School Education Act. The so-called "T&E" law (named for the "thorough and efficient" clause in the state constitution) introduced a new funding system that included the state's first income tax. After complying with the court's dictate by passing the T&E law, the legislators changed course and scuttled the bill by refusing to appropriate funds for implementation. The court responded in 1976 by enjoining spending for all schools until the legislature complied with the new act. The legislature relented and financed the new law with a 2 percent state income tax.

The Education Law Center (ELC), an education advocacy organization founded in 1973 by Paul Tractenberg, a young Rutgers law professor, has been a key force in New Jersey school finance litigation. The ELC was not satisfied with the outcome of the equity litigation, insisting that, even if the T&E remedy were fully funded, it would not go far enough to address inequities. Representing children from some of the state's poorest districts, the ELC again challenged the state system in 1981 in a suit entitled *Abbott* v. *Burke* (later referred to as *Abbott I*).[40] The suit was filed in the name of Raymond Abbott, a Camden seventh grader. Arguing that districts with large numbers of disadvantaged students were entitled to additional money, the lawsuit foreshadowed the adequacy strategy that would dominate school finance litigation later in the decade. The thirty districts that the ELC represented, including Newark, Jersey City, Trenton, and Camden, would be officially designated the *Abbott* districts.

In 1990 in *Abbott II*, the court issued its first mandates, directing the state to ensure that per-pupil expenditures were "substantially equivalent" and then requiring the state to move beyond equal funding to provide enough money to meet the special needs of the *Abbott* districts. Democratic governor Jim Florio responded by proposing the bold Quality Education Act (QEA). The QEA called for a major overhaul and expansion of the New Jersey system of education funding, providing new aid totaling $1.15 billion to more than half of the state's school districts. Instead of using a tax formula to fund schools, QEA provided a basic level of aid of $6,835 per pupil and ensured that newly defined "special needs" districts would receive additional funds.[41] The Democratic legislature quickly enacted the legislation despite vocal opposition from the New Jersey Education Association (NJEA). Florio pitched the QEA as leveling the playing field and bringing property tax relief, but the public saw a tax increase of nearly $1.3 billion in the midst of a recession.[42] While Florio had been elected in a landslide the previous year, by 1990 more than two-thirds of voters reported that they disapproved of his fiscal policies.[43] That summer, more than 6,000 turned out for a protest at the state capitol advocating Florio's recall.[44]

Beyond the tax question, several other provisions undermined support for the bill. The most politically perilous was the proposal to end the practice of having the state cover the costs of the teacher pension fund and Social Security. Traditionally, school districts negotiated teacher salary and retirement benefits with the union, but the state picked up the tab for funding pensions and Social Security taxes. This was hugely popular with the teacher unions because it gave districts cause to be generous with retirement benefits. It also meant that the state ended up subsidizing the wealthy districts that could pay higher teacher salaries. Florio's proposal to have districts pay their own costs provoked a furious response from the powerful NJEA, the largest political donor in the state, which feared that the measure would put downward pressure on teacher compensation.[45] Florio's administration lashed out at the NJEA, declaring that it would not bow to special interests and arguing that existing policy subsidized wealthy districts and rewarded undisciplined negotiating. The NJEA president said she "never thought I'd be in bed with the Republicans" but vowed to fight the governor and his legislative backers in their reelection bids.[46]

Support for the bill was hurt by the quiet opposition of some poor city districts, which were leery of being responsible for pensions and did not want to raise local taxes to comply with the minimum funding levels established by QEA. Meanwhile, wealthier districts opposed removing the state retirement subsidy and cutting state aid. The resistance prompted the legislature to strip out the controversial provisions and adopt QEA II in March 1991. QEA II boosted spending by $750 million, targeting the new funds at the *Abbott* districts, while holding other districts harmless. It reversed the one fiscally responsible piece of QEA—the measure shifting teacher pensions to districts. The backtracking, however, was too little, too late. In the fall, Republicans swept to a veto-proof majority in the previously Democratic legislature. Three years later Florio was defeated by antitax Republican Christine Todd Whitman.

Whitman promised to cut taxes, hold the line on spending, and focus on educational discipline, accountability, and standards. In 1994 the ELC again filed suit, alleging the continued absence of an adequate education in *Abbott* districts. The court ruled QEA II unconstitutional in *Abbott III* because it failed to provide supplemental programs or adequate funding for *Abbott* districts. The Republican legislature responded in 1996 by enacting the Comprehensive Educational Improvement and Financing Act (CEIFA), which sought to shift "the focus of school finance reform from inputs to outputs."[47]

The Whitman administration opted to define "thorough and efficient" using educational standards that included standards for the content of core curricula and yielded relatively low-cost estimates for adequacy in a "model school." The per-pupil cost of basic education was determined by the state Department of Education in 1996 to be $8,285, or $132 less than the state's average per-pupil spending at the time. The formula would have increased aid for 381 districts, reduced aid for 146, and left 86 unaffected.[48] The ELC charged that the proposal did not do enough for *Abbott* districts, while the NJEA again worried about downward pressure on teacher salaries. One scholar observed that irate "school districts and educational interest groups quickly went to work blasting particular components of the plan," forcing changes that "inflated the total cost."[49]

The ELC again filed suit, arguing that CEIFA did not provide adequate funding or programs for *Abbott* districts. In 1997 the court issued *Abbott IV*, declaring CEIFA unconstitutional but remanding the case to the New Jersey Superior Court, where hearings with education experts were held to determine what programs were needed to bring the *Abbott* district schools to adequacy and what they would cost. These decisions formed the basis for the *Abbott V* ruling, which specified new programs in four areas: early education, curricula, supplemental programs, and facilities. In the *Yale Law and Policy Review*, Alexandra Greif noted that *Abbott V* "increased state funding for *Abbott* preschool programs . . . and resulted in facilities legislation more ambitious than any of its kind elsewhere in the country."[50] Between 2000 and 2003, *Abbott VI, VII, VIII,* and *X* followed on *Abbott V,* dealing with the funding of preschool and school facilities and leaving questions of fiscal and educational accountability largely unaddressed. (*Abbott IX* in 2002 gave the state a one-year respite on further implementation of *Abbott* remedies.)

By 2002–03, $3,000 more per pupil was being spent in *Abbott* district schools than in wealthy districts: $13,249 compared to $10,263.[51] State average per-pupil spending of $10,291 was the third highest in the nation.[52] The mandated spending on school facilities, in particular, has been plagued by management problems. An investigation of the Schools Construction Corporation (SCC) by the state inspector general uncovered "pervasive waste and mismanagement in the school construction program" and possible illegal activity.[53] A newspaper analysis found that SCC schools cost an average of 45 percent more than non-SCC schools to build, while construction and school-opening delays caused ongoing problems.[54] In 2005 New Jersey's Democratic U.S. senator Jon Corzine declared, "The cost overruns and mismanagement of the school construction program [have] been a disgrace."[55]

Adequacy proponents have claimed that the new spending and programs produced some success in preschool provision and in schools led by skilled leaders.[56] Although *Abbott* champions have pointed to rising reading scores in *Abbott* districts, the gains actually reflect statewide improvements following an overhaul of the test, which was prompted by complaints that the test's bar for proficiency was set too high.[57] Meanwhile, despite the expensive emphasis on the *Abbott* districts, New Jersey continued to lag far behind other states in closing the achievement gap between white and black students. On the 2003 NAEP, among all states, New Jersey's gap in math achievement ranked fourth from the bottom in the fourth grade and fifth from the bottom in the eighth grade. In reading, which adequacy proponents tout as a bright spot, the state's gap among all states remained mired fourth from the bottom in the fourth grade and fifth from the bottom in the eighth grade.[58] Supporters of the litigation have blamed admittedly modest gains on the intransigence of the legislature, the resistance of the suburbs, and difficulties in implementing the court's rulings.[59]

Some supporters of the litigation have suggested that they feel like they are on a treadmill. "Every year we have this ridiculous dance with the governor, the legislature, the department, and us and the courts," said David G. Sciarra, executive director of ELC, "and we always end up in the same place."[60] Perhaps the best summary of New Jersey's adequacy effort comes from a sympathetic scholar, Georgetown University's Douglas Reed, who has noted, "The progression from the lofty rhetoric of *Abbott II* to the detailed policy prescriptions of *Abbott V* highlights the inability of the courts to do more than pump more money through the existing institutional framework of educational governance."[61]

Maryland: One-Wing Airplanes Don't Fly

When the first Baltimore adequacy lawsuit was filed in 1994, the city had been wrestling with educational reform for more than a decade. Baltimore is a poor, heavily black city in a predominantly white state. In 2000, 23 percent of Baltimore residents lived below the poverty line in a city that was 64 percent black.[62] In 1994, just 9 percent of Baltimore City third graders scored at a satisfactory level on the Maryland State Performance Assessment reading exam; by eighth grade, the percentage scoring at a satisfactory level was down to 6 percent. In comparison, about one-third of Maryland third graders and one-quarter of Maryland eighth graders were performing satisfactorily. Math scores in Baltimore were equally abysmal, with 12 percent of third graders and 9 percent of eighth graders scoring at a satisfactory level, compared to state averages of 34 and 40 percent, respectively.[63]

Maryland and Baltimore officials had long regarded the Baltimore school system as in dire need of reform. In 1978 Baltimore had joined several rural districts to file an equity suit against the state Board of Education (*Hornbeck* v. *Somerset County Board of Education*).[64] The case sought to address statewide funding inequities. The plaintiffs won the initial suit, but ultimately their victory was overturned in the Court of Appeals.

In the early 1990s the effort to reform Baltimore schooling took wing when Democratic delegate Howard Rawlings of Baltimore, the intimidating chairman of the House Appropriations Committee, pressed the district to reorganize its notoriously ineffective management. The Department of Education and an alliance of nonprofits hired a management consultant to craft a reform proposal, which called for delegating budgeting and resource management to individual schools and increasing the authority of principals. Baltimore superintendent Walter Amprey rejected the measures as unduly harsh. Rawlings responded by using his appropriations post to withhold $5.9 million in state funds earmarked for school administrative benefits and salaries.[65]

In 1994 the American Civil Liberties Union (ACLU) filed Maryland's first adequacy lawsuit (*Bradford* v. *Maryland State Board of Education*) on behalf of a "class of at-risk students in Baltimore."[66] In the words of lead attorney Alan Baron, the ACLU opted to focus on "adequacy" because, "this suit is about how well Baltimore City students are doing." Baron said, "This isn't a replay of the [earlier equity suit]. That suit was about input. This suit is about output. Good education is more than a question of money."[67] The ACLU hoped that its independent role would allow it to be uncompromising in its litigation. Baron elaborated, "The city, as a political entity, has considerations in its relations with other political jurisdictions that we don't have. One of our luxuries is that we don't have to worry about politics."[68]

Baltimore followed the ACLU's lead and filed its own suit nine months later. Baltimore's mayor, Kurt Schmoke, hoped that litigation would allow the city to skirt political pressures, unite quarrelsome local interests, and spur reform in the city's schools. The ACLU's and the city's cases ultimately were combined. In its defense, the state claimed that city mismanagement was responsible for mediocre school performance and the absence of meaningful reform and that this ought to be addressed before calling for new funding. Ultimately, in a settlement reached just before the case went to court, Baltimore received new funding and promised some management reform. The settlement, the 1996 consent decree, determined that the state's funding system was inadequate and was not fulfilling its responsibility to maintain a "thorough and efficient education system." Maryland would provide the city with an additional $230 million over five years. At the time, Baltimore's total school spending totaled roughly $640 million a year, or about $5,500 per student.[69] The decree also specified that the plaintiffs could seek additional funding in 1999 should it be necessary and promised that the state would make its "best efforts" to satisfy such a request.

Meanwhile, the judge required the city to submit a master plan for management reforms and stipulated that the reforms be evaluated in public progress reports. The school governance system was to be completely overhauled, replacing the old mayor-appointed school board with one selected jointly by the mayor and governor. Candidates for the board would be proposed by the state Board of Education and were to include members representing various interests (that is, one parent, one student, multiple school administrators, and so forth). The consent decree also abolished the position of superintendent and established a leadership triumvirate—a chief executive officer, a chief financial officer, and a chief academic officer—that would report to the board. Finally, the consent decree established a fourteen-member Parent and Community Advisory Board. While these measures were hailed as evidence of dramatic change, what they actually meant for management or governance was unclear.

Given city-state tensions and heated opposition from suburban legislators who wanted additional funds for their schools, a compromise was not reached until the end of 1997. It was enacted only after an additional $32 million was added for districts outside Baltimore.[70] Some prominent Baltimore residents criticized the settlement for sacrificing too much autonomy. A public letter of protest, signed by representatives of the Maryland Parent Teacher Association and the NAACP, among others, read, "We will not accept Baltimore becoming a colony of the State, with its citizens having no say in the education of their children. House Bill 312 and Senate Bill 795 are anti-democratic and smack of racist paternalism."[71] Maryland's largest teacher union, the Maryland State Teachers Association, supported the provisions on spending and smaller class size but staunchly opposed proposals to link school accountability to student achievement.

Robert Schiller, Baltimore's interim chief executive officer (CEO), had a reputation for tough-minded management. Because the settlement stipulated that Schiller was ineligible to serve as permanent CEO, he appeared to enjoy the freedom to resist political pressure. Proponents hoped he would use the window afforded by the legislation to clean house. Schiller's big reforms, however, proved to be surprisingly mild. He tweaked teacher evaluation so that it would begin to include measures of student achievement, reduced class size, created new after-school programs for at-risk students, and hired more than 1,000 new teachers.[72] Skeptics noted that only the decision to tweak teacher evaluation actually challenged the status quo; the rest of the measures simply involved new spending and new programs.

In 1999 the Board of School Commissioners returned to the state to request more funds. The state rejected the request, saying that Baltimore needed more time to install the reforms before requesting additional money. The city and the ACLU returned to court. Ultimately, the state agreed to provide more than $200 million in additional funding. As a result of the settlement, the governor and the General Assembly established the Thornton Commission to review state funding. In January 2000 the commission concluded that the state had substantially increased aid but that a gap of nearly $2,500 remained between per-pupil spending in the wealthiest and poorest districts. In its 2002 final report, the commission advocated more spending, especially for "special populations," and endorsed new funding "of about $1.1 billion by fiscal 2007."[73] The proposal was backed by the Coalition to Support the Thornton Commission, a group that included the Maryland Parent Teacher Association and the new Baltimore school board.

In 2002 the commission's plan to increase funding was enacted, but only after including a provision granting Montgomery County $80 million in additional funding. Chris Maher, education director of the Advocates for Children and Youth, described the vote: "It was an absolute pure political buyout . . . We could give Montgomery their money and give everyone else in the state a lot more money, or we could trash it all."[74] The adequacy proponents successfully secured additional funding for Baltimore. In 1998 Baltimore spent less per pupil than the statewide average of $6,964. By 2003 district per-pupil spending exceeded the state average of $9,639 by nearly $500.[75]

It is harder to make the case that the governance shuffle yielded meaningful management reform in Baltimore. In November 2003 the district had to frantically lay off 710 personnel when it faced bankruptcy due to a multiyear

$52 million deficit. Even as she announced the layoffs, CEO Bonnie Copeland reported that she was still uncertain how much the system owed and pleaded with staff to turn in invoices, which might amount to $13 million or more. The hurried cuts were concentrated in the central office, which the district had failed to trim even as enrollment had shrunk. By 2001–02, Baltimore had 581 central staff for 94,000 students, while larger Maryland systems, including Baltimore County and Prince George's County, needed less than 300 central staff for more than 100,000 students. Reducing administration to a comparable level would have saved Baltimore $15 million a year.[76]

In spring 2004, the governor and mayor clashed over news that the Baltimore deficit now amounted to $58 million—or more than 6 percent of its $914 million budget. When the governor insisted on more state control of the district's finances as a condition for a state loan, Baltimore's mayor, Martin O'Malley, rejected the offer and opted to have the city cover the shortfall. Ultimately, there was limited evidence that much had changed. In July 2005 a federal judge found that district efforts to improve special education services had resulted in "massive failure" and handed control over special education to the state Department of Education.[77]

Critics traced continued problems to a failure to fix district management. Years before, delegate Barrie Ciliberti had said of the Thornton effort that putting more money into a mismanaged system is "like putting millions of dollars into a one-wing airplane. One-wing airplanes don't fly. It's just good money after bad."[78] Adequacy sympathizers took a very different perspective. In 2004 one lead teacher in Baltimore explained, "Underfunding of this magnitude necessarily leads to poor management . . . The deficit grew principally not from mismanagement but from the emergencies that arise every day in a city desperately poor."[79]

Assessing the actual outcomes in Maryland and Baltimore is not easy. Adequacy proponents point to new spending and Baltimore initiatives intended to attract high-quality educators and improve elementary education. The extra dollars reduced class size in early grades, expanded pre-kindergarten programs, purchased new textbooks, funded a reading curriculum, and raised teacher salaries. However, adequacy advocates made clear from the start that they were interested in outcomes, not inputs. On that score, the results are meager.

The scores on the Maryland School Performance Assessment Program (MSPAP), which tested students in grades three, five, and eight during 1997–2002, evinced, at best, a very modest improvement in the performance of Baltimore's students. For third graders, the percentage of students scoring satisfactory in reading inched from 12 percent in 1996–97 to 13 percent in 2001–02. Over the same period, the percentage scoring satisfactory in math crept from 11 to 13 percent. The percentage of fifth graders scoring satisfactory in reading climbed from 14 to 18 percent and in math from 14 to 19 percent; at the eighth-grade level, the percentage slipped from 12 to 11 percent in reading and rose from 11 to 14 percent in math.[80] (The MSPAP was last used in 2001–02, before Maryland adopted a new assessment system more attuned to the federal No Child Left Behind Act. Results from that point cannot be compared readily to earlier outcomes.)

Baltimore's school performance remained so dismal that, in March 2006, the state Board of Education moved to seize control of four Baltimore high schools and strip Baltimore of the direct operation of seven more middle schools. Maryland deputy superintendent Ronald Peifer said the move was necessary because the schools in question had failed to show improvement for nine years, pointing out, "Some of these schools have been failing for twelve years under three different governors."[81] State superintendent Nancy S. Grasmick said, "We're talking about 10,000 students. Ten thousand students that are in schools that are persistently low-performing . . . We have an obligation under the law and ethically to address that situation on behalf of the children." Grasmick said the problem was not only with the schools in question, but with a district that had not taken strong action to turn those schools around.

Baltimore officials, including city schools chief Bonnie Copeland, said they were disappointed by the action, protested that reform efforts were under way, and argued that the state's move reflected impatience and a lack of appreciation for the district's reform strategy. Republican governor Robert Ehrlich Jr. rejected district complaints, arguing that there was little evidence that Baltimore's schools were improving and that "all extraordinary means" were justified to improve "a system that is this dysfunctional."[82]

The state board was overridden in the state legislature, at the behest of Baltimore's delegates. The governor vetoed the legislature's decision, but the legislature then overrode Ehrlich's veto, ensuring that all eleven schools would remain under district control for at least another year. Maggie McIntosh, a former schoolteacher and Democratic delegate from Baltimore, explained that it was wrong to deem the eleven schools "failures" and that it was impossible to compare Baltimore's performance to that of other urban school districts. State senator Nathaniel McFadden, a Democrat from Baltimore, said the city's schools needed to improve but insisted that it was necessary to allow the school system to continue its restructuring plans before taking more dramatic steps. The city's reform strategy included altering the organizational chart so that all eleven schools would report directly to the CEO; having district staff visit the schools weekly, observe teachers, conduct regular reviews,

and mentor principals; offering financial incentives to principals in the targeted schools; spending an additional $22 million in fiscal 2007 on the eleven
schools and on other low-performing schools; and continuing its effort to
transform the four high schools into small schools.[83] These reforms, individually and collectively, seemed more than a little familiar to skeptics who had
seen the fruits of a decade's worth of Baltimore school reform.

Ohio: Why Don't the Attorneys Run for Office?

Ohio's experience highlights the critical role of elected officials in breathing life
into adequacy judgments by illustrating how readily legislatures can refuse to
respond to court mandates. In four separate rulings over more than a decade,
the Ohio Supreme Court ruled that the legislature was failing its constitutional duty to provide a "thorough and efficient system of common schools
throughout the state." None of the rulings prompted the state's elected officials
to raise taxes and enact the measures endorsed by the court.

The first Ohio adequacy lawsuit, *DeRolph* v. *The State of Ohio*, was filed in
1991 by the Ohio Coalition for Equity and Adequacy in School Funding
(E&A Coalition). The E&A Coalition represented 553 of the state's 611 districts, or about 90 percent of the state's schools. In 1994 a Common Pleas
Court judge ruled in favor of the plaintiffs. The state appealed and lost in
1995, pushing the case to the state supreme court. In 1997 in a 4-3 vote, the
court ruled the education funding system to be unconstitutional. It struck
down the system's reliance on property taxes and ordered the state to narrow
spending disparities between rich and poor districts (per-pupil expenditures
ranged from $4,000 in the lowest-spending districts to $12,000 in the highest-
spending ones).[84]

Republican governor George Voinovich and the Republican legislature
responded half-heartedly. Voinovich used a $280 million budget windfall that
resulted from a national tobacco settlement to fund capital improvements in
outdated schools, slightly increase per-pupil funding, and establish a modest
testing and accountability system. One analyst declared in a *Columbus Dispatch*
editorial that the state's response consisted of "duct tape and a little wire."[85]

In a hostile environment, the Ohio Supreme Court had little luck over-
coming legislative resistance. In the heavily Republican state, in which justices
are elected to six-year terms, the Republican leadership, including the governor, Senate president, and House speaker, made clear its displeasure with the
court's verdict.[86] Members of the *DeRolph* majority were reportedly subjected
to "extreme political pressure."[87] Republican Senate Finance Committee chair
Roy Ray fumed, "I always appreciate it when attorneys try to tell us what to

do. Why don't they run for office?"[88] Republican and antitax organizations began a coordinated effort to unseat pro-*DeRolph* justices and reverse the one-vote court majority.[89]

The *Akron Beacon Journal*, in a 1997 news series, and the Public Broadcasting Service, in a 1996 documentary, had focused attention on educational inequity in Ohio. After the court ruling, however, the weight of editorial-page opinion inveighed against judicial overreach. The *Toledo Blade* branded the majority justices the "gang of four," language echoed in the *Columbus Dispatch* and the *Cleveland Plain Dealer*.[90] The *Dispatch* dismissed one ruling as "one of the most poorly reasoned, overreaching decisions to emanate from the high court in a long time . . . It displays a cool dismissal of original intent, separation of powers, prior court decisions, and nearly 200 years of educational progress in Ohio . . . This is both a tragedy and travesty."[91]

With the editorial pages of the major papers in their corner, a public resistant to tax increases, a politically vulnerable state supreme court, and the one-vote *DeRolph* majority, legislators felt little pressure to act. As part of the *DeRolph I* ruling, the lower-court judge who initially heard the case was charged with reevaluating the state's funding mechanism in twelve months. After review, the judge maintained that the revised system was still unconstitutional and that the legislature needed to address structural deficiencies. In May 2000 the Ohio Supreme Court issued *DeRolph II*, which upheld the lower court's ruling and gave the General Assembly another year to respond. The legislature's response was again minimal; it adjusted the funding mechanism to include a "parity aid" formula intended to reduce the gap between property-rich and property-poor districts and continued to increase spending in line with the 6–7 percent rate at which it had been boosting annual school spending.

In September 2001, in *DeRolph III*, the court found the newly created funding system constitutional so long as funding was increased. Estimates of the cost of implementing the decision varied widely. When Ohio Supreme Court justice Andy Douglas and E&A Coalition executive director William Phillis predicted that compliance would cost between $750 million and $1.2 billion annually, elected officials fired back, declaring that the state did not have that kind of money.[92]

In late 2001, hoping to resolve the standoff, the court ordered the parties to a settlement conference with a court-appointed special commissioner. In March 2002 the talks were halted for lack of progress. Finally, in December 2002, the court followed the failed special commission and three consecutive 4-3 court rulings with one last 4-3 ruling in *DeRolph IV*. The court again ruled the finance system to be unconstitutional. However, it refused jurisdiction over subsequent appeals regarding enforcement and implementation, essentially throwing up its hands. One scholar concluded simply that the adequacy victories had been overturned by "political realities" because Republican legislators lacked "the political will or desire to provide for the complete systematic overhaul mandated in *DeRolph*."[93] The *DeRolph IV* ruling effectively ended the court's involvement.

In spring 2003, anticipating a recession-related state budget deficit and seeking to minimize spending cuts, Governor Bob Taft proposed a tax increase and created a blue-ribbon commission to study school funding. The tax proposal was rebuffed by the General Assembly. The E&A Coalition filed a petition asking the Common Pleas Court to step in and oversee the development of a new constitutional funding mechanism. The supreme court responded, in May 2003, by rejecting further judicial involvement.

While adequacy proponents explain that one purpose of litigation is to educate the public, public opinion polls suggest that the Ohio public remains uninformed about education finance even after years of high-profile litigation. In September 2001 a statewide poll found that 70 percent of 505 Ohioans surveyed said that they had not heard of the *DeRolph* lawsuit. More than half inaccurately believed that state funding for schools had not increased in five years, although an additional $2 billion had been appropriated since 1997. In 2002, when asked whether the state supreme court was deciding whether to find the Ohio "system of school funding to be unconstitutional," 50 percent of respondents said it was, 35 percent said that it was not, and 15 percent did not know. In 2002, after years of litigation and despite the belief of most Ohioans that state aid for schooling had been static for five years, just 15 percent of respondents said "lack of funding" was "the most important obstacle" to improving local schooling.[94]

A Quick Look at the Numbers

The case studies suggest that the bulk of reform involved new spending and new programs, rather than modifying existing routines. It is therefore useful to consider the degree to which adequacy victories have helped these four states to gain ground relative to their peers on input metrics like per-pupil spending, teacher salaries, and class size. Given that other states, even in the absence of a court judgment, were also making changes to their school systems during this period, it is most useful to compare state changes to the national norm. The utility of this comparison benefits from the fact that adequacy plaintiffs were victorious in only a small number of states during the period under consideration. Because the adequacy movement has focused on systemic improvement rather than redistribution, it is more appropriate to consider statewide results than within-state comparisons.

How much have adequacy wins boosted overall state spending? In 1985, when the *Rose* v. *Council* suit was first filed, Kentucky's per-pupil spending equaled 64 percent of the national average. By 1993, three years after KERA, that was up to 85 percent, before beginning a slight decline. In 2002 the figure stood at 83 percent (see table 7-1). New Jersey spent 148 percent of the national average per pupil in 1985, a figure that grew modestly to 156 percent by 2002. In Maryland, where the adequacy effort targeted only Baltimore, per-pupil spending remained relatively stable; it was 113 percent of the national average in 1985 and 114 percent in 2002. Finally, in Ohio, where the legislature balked at the *DeRolph* ruling, spending nonetheless increased from 94 percent of the national average in 1985 to 107 percent in 2002. In other words, spending growth in Ohio outpaced that in both Maryland and New Jersey. Spending in the four states grew slightly more rapidly than in the nation as a whole during 1985–2002.

Employee compensation consumes about 80 percent of education spending, and boosting teacher pay has frequently been a key rationale for adequacy. How big an impact did these four victories have on teacher salaries? In 1987 Kentucky paid teachers 87 percent of the national average (see table 7-2). In 1992, two years after KERA, that figure was 89 percent. It slipped to 85 percent by 2002. In Maryland the figure was 110 percent in 1987 and remained almost unchanged, at 108 percent, in 2002. New Jersey's pay grew rapidly during the late 1980s and early 1990s, rocketing from 110 percent of the national average in 1987 to 122 percent in 1992. Ironically, this period preceded the legislative package designed to comply with *Abbott*. Pay actually declined slightly in the decade after the *Abbott* reforms, to 118 percent of the national average in 2002. In Ohio salaries were flat through the 1990s. Nowhere did the adequacy victories translate into a sustained increase in teacher pay relative to the national average.

A third measure of inputs worth a cursory look is the teacher-student ratio, a rough proxy for class size. This is instructive not only because it reflects the degree to which new spending is used to add staff, but also because it is an especially popular school reform. In 1998 the American Federation of Teachers observed, "There's no more popular educational initiative across the country . . . than cutting class size."[95] In 2001 the NAACP urged lawmakers to "aggressively target class-size reductions for the highest-minority and concentrated-poverty schools."[96] In Kentucky classes were about 3 percent larger than the national average in 1987 (see table 7-3). After KERA, they shrank slightly, but by 2002 classes were again larger than the national norm. Maryland's

Table 7-1. *Per-Pupil Spending in Select States in Unadjusted Dollars and as a Percentage of National Average, 1969–2003*

Year	United States	Kentucky Amount	Kentucky Percent	Maryland Amount	Maryland Percent	New Jersey Amount	New Jersey Percent	Ohio Amount	Ohio Percent
1969–70	751	502	67	809	108	924	123	677	90
1979–80	2,088	1,557	75	2,293	110	2,825	135	1,894	91
1985–86	3,479	2,229	64	3,923	113	5,139	148	3,265	94
1989–90	4,643	3,384	73	5,573	120	7,546	163	4,531	98
1993–94	5,327	4,505	85	6,191	116	9,075	170	5,319	100
1997–98	6,189	5,213	84	7,034	114	9,643	156	6,198	100
2000–01	7,376	6,079	82	8,256	112	11,248	152	7,571	103
2002–03	8,041	6,661	83	9,153	114	12,568	156	8,632	107

Source: U.S. Department of Education, National Center for Education Statistics. Figures for 1969–2001 are from Thomas D. Snyder, *2003 Digest of Education Statistics* (2003), table 170. Figures for 2002–03 are from *Revenues and Expenditures for Public Elementary and Secondary Education: School Year 2002–03* (2005), table 5.

Table 7-2. *Annual Teacher Salary in Public Elementary and Secondary Schools in Select States in Unadjusted Dollars and as Percentage of National Average, 1972–2003*

Year	United States	Kentucky		Maryland		New Jersey		Ohio	
		Amount	Percent	Amount	Percent	Amount	Percent	Amount	Percent
1972–73	10,174	7,796	77	11,159	110	11,739	115	9,628	95
1977–78	14,198	11,723	83	15,810	111	15,369	108	13,306	94
1982–83	20,695	18,385	89	22,922	111	21,536	104	20,004	97
1987–88	28,034	24,253	87	30,933	110	30,720	110	27,606	98
1992–93	35,030	31,115	89	38,753	111	42,680	122	34,519	99
1997–98	39,454	34,613	88	41,739	106	50,442	128	38,985	99
2002–03	45,822	38,981	85	49,677	108	54,166	118	45,452	99

Source: U.S. Department of Education, National Center for Education Statistics. Figures for 1972–93 are from Thomas Snyder, Charlene Hoffman, and Claire Geddes, *State Comparisons of Education Statistis: 1969–70 to 1996–7* (1998), table 27. Figures for 1997–98 are from Thomas Snyder and Charlene Hoffman, *2000 Digest of Education Statistics* (2001), table 76. Figures for 2002–03 are from Snyder, *2003 Digest of Education Statistics* (2003), table 78.

Table 7-3. *Pupil-Teacher Ratios in Public Elementary and Secondary Schools in Select States and as a Percentage of National Average, 1972–2003*

Year	United States	Kentucky		Maryland		New Jersey		Ohio	
		Ratio	Percent	Ratio	Percent	Ratio	Percent	Ratio	Percent
1972–73	21.7	22.7	105	22.1	102	19.0	88	23.4	108
1977–78	19.7	21.2	108	19.6	99	17.6	89	20.7	105
1982–83	18.6	20.2	109	18.5	99	15.8	85	19.8	106
1987–88	17.6	18.2	103	17.1	97	14.0	80	18.0	102
1992–93	17.4	17.3	99	16.9	97	13.6	78	16.9	97
1997–98	16.8	16.5	98	17.2	102	13.9	83	16.7	99
2001–02	15.9	16.2	102	16.0	101	12.9	81	15.0	94
2002–03	15.9	16.3	103	15.7	99	12.8	81	14.7	92

Source: U.S. Department of Education, National Center for Education Statistics. Figures for 1972–92 are from Snyder, Hoffman, and Geddes, *State Comparisons of Education Statistics: 1969–70 to 1996–97* (1998), table 24. Figures for 1997–2001 are from Snyder, *2003 Digest of Education Statistics* (2003), table 66. Figures for 2002–03 are from Thomas Hoffman and others, *Public Elementary and Secondary Students, Staff, Schools, and School Districts: School Year 2002–03* (2005), table 5.

classes were slightly smaller than the national average in 1987 and 1992, were larger than the national average by 1997, but were slightly smaller again by 2002. New Jersey's classes were 20 percent smaller than the national average in 1987. In 2002, after a decade of *Abbott* litigation, they were 19 percent smaller. Finally, in Ohio, classes were slightly larger than the national average in 1987 but 8 percent smaller by 2002. Adequacy victories in these four states did not lead to smaller classes, with the exception of Ohio, where class sizes declined more than in the nation as a whole, even as the legislature resisted the adequacy ruling.

It appears that even successful adequacy efforts modestly boosted total spending but had no discernible effect on teacher pay or class size. These spending figures raise provocative questions about where the new dollars were actually spent in Kentucky, New Jersey, and Ohio. It is not clear whether the dollars were spent on administration or facilities, were wasted, or were spent in some other way. The requisite analysis is not possible here, but the issue is ripe for future research. The evidence from New Jersey and Kentucky, where even ambitious court decisions had only a modest or short-term impact, also raises questions about whether adequacy judgments can overcome entrenched political dynamics. Early adequacy victories had only a modest impact on spending, with implementation marked by foot dragging and ongoing court battles. Meanwhile, the performance of students in the *Abbott* districts and in Baltimore suggests that new resources and reforms have not been sufficient to boost school quality significantly, even where they have been applied most assiduously.

Adequacy and School Reform

Ultimately, the record suggests that adequacy victories have led consistently to accommodative rather than disruptive reforms. More surprising is the degree to which they appear to have had a limited impact even on statewide inputs, despite the proclaimed goal of using adequacy to "level everyone up." Victories in New Jersey and Maryland primarily served to direct resources to select urban districts, with little evidence of spurring meaningful reform.

Accommodative changes were widespread, with the courts and legislatures favoring the addition of new, popular supplemental programs. In Kentucky, New Jersey, and Maryland, this included new preschool programs, professional development resources, services for at-risk students, and construction. However, the most expensive accommodative reforms—namely, more teacher hires and increased teacher pay—were rarely evident. Meanwhile, the record of potentially more disruptive reforms is one of ineffectual or symbolic steps.

Kentucky's bonus system was permitted to atrophy, and not a single educator was terminated under the state's heralded accountability sanctions; New Jersey backed off its effort to reform pension bargaining; Baltimore and the *Abbott* districts remained mired in dysfunction, and Baltimore's mayor opted to bail out a district plagued by continued incompetence or malfeasance rather than accept the more wrenching changes demanded by the governor as a condition for a state loan.

There is little evidence that adequacy led to any of the most widely discussed disruptive reforms of the past fifteen years, including enhancing teacher quality by revamping licensure, adopting competency tests, or encouraging effective teachers to work in troubled schools; increasing managerial flexibility and district efficiency; adopting choice-based arrangements; or enacting consequential accountability systems. Measures to remove ineffective teachers, link compensation to performance, or shutter low-performing schools met with little success.

KERA indisputably wrought real changes in Kentucky, and the state routinely was hailed as the proof point for the potential of adequacy suits. The decision to monitor school progress and link modest consequences to performance was a truly disruptive step, while KERA also overhauled a corrupt and ineffective state bureaucracy. Additionally, KERA enacted a lasting commitment to site-based councils, though, tellingly, scholars have suggested that site-based management was popular in the 1990s precisely because of its symbolic appeal.[97] KERA shows that a ruling backed by active business support, widespread public consensus, and a sympathetic legislature did boost spending, modernize a corrupt bureaucracy, and bring a nineteenth-century school system into the twentieth century. However, even with all its advantages, KERA had little success in transforming education, producing long-term changes in school spending, or sustaining reforms that educators deemed unwelcome. In the other states, modest reform on even that scale proved unattainable.

The cases suggest a substantial gap between the rhetoric of adequacy proponents and the actual effects of the lawsuits. Proponents have explained that they are not simply seeking more money; instead, they want to ensure that states provide productive, efficient, and effective K–12 school systems. Recall the quote from plaintiff's attorney Alan Baron describing the ACLU suit in Maryland: "This suit is about output. Good education is more than a question of money." Adequacy impresario Michael Rebell has explicitly asserted, "More and more, these litigation efforts are tied to a basic political organizing campaign" and has even cited Maryland as one of two examples where simply filing a suit spurred reform.[98] However, the cases examined here raise doubts about the validity of such claims. After all, if Baltimore's failing schools and political paralysis represent the fruits of an effective organizing campaign, the prospects for such a tack appear dim.

The reality and appeal of adequacy suits are that their courtroom journey typically unites diverse education constituencies, all of which can agree on the desirability of more resources. Where earlier equity suits could draw fierce opposition from suburban districts that feared they would lose dollars, adequacy suits avoid identifying losers and make it less likely that concerted opposition will arise. Moreover, an emphasis on "effectiveness" makes adequacy more palatable to business interests and suburban voters than the earlier generation of purely redistributive equity cases.

The initial political success of adequacy suits, however, lasts only so long. The legislative aftermath—in which taxes must be raised, remedies must identify losers and winners, and serious efforts to reinvent the status quo imply disruptive reforms that require certain constituencies to swallow concentrated costs—is far more difficult. The result is an incentive to embrace accommodating measures that will not trigger opposition; this explains the preference of plaintiffs, courts, and legislators for broadly popular measures like general pay increases, preschool classes, construction, and professional development. To the extent that more controversial measures are proposed, as with the Kentucky accountability system, they appear to include significant safeguards for educators. The record also suggests that potentially disruptive features adopted in the aftermath of the adequacy decision are delayed, softened, or rescinded with time.

Finally, to put a finer point on the possibility that adequacy victories could weaken the case for disruptive change, consider the case of charter schooling, perhaps the most widely adopted disruptive reform of the past fifteen years. On this front, Ohio was significantly more active than the other three states. Ohio, with 255 charter schools in early 2005, had embraced charter schooling much more aggressively than Kentucky, which had none, and Maryland and New Jersey, which had one and fifty-two charter schools, respectively.[99] Meanwhile, some Kentucky observers suggested that popular reforms like site-based councils diminished support for disruptive reforms like charter schooling.[100] The case of charter schooling at least raises the question of whether adequacy litigation might be a balm that tempers more aggressive reform efforts. A similar point emerges with regard to Ohio school voucher legislation. Ohio vouchers were first introduced in Cleveland in 1995, and in 2005 the state adopted a new statewide voucher for students in schools that were persistently labeled as failing under Ohio's accountability system. The statewide voucher program could accommodate up to 14,000 students at an annual cost of up to $70 million. Again, the enactment of the Ohio voucher shortly after the state supreme court withdrew from the adequacy case raises questions about how litigation affects efforts to pursue disruptive reforms. The Ohio experience raises the possibility that disruptive reforms may be more politically palatable where adequacy-fueled accommodation is less prevalent.

Conclusion

Adequacy suits backed by a strong political coalition in favor of structural change do indeed have the potential to drive fundamental reform. Court orders "forcing" legislators to act, providing political cover, and promising additional resources could pry open a window of opportunity that helps a mobilized reform coalition to win deep-seated changes in how public schools are governed, managed, structured, and held accountable. However, to date, even adequacy suits hailed as "landmark" show little evidence of producing such change.

Adequacy champion Peter Schrag wryly conceded in 2003, "The battles of the past decades demonstrate . . . that the courts are rarely great places to make educational policy. They can declare a state fiscal structure unconstitutional and order the legislature to fix it, but where the political system is reluctant . . . that can be like trying to push string uphill."[101]

Scant research has explored the effects of adequacy litigation on attitudes toward schooling, and what is known about public opinion offers reason to question whether it will foster or retard substantive reform. Some evidence questions whether adequacy suits even have the potential to roil underlying political dynamics or spur public action. In Ohio, in fact, after a decade of litigation and a series of controversial state supreme court decisions, adults were still unsure as to whether the lawsuit existed. Other data, like the 2005 Phi Delta Kappa/Gallup poll, found that the public tends to finger a lack of spending as the nation's leading educational problem.[102] This line has enjoyed broad support among political elites, editorial boards, and education experts. At times, such sentiment may foster an emphasis on resources rather than results. For instance, a 1992 Kentucky survey asked respondents whether equal educational opportunity or high academic achievement was most important and found that 73 percent of respondents opted for equality over achievement.[103] Not only the public leadership but also the news coverage accompanying an adequacy decision may significantly affect public opinion in such cases. Preliminary data suggest that adequacy suits may focus newspaper coverage on inputs and thus distract public attention from issues like accountability or teacher quality.[104] It is at least possible that litigation may substitute legal appeals for political mobilization and hamper the formation of "reform" coalitions committed to disruptive change.

Because the general public has mixed feelings when it comes to disruptive reforms like establishing charter schools or linking teacher compensation to student performance but is receptive in principle to reforms like merit pay and increased school accountability, such a dynamic is no minor consideration.[105] The evidence suggests that the public is willing to contemplate aggressive reform but is quite eager to turn aside from conflictual or disruptive strategies. Adequacy suits seem to provide the public with just such an opportunity and excuse.

The window for transformational change opens not because educators are sweet-talked or browbeaten into going along, but because frustration with the status quo leads self-interested educators to prefer change, even with all its uncertainties. In any line of work, decisionmakers want to avoid unpopular decisions that anger employees or constituents. But radical change sometimes requires leaders to make painful choices: to fire a popular principal, terminate ineffective teachers, close a troubled school, or dismantle and then remake managerial operations. In each case, the easiest course is not to act. The way to compel action is to make inaction unpalatable.

The challenge for adequacy proponents is that the new money and the symbolic commissions, takeovers, new programs, and assessments their victories entail may have the effect of reassuring observers, soothing concerns, and making it easier for parties to push off tough decisions while leaving fundamental problems unaddressed. The result is that staggering dysfunction, incompetence, bureaucracy, and even corruption can remain largely unaddressed by "dramatic" reforms. There is reason to wonder whether adequacy victories may shift attention to inputs, undermine efforts to promote structural change, and erode the incentive for educators or education officials to contemplate disruptive reform.

The tendency for litigants to chalk ensuing disappointments up to "implementation problems" or "politicking" may well illustrate the limitation of their chosen remedy. In fall 2005 Bebe Verdery, education director for the ACLU in Maryland, shrugged off questions about the workability and coherence of the Baltimore governance reforms, declaring, "Children should not be part of a political football game. Both the city and the state have a role in ensuring the students get a quality education. I expect them to work more collaboratively than they have over the last couple of years, or the children will suffer."[106]

What would-be reformers of all stripes must confront is the frustrating reality that the provision of K–12 schooling is ultimately a product of democratic decisionmaking. Decades of experience have shown that the hardest part of school reform is not getting public officials to act, but getting them to act in a manner that displaces ineffective routines and overhauls anachronistic arrangements. Suits intended to force more money into that decisionmaking apparatus and change policy succeed to the extent that the dominant educational constituencies support implementation. Of course, those same constituencies tend to resist change they regard as "disruptive." Ultimately, then, if reformers believe that the K–12 status quo is fundamentally problematic, the courts are unlikely to provide much succor, unless the reformers work to build politically effective coalitions. Of course, the irony is that such success would likely render judicial intervention unnecessary, except as a lever for new spending.

Notes

1. Michael Rebell, "Why Adequacy Lawsuits Matter," *Education Week*, August 11, 2004, p. 40.

2. See Lawrence O. Picus, "Adequate Funding," in *School Spending: The Business of Education* (National School Boards Association, 2000) (www.asbj.com/schoolspending/picus. html [September 2006]).

3. Eric Hanushek, "Pseudo-Science and a Sound Basic Education," *Education Next* 5, no. 4 (Fall 2005): 67–73.

4. Peter Schrag, *Final Test: The Battle for Adequacy in America's Schools* (New York: New Press, 2003), pp. 9–11.

5. For the classic explanation of policy windows, see John W. Kingdon, *Agendas, Alternatives, and Public Policies* (Glenview, Ill.: Scott Foresman, 1984).

6. See Frederick M. Hess, *Spinning Wheels: The Politics of Urban School Reform* (Brookings, 1999).

7. Melissa C. Carr and Susan H. Fuhrman, "The Politics of School Finance in the 1990s," in *Equity and Adequacy in Education and Finance: Issues and Perspectives*, edited by Helen F. Ladd, Rosemary Chalk, and Janet S. Hansen (Washington: National Academy Press, 1999), p. 142.

8. Molly Burke and Michael Griffith, "School Funding Adequacy Cases," *State Notes: Finance/Litigation* (Education Commission of the States, February 2005) (www.ecs.org/ clearinghouse/59/07/5907.doc [December 2005]).

9. Rebell, "Why Adequacy Lawsuits Matter," p. 40.

10. See Daniel C. Vock, "Standards Push Helps Lawsuits," *Catalyst Chicago* (April 2004) (www.catalyst-chicago.org/arch/04-04/0404else.htm [December 2005]).

11. Reagan Walker, "Entire Kentucky's School System Is Ruled Invalid," *Education Week*, June 14, 1989 (www.edweek.org [December 2005]).

12. Carr and Fuhrman, "The Politics of School Finance in the 1990s," pp. 155–57.

13. *Rose* v. *Council for Better Education*, 790 S.W.2d 186, 198 (Ky. 1989).

14. Thomas D. Snyder and Charlene M. Hoffman, *1990 Digest of Education Statistics* (U.S. Department of Education, National Center for Education Statistics, 1990), table 12.

15. Snyder and Hoffman, *1990 Digest of Education Statistics,* tables 66, 155. The data presented in table 66 were originally from Carnegie Foundation for the Advancement of Teaching, *The Condition of Teaching: A State-by-State Analysis* (New York, 1988).

16. As said by Ray Corns, the circuit court judge who first declared the state's finance system to be unconstitutional in 1988, in Lonnie Harp, "After First Year, Ky. Reforms Called 'On the Move,'" *Education Week*, April 10, 1991 (www.edweek.org [December 2005]).

17. As said by Elissa Plattner, a long-time member of the Prichard Committee, a prominent and influential organization that focuses on Kentucky education reform issues, in Crystal Harden, "Dusting off the Armor," *Kentucky Post*, November 15, 2003.

18. Michael Paris, "Legal Mobilization and the Politics of Reform: Lessons from School Finance Litigation in Kentucky, 1984–1995," *Law and Social Inquiry* 26, no. 3 (Summer 2001): 649.

19. Reagan Walker, "Lawmakers in Ky. Approve Landmark School-Reform Bill," *Education Week*, April 4, 1990 (www.edweek.org [December 2005]).

20. Groups such as Families United for Morals in Education and Parents and Professionals Involved in Education expressed concerns that state curricula would teach their children "to embrace any lifestyle and support extreme environmentalism." Lonnie Harp, "The Plot Thickens," *Education Week*, May 18, 1994 (www.edweek.org [December 2005]).

21. Paris, "Legal Mobilization and the Politics of Reform," pp. 666–67.

22. Kentucky Legislative Research Commission, *A Citizen's Handbook: The Kentucky Education Reform Act* (Frankfort: Kentucky Legislative Research Commission, 1994).

23. Kentucky Department of Education, *Results Matter: A Decade of Difference in Kentucky's Public Schools, 1990–2000* (Lexington, 2000), p. vi.

24. "Budget Imperils Education Reform," *Lexington Herald Leader*, February 26, 1992, p. A6.

25. Lynn Olson, "From Risk to Reform: Kentucky Moves to Enact Reform Plan," *Education Week*, April 21, 1993 (www.edweek.org [December 2005]).

26. The poll reported that the percentage responding that "school councils work very/moderately well in improving teaching and learning" had increased among all answering groups. In the five-year period between 1994 and 1999, the percentage of principals answering this way grew from 75 to 82 percent, the percentage of teachers grew from 64 to 76 percent, and the percentage of parents grew from 63 to 64 percent. The poll was conducted by the Kentucky Institute for Education Research in November 1999 and cited in Kentucky Department of Education, *Results Matter*, p. 63.

27. Phone and e-mail correspondence with Dr. Robert Sexton, executive director of the Prichard Committee, September and December 2005.

28. Kentucky Legislative Research Commission, *A Citizen's Handbook*, p. 13.

29. See, for instance, Daniel M. Koretz and Sheila I. Barron, "The Validity of Gains in Scores on the Kentucky Instructional Results Information System (KIRIS)" (Santa Monica, Calif.: Rand Corporation, 1998) (www.rand.org/publications/MR/MR1014/#contents [December 2005]).

30. Kentucky Department of Education, "Commonwealth Accountability Testing System" (last updated May 21, 2005) (www.education.ky.gov/KDE/Administrative+Resources-Testing+and+Reporting+/CATS/default.htm [December 2005]).

31. Nancy C. Rodriguez, "Fiscal Trouble, Doubts Put School-Reward System at Risk," *Courier-Journal*, January 29, 2004, p. A1.

32. Ibid.

33. Ibid.

34. David J. Hoff, "Capitol Recap: Despite Rise in Spending, Reform Effort Takes Hits," *Education Week*, May 21, 2003 (www.edweek.org [December 2005]).

35. Rodriguez, "Fiscal Trouble, Doubts Put School-Reward System at Risk," p. A1.

36. Harden, "Dusting off the Armor."

37. Linda B. Blackford, "Superintendents Uneasy about Added Expenses," *Lexington Herald Leader*, January 17, 2002, p. B1.

38. Monica Richardson-Roberts, "March on Frankfort Set Feb. 12," *Lexington Herald Leader*, December 25, 2002, p. A1.

39. Lisa Deffendall, "Study: State Schools Need $740 Million," *Lexington Herald Leader*, April 4, 2003, p. B1.

40. *Abbott* v. *Burke*, 495 A.2d 376, 390 (N.J. 1985).

41. Margaret E. Goertz, "The Development and Implementation of the Quality Education Act of 1990" (Center for Educational Policy Analysis, 1992).

42. Peter Kerr, "Florio's Tax-Increase Plan Is Passed by Senate, 21-17," *New York Times*, June 21, 1990, p. B1.

43. Peter Kerr, "The 1990 Elections: New Jersey; A Governor's Response," *New York Times*, November 8, 1990, p. A1.

44. Anthony DePalma, "Anti-Tax Protesters Demand Florio's Recall, for Starters," *New York Times*, July 2, 1990, p. B4.

45. Barbara G. Salmore and Stephen A. Salmore, *New Jersey Politics and Government: Suburban Politics Comes of Age* (University of Nebraska Press, 1993).

46. Peter Kerr, "The 1990 Elections," p. A1.

47. Alexandra Greif, "Politics, Practicalities, and Priorities: New Jersey's Experience Implementing the *Abbott V* Mandate," *Yale Law and Policy Review* 22, no. 2 (Spring 2004): 623.

48. Douglas S. Reed, *On Equal Terms: The Constitutional Politics of Educational Opportunity* (Princeton University Press, 2001), p. 154.

49. Reed, *On Equal Terms*, p. 152.

50. Greif, "Politics, Practicalities, and Priorities," p. 656.

51. Philip E. Mackey, "New Jersey's Public Schools: A Biennial Report for the People of New Jersey, 2002–2003 Edition" (Public Education Institute, State University of New Jersey, Rutgers, September 2002) (www.policy.rutgers.edu/cgs/PDF/NJPS02.pdf [December 2005]), A.4.

52. Ibid., p. 21.

53. Dunstan McNichol, "Builders' Lobbyist Quits School Construction Board," *Star-Ledger*, September 23, 2005.

54. Dunstan McNichol and Steven Chambers, "Jersey's Schools of Hard Knocks," *Star-Ledger*, September 8, 2005.

55. John Mooney, "Corzine: School Program 'A Disgrace,'" *Star-Ledger*, September 9, 2005.

56. Greif, "Politics, Practicalities, and Priorities."

57. Bill Shralow and Frank Kummer, "Abbott Schools Make Strides on State Tests," *Courier-Post*, January 11, 2002.

58. Education Trust, "Achievement Gap Summary Tables," *Education Watch* (Spring 2004): 13–17.

59. Greif, "Politics, Practicalities, and Priorities."

60. Dana E. Sullivan, "Court Still Rides Herd on Abbott Plan," *New Jersey Lawyer* 14, no. 33 (August 15, 2005): 4.

61. Reed, *On Equal Terms*, p. 160.

62. Census Bureau, "Census 2000 Demographic Profile Highlights" (www.census.gov/main/www/cen2000.html [September 2006]) for Baltimore City, Maryland.

63. Michael Casserly, Jack Jepson, and Sharon Lewis, "Adequate Financing of Urban Schools: An Analysis of Funding of the Baltimore City Public Schools" (Council of the Great City Schools, January 2000) (www.cgcs.org/pdfs/BaltimoreFinanceReport.pdf [December 2005]), pp. 12–16.

64. *Hornbeck* v. *Somerset County Board of Education*, 295 Md. 597 458A.2d 758 (1983).

65. Jean Thompson, "Rawlings Again Proposes Money Squeeze on Schools," *Baltimore Sun*, March 15, 1995, p. B5.

66. *Bradford* v. *Maryland State Board of Education*, 94340058/CE 189672 (Circ. Ct. for Baltimore City, Oct. 1996).

67. Mike Bowler, "ACLU Sues State over School Funding," *Baltimore Sun,* December 7, 1994, p. B2.

68. Ibid.

69. In 1993–94, Baltimore City's total expenditures on public schools amounted to $639,683,000, and per-pupil spending was $5,471, as reported by Thomas D. Snyder, Charlene M. Hoffman, and Claire M. Geddes, *1997 Digest of Education Statistics* (U.S. Department of Education, National Center for Education Statistics, 1997), table 92.

70. Diane W. Cipollone, "Gambling on a Settlement: The Baltimore City Schools Adequacy Litigations," *Journal of Education Finance* 24, no. 1 (Summer 1998): 105.

71. See Thomas W. Waldron and William F. Zorzi Jr., "Blacks Denounce Schools Package," *Baltimore Sun,* April 4, 1997, p. A1.

72. Thomas Saunders, "Settling without 'Settling': School Finance Litigation and Governance Reform in Maryland," *Yale Law and Policy Review* 22, no. 2 (Spring 2004): 19.

73. The Thornton Commission on Education Finance, Equity, and Excellence, "Preliminary Report" (January 3, 2000), app. 1, exhibit 12; Thornton Commission on Education Finance, Equity, and Excellence, "Final Report" (January 18, 2003), sec. 2.6 and 3.3. Both are available at the Maryland State Archives (www.mdarchives.state.md.us/msa/mdmanual/26excom/defunct/html/13edfin.html [December 2005]).

74. Saunders, "Settling without 'Settling,'" p. 28.

75. The figure for Baltimore's 1998 per-pupil spending is from the Thornton Commission, "Preliminary Report," exhibit 12. All figures for 2003 per-pupil spending are from Census Bureau, *Federal, State, and Local Governments 2003 Public Elementary-Secondary Education Finance Data* (March 2005), table 17, fig. 4.

76. Liz Bowie and Tanika White, "710 City School Employees Get Notice of January 1 Layoffs," *Baltimore Sun*, November 26, 2003, p. A1.

77. John Gehring, "Looming Race Fuels Sniping over Baltimore Schools," *Education Week,* September 14, 2005, p. 8.

78. Thomas W. Waldron and William F. Zorzi Jr., "House Passes Measure on City Schools," *Baltimore Sun*, April 6, 1997, p. A1.

79. Jay Gillen, "Pay up, Maryland," *Baltimore Sun*, February 6, 2004, p. A17.

80. Mary E. Yakimowski and Carol L. Wilson, "Student Performance on the Maryland School Assessment Program: 1996–97 through 2001–02," report prepared for the Board of School Commissioners (Baltimore City Public School System, Division of Research, Evaluation, and Accountability, December 10, 2002).

81. Diana Jean Schemo, "Maryland Acts to Take over Failing Baltimore Schools," *New York Times*, March 30, 2006.

82. Nick Anderson, "Control of 11 Schools Seized," *Washington Post*, March 30, 2006, p. B1.

83. Vaishali Honawar, "Baltimore Takeovers Prevented," *Education Week,* April 19, 2006, p. 1.

84. Catherine Candisky, "School Funding: Where Is Ohio Headed?" *Columbus Dispatch,* March 30, 1997, p. B1.

85. Andrew Benson, "Ohio's School-Funding Dilemma: Is the Court on the Right Track?" *Columbus Dispatch,* May 15, 2000, p. A9.

86. William L. Phillis, "Ohio's School Funding Litigation Saga: More Money and Some New Buildings but the Same Unconstitutional School Funding Structure," *Journal of Education Finance* 30, no. 3 (Winter 2005): 313–20.

87. Ibid., p. 319.

88. Dennis J. Willard and Doug Oplinger, "Battle Is Still Raging, Leveling Up, Not Leveling Down," *Akron Beacon Journal,* March 25, 1997, p. D3.

89. Sandra K. McKinley, "The Journey to Adequacy: The DeRolph Saga," *Journal of Education Finance* 30, no. 4 (Spring 2005): 321–81.

90. Ibid., p. 322.

91. "Judicial Lawmaking High Court Wreaks Havoc in Ohio Schools," *Columbus Dispatch,* March 25, 1997, p. A14.

92. McKinley, "The Journey to Adequacy," p. 349.

93. Ibid., p. 377.

94. KnowledgeWorks Foundation, "Ohio's Education Matters: KnowledgeWorks Foundation 2001–02 Poll" (www.kwfdn.org/poll/2002/images/summary.pdf [December 2005]), pp. 31, 42.

95. Daniel Gursky, "Class Size Counts: The Research Shows Us Why," *American Teacher* (April 1998) (www.aft.org/topics/classsize/at98-sizecounts.htm [December 2005]).

96. NAACP, "Call for Action in Education" (October 2001) (www.naacp.org/inc/docs/education/education_call_to_actn_2.pdf [December 2005]), p. 11.

97. Frederick M. Hess, "A Political Explanation of Policy Selection: The Case of Urban School Reform," *Policy Studies Journal* 27, no. 3 (1999): 459–73.

98. Vock, "Standards Push Helps Lawsuits."

99. Center for Education Reform, "Charter Schools" (2005) (www.edreform.com/index.cfm?fuseAction=stateStatChart&psectionid=15&cSectionID=44 [December 2005]).

100. Nancy C. Rodriguez, "Kentucky Receives an 'A' on School Testing," *Courier-Journal,* January 8, 2004, p. B1.

101. Schrag, *Final Test,* p. 233.

102. Lowell C. Rose and Alex M. Gallup, "The 37th Annual Phi Delta Kappa/Gallup Poll of the Public's Attitudes toward the Public Schools," *Phi Delta Kappan* 7, no. 1 (September 2005): 41–57.

103. Reed, *On Equal Terms,* pp. 97–98.

104. Frederick M. Hess, *Stimulant or Salve? The Politics of Adequacy Implementation* (Harvard University, Kennedy School of Government, 2005), pp. 29, 43.

105. Rose and Gallup, "The 37th Annual Phi Delta Kappa/Gallup Poll," pp. 41–57.

106. Gehring, "Looming Race Fuels Sniping over Baltimore Schools," p. 8.

8

JOE WILLIAMS

The Non-Implementation
of New York's Adequacy Judgment

F OR AS LONG as newspapers have been cranking out front pages, there has
been a certain pressure on those who write the "first draft of history" to
publish accounts of verifiable happenings. Nearly every headline that has ever
been written implies that some sort of action has occurred: a hurricane ripped
through the Gulf Coast, a fire blazed its way through an apartment building, an
election was held in which voters selected one person over another to lead a
community. Very rarely are consumers of news media treated to accounts of
equally verifiable non-happenings. Not only does the proverbial tree that did
not fall in the forest not make much of a sound, but it also has about the same
chances of getting covered in the press as the rainstorm that never came, the airplane that did not crash, or the cure for cancer that has not yet been discovered.

For most segments of society, these ironclad rules of newsworthiness work
just fine. But in other subject areas, like education, the things that *don't* happen often are as important as the things that do. The conventional rules of
journalism, for example, make it difficult for news outlets to produce stories
about why kids are not performing on grade level, why school leaders are not
providing schools with the levels of support necessary for reform to take place,
and why the public is seemingly content to settle for education systems that
clearly are not getting the job done for millions of kids who need an education.

This chapter looks at one of the most noteworthy events in New York City
education that never happened: the distribution of billions of additional dollars in tax money to the city's 1.1 million–student school system. Despite a

court ruling requiring this massive infusion of cash to provide for an "adequate" education for the city's schoolchildren, a complicated set of factors has combined in the Empire State to create what has up to now been a stalemate of sorts. This stalemate, depending on your perspective, is viewed either as a welcome delay by fiscal conservatives, who have long argued that the *Campaign for Fiscal Equity* v. *State of New York* was an illogical and dangerously bad form of judicial intrusion, or as a frustrating exercise that has continued to delay the moment when justice will ultimately be served to the unfortunate students who have been denied a "sound basic education" by the city's school system.

To be sure, New York's case and the complicated factors affecting it have swirled in uncharted territory and have been difficult to comprehend, even for seasoned political and educational observers. "I didn't think that we would be at this point, so long after the judge's order, wondering what is going to happen," said Diana Fortuna, of the Citizens Budget Commission, at a June 2005 forum on the case that was sponsored by the Manhattan-based education advocacy group PENCIL. Remarked Michael Rebell, the attorney who filed the original lawsuit seeking additional funding for city schools, in comments to reporters in September 2005: "We want this matter resolved . . . If we have to wait for a new governor in 2007 it will mean the schoolchildren will have had to have waited another year."

Simply put, the politics that lead to legal decisions regarding school adequacy can become so complicated that they contribute to a political climate that makes settling these cases difficult, if not impossible. Rifts can open up within the adequacy coalition, as the focus shifts from proving "inadequacy" to determining precisely how much money will correct the problem, who should get their hands on that money, and what it should be used to fund. In addition, the adequacy coalition in cases like New York's has itself been forced to contend with an increasingly fragmented political system that has trouble paying its existing bills, much less supporting massive and sudden increases in school spending. As a result, the promised windfall of new school cash becomes a doubtful reality, along with the reforms the adequacy lawsuit was intended to unleash.

One's views of this particular case, for reasons that are fully explained elsewhere in this chapter, often are influenced by the geographic vantage point one assumes at the start. In New York City, for example, there has been a relatively widespread willingness to concentrate on the potential funding increase for city schools and the shortcomings it might resolve. Outside of the city, the case has raised more questions about what will happen to funding streams for other school districts as a result of the case, not to mention the potential impact of any significant new school spending on programs like Medicaid, capital improvements to the subway system, and other significant portions of an already cash-strapped state budget.

Background

Like all adequacy cases nationwide, the Campaign for Fiscal Equity (CFE) case in New York has been about one thing: money. Although it has indirectly touched on issues like facilities and access to qualified teachers, from the outset all of these issues have been linked back to the concept of resources and whether or not they are adequate for the delivery of a constitutionally guaranteed "sound basic education." What has made New York's case worth watching is the eye-popping amount of dollars being touted. On February 14, 2005, state supreme court justice Leland DeGrasse, who had overseen the case from the beginning, awarded the city a staggering $5.6 billion more per year for its schools, a 43 percent increase to the city's $12.9 billion school budget, an amount that would raise per-pupil spending to more than $18,000 a year and make New York City's huge school district (with more than a third of the children in the state) among the richest in the state, if not the country. (In fact, it would propel per-pupil spending to the top 3 percent of districts nationwide.)

While the players in this multibillion-dollar drama wrangled over DeGrasse's order in the winter of 2005, the question at the heart of the New York case was the one debated across the country: Will more money improve children's education or simply feed an already bloated and ineffectual bureaucracy? How much is enough? Does money buy adequacy? Just as important were debates that played out locally about the role of the courts in establishing policies regarding state spending and specifically questions about whether the governor and legislature could be forced to make major policy decisions that were ordered by the court.

These questions were complicated further by New York State's precarious financial situation at the time of the decision, with a projected $6 billion structural deficit and the failure of legislators to identify potential areas for budget cuts. In fact, while the *Campaign for Fiscal Equity* v. *State of New York* poses the question of adequacy with characteristically New York bluntness and extravagance, many wonder whether the case has become a victim of those excesses and, during the twelve-year brawl over the merits of linking financial input with academic output, been overtaken by events.

Much has changed since the fledgling CFE, fourteen New York City community school boards, and twenty-three individual parents and their children lodged the initial complaint charging the state of New York with denying "thousands of public school students in the City of New York their constitutional rights to equal educational opportunities." Indeed, the city's fiscal disadvantage in 1993 was clear to everyone: its schoolchildren received some 12 percent fewer dollars than their counterparts elsewhere in the state; 11.8 percent of the city's teachers were not certified, compared with 7.3 percent statewide; the city's students had one computer for every nineteen students, compared with one for every thirteen students statewide; there was one guidance counselor for every 700 city students, compared with one per 350 students in the rest of the state; there were 16.5 library books per pupil in the state, but only 10.4 in the city. In the year preceding the suit, New York City, which then had 37 percent of the state's students, received less than 35 percent of the state's education dollars; the city got some $3,000 per student, while areas outside of New York got $3,400 on average.

The bottom line, said the plaintiffs, was that the state aid formula for school districts (at the time the state provided 42 percent of the total spent by the districts) was "an incoherent, unsystematic aggregation of approximately 50 different formulas" that were "reformulated each year." It was a poorly kept secret that the governor and the state's two top legislative leaders sat down each year with a spending scheme that met their political needs and then came up with funding streams to provide the same result.

While the plaintiff's name, Campaign for Fiscal Equity, suggests that the case is somehow about equity, New York's court of appeals, the state's highest appeals court, had rejected equity as grounds for reforming education finance in 1982 (in *Levittown* v. *Nyquist*), concluding that the state's constitution did not require equitable funding of schools across the state.[1] But as CFE and its lead attorney, Michael Rebell, knew, the court had left a door open: the possibility of reconsidering that ruling if the state's financing system was shown to have "gross and glaring inadequacy." Expressed positively, the court laid down a new constitutional standard: a sound basic education. (As proof of the vicissitudes of the judicial enterprise, the actual article in the state constitution that formed the basis of this conclusion, and the Herculean struggles surrounding the CFE suit, contains these twenty-six words: "The legislature shall provide for the maintenance and support of a system of free common schools, wherein all the children of this state may be educated." The phrase "sound basic education" was introduced later by the Court of Appeals as an explanation of what the constitution requires.)

Although the distinction between equity and adequacy would become more significant in later years, in 1993 few education observers would dispute CFE's list of the education crimes perpetrated on New York City's schoolchildren or the incoherence of the system that delivered them. Still, it took two years before the Court of Appeals ruled that CFE's complaints met the adequacy standard (questioning that the state provided a sound basic education) and six more years to bring the case to trial. When DeGrasse finally ruled in CFE's favor, declaring New York State's system of education financing to be unconstitutional, on January 10, 2001, school advocates, politicians, and the teacher union celebrated a victory they were sure would bring a bundle of cash to the city's struggling schools.

But something happened on the way to the chancery—something more than just the back-and-forth struggles between contending parties arguing and appealing and rearguing. Inequity was one thing. The difference between ten library books and sixteen was clear. But were sixteen adequate for a sound basic education, or were ten enough? Or should there be twenty? Beyond those questions was a portal leading through the looking glass.

In fact, those questions had been all but cast aside during the country's headlong pursuit of academic results and student outcomes in the previous decade. Between 1993 and 2005, the "no-more-excuses" standards and accountability movements swept through the education establishment, culminating with the passage (381-41 in the House and 87-10 in the Senate) of the federal No Child Left Behind Act in 2001. In New York not only was a different governor in the statehouse—a Republican—but he had pushed through a charter school bill and was now serving his third four-year term. The key players in the state's Education Department, including its commissioner, had all been replaced; the new administrators were issuing challenging curriculum standards, requiring new statewide tests, and demanding more accountability.

The changes in New York City were even more dramatic, especially on the financial front. The long-standing practice whereby the city received a disproportionately small share of state aid had been reversed, with the city receiving 37.1 percent of state education dollars in 2004–05, despite enrolling only 36.5 percent of the state's students. In fact, the state's payments to New York City schools had increased faster than the city's own contributions to its schools: a 289 percent increase from the state, or more than $4 billion a year, compared with the city's 127 percent increase, between 1982 and 2001. In the previous ten years alone, the state had increased education spending overall some 60 percent.

Twelve years after the CFE suit—and without a penny from it—the city was spending some $13,600 per student, about $100 above the state average, which was already the highest in the nation, and more than $5,000 above the national average. In fact, between 1997 and 2004 alone, the city schools' annual budget increased more than $6 billion.

On the governance front, the state legislature granted control of the city's 1,300 public schools to Republican mayor Michael Bloomberg in 2002. Bloomberg hired a prominent litigator and former White House lawyer, Joel Klein, to implement a broad set of structural and curriculum reforms called Children First. In many respects, the New York City school system that existed when the CFE case was originally launched, some argued, was a relic of the past.

What had not changed, it appeared, were the academic numbers: the city's dropout rate, over 11 percent, was more than four times greater than the state average, and only 47 percent of its fourth graders passed the state's English language arts exam in 2001–02. This was 24 percentage points below the pass rate in the rest of the state. As New York City councilwoman Eva Moskowitz noted in a 2005 letter to Justice DeGrasse, "Education spending has increased by about a third since I took office in 1999, yet our schools have not improved by a third."

DeGrasse's 2001 ruling in the CFE case established that the city's students were not receiving a sound basic education as stipulated in the state constitution and placed the blame squarely on the state's method of funding the schools. Governor George Pataki appealed, and an intermediate appeals court overturned the decision, ruling that a decent education only amounted to being taught on an eighth- or ninth-grade level.

But the plaintiffs—the Campaign for Fiscal Equity—persisted, and on June 26, 2003, the Court of Appeals found the state's school aid formula to be unconstitutional because city schools were left with less money than necessary to provide students with what they need for the real world. Wrote Chief Judge Judith Kaye, "Tens of thousands of students are placed in overcrowded classrooms, taught by unqualified teachers, and provided with inadequate facilities and equipment. The number of children in these straits is large enough to represent a systemic failure." Even critics of the lawsuit did not quibble with the extent of the problem. Still, they argued that spending was neither the cause of nor the solution to what ailed the city's 1,300 public schools.

While it may never be known how many of the spending and reform changes that were introduced in the city over the course of the lawsuit were made because of the threat posed by the lawsuit, the CFE case highlights, if nothing else, the many—and many significant—contending powers that locked horns in the legal and political battle that played out. This was a heavyweight contest, with extravagant resources in all corners and no one willing to take a technical knockout.

The CFE

Founded in 1993 by Robert Jackson, who was then president of one of the city's thirty-two community school boards, and Michael A. Rebell, the attorney for the same school board, the organization's own name obscures the nature of the case it successfully argued. Equity is a concrete concept that the public can easily grasp and monitor. Anyone can look at a list of per-pupil spending by the state and local municipalities and be armed for a debate about whether all students are backed by the same resources. Adequacy is considerably more complicated. Still, the CFE was often able to point to myriad examples of ways in which city students were being denied access to the kinds of learning and equipment that were commonplace elsewhere in the state, and the case resonated with many New Yorkers.

The organization's name is not its only area of conflict in the case. Even though the lawsuit sought more money specifically for city schools, the Campaign for Fiscal Equity's articulated mission is to secure adequate funding for all students in the state, not just to settle the New York City case. "We are committed to a statewide remedy," Rebell said in the fall of 2004, as the legislature and the plaintiffs were attempting to negotiate a settlement in the case. CFE leaders argued that a statewide remedy was one way to build support for the cause among upstate legislators, who otherwise would not be inclined to support dumping more cash in the city.

Starting as a small shop to coordinate the legal case, CFE eventually grew to become an impressive organization, taking in more than $7.4 million in contributions and grants between 1999 and 2003, according to tax records. Among those who opened their wallets to the cause: the Atlantic Philanthropies, the Ford Foundation, the Bill and Melinda Gates Foundation, the Robin Hood Foundation, and the Rockefeller Foundation. The CFE employs a small army of staff people with an eye toward working with districts statewide and across the nation. The lawsuit they are trying to settle, however, only resulted in a court order to increase funding levels in the city.

Although it received pro bono legal help, that help was from Simpson, Thacher, and Bartlett, a 122-year-old, seventy-five-lawyer firm with a midtown Manhattan address and a laundry list of affluent corporate clients. The CFE's board of directors included a former city borough president, a former chancellor of the state Board of Regents, and two former members of the Board of Regents. Among its advisory board were education celebrities like Linda Darling-Hammond (Stanford education professor), Harold Levy and Frank Macchiarola (former city school chancellors), Deborah Meier (author and educator), Thomas Sobol (former state commissioner of education), and Randi Weingarten (president of the United Federation of Teachers).

These were the kinds of people whose involvement in schooling issues transcended the typical revolving-door style of leadership that plagued the top of the school system's administration. Thus an appellate court reversal of DeGrasse's 2001 ruling was only a minor setback, as CFE pursued an appeal and won. The Court of Appeals weighed in again, this time with a ruling that ordered the state to determine the cost of a sound basic education in New York City and make sure to provide it. It gave the state until July 30, 2004, to come up with a number.

By now it was clear that the case had nothing to do with equity and little to do with changing the way education is delivered to children. And so the argument shifted, with some finality, to the ambiguous standard of adequacy. The difficulty in defining that term was a clear invitation to the forces driving politics in New York to continue the fight. And in New York fashion, the fight was anything but genteel.

The court, moving forward, ordered the state by July 30, 2004, to determine the actual cost of a sound basic education in New York City and to alter its school aid formula to bring spending in the city immediately up to that level. The deadline came and went, with no agreement between the governor and the legislature on how to proceed. DeGrasse responded by creating his own panel to "ascertain the actual cost of providing a sound basic education in New York City."

By this time, it had long been clear that education reform was not what this case was about. In fact, at one point during testimony before the referees, in the fall of 2004, lawyers for the city requested that the panel include a recommendation for the legislature to remove a statutory cap limiting the number of charter schools in the state, arguing that charter schools were one part of its strategy for overhauling the city's school system. William Thompson, a retired judge who was serving on the referee panel, dismissed the request, saying, "This is about money."

Both the CFE and the state, to their collective credit, developed accountability plans to accompany new cash for city schools. Those plans ultimately were ignored by both the referees and DeGrasse. A panel appointed by Governor Pataki, for example, recommended changes to the state's Wicks laws pertaining to costly bidding procedures for school construction projects. The panel also set the state's tenure laws for teachers and principals in its sights and even took on the issue of the monopoly of teacher certification, using the possibility of a CFE settlement as a wedge to broaden the entry points to the teaching profession. The governor's panel also addressed issues such as giving control to the mayors of the five largest cities. For its part, the CFE recommended that any settlement should examine all existing "statutory, regulatory, and contractual impediments to providing a sound basic education and concerted efforts to negotiate new ways to promote policy initiatives, while recognizing employee job protection needs in the changed constitutional context." The CFE also called for an overhaul of information systems to make it easier to track student performance accurately.

Even the state's Court of Appeals stressed in the case that school management structures should be altered to make them more accountable for student learning and for more efficient school spending. Both DeGrasse and his judicial referees showed that they were sticking to William Thompson's guiding philosophy that this case ultimately was not about reforming schools but rather about sending them more money. Neither the referees' recommendations nor DeGrasse's final order set guidelines for accountability measures or managerial reforms, leaving both up to the stalemated legislature to figure out.

The process of determining what a sound basic education was, much less how much it should cost, seemed equal parts science and voodoo. As the consultants who provided the plaintiffs' analysis explained, their job was to "identify and measure the impact of the major, systematic factors that underlie the variations in costs of achieving a specific set of outcome standards across the schools in New York State." This meant that "state aid that districts receive should be sufficient to provide an opportunity for all of its students to meet the Regents Learning Standards and should be adjusted for variations in educational costs that are essentially beyond the control of local school districts."

Such "costing out" analysis was done in two basic ways: the professional judgment method and the successful schools method. The former asks educators (the professionals) to construct an adequate school budget from the bottom up; the latter applies the observed spending levels in high-performing districts to low-performing districts. Although neither method offers much in the way of credibility from the perspective of a causal relationship, plenty of numbers can be fed into many different calculations. And so the plaintiffs and defendants did.

Using the successful schools model, the state's analysts determined that it would cost $14.55 billion to deliver a sound basic education to New York City's students, $1.93 billion more than was currently being spent.

The referees disagreed. They accepted the analysis of the plaintiffs' consultants, who used a combination of approaches, and on November 30, 2004, issued a fifty-seven-page report concluding that it would take $5.63 billion more state aid each year to make New York City schools "adequate." They also determined that the city required an additional one-time infusion of $9.2 billion to build and repair school facilities. As mentioned, even setting aside the money for facilities, these numbers would drive the city's per-pupil spending to over $18,000 per student per year. And they formed the basis of Justice DeGrasse's Valentine's Day ruling. (Also staggering was the $353,000 bill submitted by the referees: public service that amounted to $500 per billable hour for each referee.)

To some, the CFE case had become an irrelevancy, with the original complaints swept aside by twelve years of massive education reform in New York and the nation. For the plaintiffs, it was quite the opposite. And the Campaign for Fiscal Equity continued to express its intention to secure adequate funding for students throughout the state.

City versus Statewide Interests

It has widely been assumed for several years that the fastest and most desirable way to end the CFE case would be to reach a settlement between all of the parties. Such a settlement would eliminate the potential for more drawn-out litigation that would prolong any remedy and would allow elected officials, who are theoretically accountable to voters, to make the actual spending and policy decisions rather than the court. Such a settlement, which continued to be something the parties sought even after DeGrasse's order, would conceivably involve less money, some sort of accountability, and a shared payment plan involving both the city and state. It also likely would include a statewide change in the state's school funding formula that would reduce the chances that other districts around the state would file adequacy lawsuits of their own.

To get a sense for how heated the issue became among those charged with negotiating it, consider what state senator Joe Bruno had to say outside a teacher union gathering at the capital in April 2005. Suggesting that the task of legislating ought to be left to legislators who are accountable to voters, Bruno lashed out at DeGrasse and the judicial referees in the case: "These people are grandiose in what they propose, and they're not specific, and then they leave it with us, and it's all over the place . . . I think it's going to go on forever in the courts. The bottom line is to get money to the schools—not to litigate."[2]

A settlement between the state and New York City would be difficult enough by itself, sources in the state capital have said, but the lingering possibility that most other school districts outside the city would be able to use the case as a precedent for their own adequacy lawsuits made it impossible for the legislature to cough up the money without a fight.

Even some of its allies in the city, including parent activists, complained that CFE's insistence on a statewide solution, while noble on its face, lessened the odds that the city would ever see the billions of dollars being dangled in front of its face by friendly courts, because tax money that could be coming to the city would have to be shared with other "underfunded" districts statewide. CFE leaders have countered that this is one way to build support for the cause among upstate legislators, who would otherwise not be inclined to support dumping more cash in the city.

Using the formula for determining the cost of an adequate education that was accepted by the judicial referees, CFE has estimated that 517 of the state's 698 school districts were funded at inadequate levels and, conceivably, would be entitled to a corresponding bump in state aid. Some speculated that this could increase the state's obligation by another $3 billion to $4 billion a year. With this reality looming over the heads of legislators, who were already looking at a projected $6 billion deficit in the state budget, it becomes easier to understand why a costly settlement with the city has been so elusive. The precedent alone could cost billions beyond what makes its way to city coffers if those other districts were to sue and win. As David Ernst, a spokesman for the New York State School Boards Association, put it, "There will be CFE clone suits on behalf of the other high-needs districts in the state."

Indeed, in 2005, CFE representatives toured the state, pitching the potential windfall for small, "underfunded," upstate communities. "We are at a historic moment in time," Rebell told a crowd in Binghamton, estimating that the upstate community stood to gain $39 million, or 147 percent, over four years.[3] The CFE tour also touted, and was able to get sponsored, legislation known as the Schools for New York's Future Act, which called for a base level of funding for every student in the state, along with adjustments for the cost of education.

What Is the City's Responsibility?

Given control of the city's schools in 2002, Mayor Bloomberg stands to win billions of dollars for education on his watch, but he has alienated even the plaintiffs in the case at times by arguing that the city should not be forced to increase its own contributions to bring school spending to adequate levels. (The special masters in the case left it to the legislature to decide how much of the spending increase should come from the city's budget, an omission that many supporters of CFE found to be disappointing for its failure to eliminate a significant stumbling block.) In arguments before Justice DeGrasse in January 2005, the city's corporate counsel, Michael Cardozo, went as far as suggesting that the city might not want any of the $5.6 billion annual spending increase if it was forced to pay any share of it. "If we have to pay any portion of this, no thanks," Cardozo told DeGrasse.

Bloomberg himself warned that if the city had to pay, it would likely come at the expense of after-school programs, libraries, and other essential city services that he would be forced to cut. The mayor described it as "robbing Peter to pay Paul." Said the mayor, "Such actions would harm the very children this lawsuit is designed to help."[4]

The CFE, working closely with the city on a settlement, called the city's position "untenable" and called for the city to contribute up to 25 percent of the new spending. "The idea of no thanks is O.K. for the mayor, but it's not O.K. for the children," said Joseph Wayland, a partner at Simpson, Thacher, and Bartlett, who represents the CFE.

Currently, the city's Independent Budget Office estimates that the city pays only 40 percent of the cost for local schools. The state picks up 45 percent of the tab, and the remainder comes from the federal government. Even with the city picking up just a quarter of whatever new spending results from the CFE case, the state's share of school funding would increase sharply, making its funding of city schools inequitable compared with that of the rest of the state. As it already stands, New York City schools in 2005–06 got 37.1 percent of the state's education aid, despite enrolling only 36.5 percent of the state's students, according to figures provided by Governor Pataki's budget office. What's more, the state's payments to New York City schools have increased much faster than the city's contributions over the last two decades. Between 1982 and 2001, state aid to the city increased 289 percent, or more than $4 billion a year. For the same time period, the city's share rose only 127 percent. Municipalities outside the city saw their contributions to local schools increase by an average of 160 percent for the same time period.[5]

The mayor's posturing over the city's ability to pay was itself tricky politically. Heading toward reelection in November 2005, Bloomberg sought to portray himself as a strong manager who helped the city to turn the corner from the economic crisis it faced after the September 11, 2001, attacks on lower Manhattan. Bloomberg's argument that the city could not afford to pay a penny more for its schools not only conflicted with the message he was sending that the budget was fiscally sound but also put him in the hot seat among parents and school employees for his enthusiastic support of massive development projects like a new stadium for the New York Jets on Manhattan's west side. The stadium would require $600 million in public subsidies—again, at a time when Bloomberg was arguing that no more money was available for schools.

But the mayor's position was more than just political posturing regarding the budget. After all, he had promised to reform the city's schools with radical management and organizational change if he were given control over them. And as he geared up to run for a second term, he was claiming success: the city's schools had been fundamentally reformed, and dramatic educational changes were under way, his campaign argued. He had never said a radical transformation required billions more per year when he asked to be held responsible for the fate of the city's schoolchildren.

In fact, Bloomberg originally argued that better use of existing resources was the key. "If I can show that in a very diverse inner city we can take the resources and apply them better and focus better and not just keep adding money but really try to say this is what we're going to do and hold ourselves accountable— if I can do that, then not only will I have done something for New York City, but New York City will have done something for the rest of the country and maybe the rest of the world," Bloomberg told 60 Minutes in April 2003.

The mayor's school reforms, called Children First, supposedly restructured the system's entire $15 billion budget around meeting the needs of students. The campaign message was that good things were starting to happen in the schools. This optimistic positioning ran counter to the core of CFE's legal argument: that spending in city schools was so low that a sound basic education was not achievable. The essence of the legal case was the notion that the only thing preventing students from learning in New York City was a few billion dollars a year and that, without an infusion of cash, meaningful reform could not be achieved. Essentially, Bloomberg was arguing that he had made changes that the plaintiffs contended in court were not possible without billions more in spending.

All of this was further complicated by the issue of victimization. The CFE case was built on the notion that the city's 1.1 million schoolchildren were the victims of a system that failed to provide them with an adequate education, and yet the remedy from the court provided direct relief not to those child victims, but to the same school system that presided over their victimization in the first place. Because New York City's long history of corruption and mismanagement of schools was considered inconsequential in the case, the entire ruling left doubts among many New Yorkers about the reasonableness of the judicial remedy.

It is easy to understand why Bloomberg felt a need to join the CFE bandwagon in demanding billions more per year for his schools. Not doing so would have left him extremely vulnerable to political attacks from Democratic opponents who generally accept without question the argument that the state has shortchanged the city's schools (and its labor unions).

But the tension in the CFE case was not just between the city and the state. The city also butted heads with its partner, CFE, and the lawyers for the state over the issue of accountability in the case. Part of the argument in favor of giving statutory control of the schools to the mayor in 2002 was that it would finally create clear lines of accountability in a massive school system in which authority was so diffused that it was systemically unresponsive. The state had concerns that giving billions of dollars to the city with no strings attached was dangerous and irresponsible. The city argued that mayoral control would ultimately allow the voters to decide whether the mayor had made good use of the money. "I don't think you can make a good case that we need another level of accountability or oversight," Bloomberg told the special masters in the case in 2004. "If anything, I would argue that we have too much now." The conflict was a major sticking point in negotiations between the parties to reach a settlement.

The city's position in the CFE case was further complicated by Chancellor Klein's involvement as an attorney in the 1980s in a school equity lawsuit in Missouri. Representing the state, Klein argued at the time that more money was not the answer to the education problem.[6] Klein and his administrative team in New York City nonetheless pressed hard publicly for the additional funding, even framing it as a civil rights issue. "This is not a question of policy. It is a question of constitutional law," Klein told legislators in April 2004, warning that if they failed to deliver new cash to the city's schools, he would be in court "cheek by jowl with the plaintiffs."[7]

To create pressure on the state to settle the case, school administrators created a $13 billion capital plan that was passed by the city council in June 2004, even though it relied on half of the bill to be paid by the state as part of the CFE settlement and despite strong indications from some legislators that the case would never be settled within the five-year time frame for the capital plan. (Senate Education Committee chairman William Saland, an upstate Republican, for example, told business leaders in a 2003 speech that it would take decades to settle and that no one in the current legislature would be alive to see the settlement in the case.) By promising billions of dollars' worth of new school construction projects and repairs in communities around the city, Bloomberg and Klein were setting up the state for taking the blame if those projects never materialized.

Both Sides of Pataki's Mouth

Because it is the governor who proposes the state's annual budget (and has veto power over it), the third-term governor has largely assumed the role of "the state of New York" in the case, even though any settlement would also require the legislature's approval. Like Bloomberg, politics has also forced Governor Pataki into taking contradictory positions at times regarding schools and money. Although he has argued that the problem with the city's schools is not a lack of money but a lack of managerial safeguards, he also has taken credit for "massive increases" to education budgets as proof that he has supported educational improvement. On unveiling his proposed state budget in January, for example, aides to the governor noted that, with the $526 million increase he proposed for education, the total amount spent on schools will have risen more than $6 billion a year—or 61 percent—since 1994–95. The same governor who argued that money does not matter was bragging about how much money he had chipped in over the years.

Unlike Bloomberg, whose interests are more narrow in comparison, Pataki must represent the interests of the entire state in attempting to resolve the case. He has continually called for reforms to the overall state funding formula, changes that ultimately could result in less money for New York City than promised by the court but additional funding statewide. But his negotiators consistently have floated plans that were backed by considerably less funding than CFE and its supporters were seeking.

On a practical level, the governor's staff has been mindful of the costly statewide precedent that would be established by any settlement with the city that relied on a costing out formula that could also be applied to other districts. Politically, Pataki has been forced to look after the needs of Republican-friendly upstate voters who tend to view New York City as a bottomless pit for tax money. Put in these contexts, it is easy to understand how doing nothing in the case becomes an appealing option for a politician in Pataki's shoes.

The backdrop for all of this tension is the projected $6 billion deficit the state is facing in its $105 billion budget. Even without a few billion more for the state's share of the CFE case, closing a gap of this magnitude would require a level of sacrifice heretofore unknown in the state capital. The political pressure to protect other big-ticket items like Medicaid makes the situation even more dire. The Metropolitan Transit Authority (MTA), in particular, which is controlled by the governor, was poised to compete with the CFE for massive infusions of state funding. The MTA, which includes the city's subways and buses, the Long Island Railroad, and MetroNorth Railroad, among other transit entities, originally asked for $27.7 billion for its five-year capital budget starting in fiscal 2006. State controller Alan Hevesi, at a December 2004 summit on education funding sponsored by the Citizens Budget Commission, remarked that legislators would be forced to tighten their belts as never before to pay for all the bills that were coming due. "I don't know how we're going to do it," Hevesi said.

Making things even more interesting throughout the case, Pataki's interests have been represented by the New York Attorney General's Office, whose boss, Eliot Spitzer, went on to be elected governor in November 2006.

One example of what some considered the utter frustration felt by participants in the case—and what others considered a sign that the CFE was a less than noble adversary in negotiations—came in 2005 shortly after DeGrasse's ruling, when city councilman Robert Jackson, one of the original CFE plaintiffs, twice called Governor Pataki a jackass during a widely covered press conference, holding up a picture of the governor with devil horns superimposed over his head.

The Legislature

Aside from the fact that New York's state legislature is widely regarded as one of the most ineffective forms of government in American history, a host of other conflicts have also contributed to the stalemate. Senate president Joe Bruno, an upstate Republican, has tended to align with Pataki and others who are interested in finding a statewide solution to funding formulas that neither results in tax increases nor breaks the bank. Assembly speaker Sheldon Silver, a Manhattan Democrat tightly aligned with the teacher union, was said to be willing to allow negotiations with Bruno and Pataki to fall apart, if necessary. He understood that a friendly city judge would be likely to order more funding than upstate Republicans would ever agree to on their own. At one point during the stalled talks in 2004, *New York Sun* columnist Jack Newfield referred to the two legislative leaders, the governor, and the mayor as "The Four Horsemen of Paralysis."

Such was the stalemate between these elephantine contenders that the courtroom erupted in laughter in January 2005 after DeGrasse asked the lawyers in the case about the likelihood that the state would file an appeal. And, a week later, answering the question once and for all, Pataki proposed a state budget that all but ignored the payments required in the CFE case. The governor's office eventually filed an appeal of DeGrasse's order, an appeal the CFE regarded as little more than a delaying tactic. A year later, in 2006, Pataki signed off on his final budget as governor, sending $4.7 billion in state-backed financing to the city to help meet Mayor Bloomberg's school construction costs (which essentially met the mandates of CFE for facilities funding) and increasing state operating aid to the city's schools by approximately $400 million (which was well shy of the $5.6 billion called for in DeGrasse's order.) The state's appeal of DeGrasse's order was struck down by the mid-level appellate division on March 23, 2006. The judges ordered that the state needed to ensure that between $4.7 billion and $5.63 billion more per year was spent on city schools. That decision was appealed to the state's highest court, which ruled on November 20, 2006, that DeGrasse's use of the high $5.63 billion costing out estimate was inappropriate. The Court of Appeals ruled that the state should increase spending for city schools by at least $1.93 billion instead, the lower of the two costing out estimates and less than even Pataki had proposed in previous negotiations.

Justice DeGrasse

Justice DeGrasse, meanwhile, has attempted to walk a fine line between showing the state he means business (by ordering that the state simply cough up the additional funding) and setting the stage for a constitutional battle that might overturn his order or, even in the best-case scenario, prolong its implementation for the foreseeable future while the case is being appealed. Lawyers for the state have consistently argued that only the legislature may legislate and that the judge was overstepping his boundaries by threatening to issue a specific remedy for the city schools. DeGrasse's only possible response to government inaction in the case was the court order, which was widely known would trigger an appeal from the state and lead to more delays.

Because of this, the city, state, and CFE have attempted to reach a settlement on their own to avoid a drawn-out appeal on the constitutionality of a judge setting spending levels for a government entity. The parties reported that they were close to a settlement over the Thanksgiving weekend in 2004, but the city would not budge from its position that the state should shoulder the bulk of the cost and that the city should be given the latitude to spend the money as it saw fit.

Further complicating the issue for the Republican governor (and the Republican-controlled state Senate) is the reality that DeGrasse himself is a creature of the local Democratic Party machine. Judges in New York City are placed on the ballot by local party leaders and generally run unopposed. When it came time to appoint a panel of three special masters to make recommendations in the case, DeGrasse appointed three Democrats, one of whom, William Thompson Sr., is the father of city controller William Thompson, a former Board of Education president who has his eye on the mayor's office.

Whether city schools will ever see the billions of dollars in new funding promised by the CFE case is anyone's guess. Where once there was hope that the Campaign for Fiscal Equity case would radically alter the way education is delivered in the city, critics have argued that crucial issues like accountability, choice, and much-needed changes to bargaining contracts have been virtually swept aside by New York–style interest group politics. After more than a decade of legal wrangling, including stacks of constitutional briefs, expert testimony, dueling costing out studies, and the like, one of the most significant school adequacy cases in American history has been reduced to little more than a wire transfer.

Notes

1. *Levittown Union Free School District* v. *Nyquist*, 57 N.Y.2d 27 (N.Y. 1982).

2. Joe Mahoney, "Bruno Slams Judge, Suit on School Funding," *New York Daily News*, April 6, 2005, p. 44.

3. George Basler, "Group Seeks More Aid for Schools," *Binghamton Press and Sun Bulletin*, April 22, 2005, p. A1.

4. Adam L. Cataldo, "Panel: NY Should Boost NYC Funds," *Bond Buyer*, December 1, 2004, p. 1.

5. Raymond Domanico, "No Strings Attached? Ensuring That 'CFE' Funds Are Spent Effectively," *Civic Report* [Manhattan Institute for Policy Research] 42 (July 2004).

6. Sol Stern, "Potemkin Education Reform," *City Journal*, November 17, 2004.

7. Carl Campanile, "Klein Tells Albany: Pay up or I'll Sue," *New York Post*, April 14, 2004, p. 2.

9

CHRISTOPHER BERRY

The Impact of School Finance Judgments on State Fiscal Policy

B EGINNING WITH CALIFORNIA'S *Serrano* v. *Priest* in 1971, the constitutionality of school finance systems in U.S. states has been under attack for nearly thirty-five years.[1] During this time, thirty-seven states have had their system of education funding challenged on constitutional grounds. In twenty-five of these states, the system has been ruled unconstitutional in one or more court challenges. Taken together, these school finance judgments represent perhaps the most important reform movement in American public education since 1954, when *Brown* v. *Board of Education* ended racial segregation in schools.[2]

With *Rose* v. *Council for Better Education* in Kentucky in 1989, challenges of school finance on constitutional grounds changed importantly.[3] Prior to *Rose*, court challenges to school finance systems rested mainly on equity grounds—that is, the argument that equality of educational opportunity, as guaranteed in many state constitutions, requires equality of educational resources. *Rose*, however, ushered in a series of cases challenging state funding systems on adequacy grounds. These adequacy cases are based on the argument that an adequate education, as guaranteed in many state constitutions, requires adequate resources. According to this line of reasoning, students with greater "needs" may in fact require greater resources in order to obtain an adequate education. Although both equity and adequacy cases have usually been grounded in a demand to provide greater resources for poor students, adequacy cases acknowledge that resources may be distributed unequally to the extent that high-need students require greater resources to obtain a satisfactory level of education.[4]

The existing literature on the empirical effects of school finance judgments typically has not differentiated between equity and adequacy cases. In this chapter, I review the previous studies and reestimate some their most important results, allowing for differential equity and adequacy effects. In addition, because few of the prior studies on school finance judgments using panel data have accounted for serial correlation when estimating standard errors, I reestimate some of the most influential models using state-clustered standard errors. The results indicate that several key findings from prior studies are based on standard errors that were likely too small, leading to overconfidence in the statistical significance of the estimated effects of school finance judgments.

In contrast to much of the rhetoric about the revolutionary impact of school finance judgments, I find that they have had relatively small or no effects on most school finance outcomes. On a variety of fiscal measures, ranging from total spending to spending inequality, I find substantively small or statistically insignificant effects of school finance judgments. The most important effect, according to this analysis, has been to accelerate the centralization of school funding to the state level. In short, school finance judgments on the whole have not resulted in the broad-ranging changes to school funding sought by plaintiffs.

Previous Research on the Fiscal Effects of School Finance Judgments

Although school finance equalization lawsuits have attracted significant attention in the legal community, and a variety of state-specific studies have been produced, nationwide empirical studies of the effects of school finance judgments on school finance have been relatively few. The first major study on a national scale was by Murray, Evans, and Schwab.[5] Studying the period from 1972 to 1992, these authors use district-level spending data to compute within-state inequality measures, which they then regress on a school finance judgment indicator and control variables. They conclude that school finance judgments have reduced within-state spending inequality by 19 to 34 percent. They argue that gains in spending equality were achieved by increasing spending in the poorest districts, while leaving spending in the richest districts unaltered. All of the increased spending, they find, was financed by aid from the state government rather than local sources. In addition, they argue that additional state funding for education was financed through higher taxes rather than by shifting resources from other functions.

Card and Payne study the effects of school finance judgments on the distribution of school spending and student test scores.[6] Using district-level data on school spending and state aid for 1977 and 1992, they find that states redistribute aid in favor of poor districts after school finance judgments. Specifically, they find that the slope of the relationship between state aid and local income becomes more negative after school finance judgments and show that total spending increases in poor districts relative to rich districts. Card and Payne also demonstrate that only those court decisions in which the system of school financing is found to be unconstitutional have these effects; cases in which a state's system is challenged but upheld have no measurable effects. They go on to provide evidence that the equalization of spending resulting from school finance judgments leads to a modest narrowing of SAT test scores across family background groups.

Baicker and Gordon examine how increased state aid for education resulting from school finance judgments affects total local revenue and spending.[7] Using county-level data for 1982 to 1997, they find that when states increase spending on education as a result of school finance judgments, they reduce aid to localities for other programs. Baicker and Gordon estimate that each dollar of increased state aid for education reduced state aid for other purposes by about 20 cents. They also find that local governments respond to increases in state education spending by reducing their own revenue and spending on education as well as other programs. These authors estimate that only about 53 cents of each dollar in additional state aid for education ends up in local spending. In other words, there is evidence that localities "undo" state efforts at increasing education spending after school finance judgments.

Springer, Liu, and Guthrie were the first to attempt to differentiate the effects of equity- and adequacy-based school finance judgments on spending inequality.[8] Using data from 1972 to 2002, these authors undertake an analysis similar to that of Murray, Evans, and Schwab but allow for different effects of equity and adequacy school finance judgments.[9] The evidence of a difference is mixed. Over the entire study period, the authors do not find a statistically significant difference in the effects of adequacy relative to equity reform on any of their inequality measures. For the period 1990 to 2000, and using a different data set, they find a significant difference, with adequacy reform having a smaller effect in reducing inequality. However, for the same period, when the authors look at the effects of school finance judgments on the correlation between state aid and local resource needs, measured by the percent of students with free or reduced-price lunch status, they find no significant difference between equity- and adequacy-based reforms. The authors conclude that the evidence is too muddled at present to make firm conclusions about differential effects of the two types of school finance judgments.

In an important paper that differs methodologically from the others described thus far, Hoxby abandons the use of a single dummy variable to characterize school finance judgments in favor of computing economically meaningful parameters of school finance equalization plans on a state-by-state basis.[10] Hoxby emphasizes that reforms can have quite different effects depending on the price and income effects they impose, whereas the dummy variable estimates capture at best the average effects. Depending on the tax price of local spending imposed on the financing system, reforms may have "leveling up" or "leveling down" effects. In states that make the tax price of additional school spending too high, such as California and New Mexico, students in poor districts may actually end up with less education spending than before the equalization plan was imposed. Hoxby's analysis of the unintended effects of school finance reforms on housing values and private school attendance is another significant contribution. The most important conclusion from her paper for this analysis is that the common approach of using a single dummy variable to characterize school finance judgments masks significant heterogeneity in the experiences of different states implementing court-ordered school finance equalization reforms.

Motivation and Objectives

This chapter's motivation is threefold. First, the various papers on the fiscal effects of school finance judgments described above use different time periods, data sources, and model specifications, making comparison of results across the analyses less straightforward than one would like. Thus one objective is to estimate the most important models in the existing literature using a common time frame and set of control variables. In addition, this allows me to update some of the results that are now dated, considering the pace of school finance litigation.

Second, with the exception of the recent paper by Springer, Liu, and Guthrie, prior studies have not attempted to differentiate the effects of equity- and adequacy-based school finance judgments. In part, this is because adequacy-based judgments did not become widespread until the mid-1990s. Therefore, I reestimate some of the important models from prior studies, allowing for differential equity and adequacy effects. Although adequacy-based judgments are still relatively new, there is now a sufficient track record—177 state-years of post-judgment experience—to allow their effects to be differentiated from those of equity-based judgments, which have accumulated 301 state-years of experience.

Third, recent work by Bertrand, Duflo, and Mullainathan underscores the importance of accounting for serial correlation in panel data analyses of the sort that have been used to study the effects of school finance judgments.[11] Although it has long been known that ordinary least squares (OLS) standard errors are inconsistent when residuals are serially correlated, these authors demonstrate the dramatic possible consequences of ignoring the problem in a typical analysis of state panel data. For instance, they randomly generate "placebo laws" in state-level data and find "effects" on female wages that are statistically significant at the 5 percent level for up to 45 percent of the sample using OLS. The authors use Monte Carlo simulations to test various remedies to the serial correlation problem and show that clustering standard errors by state to allow for arbitrary autocorrelation provides an easily implemented solution to this problem.[12] They recommend that clustered standard errors become the customary practice in applied work.

Unfortunately, of the studies discussed above, only Hoxby takes account of serial correlation. All of the other studies use OLS standard errors, ignoring serial correlation. In other words, the standard errors reported in much of the existing literature are likely to be too small, leading to overconfidence in the estimated effects of school finance judgments. Thus an important objective of this chapter is to reestimate several of the important models in the literature, while allowing for state-clustered standard errors.

Data and Empirical Strategy

I compiled several data sets for this chapter. To begin, I assembled variables related to school finance judgments by state for the years 1970 to 2003. The first is simply a dummy variable set equal to 1 if the state had a court decision overruling the school finance system on equity or adequacy grounds in the current year or a prior year. Second, I created two separate dummy variables for equity-based and adequacy-based school finance judgments. Third, I created a variable counting the number of years since a decision, set to 0 for states without a decision. Finally, I created another dummy variable indicating whether the state's school finance system was upheld as constitutional in a court challenge in a prior or the current year.[13] The information for creating all of these variables was taken from the paper by Springer, Liu, and Guthrie, who updated, and in some cases corrected, information used by Card and Payne and Baicker and Gordon.

I next compiled several data sets of fiscal and demographic variables over time. Summary statistics of the main outcome and control variables are provided in appendix table 9A-1. First, from the National Center for Education Statistics (NCES), I obtained state-level data on the sources of public school revenue for the years 1971 to 2002. Published first in the *Digest of Education Statistics* and later in the *Common Core of Data*, these data show the level and proportion of revenue received by public elementary and secondary schools from local, state, and federal sources.[14] I used this data set to analyze the effects of school finance judgments on state and local funding for education.

Second, from the *Census of Governments*, I collected a variety of additional state finance data. Published as *State Government Finances*, these data are available as an interrupted time-series starting with 1972 and then annually from 1977 to 2003.[15] I used this data set to analyze the effects of school finance judgments on own-source revenue of state governments as well as non-education spending by state governments.

Third, I compiled a district-level data set with a variety of fiscal variables, also from the *Census of Governments* and covering the years 1972 and 1977 through 2002. I used this data set to compute four within-state measures of inequality in school spending: the Gini coefficient, coefficient of variation, Theil index, and log of the ratio of spending by the ninety-fifth-percentile district to the fifth-percentile district.[16] Because several of these inequality measures are highly sensitive to extreme values, I followed Murray, Evans, and Schwab in using the following algorithm to delete potential outliers. Within each state and year of observation, I identified the fifth-percentile and ninety-fifth-percentile district in terms of per-pupil spending. I deleted any district whose spending was greater than 150 percent of the ninety-fifth-percentile value or less than 50 percent of the fifth-percentile value. In addition, I weighted districts by their enrollment in computing the inequality indexes. These state-level aggregate measures of inequality then became the dependent variables in second-stage models, wherein inequality is related to school finance judgments.

For each of the dependent variables mentioned, I estimated the same four basic model specifications. In the first model, the dependent variable of interest was regressed against a dummy variable indicating whether a court decision ruled the state's school financing system to be unconstitutional in the current year or a previous year, state and year fixed effects, and demographic controls including the proportion of the population over sixty-five years of age, proportion of the population five to seventeen years of age, per capita income and its square, and population and its square. In the second specification, an additional dummy variable was added, indicating whether the state's school finance system was upheld, as described above. If it is the ruling itself that matters, rather than other unobservable characteristics that make a state susceptible to a challenge, then it should be possible to demonstrate that decisions overruling the school finance system have different effects than decisions upholding it. In the third model, I used a variable counting the number of years since the school finance system was overruled, rather than the dummy variable. This specification is intended to capture the possibility that decisions take time to have an effect, and so their impact may increase over time.[17] In the final model, I used separate dummy variables for equity- and adequacy-based decisions overruling the state's school finance system in the current or earlier years. If the two types of cases have different impacts, it should be possible to reject the hypothesis that these coefficients are equal.[18]

Each of the models described above was estimated twice. First, the models were estimated using robust (Huber-White) standard errors to account for heteroskedasticity, but ignoring serial correlation. The models were estimated a second time using robust, state-clustered standard errors, to account for both heteroskedasticity and serial correlation. In tables 9-1 to 9-6, I report both types of standard errors below the regression coefficients. Although the state-clustered standard errors are preferred, I show both so as to demonstrate when accounting for serial correlation makes it impossible to reject a null hypothesis that otherwise would be rejected.

It is important to keep in mind what this empirical strategy is designed to do and what it will not do. Some states may implement major reforms as a result of court rulings, whereas others may only tinker at the margins or do nothing at all. While acknowledging Hoxby's key point that all school finance judgments are not created equal, the dummy variable approach is designed to uncover the average impact of having a court ruling overturn a state's school finance system. This approach is analogous to an intent-to-treat analysis in experimental analyses. By contrast, Hoxby's approach uncovers the effects of specific fiscal reforms, but not the effects of court rulings per se. Her approach is useful in understanding the impact of particular types of finance reforms and should be of interest, for instance, to legislators considering how to respond to a school finance judgment. In contrast, the approach used here is useful in assessing the overall impact of school finance judgments per se and presumably would be of greater interest to a plaintiff considering whether to file a lawsuit.

Aggregate Budgetary Effects of School Finance Judgments

Table 9-1 shows the relationship between school finance judgments and total funding for public schools. The data are from NCES and represent the revenue

Table 9-1. *Total Education Revenue*[a]

Indicator	Model 1	Model 2	Model 3	Model 4
SFJ indicator	260.95 {62.25} [182.34]	290.17 {72.74} [210.26]		
Upheld indicator		49.39 {50.31} [130.14]		
Years since SFJ			29.69 {5.39} [15.2]	
Equity indicator				441.09 {89.42} [244.81]
Adequacy indicator				97.74 {68.38} [185.73]
Proportion of the population less than 65 years of age	−131.17 {49.03} [141.39]	−131.89 {49.09} [141.5]	−118.49 {52.06} [155.36]	−100.02 {50.73} [144.23]
Proportion of the population 5–17 years of age	−252.52 {21.76} [43.56]	−254.5 {21.92} [43.83]	−246.42 {21.56} [42.45]	−245.99 {22.27} [46.05]
Per capita income (thousands of dollars)	81.19 {44.42} [102.39]	76.09 {45.06} [103.81]	133.87 {45.89} [103.59]	59.31 {45.16} [103.46]
Per capita income squared	1.95 {0.6} [1.52]	2.02 {0.61} [1.54]	1.05 {0.62} [1.45]	2.13 {0.61} [1.5]
State population (millions)	−294.33 {47.68} [137.89]	−291.5 {47.42} [135.47]	−237.76 {48.26} [141.31]	−279.75 {47.34} [132.59]

(continued)

received by public elementary and secondary schools from all sources, including federal, state, and local revenue. In model 1, the school finance judgment (SFJ) indicator—that is, a dummy variable equal to 1 if the state's school finance system was ruled unconstitutional in the current year or a previous year—has a coefficient of $261 and an unclustered standard error of $62, a relationship that is highly significant statistically. This effect represents about 4 percent of average education revenue in the sample, which is $6,900 per pupil. However, the state-clustered standard errors, shown in brackets, are about three times as large as the unclustered standard errors. In other words, when serial correlation is accounted for by clustering standard errors by state,

Table 9-1. *Total Education Revenue*[a] *(Continued)*

Indicator	Model 1	Model 2	Model 3	Model 4
State population squared	4.41 {0.96} [2.56]	4.4 {0.96} [2.53]	2.6 {1.02} [2.71]	4.1 {0.95} [2.46]
Constant	12,286.45 {1,484.93} [3,681.4]	12,377.79 {1,503.17} [3,734.77]	10,792.16 {1,598.15} [4,069.1]	12,188.17 {1,532.84} [3,828.1]
Summary statistic				
Adjusted R^2	0.88	0.88	0.88	0.88
Number in sample	1,436	1,436	1,436	1,376
F tests		Overturned = upheld		Equity = adequacy
F statistic without state-clustered standard errors		14.8		8.25
p value		0.000		0.004
F statistic with state-clustered standard errors		1.78		1.14
p value		0.189		0.291

Source: NCES data.

a. Data represent annual observations of the forty-eight mainland U.S. states for 1971–2002, missing 1981. Robust standard errors are in curly braces; robust state-clustered standard errors are in brackets. Regressions include year and state fixed effects, percent of the population over sixty-five years of age, percent of the population five to seventeen years of age, per capita income, per capita income squared, population, and population squared. All dollar figures are in thousands of per capita, real-year 2004 dollars. Model 4 excludes Montana and Vermont, as explained in the text. Data for Virginia were not reported in 1985–87.

the relationship between school finance judgments and total education revenue is no longer statistically significant at conventional levels.

In model 2, I added a dummy variable equal to 1 if the state's education system was ever challenged and upheld. The upheld indicator is not significant under either version of the standard errors and, once again, the SFJ indicator fails to obtain statistical significance when using state-clustered standard errors. Moreover, it is not possible to reject the hypothesis that the effect of being overruled and being upheld is equal when standard errors are clustered by state.

Model 3 replaces the SFJ indicator with a variable measuring the number of years a judgment has been in place; that is, the number of years since the state's school finance system was found unconstitutional. The point estimate suggests that a judgment increases per-pupil education revenue by $30 each year that it is in place. This relationship is highly significant using conventional standard errors and remains significant at the 6 percent level when using state-clustered standard errors. This result suggests that school finance judgments may take time to have an effect on education funding, and the simple SFJ dummy variable, which measures the average effect of school finance judgments over all years, may understate their long-term impact.

In model 4, I used separate indicator variables for equity-based and adequacy-based school finance judgments. The point estimates indicate that equity-based decisions have a much greater impact on education revenue than adequacy-based decisions. However, neither of these variables is significant with state-clustered standard errors, nor is it possible to reject the hypothesis that the effects of equity- and adequacy-based reforms are equal.

In sum, of the various school finance judgments and revenue relationships examined in table 9-1, only the years since judgment variable remains significant using state-clustered standard errors, and even this is just shy of the conventional 5 percent threshold of statistical significance. At the same time, it is worth noting that other variables are also affected importantly by the serial correlation correction. For instance, the proportion of the population over sixty-five years of age shows a highly significant negative effect on education revenue in all of the models in table 9-1 using conventional standard errors but is never significant using state-clustered standard errors. In contrast, the proportion of the population five to seventeen years of age is highly significant in all of the models regardless of the form of the standard errors.

Previous studies have found that school finance judgments have greater effects on funding by state governments than on funding by local governments, and table 9-2 examines state and local revenue separately.[19] Again, the revenue data are from NCES and represent funding for public elementary and secondary schools received from the state government and from local sources. Table 9-2 repeats the model specifications shown in table 9-1 with state and local government revenue as the dependent variables. For brevity, the coefficients for the control variables are not shown in table 9-2 or subsequent tables. Model 1 shows a positive effect of school finance judgments on state education revenue, which is statistically significant under either version of the standard errors. States after decisions provide roughly $450 per pupil in additional revenue. This effect represents about 14 percent of mean per-pupil state education revenue of $3,209 in the estimation sample. Model 2 reveals a negative coefficient for the upheld indicator. This result suggests that states spend less on education after the school finance system has been upheld as constitutional, although the effect is not significant with state-clustered standard errors. We can, however, reject the hypothesis that upholding and overturning a state's system of education finance have the same effects. In addition, the variable for years after the school finance judgment is again highly significant in model 3, even with state-clustered standard errors, and indicates that states increase education revenue by nearly $50 a year after a decision. Finally, model 4 examines equity- and adequacy-based school finance judgments separately. Neither is significant individually, nor is it possible to reject the hypothesis that the two coefficients are equal, after state clustering. In other words, while I am able to get fairly precise estimates of the overall effects of school finance judgments on state education revenue, I do not obtain precise estimates for the two types of school finance judgments individually.

Models 5 through 8 of table 9-2 repeat the specifications using local education revenue as the dependent variable. The coefficients are generally negative, indicating that local governments reduce their education funding after a decision, consistent with the findings of Card and Payne and Baicker and Gordon, discussed above. However, none of the relationships between local education revenue and school finance judgments is significant after accounting for serial correlation via state-clustered standard errors.

One provocative result is that the upheld indicator in model 6 carries a positive coefficient, suggesting that court judgments upholding school finance systems lead to lower state funding and higher local funding, exactly the inverse of the results for judgments overruling finance systems. These results are only provocative, however, as we cannot reject that the upheld and overturned indicators are equal using state-clustered standard errors. Also intriguing are the results of model 8, which show a positive effect of equity-based reforms on local revenue, suggesting that equity-based reforms lead to increases in both state and local revenue, while adequacy-based reforms generate higher state revenue, but offsetting decreases in local revenue. These results account for the much larger effect of equity-based reforms on total revenue estimated in model 4 of table 9-1. Unfortunately, it is not possible to draw such conclusions with much confidence, as it is not possible to reject the possibility that equity- and adequacy-based judgments have the same effect after state clustering.

To summarize the results of tables 9-1 and 9-2, school finance judgments lead to significant increases in state revenue for public education, but it is not possible to estimate precisely the effects of school finance judgments on local education revenue. Given the imprecision in the estimates for local education revenue, it is not surprising that it is not possible to estimate confidently the effects of school finance judgments on total education revenue in table 9-1. In other words, it is not certain whether local changes in education revenue after school finance judgments offset state increases partially or completely. Based on these results, however, it should be possible to show that the state's share of education revenue increases after school finance judgments, and indeed this is the case in model specifications with the state's share of funding as the dependent

Table 9-2. *Sources of Education Revenue*[a]

| | Education revenue from state | | | | Local education revenue | | | |
Indicator	Model 1	Model 2	Model 3	Model 4	Model 5	Model 6	Model 7	Model 8
SFJ indicator	452.92 {77.72} [196.03]	379.98 {84.5} [213.79]			−201.2 {74.44} [184.24]	−100.11 {81.43} [198.78]		
Upheld indicator		−123.22 {48.12} [136.92]				170.88 {51.06} [146.4]		
Years since SFJ			46.81 {4.32} [9.24]				−18.79 {4.64} [13.09]	
Equity indicator				332.44 {73} [205.63]				98.39 {71.11} [162.79]
Adequacy indicator				237.88 {80.38} [167.83]				−135.25 {79.63} [191.85]

Summary statistic

Adjusted R^2	0.72	0.72	0.73	0.74	0.54	0.54	0.54	0.57
Number in sample	1,437	1,437	1,437	1,377	1,436	1,436	1,436	1,376
F tests		Overturned = upheld		Equity = adequacy		Overturned = upheld		Equity = adequacy
F statistic without state clustering		40.7		0.6		12.7		3.49
p value		0.000		0.439		0.000		0.0619
F statistic with state clustering		6.18		0.12		1.91		0.62
p value		0.0165		0.729		0.174		0.435

Source: NCES data.

a. Data represent annual observations of the forty-eight mainland U.S. states for 1971–2002, missing 1981. Robust standard errors are in curly braces; robust state-clustered standard errors are in brackets. Regressions include year and state fixed effects, percent of the population over sixty-five years of age, percent of the population five to seventeen years of age, per capita income, per capita income squared, population, and population squared. All dollar figures are in thousands of per capita, real-year 2004 dollars. Model 4 excludes Montana and Vermont, as explained in the text. Data for Virginia were not reported in 1985–87.

Table 9-3. *Education as a Share of State Spending*[a]

Indicator	Model 1	Model 2	Model 3	Model 4
SFJ indicator	1.72 {0.38} [0.9]	1.81 {0.41} [0.97]		
Upheld indicator		0.15 {0.26} [0.62]		
Years since SFJ			0.17 {0.03} [0.06]	
Equity indicator				1.02 {0.41} [0.91]
Adequacy indicator				1.30 {0.41} [0.89]
Summary statistic				
Adjusted R^2	0.2	0.2	0.21	0.21
Number in sample	1,437	1,437	1,437	1,377
F tests		Overturned = upheld		Equity = adequacy
F statistic without state clustering		18.42		0.17
p value		0.000		0.677
F statistic with state clustering		3.04		0.04
p value		0.0875		0.845

Source: NCES data and Census Bureau, *Census of Governments*.

a. Data represent annual observations of the forty-eight mainland U.S. states for 1971–2002, missing 1972 and 1981. Robust standard errors are in curly braces; robust state-clustered standard errors are in brackets. Regressions include year and state fixed effects, percent of the population over sixty-five years of age, percent of the population five to seventeen years of age, per capita income, per capita income squared, population, and population squared. All dollar figures are in thousands of per capita, real-year 2004 dollars. Model 4 excludes Montana and Vermont, as explained in the text.

variable. The results (not shown) indicate that the state's share of education revenue increases by about 4 percentage points after school finance judgments, which represents just under 10 percent of the sample mean state share of funding (47 percent). It is possible to reject the hypothesis that decisions upholding and overturning school finance systems have equal effects, but not the hypothesis that equity-based and adequacy-based decisions have equivalent effects on the state's share of education revenue.

As the final analysis in this section, in table 9-3 I examine the effect of school finance judgments on the share of the state's total budget devoted to education. The dependent variable is education revenue from the state government (NCES data) divided by total general expenditures of the state government (*Census of Governments* data). Model 1 of table 9-3 indicates that the share of the state government's budget devoted to education increases by about 1.7 percentage points after a school finance judgment, and the relationship is significant at the 10 percent level with state-clustered standard errors. The hypothesis that court decisions upholding and overruling the school finance system have equal effects on the share of the budget devoted to education can also be rejected at the 10 percent level. In addition, the years after a school finance judgment variable in model 3 remain highly significant with appropriate standard errors, indicating that school finance judgment decisions have increasing effects over time in shifting spending toward education. It is not possible to reject the hypothesis that equity- and adequacy-based reforms have equal effects on the share of the budget devoted to education.

The Allocation of State Aid for Education

The one robust finding documented in the preceding section is that school finance judgments lead to greater educational spending by state governments. The effects of this increased state spending likely depend not just on how much money is spent, but on how it is allocated. In this section, using data from the *Census of Governments*, I aggregate intergovernmental revenue for education received from the state by all local governments in a county. With seven time points at five-year intervals from 1972 to 2002, I have just over 20,000 county-year observations. I then regress state education revenue per pupil in a county on county per capita income, SFJ-related variables, and interactions between judgments and income. The models also include county and year fixed effects. The interaction terms are of primary interest and indicate the extent to which school finance judgments alter the slope of the relationship between state aid and local income. A more negative slope is taken to signify greater progressivity in state education spending.[20]

Table 9-4 presents the analysis of the effects of school finance judgments on the progressivity of state education spending. In model 1, all of the variables take the expected sign. The main effect of income is negative, indicating that state aid is targeted disproportionately to low-income areas. The SFJ indicator is positive, suggesting that school finance judgments increase the overall level of state education aid received, which is consistent with the analyses shown in the preceding section. And the SFJ-income interaction is negative, suggesting that state education aid becomes more progressive after a court decision ruling the

Table 9-4. Progressivity of State Aid

Indicator	Education revenue from state				Noneducation revenue from state			
	Model 1	Model 2	Model 3	Model 4	Model 5	Model 6	Model 7	Model 8
Income per capita (thousands of dollars)	-0.0309 {0.0038} [0.0225]	-0.0184 {0.0041} [0.0213]	-0.015 {0.0038} [0.0139]	-0.0327 {0.0039} [0.0218]	-0.002 {0.0007} [0.0019]	-0.0036 {0.0008} [0.0023]	-0.0025 {0.0007} [0.0017]	-0.0019 {0.0007} [0.0019]
SFJ indicator	0.2716 {0.0488} [0.2737]	0.3343 {0.049} [0.2642]			-0.0302 {0.006} [0.0244]	-0.0468 {0.0067} [0.0275]		
SFJ × income	-0.0037 {0.0042} [0.0264]	-0.0184 {0.0044} [0.0234]			0.0027 {0.0005} [0.0019]	0.0039 {0.0006} [0.0021]		
Upheld indicator		0.0289 {0.0368} [0.1405]				-0.046 {0.0065} [0.0199]		
Upheld × income		-0.0143 {0.0031} [0.0105]				0.0035 {0.0006} [0.0018]		
Years since SFJ			0.0477 {0.0028} [0.0074]				-0.0036 {0.0005} [0.0013]	

	(1)	(2)	(3)	(4)	(5)	(6)	(7)	(8)
Years since SFJ × income			−0.0021 {0.0002} [0.0005]				0.0002 {0.0000} [0.0001]	
Equity indicator				0.1348 {0.0559} [0.3974]				−0.0432 {0.0072} [0.0334]
Equity × income				0.0005 {0.0048} [0.0381]				0.0025 {0.0006} [0.0028]
Adequacy indicator				0.5544 {0.067} [0.18]				−0.0114 {0.0072} [0.0177]
Adequacy × income				−0.0214 {0.0056} [0.0198]				0.0017 {0.0006} [0.0012]
Constant	1.2948 {0.0359} [0.1972]	1.1851 {0.0377} [0.1903]	1.1587 {0.0353} [0.13]	1.3225 {0.0361} [0.1926]	0.1317 {0.0064} [0.0166]	0.1474 {0.0069} [0.0186]	0.1374 {0.0064} [0.0152]	0.1337 {0.0065} [0.0165]
Summary statistic								
Adjusted R^2	0.70	0.70	0.70	0.71	0.10	0.11	0.10	0.1
Number in sample	20,377	20,377	20,377	19,916	20,189	20,189	20,189	19,736

Source: Census Bureau, *Census of Governments*.

a. Data represent annual county-area observations for 1972, 1977, 1982, 1987, 1992, 1997, and 2002. All models include county and year fixed effects. Robust standard errors are in curly braces; robust state-clustered standard errors are in brackets. All dollar figures are in thousands of per capita, real-year 2004 dollars.

state's school financing system to be unconstitutional. However, none of these relationships is statistically significant when state-clustered standard errors are used, and in fact the SFJ-income interaction is insignificant under either version of the standard errors. Similar results are obtained when the upheld indicator is added in model 2 of table 9-4: the coefficients take the expected signs, but none is significant with state-clustered standard errors. Nor is it possible to reject the hypothesis that the upheld-income and SFJ indicator–income interaction terms are equal.

When the years after SFJ variable is used rather than the indicator, both its main effect and its interaction with income are highly significant under both versions of the standard errors. The main effect indicates that local governments receive an increase of $48 per pupil in state aid each year after a school finance judgment ruling. More to the point, the negative interaction effect suggests that the distribution of state aid becomes increasingly progressive after a decision. That the years after SFJ variable attains significance where the indicator variable does not may imply that the effects of school finance judgments increase over time and therefore that the average effect may not approximate the long-term effect of school finance judgments.

Finally, model 4 of table 9-4 shows that the adequacy-income and equity-income interaction terms carry different signs, suggesting that only adequacy-based reforms produce greater progressivity in state education aid. However, neither of the interaction terms in model 4 is significant, nor is it possible to reject the hypothesis that the two terms are equal when state-clustered standard errors are used.

Models 5 through 8 in table 9-4 repeat the same specifications using state noneducation aid as the dependent variable, which is computed by subtracting local intergovernmental revenue from the state for education from total intergovernmental revenue from the state. Interestingly, the signs of the school finance judgment–related variables generally carry the opposite signs from what was seen in models 1 through 4. In model 5, for instance, the main effect of school finance judgment is negative, while its interaction with income is positive, which suggests that local governments receive less noneducation aid from the state after a school finance judgment decision, but that it is distributed less progressively. Again, these results fall short of statistical significance when serial correlation is addressed.

As with the analysis of education aid, however, the years after SFJ variable is highly significant under both forms of standard errors in model 7 of table 9-4. The positive interaction term between years after SFJ and income indicates that state noneducation aid becomes increasingly less progressive after

a school finance judgment. In other words, states may compensate more affluent areas for relative losses in education aid by providing additional noneducation aid.

School Finance Judgments and Spending Inequality

The ultimate goal of many school finance lawsuits is to reduce inequality in
per-pupil spending. However, some adequacy-based suits seek to increase
resources for needy students without regard for spending inequality per se.
This section investigates the effects of school finance judgments on spending
inequality. Using district-level data from the *Census of Governments*, I compute
four measures of within-state inequality in per-pupil spending: the Gini coefficient, the coefficient of variation, the Theil coefficient, and the log of the
ratio of the ninety-fifth-percentile district's spending to the fifth-percentile district's spending. I multiply each of these indexes by 100 to facilitate presentation of the results. Maryland, North Carolina, and Virginia are omitted from
this analysis because they contain no independent school districts as classified
by the *Census of Governments*. Montana and Vermont are also excluded, following Springer, Liu, and Guthrie, because they have very few unified school
districts. This analysis uses a panel of school districts observed at seven time
points in five-year intervals from 1972 to 2002. Producing state-level summary measures of inequality based on the district-level spending data yields a
panel of forty-two states at seven time points for a total of 294 observations.

Table 9-5 presents four models of the effects of school finance judgments on
the Gini coefficient of spending inequality. The SFJ indicator in model 1 of
table 9-5 is highly statistically significant using either version of the standard
errors. The point estimate indicates that, in states with a school finance judgment, inequality is reduced by 1.2 Gini points, which amounts to 16 percent
of the mean Gini value of 7.5 in the estimation sample. In model 2, the hypothesis that a court decision upholding the state's school financing system has the
same effect as a decision overturning the system is soundly rejected, as shown
at the bottom of table 9-5. However, neither the equity- nor the adequacy-
based reform indicator is individually significant, and it is impossible to reject
that the two are equal.

The results shown in table 9-5 indicate that school finance judgments have
had a significant effect in reducing spending inequality as measured by the
Gini coefficient. Analyses of the coefficient of variation and the Theil index
of inequality yield similar results (not shown). An exception is the analysis of

Table 9-5. *Education Spending Gini Coefficient*

Indicator	Model 1	Model 2	Model 3	Model 4
SFJ indicator	−1.2312 {0.3328} [0.3982]	−1.0623 {0.3563} [0.4037]		
Upheld indicator		0.2868 {0.2849} [0.3533]		
Years since SFJ			−0.0752 {0.0215} [0.0288]	
Equity indicator				−1.0498 {0.4916} [0.6425]
Adequacy indicator				−0.5786 {0.3511} [0.4692]
Summary statistic				
Adjusted R^2	0.76	0.76	0.75	0.75
Number in sample	294	294	294	294
F tests		Overturned = upheld		Equity = adequacy
F statistic without state clustering		13.92		0.47
p value		0.000		0.492
F statistic with state clustering		8.68		0.28
p value		0.005		0.6

Source: Census Bureau, *Census of Governments.*

a. Data represent annual observations of forty-three U.S. states for 1972, 1977, 1982, 1987, 1992, 1997, and 2002. Excluded are Alaska, Hawaii, Maryland, Montana, North Carolina, Vermont, and Virginia. Robust standard errors are in curly braces; robust state-clustered standard errors are in brackets. Regressions include year and state fixed effects, percent of the population over sixty-five years of age, percent of the population five to seventeen years of age, per capita income, per capita income squared, population, and population squared. All dollar figures are in thousands of per capita, real-year 2004 dollars.

the log of ninety-fifth-/fifth-percentile spending (not shown). Although the coefficients carry the same signs as in the other inequality analyses, they are never statistically significant, using either form of the standard errors.

Aside from the anomalous results for the ninety-fifth-/fifth-percentile spending, the preceding analysis suggests that school finance judgments have reduced within-state spending inequality. However, given the simplicity of the inequality indexes, it is not clear how the reductions have occurred. On the one hand, a reduction in spending by high-spending districts, without changing spending at the low end of the distribution, would lead to a lower inequality index. On the other hand, starting from a relatively equal distribution of spending, a significant increase in spending at the low end could conceivably increase inequality.

In order to better understand how school finance judgments might reduce spending inequality, I conclude my analysis by estimating the effect of school finance judgments on spending by the fifth-, fiftieth-, and ninety-fifth-percentile districts in each state. Again, the data are from the *Census of Governments* and cover the period 1972 to 2002 at five-year intervals. For each state, I identify the district at the fifth percentile of spending for each of the seven time points. And so, too, for the fiftieth- and ninety-fifth-percentile districts. I then regress spending at each point in the distribution on the same SFJ-related variables and controls.

Table 9-6 shows the results. The SFJ indicator in model 1 shows a positive effect on spending, which is significant under either version of the standard errors. In model 2, the hypothesis that court decisions upholding and overruling school finance systems have the same effects is easily rejected. However, the years after SFJ variable in model 3 does not approach statistical significance, regardless of the form of standard errors used.

I then repeat the same sequence of analyses for the median and ninety-fifth-percentile districts' spending. The school finance judgment effect declines for the median district and again for the ninety-fifth-percentile district, suggesting that school finance judgments increase spending more at the low end of the distribution. Although the hypothesis that the school finance judgment coefficients in models 1, 5, and 9 are equal cannot be rejected, these point estimates suggest a plausible explanation for how school finance judgments might lead to a reduction in spending inequality. For the years after SFJ variable in models 3, 7, and 11, the hypothesis that the coefficients are equal at conventional significance levels cannot be rejected either.[21] In none of the analyses is it possible to reject the hypothesis that equity- and adequacy-based reforms have equal effects.

Summary and Conclusion

Across a wide range of fiscal outcomes measuring both the level and distribution of education spending, the analysis presented here generally reveals substantively small and statistically insignificant effects of school finance judgments. The exceptions are an increase in the state's share of education funding and a modest (perhaps 16 percent) decline in spending inequality related to school finance judgments. Whether these results indicate that school finance

Table 9-6. Spending by Fifth-, Fiftieth-, and Ninety-Fifth-Percentile Districts

Indicator	Fifth-percentile district spending				Median district spending				Ninety-fifth-percentile district spending			
	Model 1	Model 2	Model 3	Model 4	Model 5	Model 6	Model 7	Model 8	Model 9	Model 10	Model 11	Model 12
SFJ indicator	0.1053 {0.0309} [0.0317]	0.0969 {0.0333} [0.0359]			0.0756 {0.0161} [0.0248]	0.0774 {0.0181} [0.026]			0.0454 {0.0329} [0.0409]	0.0589 {0.0323} [0.0465]		
Upheld indicator		−0.0141 {0.0318} [0.0417]				0.0032 {0.0151} [0.0219]				0.0229 {0.0281} [0.0315]		
Years since SFJ			0.0025 {0.0029} [0.0032]				0.0041 {0.0013} [0.0017]				0.0004 {0.0018} [0.0022]	
Equity indicator				0.1019 {0.0505} [0.0536]				0.0962 {0.0198} [0.0253]				0.0737 {0.0351} [0.0516]
Adequacy indicator				0.0508 {0.0334} [0.036]				0.0352 {0.0176} [0.0285]				0.0153 {0.0387} [0.0438]

Summary statistic

	Overturned = upheld	Equity = adequacy	Overturned = upheld	Equity = adequacy	Overturned = upheld	Equity = adequacy
Adjusted R^2	0.79 / 0.79	0.79 / 0.79	0.96 / 0.96	0.96 / 0.96	0.93 / 0.93	0.92 / 0.93
Number in sample	294 / 294	294 / 294	294 / 294	294 / 294	294 / 294	294 / 294
F tests	Overturned = upheld	Equity = adequacy	Overturned = upheld	Equity = adequacy	Overturned = upheld	Equity = adequacy
F statistic without state clustering	9.76	0.49	17.82	4.32	0.89	0.98
p value	0.00	0.483	0	0.039	0.345	0.323
F statistic with state clustering	7.94	0.55	7.19	1.8	0.73	0.65
p value	0.007	0.464	0.011	0.187	0.399	0.425

Source: Census Bureau, *Census of Governments*.

a. Data represent annual observations of forty-three U.S. states for 1972, 1977, 1982, 1987, 1992, 1997, and 2002. Excluded are Alaska, Hawaii, Maryland, Montana, North Carolina, Vermont, and Virginia. Robust standard errors are in curly braces; robust state-clustered standard errors are in brackets. Regressions include year and state fixed effects, percent of the population over sixty-five years of age, percent of the population five to seventeen years of age, per capita income, per capita income squared, population, and population squared. All dollar figures are in thousands of per capita, real-year 2004 dollars.

judgments are a major or a minor force in education finance depends perhaps on one's prior expectations. The idea that school finance judgments represent a revolutionary force in education appears untenable in light of these findings. That said, in a policy domain with a long history of failed attempts at reform, reducing inequality by any measurable amount is nothing to sniff at.

To return to an issue raised earlier in the chapter, the results presented based on SFJ-related dummy variables reveal the average effects of school finance judgments across states and over time. As Hoxby rightly emphasizes, however, all school finance judgments do not have equal effects.[22] Substantial hetero-geneity in state experiences with school finance judgments is hidden with the dummy variable coefficients in the models presented in this chapter. Better understanding of the differences in state outcomes is probably a more impor-tant line of future research than further work attempting to refine the SFJ dummy variable–style models presented here and in much of the earlier liter-ature. For instance, it is important to understand the institutional and politi-cal factors that cause states to create and apply school finance equalization plans that differ so widely from one another. And finally, regardless of the fis-cal effects of school finance judgments, the question remains, Does the in-cremental spending associated with school finance reform improve student achievement?

Table 9A-1. *Summary Statistics, Various Years, 1972–2002*[a]

Variable	1972[b]		1982		1992		2002	
	Mean	*Standard deviation*	*Mean*	*Standard deviation*	*Mean*	*Standard deviation*	*Mean*	*Standard deviation*
Outcome variables								
Total education revenue per pupil	4,664.05	980.59	5,717.45	1,354.30	7,526.78	1,645.56	9,421.96	1,846.12
State education revenue per pupil	1,786.43	645.23	2,667.56	824.69	3,433.33	987.62	4,637.25	1,269.36
Local education revenue per pupil	2,401.63	1,068.35	2,639.98	1,328.56	3,569.51	1,588.63	3,953.62	1,538.19
State share of education revenue	39.10	13.34	47.71	13.79	46.63	13.13	49.49	10.71
State own-source revenue per capita	1,533.29	286.27	1,780.71	525.25	2,347.54	474.53	2,745.95	529.46
Local noneducation revenue from state per capita	209.55	193.30	222.65	178.47	280.75	208.74	324.07	218.58
Education revenue as a percent of state spending	19.99	5.84	20.42	5.77	18.37	4.73	18.44	3.71
Gini coefficient ($\times$ 100) of per-pupil spending	7.64	2.87	8.09	2.93	7.68	2.96	6.81	2.24
Coefficient of variation ($\times$ 100) of per-pupil spending	14.57	5.63	15.28	5.64	14.79	5.84	13.37	4.67
Theil coefficient ($\times$ 100) of per-pupil spending	1.25	1.28	1.27	0.85	1.17	0.89	0.92	0.65
ln(ninety-fifth-percentile spending/ fifth-percentile spending)	0.63	0.61	0.57	0.24	0.55	0.22	0.52	0.20

(continued)

Table 9A-1. *Summary Statistics, Various Years, 1972–2002*[a] *(Continued)*

	1972[b]		1982		1992		2002	
Variable	*Mean*	*Standard deviation*	*Mean*	*Standard deviation*	*Mean*	*Standard deviation*	*Mean*	*Standard deviation*
Control variables								
Percent of the population over sixty-five years of age	10.04	1.67	11.51	1.83	12.81	1.79	12.62	1.60
Percent of the population five to seventeen years of age	25.46	1.25	20.00	1.23	18.85	1.93	18.31	1.03
Income per capita (thousands of dollars)	19.01	2.62	20.72	2.73	25.74	3.78	31.18	4.55
State population (millions)	4.30	4.43	4.79	4.89	5.27	5.67	5.95	6.43

Source: NCES data and Census Bureau, *Census of Governments.*
a. All dollar figures have been adjusted to 2004 dollars using the consumer price index.
b. Total, state, and local education revenues, as well as state share of education revenue, are reported for 1971, as 1972 data were not available.

Notes

1. *Serrano* v. *Priest,* 5 C3d 584 (L.A. 29820 Calif. Sup. Ct. August 30, 1971).

2. *Brown* v. *Board of Education of Topeka,* 37 U.S. 483 (1954).

3. *Rose* v. *Council for Better Education,* 790 S.W.2d 186, 198 (Ky. 1989).

4. For a discussion of the underlying conceptualization of resource distribution in equity and adequacy lawsuits, see J. W. Guthrie, "Twenty-First-Century Education Finance: Equity, Adequacy, and the Emerging Challenge of Linking Resources to Performance," in *Money, Politics, and Law: Intersections and Conflicts in the Provision of Educational Opportunity; 2004 Yearbook of the American Education Finance Association,* edited by Karen DeMoss and Kenneth K. Wong (Larchmont, N.Y.: Eye of Education, 2004).

5. Sheila Murray, William N. Evans, and Robert Schwab, "Education Finance Reform and the Distribution of Education Resources," *American Economic Review* 88 (September 1998): 789–812. A similar paper was published as William N. Evans, Sheila E. Murray, and Robert M. Schwab, "Schoolhouses, Courthouses, and Statehouses after *Serrano,*" *Journal of Policy Analysis and Management* 16, no. 1 (1997): 10–31.

6. David Card and A. Abigail Payne, "School Finance Reform, the Distribution of School Spending, and the Distribution of Student Test Scores," *Journal of Public Economics* 83, no. 1 (2002): 49–82.

7. Katherine Baicker and Nora Gordon, "The Effect of Mandated State Education Spending on Total Local Resources," NBER Working Paper 10701 (Cambridge, Mass.: National Bureau of Economic Research, 2004).

8. Matthew Springer, Keke Liu, and James Guthrie, "The Impact of Education Finance Litigation Reform on Resource Distribution: Is There Anything Special about Adequacy?" Working Paper (Vanderbilt University, Peabody Center for Education Policy, 2005).

9. Murray, Evans, and Schwab, "Education Finance Reform."

10. Caroline M. Hoxby, "All School Finance Equalizations Are Not Created Equal," *Quarterly Journal of Economics* 116, no. 4 (2001): 1189–231.

11. Marianne Bertrand, Esther Duflo, and Sendhil Mullainathan, "How Much Should We Trust Differences-in-Differences Estimates?" *Quarterly Journal of Economics* 119, no. 1 (2004): 249–75.

12. In the Stata statistical software, for instance, this correction can be estimated by using the *cluster* option. The theory is explained in Manuel Arellano, "Computing Robust Standard Errors for Within-Groups Estimators," *Oxford Bulletin of Economics and Statistics* 49, no. 4 (1987): 431–34; Halbert White, *Asymptotic Theory for Econometricians* (San Diego, Calif.: Academic Press, 1984).

13. Some states faced initial challenges in which the school system was upheld, only to be ruled unconstitutional later. In cases where the financing system is first upheld and later overruled, the upheld dummy variable is switched back to 0 at the point when the system is overruled.

14. National Center on Education Statistics, *Digest of Education Statistics* (U.S. Department of Education, Institute of Education Sciences, various years) (www.nces.ed.gov/programs/digest [September 2006]); National Center on Education Statistics, *Common Core of Data* (U.S. Department of Education, Institute of Education Sciences, various years) (www.nces.ed.gov/ccd [September 2006]).

15. Census Bureau, *Federal, State, and Local Governments: Census of Governments* (various years) (www.census.gov/govs/www/state.html [September 2006]).

16. These four indexes of inequality are reviewed in Murray, Evans, and Schwab, "Education Finance Reform," and discussed in detail in Robert Berne and Leanna Stiefel, *The Measurement of Equity in School Finance: Conceptual, Methodological, and Empirical Dimensions* (Johns Hopkins University Press, 1983).

17. Of course, there is no reason to expect the effects of school finance judgments to grow linearly over time. I take the linear specification to capture the idea that the effects grow over some finite time horizon, rather than as a precise depiction of the functional form of this growth.

18. Some states have had both equity- and adequacy-based school finance judgment decisions, and in principle an interaction term could also be included to estimate the multiplicative effect of having both types of judgments. However, given that there are relatively few observations of states operating after both equity and adequacy school finance judgments, I have not attempted to estimate this interaction.

19. Card and Payne, "School Finance Reform"; Murray, Evans, and Schwab, "Education Finance Reform."

20. This approach is modeled after Card and Payne, who use school district–specific data for 1977 and 1992. They are able to compute district-level income by matching districts to census data for 1980 and 1990. Unfortunately, district-level income measures are not available for all the time points in my panel, and so I must aggregate the data to counties in order to match them with local income data. I use county-level per capita income data from the Regional Economic Information System of the Bureau of Economic Analysis (www.bea.gov/bea/regional/reis [September 2006]).

21. In order to test these hypotheses, I estimated the equations for the fifth, fiftieth, and ninety-fifth percentiles by seemingly unrelated regressions and then tested the equality of the school finance judgment coefficients. For models 1, 5, and 9, the chi-square statistic is 4.52, with a p value of 0.105. For models 3, 7, and 11, the chi-square statistic is 4.04, with a p value of 0.13.

22. Hoxby, "All School Finance Equations Are Not Created Equal."

PART IV

Predictions

10

ANDREW RUDALEVIGE

Adequacy, Accountability, and the Impact of the No Child Left Behind Act

AFTER THE SUPREME Court held in 1973 that education was not a fundamental right under the U.S. Constitution, the battle shifted to the states. Since then, forty-five states have faced lawsuits charging that their funding levels and formulas for education failed to meet their own constitution's commitment to their children. These efforts, aimed first at fiscal equity and then at educational "adequacy," continue apace: twenty-four were pending at wildly different stages of completion as of February 2006. In the aggregate, they represent a steady, but relatively stealthy, brand of national education reform.[1]

At the same time, with much more fanfare, states find themselves subject to the requirements of the 2001 reauthorization of the Elementary and Secondary Education Act (ESEA), known as the No Child Left Behind (NCLB) Act. NCLB was the cumulative manifestation of nearly two decades of efforts by "new Democrats" and "compassionate conservatives" alike to place standards and accountability at the heart of education policy at both the state and federal levels. The resulting law required districts receiving funds from ESEA's Title I to provide all students with "highly qualified" teachers, to devise "challenging" academic standards, to test students against those reading and math

A substantially different version of this chapter was presented at the conference "Adequacy Lawsuits: Their Growing Impact on American Education," at Harvard University. The author wishes to thank Checker Finn, Al Lindseth, Paul Peterson, Michael Rebell, Andy Rotherham, and especially Ashley Osment and Marty West for helpful conversations.

standards every year between grades three and eight and again in high school, and to make "adequate yearly progress" in bringing all students to proficiency on those standards by 2014 or face a variety of escalating sanctions. All this built on states' own labors in defining and enforcing standards, but NCLB raised both the stakes for schools aiming to narrow the gaps in student achievement and the profile of the federal government in education policy generally.[2]

How do these two developments relate to each other? That is, how has accountability politics at the national level intersected adequacy politics at the state level? One quick answer might be not at all. After all, the adequacy movement long predates NCLB, and only a handful of suits to date have been filed since NCLB's enactment. They are grounded in state, not federal, constitutional language.

Yet closer examination shows that NCLB has made—and will make—a difference, although the evidence is necessarily preliminary and in some areas that difference is one of degree rather than of kind. Since 1989, when President George H. W. Bush's National Education Summit heralded state and federal commitment to standards-driven accountability, the number of cases filed by adequacy advocates, as well as their legal success rate, has skyrocketed. By providing judges with accessible evidence for gauging the quality of state education systems (often linked to the quantity of state education dollars), student proficiency measurements have added greatly to judicial willingness both to pass judgment on legislative behavior and to impose sanctions to remedy it. NCLB, by providing more, more consistent, and more detailed data on student performance, gives adequacy advocates new ammunition of this type. It effectively declares as federal policy that every child can learn, if given the resources to do so. Small wonder that a draft report from a major adequacy advocacy group, the Campaign for Educational Equity, is entitled *Opportunity Knocks*. Or, given the potential fiscal exposure facing state governments as lawsuits proceed, that the reaction of the National Conference of State Legislatures has been, "We're very afraid."[3]

This development is a key aspect of NCLB's impact on education politics. However, adequacy advocates' dealings with the states are only one leg of a triangle of relationships that also includes the politics of state-federal relations in the education arena and the state-based advocates' new interest in, and concerns about, federal policymaking. Adequacy politics, in short, go beyond traditional adequacy lawsuits. NCLB may not serve as legal tender in the same way in each set of relationships, but it both drives and constrains behavior—and contributes to political pressures—that may accomplish some of the same ends. The remainder of this chapter explores these ramifications.

NCLB and Adequacy Politics

The theme of "adequacy" in education has evolved from the landmark *Brown* v. *Board of Education* decision in 1954 to the ongoing state suits grounded in standards-based accountability.[4] While early cases seeking educational spending equity (for example, California's *Serrano* v. *Priest*) found that funding disparities could violate the state constitution's equal protection clause, such equity, it transpired, could be of the lowest-common-denominator variety. Advocates thus shifted ground somewhat, arguing that the real educational shortfall was "by reference to some absolute standard and not in comparison with others."[5]

Still, it was not obvious what that absolute standard should be. Fiscal equity, whatever its substantive faults, had the virtues of mathematical clarity: funding was equal, or it was not. Once adequacy was mandated, its connection to funding seemed less linear. Judges found it difficult to define an "adequate" education given the vague guidance found in most state constitutions.

As a result, state defendants won about two-thirds of these cases prior to 1989. However, even as the initial flurry of court success faded, the accountability movement noted in the previous section had begun to define student achievement in a crucially specific way. States adopted standards that demarcated actual things students had to know, along with ways to test that knowledge. Once educational output could be measured, inequitable outputs provided a rationale for finding state education funding systems to be unconstitutional: it was a short logical step from requiring proficiency against state standards to assuming that proficiency was what an adequate education entailed. "Judicially manageable standards" were now available. Better yet, judges could say they were simply following political actors' own determinations: a Kansas court said in 1994, for example, that it would "not substitute its judgment of what is 'suitable' but will utilize as a base the standards enunciated by the legislature and the state department of education." Standards-based reforms thus became quickly and closely intertwined with adequacy-driven legal strategies.[6]

NCLB, Adequacy, and State Governments: What Value Added?

Even as adequacy suits began to succeed, their legal basis remained states' alleged failure to live up to the education promised all their citizens in their own state constitutions. Despite the passage of NCLB, the various constitutional clauses parsed by advocates and judges remain in place, as does the lack of such language in the U.S. Constitution. The plaintiffs in the Georgia case brought in 2004, for example, barely mention NCLB in their basic recital of the state's supposed dereliction of duty; by contrast, Article VIII, Section 1, of Georgia's constitution is front and center.[7] NCLB is in itself neither necessary nor sufficient to fuel new state-level suits.

Nonetheless, adequacy advocates have applauded its passage. The Campaign for Educational Equity, which has become a central player in organizing the adequacy movement nationally, calls "the central goals and the implementing principles [of NCLB] a tremendous asset in school-funding adequacy cases"; they are "enormously helpful to us," as executive director Michael Rebell has noted, "from a litigation point of view." David Sciarra, executive director of the New Jersey group that represented parents in *Abbott* v. *Burke*, argues that NCLB "is reinforcing the trend that the states are ultimately responsible for making sure there's a rigorous education system in place. The courts are saying: 'Now that you've assumed the responsibility for the substance of education, you've got to make sure there are resources to support that.'"[8]

States, too, see NCLB as significant. The National Conference of State Legislatures hired a Washington law firm in 2003 to examine the law's impact, which warned that "NCLB is likely to accelerate those kinds of [adequacy] lawsuits." The conference's Task Force on No Child Left Behind likewise noted its concern that "NCLB could embolden the advocates who see school finance court challenges as the answer to the social disparities that underscore much of the achievement gap."[9]

At least two major aspects of NCLB make it an emboldening addition to the adequacy arsenal: its principles and its data.

PRINCIPLES OF GOVERNANCE. First, quite simply, is the moral clout NCLB implies for those seeking to enforce the promise of its name. Indeed, the terms of the debate over NCLB were congruent with, even identical to, the arguments made on behalf of educational adequacy. Consider the "statement of purpose" laid out in Section 1001 of the law: "The purpose of [Title I] is to ensure that all children have a fair, equal, and significant opportunity to obtain a high-quality education and reach, at a minimum, proficiency on challenging state academic achievement standards and state academic assessments." This could be achieved, Congress went on to declare, by aligning "high-quality academic assessments [and] accountability systems" with "challenging state academic standards" to make it easy to "measure progress against common expectations for student academic achievement." Special attention was to be paid to "meeting the educational needs of low-achieving children in our Nation's highest poverty schools" and "closing the achievement gap between high- and low-performing children, especially . . . between minority and nonminority students, and between disadvantaged students and their more advantaged peers," as well as "providing children an enriched and accelerated educational program."

President Bush consistently pressed these themes as well. Districts with average high performance, the president argued repeatedly, concealed pockets of neglect. "An equal society begins with equally excellent schools," Bush told the National Urban League in August 2001. In a press conference early in his second term, President Bush recalled that, in formulating NCLB, "We said, 'Let's change the attitude. We ought to start with the presumption every child can learn, not just some.'"[10]

The Campaign for Educational Equity or the Campaign for Fiscal Equity, which organized the lawsuit against New York State, could not have put it better, and in courtrooms they have not put it much differently. In New York, adequacy attorneys argued that NCLB language meant that states are responsible not only for overall performance but also "specifically for the achievement of 'economically disadvantaged students,' 'students from major racial and ethnic groups,' 'students with disabilities,' and 'students with limited English proficiency'"; any extra services these subgroups required became "an inherent part" of any curriculum "intended to impart minimal competency."[11]

Clearly, this line of argument raises the stakes for the states. The National Conference of State Legislatures criticizes the "possible confusion" that arises from state cases that use "adequacy and proficiency indistinguishably" and warns that adequacy should not be equated with 100 percent proficiency, given that judicial analysis had previously rested on lower figures. For example, Ohio had planned to achieve a level of 75 percent proficiency under its pre-NCLB standards; now it must raise that aim dramatically.[12] The last 5 or 10 percent of students will be the most difficult, and most expensive, to make proficient. Many argue that the 100 percent figure is simply utopian and must be amended.

At present, though, the universality of the law, backed by a date certain, is at the least a powerful ideal. At worst (for the states), it is a powerful legal instrument aimed at them a decade hence. As such, its consequences are in the here and now, creating urgency and potentially pressuring states to settle adequacy suits. Even if achieving 100 percent proficiency is unrealistic, the adequacy movement has little incentive to settle on a lower standard. At the least, advocates argue, "100 percent *opportunity*" must be available, at which point policymakers can better calibrate absolute progress in proficiency.[13]

JUDICIALLY MANAGEABLE STANDARDS. It is true that grand statements of principle only go so far in court. However, NCLB also provides adequacy advocates with more tangible benefits. Most of all, the law is a boon to the construction of the "judicially manageable standards" that are so crucial to the adequacy argument. While many states had begun to implement accountability systems prior to 2002, progress was often glacial within states and very uneven across them. But NCLB is, above all, about measurement: about setting clear state standards, making them the primary means of evaluating adequate yearly progress (and thus, by implication, adequacy), testing that progress frequently, and publishing the results. Further, while its 1994 forerunner, the Improving America's Schools Act, was executed slowly at the state level, implementation of NCLB has been immediate and highly salient.

NCLB advocates, led by President Bush, have consistently equated measurement with testing. Thus instead of six tests (across two subjects) between grades three and twelve, by 2005–06 at least fourteen tests (across three subjects) were required. Results are tracked not just in the overall student population but also in subgroups disaggregated by income, race, English proficiency, and special needs. And by elevating—some would say reifying—tests as the principal element of adequate yearly progress, NCLB enshrines their results as the juridically appropriate unit of analysis. The robust academic debate over the validity of standardized tests as assessments of performance is not reflected in the calm print of the law: such tests are defined in statute as indicative of a school's value. The states, through the National Conference of State Legislatures, have objected "that it is inappropriate to impose high stakes on schools and districts based primarily, if not entirely, on the annual test results of students."[14] That is an argument lost, thus far at least.

Still, other aspects of adequate yearly progress may not give states much comfort either. Consider high school graduation rates. At present, as a legal defense, the states must generally say that their own standards are "aspirational," not definitive, measures of student abilities or education inputs. They must argue, as North Carolina did in the *Hoke* case, that an education failing to enable children to meet the state's own standards is nonetheless "adequate." Likewise, New York argued that the equivalent of an eighth-grade education would be sufficient for constitutional adequacy. Yet adequacy attorneys were able to point out that this was strikingly at odds with "the fact that Congress recently enacted legislation providing for assessments based, in part, on high school graduation rates."[15]

The results of adequate yearly progress measures must, of course, be made very public. By late 2003, a survey by the journal *Education Week* found that the law had "produced one unambiguous result: an avalanche of data on the performance of public schools in the United States." It suggested that this was NCLB's "most visible change so far."[16] The data themselves do not guarantee change, but they can be organized to lead to change. Among other things, they help advocates to locate possible plaintiffs, since organizers can see where the worst performance is, school by school, group by group. "With the supplemental disaggregated data on certain student populations," National Conference of State Legislatures analyst Steven Smith noted, "plaintiffs will be able to narrowly focus and highlight specific damage accrued by certain populations and bring claims on their behalf."[17] And they will be able to use the data subsequently as courtroom ammunition mustered to bolster substantive claims. In South Carolina, for example, the plaintiffs' lead attorney looked to NCLB's requirement for "highly qualified" teachers and noted that, in court, "we are showing that our school districts have the least experienced teachers." One local superintendent translated that directly into adequacy terms: "Our students aren't being given the opportunity to attain an adequate education."[18]

Recent filings in Nebraska's *Douglas County School District* v. *Johanns* case highlight these points: the districts bringing suit, note the plaintiffs, "are required to comply with state academic standards, assessment measures, and reporting requirements" and "are held accountable for whether students are meeting the expected level of proficiency on state standards." Further, "The state of Nebraska requires significant increases over time in the number of students meeting proficiency levels as a measure of 'adequate yearly progress' until it requires by 2013–14 that all students are at least 'proficient.'" Further, "State law requires that all students . . . be assessed individually. The data [are] then required to be reported by demographic groups." And "The state of Nebraska requires schools to have a graduation rate of 83.97 percent in the aggregate, and in each separate category of students, in order to be considered to have made [adequate yearly progress]." All of this, of course, is required by NCLB, but when translated instead as state requirements, it has direct relevance to the state's constitutional duties toward education. "Thousands of students" in the plaintiff districts, the brief continues, "are not proficient; . . . are not graduating from high school; and are not meeting [adequate yearly progress] standards as defined by Nebraska's Department of Education and the No Child Left Behind Act." The answer? "Improving student achievement requires increased funding." Other ongoing cases (as in Georgia) follow similar reasoning and reach similar conclusions.[19]

The upshot is that, while proficiency is an output, it has distinct implications for inputs. When states accept, through legislation or by judicial fiat, that they are accountable for student performance, to be measured by standardized tests against specified content standards, they may be assumed to accept the fiscal responsibility for making that performance possible. The 2002 final report of the Maryland Commission on Education, Finance, Equity, and Excellence (the Thornton Commission) notes the circular nature of the input-output relationship in finding that "schools are being adequately funded when the amount of funding provided is sufficient to allow students, schools, and school systems to meet prescribed state performance standards." Or, as a Montana district court judge wrote in 2004, in an opinion affirmed the next year by that state's supreme court, "For the standards-based approach to have any chance of success, the state must assure that districts have sufficient resources available so that they can reasonably be expected to meet the state's standards concerning student performance."[20]

NCLB, then, intersects with, and accelerates, adequacy advocates' ongoing strategy of alliance with the accountability movement. As NCLB continues to produce more data, and more schools are deemed to be failing, even states where adequacy judgments have already been pursued may be revisited. That might apply both to states where adequacy claims were once rejected and to those where earlier remedies now appear insufficient.

State Governments and the Federal Government: The Scope of Conflict

The National Conference of State Legislatures' 2003 analysis of NCLB argued, "As a result of No Child Left Behind, the states will likely face court challenges to their school finance systems just as the federal government could face federal court challenges to the fiscal implication of the law."[21] The phrase "just as" is misleading: these are not the same legal arguments. But if one lesson of state accountability efforts is that any such system becomes a tool with which to leverage resources, there is ample reason to expect parallel results at the federal level.

AN UNFUNDED MANDATE? Complaints by states about federal funding and flexibility are certainly nothing new, nor are they limited to education policy. The governor who cried "unfunded mandate" is a bipartisan phenomenon, as Lance Fusarelli amply documents in a recent collation of state-level reactions to NCLB.[22]

But the sheer size of recent NCLB-related claims is striking. Representative George Miller (D-Calif.), ranking member of the House Education and the Workforce Committee, has argued that "students were shortchanged" by $40 billion over the five fiscal years (2002–06) since the law's passage. The National Education Association (NEA) claimed in January 2004 that educators needed some $42 billion that fiscal year alone. The states, given their expertise in the "costing out" exercise inherent in adequacy suits (where, ironically, they resist the more extravagant figures produced by such analyses), came up with the biggest number of all, suggesting modal spending increases of 30 to 40 percent. The National Conference of State Legislatures concluded, "New costs to give all students adequate standards-based opportunities to achieve proficiency could add up to $139 billion per year."[23] This figure, if added to fiscal 2004 spending, would have placed more than a third of that year's entire domestic discretionary budget in the Department of Education.

In contemplating (and taking) legal action, states have looked eagerly to Section 9527(a) of NCLB: "Nothing in this act shall be construed to authorize an officer or employee of the federal government to . . . mandate a state or any subdivision thereof to spend any funds or incur any costs not paid for under this act." The National Education Association, filing suit along with a scattering of school districts in three states, claimed that state and local funds had been diverted to meet NCLB mandates and that even the authorized, much less the appropriated, level of Title I funding fell short of NCLB's demands. Costs covered in the suit included the revision of curriculum standards, the development and administration of tests, the calculation of adequate yearly progress, and the enforcement of sanctions, as well as the provision of qualified personnel, for the purposes of raising student achievement to full proficiency.[24] But when a state itself (Connecticut) sued the federal government in August 2005, the claim was narrower, mainly that the additional funding granted the state was insufficient to carry out the law's new testing regime, including administrative support. That shortfall was estimated at some $6.4 million a year through fiscal 2008.[25]

The lower figure reflects the fact that the states had committed to raising their achievement levels before NCLB came along, both through state law and as guided by the 1994 reauthorization of ESEA, the Improving America's Schools Act. As regards adequacy, to claim that NCLB is an unfunded mandate is to say that NCLB requires proficiency, but that state constitutions do not; many state courts, at least, have already dismissed the latter half of that.

Nor should the Tenth Amendment's reservation of powers to the states offer much hope. While Congress cannot regulate local education directly, except as it plausibly affects interstate commerce, the federal government's spending power encompasses the power to place strings on the funds it sends the states. The Supreme Court's most thorough recent discussion of this point, in the drinking age case of *South Dakota* v. *Dole* in 1987, suggests that the ability of Congress to spend on behalf of the general welfare is sufficiently permissive as to resist judicial enforcement.[26] Even the Unfunded Mandates Reform Act (UMRA), passed with great fanfare by the 104th Congress, excludes from its treatment the cost of complying with legislative conditions for receipt of federal aid. In dismissing the NEA lawsuit in November 2005, the district court noted that Section 9527(a) applied to departmental administrators, not legislators, and was thus insufficient to show that "Congress intended for these requirements to be paid for *solely* by the federal appropriations." In September

2006, a federal judge likewise dismissed most of Connecticut's suit, holding that it was too early to gauge the accuracy of the Education Department's claim that federal funding would, in fact, cover the state's additional testing requirements and that a "pre-enforcement declaratory ruling" in the opposite direction would be inappropriate.[27]

But even if the states cannot make the same legal claim as adequacy advocates, they can nonetheless make analogous political arguments that themselves could have real bite. As the National Conference of State Legislatures (NCSL) admits, "By federal statutory definition, NCLB is technically not a mandate. . . . [But] at the very least . . . the section is a clear statement of Congress's intent not to shift costs to the states. The language, therefore, should give state officials leverage in their efforts to ensure that NCLB is not an unfunded or underfunded federal mandate."[28] The very size of the NCSL's funding claim seems designed to gain attention for those efforts. At the same time, governors and state lawmakers have begun to seed the press with comments painting NCLB as a "well-intentioned" but inflexible (even "dangerously arbitrary") "federal grab" pushed on states "without the resources" to make it work. The NEA's March 2006 appeal of its case's dismissal, for example, attracted support from elected officials in California, Connecticut, and Pennsylvania, arguing that NCLB "is, *in effect*, an unfunded mandate. . . . It is naïve to suggest states and school districts can achieve [NCLB's] ends without adequate financial assistance from the federal government." And states from Hawaii eastward have publicly resisted various aspects of NCLB implementation.[29] These arguments seem designed to gain regulatory breathing room for that implementation, as much as they are grounded in a passion for states' rights. It is no coincidence that the 2005 Connecticut lawsuit complains about the "rigid, arbitrary, and capricious" manner in which the Department of Education has interpreted NCLB in denying Connecticut waivers of the law's requirements, including the annual testing provision.[30]

"WATCH THE CROWD"? A useful injunction comes from political scientist E. E. Schattschneider, who argued that political winners and losers can often be determined by skillful manipulation of the scope of conflict. "If a fight starts," he advised, "watch the crowd."[31] Expanding that conflict to the national level has long been a part of education politics. As early as 1965 and the original ESEA, states-rights advocates argued, as Rep. John William (D-Del.) put it, "The needy are being used as a wedge to open the floodgates . . . You may be absolutely certain that the flood of Federal control is ready to sweep the land." NCLB certainly doesn't stem that tide.[32]

Yet the very scope of the federal commitment, which aids adequacy advocates vis-à-vis the states, may also aid the states vis-à-vis the federal government. In Schattschneider's theory, "Every change in scope changes the equation," and what may seem the stronger force may lose control.[33] In practical terms, the Bush administration has strong incentives to keep its signature domestic policy achievement on track and certainly to forestall its ideological allies from turning on the administration. "The White House does not want the state that had the largest margin for Bush backing out of a program," observed Utah Congressman Chris Cannon, an incentive heightened as the president's political difficulties in other areas have mounted.[34] The publicity of pulling a state's entire allotment of Title I funding (as opposed to the smaller penalties imposed thus far) would almost certainly provoke a backlash. After all, NCLB makes clear a commanding commitment to education that transcends localism. "Education is a local responsibility," President Bush noted in 2001, "yet improving our public schools is a national goal." He asked his audience to join him "in building a system of education worthy of all America's children, so that every child has a chance in life, and not one single child, in the greatest land on the face of this Earth, is left behind."[35] NCLB does not change the U.S. Constitution, of course, nor can statute author the compelling interest that the *Rodriguez* court failed to find. But some legislators have sought to make just those changes.[36] And even short of that, such soaring rhetoric goes some way toward a promise, toward making compelling the states' case for enhanced federal funding or increased local flexibility in the court of public opinion. In that venue the jury is still out; "the crowd" is still open to persuasion. Even as of August 2006, only 45 percent of respondents claimed to know "a fair amount" or more about the requirements of NCLB; the rest said they knew "very little" or "nothing at all."[37]

Astute states might be able to combine these trends into a compelling case for federal funds, flexibility, or both. However, the moral leverage that NCLB gives states to extract additional funding from the federal government may be offset by the simple fact that the federal government has little money to give, in light of present and projected budget deficits. If so, an alternate and more ominous path would see the states quietly continue to lower their standards or avoid testing special-needs students (perhaps with federal collusion) so that widespread proficiency can be achieved more readily. Already, states have shown great creativity in defining the subgroups whose performance they must report. After all, failing to make adequate yearly progress is punished, but undercutting its substance is not.[38]

This in turn, obviously, undercuts not only adequacy suits but also the promise of accountability. Yet to prevent it requires *more* assumption of authority by the federal government, a difficult political position given the current congressional majority's preferences regarding states' rights. It may be no accident that some states have added federal adequate yearly progress to extant measures of standards, rather than replacing them. When this practice results in two contradictory state "grades" assigned to a single school, state policymakers can argue that the school is not really underperforming, except by the unfair measures imposed by the federal government. Florida goes farthest here, perhaps; when its schools cannot meet federal adequate yearly progress but have received good grades on the state's own accountability system, the state (with federal approval) has nonetheless designated them as having achieved "provisional adequate yearly progress."[39]

Of course, some states may welcome the federal pressure that NCLB provides, even as they quarrel over its specific requirements. The Pennsylvania Department of Education, for example, went so far as to call "the timing of NCLB . . . fortuitous, because it speaks to the urgent need to act on the Governor's education plans"[40] in the face of a recalcitrant legislative majority under divided government. In Maryland, when the state sought to utilize the provisions of NCLB to restructure eleven schools in Baltimore under state or private management, the battle became a proxy for the 2006 governor's race between incumbent Robert Ehrlich and challenger (and Baltimore mayor) Martin O'Malley. Ehrlich lost that battle, at least in the short run, when the Maryland legislature overrode his veto of legislation barring state action. But his state schools chief wondered aloud whether NCLB's requirements might in fact legally trump the legislature's action.[41]

More generally, we might expect to see the centralizing changes in the federal-state relationship paralleled by intrastate shifts. After all, despite the long history of local control over education, state governments have real incentive to tighten their authority over schools failing to meet NCLB performance markers. If states are legally responsible not just for the existence of schools but also for their performance, they cannot simply set standards and let districts have their head; when North Carolina argued, for example, that it was providing sufficient funds to achieve the adequacy goals set by the court, the court held that the state was also responsible for ensuring that districts spent that money in effective ways, to the point of sending state personnel to the districts to help them implement such policies.[42] Even before NCLB, state takeovers of decimated districts and shifts to appointed school boards under mayoral control had become a familiar part of the landscape. NCLB may push additional accountability to state capitols; in states with decentralized systems of education (Pennsylvania, for example, has more than 500 school districts with independent fiscal and curricular authority), this could be a promising development.[43]

Adequacy Goes National

It is interesting to note the degree to which the adequacy movement—which relies, after all, on a state-by-state, locally grounded legal approach—has become a national movement. The states may be "laboratories of democracy," but they are also laboratories of litigation: the sheer number of adequacy cases facilitates the transfer of expertise and the sequential development of legal arguments. The Advocacy Center for Children's Educational Success with Standards (ACCESS), for example, a coalition of school finance lawyers and policy advocates, holds conferences and maintains an extensive website devoted to disseminating information about state suits. The recently formed Campaign for Educational Equity, which will house the ACCESS project, is in turn housed at Teachers College of Columbia University, with a board chaired by philanthropist Laurie Tisch and possessed of ambitious fundraising goals. The Campaign for Educational Equity gained a West Coast ally in 2005 with the creation of the Earl Warren Institute on Race, Ethnicity, and Diversity at the University of California, Berkeley.[44]

The infrastructure is there, then, for a national lobbying presence. NCLB provides an important rationale for building that presence, especially as its 2007 reauthorization approaches, since the adequacy movement shares NCLB's implied distrust of states' good faith and loves the law's strict requirements. One priority will be to maintain high standards and fend off the potential "race to the bottom" noted earlier. The Department of Education, the Campaign for Educational Equity argues, has not defined "rigorous" (as in "coherent and rigorous" state standards) in any serious way. Lower standards "could undermine both NCLB and standards-based reform" and thus "a mainstay of the adequacy movement."[45]

Further, a series of state court decisions has coalesced around what an adequate education might mean substantively as it relates to the state interest in education in the first place, including the creation of productive citizens, able to serve as competent jurors, voters, and competitors in the modern economy. Adequacy advocates argue that the standards and resources underwriting these skills should be written into NCLB. Here, as with the "highly qualified" teacher requirement, advocates hope for additional centralization of federal authority—though also for additional funds that can build long-term capacity in needy districts.

However, some advocates feel that certain aspects of the law undercut adequacy's success and the movement's traditional grounding in equity. Many are dubious about the sanctions that NCLB prescribes as accountability mechanisms, especially as regards privately provided supplemental services and school choice. Others dislike its focus on testing, either because they feel that testing does not assess the civic ability described above or because they feel generally uneasy about standardized tests. Still others complain that NCLB conceives of schools as a place unconnected to their community context—that is, it demands production targets and, when they are not met, looks within the school for change rather than to the wider, societal concerns that affect one's ability to learn: poverty, racism, access to health care, and the like.[46]

Here equity and adequacy may yet splinter. Accountability-driven reform, especially as it pushed high-stakes testing combined with flexible state spending and various forms of school choice, has often (though not always accurately) been associated with the right of the political spectrum. During the 1990s, at least, most on the left eschewed standards and testing in favor of pushing the "opportunity to learn" to be achieved by the trinity of lower class size, school renovation and construction, and teacher training. Yet while the battle for resources clearly remains at the heart of the adequacy movement, as standards-based reform and adequacy became more closely intertwined, even those who disliked testing were constrained from criticizing it too vocally—lest readily measurable (read: judicially manageable) standards be lost and resources with them. This dynamic was not created by NCLB, but NCLB reinforces it. NCLB's pragmatic obsession with measurement and assessments helps to provide the objective measures so helpful to courtroom success; its push for disaggregated data provides both the evidence and the motivation for closing the achievement gap across race and class.

Thus a "Baptist-bootlegger" coalition promoting standards-based reform has held firm over time, parallel to the odd-bedfellows arrangement created during Prohibition by those who supported banning legal liquor sales for religious reasons and those who had rather more worldy motives to support that ban. But as Peter Schrag has observed, "The joining of conservative educational practice to liberal objectives is almost entirely new and still widely misunderstood," not least, perhaps, by adequacy advocates themselves.[47] While advocacy attorneys have no interest in defining proficiency down, other allies of the movement (for example, school districts and teachers) do have such incentive, given that they are judged by their students' adequate yearly progress.[48] Can advocates of each vision cooperate in the short run and in the long? And what party is the adequacy movement's natural partner in a polarized polity? Whether the movement can manage to transcend its differences will have a lot to say for its future political success and for the success of NCLB.

That observation may stand, in fact, as the broader conclusion of this chapter. Court decisions may shape the direction of policy outcomes, but if they are not to serve, ultimately, as a "hollow hope," politics and political actors must follow suit.[49] NCLB has not rewritten the basis for adequacy lawsuits. But it has created new dynamics within which adequacy politics, more broadly conceived, must navigate. Accountability-driven reform generally has created new coalitions and invented new relationships; NCLB, in turn, has pulled state-level battles into the national spotlight as well as provided new strategies for those battles.

How things develop now may well hinge on whether the adequacy movement can be as adroit in the public sphere as in its recent legal maneuverings. As suggested above, it is time to "watch the crowd": public reaction to NCLB will have a lot to do with the shape of the 2007 reauthorization. Will the public be persuaded that the law is useful and effective? Who will win the battle of framing the issues involved? State politicians, federal policymakers, and interest groups of all stripes will be engaged in the arena, and this time around, adequacy advocates may have a crucial voice. Adequacy suits have normally involved a colloquy among courts, legislators, and educators, but in the recent (and ongoing) New York case, at least, there were serious efforts as well at grassroots organizing and public participation as the shape of the Campaign for Fiscal Equity lawsuit was formulated. How deeply those efforts took hold, and how well they can be replicated in other places, will shape the volume and effectiveness of adequacy politics in education politics generally.

There is a lot at stake in that determination for the adequacy movement as a whole. It will, most broadly, shape the tangible gains realized from the 2007 reauthorization for adequacy strategies nationally. But it also will show how unified the movement is around the definition of its historic goal of equity and how committed it is to using the tactics of standards and assessments toward that goal. Most fundamentally, it will show whether it is a movement centered on judicial decisions that could likely not be attained through representative politics—or whether its claims to represent the democratic ideal through the substantive connections between an "adequate" education and civic and economic empowerment can gain real leverage in the democratic process.

Notes

1. David J. Hoff, "Federal Law Bolsters Case for Aid Suits," *Education Week*, October 1, 2003; Molly A. Hunter, *Litigations Challenging Constitutionality of K–12 Funding in the 50 States* (Campaign for Fiscal Equity, February 2, 2006) (www.schoolfunding.info [April 29, 2006]). The U.S. Supreme Court case referenced is *San Antonio Independent School District* v. *Rodriguez*, 411 U.S. 1 (1973).

2. NCLB is Public Law 107-110. For description and background, see Diane Ravitch, *National Standards in American Education* (Brookings, 1995); Andrew Rudalevige, "Forging

a Congressional Compromise," in *No Child Left Behind? The Politics and Practice of School Accountability,* edited by Paul E. Peterson and Martin West (Brookings, 2003); Susan H. Fuhrman, "Standards, Testing, and Fear of Federal Control," in *Who's in Charge Here? The Tangled Web of School Governance and Policy,* edited by Noel Epstein (Brookings/Education Commission of the States, 2004), pp. 135–41.

3. Michael A. Rebell and Jessica R. Wolff, *Opportunity Knocks: Applying Lessons from the Education Adequacy Movement to Reform the No Child Left Behind Act,* Campaign for Educational Equity Policy Paper 2 (Columbia University, March 2006). I am grateful to Michael Rebell for permission to read an earlier version of this document prior to its formal release. Rebell is executive director of the Campaign for Educational Equity, and Wolff is the director of policy development. David Shreve, director of the National Conference of State Legislature's Education Committee, is quoted in Hoff, "Federal Law Bolsters Case."

4. See chapter 1, by West and Peterson, and chapter 2, by Briffault, in this volume as well as Michael Heise, "State Constitutions, School Finance Litigation, and the 'Third Wave': From Equity to Adequacy," *Temple Law Review* 69 (Fall 1995): 1151–76; Michael Rebell, "Educational Adequacy, Democracy, and the Courts," in *Achieving High Educational Standards for All,* edited by Timothy Ready, Christopher Edley Jr., and Catherine E. Snow (National Research Council, 2001), pp. 228–31; and Peter Schrag, *Final Test: The Battle for Adequacy in America's Schools* (New York: New Press, 2003).

5. Paul A. Minorini and Stephen D. Sugarman, "Educational Adequacy and the Courts," in *Equity and Adequacy in Education Finance: Issues and Perspectives,* edited by Helen F. Ladd and others (National Academy Press, 1999), pp. 179–80; and see William Clune, "Educational Adequacy: A Theory and Its Remedies," *University of Michigan Journal of Law Reform* 28 (Spring 1995): 485.

6. *Unified School District No. 229* v. *Kansas,* 885 P.2d 1170 (Kans. 1994); see also the decision in *Idaho Schools for Equal Educational Opportunity* v. *Evans,* 123 Idaho 573, 583, 830 P.2d 724 (Idaho 1993), and the May 2005 "Report from the Court: The High School Problem," issued by North Carolina judge Howard E. Manning Jr., in the *Hoke* case there (thanks to Ashley Osment for making this available). Rebell, "Educational Adequacy, Democracy, and the Courts," pp. 228–30; David J. Hoff, "States on Ropes in Finance Lawsuits," *Education Week,* December 8, 2004, p. 1.

7. Complaint, *Consortium for Adequate School Funding (CASF) in Georgia, Inc.* v. *State of Georgia,* no. 04-91004 (Sup. Ga. October 28, 2005), especially at 8–21, 126–39.

8. Rebell and Wolff, *Opportunity Knocks,* p. 3; phone interview with Michael Rebell, September 9, 2005; Sciarra quoted in David J. Hoff, "States on Ropes."

9. Pamela Prah, "No Child Law Could Spawn State Lawsuits," *Stateline.org,* July 9, 2003 (www.stateline.org/live/ViewPage.action?siteNodeId=136&languageId=1&contentId=15440 [September 2006]); National Conference of State Legislatures, *Final Report of the Task Force on No Child Left Behind* (February 2005), p. 47.

10. Office of the White House Press Secretary, "President Discusses Education at National Urban League Conference" (August 1, 2001); Office of the White House Press Secretary, "Press Conference of the President" (April 28, 2005).

11. Plaintiffs' Opening Brief, Court of Appeals, *Campaign for Fiscal Equity (CFE) et al.* v. *State of New York* (January 31, 2003), at 51.

12. National Conference of State Legislatures, *Final Report of the Task Force,* p. 47; David J. Hoff, "Debate Grows on True Costs of School Law," *Education Week,* February 4, 2004, p. 1.

13. Rebell and Wolff, *Opportunity Knocks*, p. 16; a November 2005 draft of the report, cited in the conference version of this chapter, discussed the politics of 100 percent proficiency in more detail (see p. 40, note 58).

14. See NCLB, §1111(b)(2), (C) and (D); National Conference of State Legislatures, *Final Report of the Task Force*, pp. 17–18.

15. Schrag, *Final Test*, pp. 159–66, 189, 196–204; Plaintiffs' Opening Brief, *CFE* v. *New York*, at 41, 49.

16. Lynn Olson, "In ESEA Wake, School Data Flowing Forth," *Education Week*, December 10, 2003, p. 1.

17. Steve Smith, "Education Adequacy Litigation: History, Trends, and Research," *University of Arkansas at Little Rock Law Review* 27 (Fall 2004): 122.

18. Steve Morrison and Superintendent Everette M. Dean, quoted in Michael Dobbs, "Poor Schools Sue for Funding: Higher Standards Are Basis for Seeking 'Educational Adequacy,'" *Washington Post*, June 7, 2004, p. A13; "Education Lawsuits Succeeding with 'No Child Left Behind' Data," July 8, 2004 (www.civilrights.org [August 26, 2005]).

19. First Amended Complaint, *Douglas County School District et al.* v. *Johanns et al.* (July 29, 2005). See also the plaintiffs' briefs in *CASFG* v. *State of Georgia* (September 14, 2004).

20. Maryland Commission on Education, Finance, Equity, and Excellence, *Final Report* (Annapolis, Md.: Department of Legislative Services, January 2002), p. x; *Columbia Falls Elementary School District No. 6* v. *State of Montana*, 04-390 (Mont. November 9, 2004), affirmed in 109 P. 3d 257 (Mont. 2005).

21. National Conference of State Legislatures, "Memorandum of the National Conference of State Legislatures on Legal Questions Regarding the NCLB" (July 7, 2003), and see Prah, "No Child Law Could Spawn State Lawsuits."

22. Lance D. Fusarelli, "Gubernatorial Reactions to No Child Left Behind: Politics, Pressure, and Education Reform," *Peabody Journal of Education* 80, no. 2 (2005): 120–36.

23. George Miller, "Bush's Broken Promise to America's Students: $40 Billion and Counting" (www.house.gov/georgemiller/eseainfo.html [September 27, 2006]); Hoff, "Debate Grows," citing a January 2004 report from the National Education Association; National Conference of State Legislatures, *Final Report of the Task Force*, p. 48, citing work by William Mathis.

24. Plaintiff's complaint, especially sec. III, and "Memorandum in Opposition to Defendant's Motion to Dismiss," in *School District in the City of Pontiac, MI* v. *Spellings*, 2:05-CV-71535 (2005), at 11.

25. This calculation reflects an estimated shortfall of $41.6 million from the period January 2002 through June 2008. See Connecticut State Department of Education, *Cost of Implementing the Federal No Child Left Behind Act in Connecticut: State-Level Costs* (Hartford, Conn., March 2, 2005); Office of Attorney General Richard Blumenthal, Connecticut, "State Sues Federal Government over Illegal Unfunded Mandates under No Child Left Behind Act," News Release (Hartford, August 22, 2005).

26. *South Dakota* v. *Dole*, 483 U.S. 203 (1987).

27. James E. Ryan, "The Tenth Amendment and Other Legal Tigers," in *Who's in Charge Here?* edited by Epstein, pp. 47–51; Opinion and Order, *Pontiac* v. *Spellings* (November 23, 2005), at 7; *Memorandum of Decision, State of Connecticut* v. *Spellings*, 3:05-CV-1330-MRK (U.S. Dist. Ct., September 2006), at 46–51.

28. National Conference of State Legislatures, *Final Report of the Task Force*, p. 10.

29. Governors Martz (R-Mont.) and Richardson (D-N.M.), Johanns (R-Neb.), and Rendell (D-Penn.), respectively, quoted in Fusarelli, "Gubernatorial Reactions," and see House

Resolution 118 of 2003, state of Hawaii; Amicus Curiae Brief of the Governor of the Commonwealth of Pennsylvania, *Pontiac* v. *Spellings* (6th Cir. Ct. of Appeals, March 31, 2006) at 1, 14–15, emphasis added (this brief and other related material may be found at www.nea.org/lawsuit/index.html [April 29, 2006]); Amanda Ripley and Sonja Steptoe, "Inside the Revolt over Bush's School Rules," *Time,* May 2, 2005.

30. Complaint for Declaratory and Injunctive Relief, *State of Connecticut* v. *Spellings* (U.S. Dist. Ct., August 2005), par. 8. The district court dismissed this charge in September 2006 but did hold that a related count in the case—the state's argument that the Department had not followed proper administrative procedures in rejecting its amended plan for testing students with limited proficiency in English—could be heard. Memorandum of Decision, at 65–66.

31. E. E. Schattschneider, *The Semisovereign People: A Realist's View of Democracy in America* (Dryden Press, 1975 [1960]), p. 3.

32. Quoted in Christopher Cross, *Political Education* (Teachers College Press, 2004), p. 28f. More generally, see Paul T. Hill, "The Federal Role in Education," in *Brookings Papers on Education Policy 2000,* edited by Diane Ravitch (Brookings, 2000).

33. Schattschneider, *The Semisovereign People,* p. 4.

34. Quoted in Fusarelli, "Gubernatorial Reactions."

35. George W. Bush, "Remarks by the President to the 2004 National Urban League Conference," Detroit, Mich., July 2004.

36. See, for example, the "Student Bill of Rights" (H.R. 2178 in the 109th Congress), proposed by Rep. Chaka Fattah (D-Penn.) with Senator Christopher Dodd (D-Conn.), which seeks to create a basis for suing in federal court states that do not meet the bill's guarantees of an "ideal or adequate" education. The language has had as many as 188 cosponsors (in its 2003 incarnation). Rep. Jesse Jackson (D-Ill.) has proposed a constitutional amendment providing that "all citizens of the United States shall enjoy the right to a public education of equal high quality" (H. J. Res. 29, 109th Congress).

37. Lowell C. Rose and Alec M. Gallup, "The 38th Annual Phi Delta Kappa/Gallup Poll of the Public's Attitudes toward the Public Schools," *Phi Delta Kappan* 88 (September 2006): 50–51.

38. Government Accountability Office, *No Child Left Behind Act: Improvements Needed in Education's Process for Tracking States' Implementation of Key Provisions,* GAO-04-734 (September 2004); Susan Saulny, "Meaning of 'Proficient' Varies for Schools across Country," *New York Times,* January 19, 2005; Paul E. Peterson and Frederick M. Hess, "Johnny Can Read . . . in Some States: Assessing the Rigor of State Assessment Systems," *Education Next* 5, no. 3 (Summer 2005): 52–53; Lynn Olson and Linda Jacobson, "Analysis Finds Minority NCLB Scores Widely Excluded," *Education Week,* April 26, 2006, p. 5.

39. See the memos included with Florida Department of Education, "Memos Regarding Provisional Adequate Yearly Progress Designation," Press Release (Tallahassee, June 14, 2005) (www.fldoe.org/news/2005/2005_06_14.asp [April 30, 2006]).

40. Pennsylvania Department of Education, *Pennsylvania's No Child Left Behind Position Paper* (Harrisburg, April 8, 2004), p. 4; see also Fusarelli, "Gubernatorial Reactions."

41. See, for example, Vaishali Hoavwar, "Baltimore Takeovers Prevented," *Education Week,* April 19, 2006, p. 1; Sara Neufeld, "With State Plans at Bay, City Acts to Save Schools," *Baltimore Sun,* April 12, 2006, p. A1; Jill Rosen, "Veto Killed, State Takeover of Schools Halted," *Baltimore Sun,* April 11, 2006, p. A1.

42. *Hoke County Board of Education* v. *State of North Carolina,* 95CVS1158 (2002); see also Smith, "Education Adequacy Litigation," p. 123.

43. Of course, state actors might also flee such responsibility: who wants to be the "education governor" as the list of "failing" schools expands? See Fusarelli, "Gubernatorial Reactions."

44. "Michael Rebell to Lead Campaign for Educational Equity at Teachers College," News Release (Teachers College, June 9, 2005) (www.tc.columbia.edu/news/article.htm?id=5184 [September 22, 2005]); the Warren Institute's online home is www.law.berkeley.edu/centers/ewi/ (December 1, 2005). See also chapter 14, by Dunn and Derthick, in this volume.

45. Rebell and Wolff, *Opportunity Knocks,* p. 8.

46. Rebell and Wolff, *Opportunity Knocks* (November 2005 draft), part II, pp. 43–68; Janice Petrovich and Amy Stuart Wells, eds., *Bringing Equity Back: Research for a New Era in American Educational Policy* (Teachers College Press, 2005); Jan Resseger's comments at the 2005 ACCESS Education Adequacy conference (www.schoolfunding.info/news/policy/7-11-05conferenceroundup.php3 [August 26, 2005]).

47. Schrag, *Final Test,* p. 241.

48. Rudalevige, "Forging," p. 33; Schrag, *Final Test,* p. 83. Note that the National Education Association, in its 2005 lawsuit, claimed it had standing to contest NCLB because its members had suffered from the "stigma" attached to those who worked in schools not making adequate yearly progress. The new emphasis of the Campaign for Educational Equity on a "full opportunity standard" (Rebell and Wolff, *Opportunity Knocks,* p. 16) may reflect a negotiated outcome on this score.

49. Gerald Rosenberg, *The Hollow Hope: Can Courts Bring about Social Change?* (University of Chicago Press, 1991).

11

MICHAEL HEISE

Adequacy Litigation in an Era of Accountability

America's quest for greater equal educational opportunity—an extension of the nation's historic drive for greater racial equality—presently involves a persistent push for large sums of money. State court decisions ordering dramatic increases in spending on education in a steadily growing number of states reflect a multi-decade nationwide litigation campaign designed to enlist the courts' assistance in extracting additional resources for public schools. The adequacy claims that constitute the most recent and aggressive line of attack in that campaign now occupy a central position in the discourse on education policy and school reform.

Adequacy litigation represents the latest iteration of an enduring struggle for and over the meaning of equal educational opportunity, a struggle ignited by the *Brown* v. *Board of Education* decision in 1954.[1] Decades ago race and school desegregation litigation forged an earlier understanding of equal opportunity. More recently, school finance litigation displaced desegregation litigation as the dominant legal strategy for enhancing equal educational opportunity. The substitution of resources for race in the legal quest for greater equal

The author wishes to thank participants in the conference Adequacy Lawsuits: Their Growing Impact on American Education at Harvard University for comments on an earlier draft. Thanks as well to Andrew C. Compton and the librarians at Cornell Law School for outstanding research assistance.

educational opportunity necessitated an alternative theoretical approach. It also stimulated a run of litigation that already spans more than three decades and traverses federal and state courts. Because judges and lawyers—prompted by litigants—are second-guessing the decisions that lawmakers and governors make about public school spending with increased regularity, this is an appropriate moment to pause and reflect on the consequences for education and public policy.

Framed by a quest for enhanced equal educational opportunity, school finance adequacy litigation raises four important issues that I consider in this chapter. First, adequacy lawsuits are structured in a manner that transforms failure in the classroom into success in the courtroom. The interaction of adequacy litigation and the No Child Left Behind Act (NCLB)[2]—notably the student achievement data developed and disseminated by NCLB—fuels this ironic metamorphosis. Second, one unanticipated consequence of the interaction between adequacy litigation and NCLB is the growing pressure on states to lower student proficiency standards so as to reduce the state's exposure to adequacy litigation. States are far less inclined to articulate bold goals for student achievement now that litigants and courts are transforming education policy goals into legal minimums. Third, the efficacy of successful adequacy lawsuits and their remedies are clouded by the inevitable political backlash that such litigation typically generates. Fourth, perhaps owing to political backlash, recent court decisions evidence an emerging hint of judicial humility. Courts in some states appear less willing for institutional, legal, or structural reasons to delve into the task of restructuring school finance regimes. Whether the judicial pullback by a few state courts signals the start of a trend or a slight detour from a drive toward greater judicial engagement with school finance policy is far from clear.

Transforming Classroom Failure into Courtroom Success

The school finance adequacy litigation movement gained critical momentum once it joined with the standards and assessments movement. Since the mid-1980s, incident to the *A Nation at Risk* report, many states began the task of reviewing and, in some instances, articulating for the first time goals for student education outcomes.[3] The emergence of the standards and assessment movement signaled a fundamental shift in the focus of educational policymaking away from inputs (resources) and toward outcomes (student achievement).

Although reasonable disagreement exists about the desirability and efficacy of the standards and assessment movement as policy, one consequence of the movement is already clear: policymakers now understand how policy goals—educational standards—can be transformed into legal entitlements to receive more resources. In state after state, school finance litigants have used evidence of shortcomings in student achievement to win favorable court decisions. In 2002, for example, only 32 percent of New York City's public high school graduates earned Regents Diplomas, although 55 percent of New York's public school graduates statewide qualified for this academic distinction.[4] The plaintiffs in New York State's adequacy litigation successfully argued that New York City schoolchildren's dismal record evidenced that the state was failing to provide a "sound basic" education.[5]

Consequently, in 2005 New York Supreme Court judge DeGrasse accepted a referees' report recommending that the General Assembly provide New York City schools with an additional $9.179 billion over the next five years for capital improvements and at least an additional $5.63 billion for operations.[6] In 2006 a somewhat ambiguous New York Court of Appeals opinion directed the General Assembly and Governor Pataki to consider allocating between $4.7 billion and $5.63 billion in additional funds to New York City schools.[7] While the New York adequacy lawsuit worked its way through the protracted appeals process, the New York General Assembly passed a state budget for fiscal 2006 that includes a provision allowing New York City schools to spend more than $9 billion over five years on capital improvements.[8]

The interaction between adequacy litigation and the standards and assessments movement took on even greater force with passage of NCLB. Under NCLB, states (that have not previously done so) must establish school accountability systems that annually assess student proficiency in math and reading. Schools must achieve adequate yearly progress as construed by NCLB or face sanctions. Although federal law says that the state standards must be "challenging," NCLB leaves states free to establish their own standards and to determine the score necessary to meet the "proficient" threshold. Thus states possess virtually complete control over the mechanisms that determine whether their students and schools achieve adequate yearly progress. State autonomy in this regard, perhaps necessary for developing political support for NCLB, frustrates comparisons between and among states.[9]

At its core, NCLB leverages state-created standards and assessments into litigation tools, increases transparency by disseminating data on progress, and imposes consequences for insufficient progress. Under NCLB, districts must test students in grades three through eight in reading and math, and schools must report and disseminate test results for all students as well as for various subgroups that contain a minimum number of students. A sliding scale of NCLB-specific consequences befalls any school that does not achieve adequate yearly progress. Thus a school's failure to achieve sufficient student achievement and progress generates liability under federal law. The full contour of a state's NCLB liability was not fully appreciated, however, until school finance activists began to advance inadequate yearly progress under NCLB as legal proof of inadequate education in school finance litigation.

The Kansas Experience

Recent adequacy litigation in Kansas illustrates how adequacy litigants synthesize state standards and NCLB consequences into a state constitutional entitlement to greater resources. The Kansas constitution, as amended in 1966, requires the legislature to "make suitable provision for finance of the educational interests of the state."[10] To discharge its constitutional duty, and prompted by a school finance lawsuit then making its way through the state's judicial system, in 1992 Kansas lawmakers passed the School District Finance and Quality Performance Act (SDFQPA).[11] SDFQPA created a statewide property tax and a statewide system for collecting and distributing property tax revenues. Although the SDFQPA begins from the presumption of equal per-pupil spending, the presumption is modified by district-specific weighting factors. As well, SDFQPA established a state-guaranteed per-pupil spending floor, along with an accountability system tied to state minimum standards of student performance in specific subjects.[12] Satisfied with Kansas lawmakers' development and implementation of SDFQPA, litigants agreed to dismiss pending school finance litigation.[13]

Satisfaction with SDFQPA was relatively short-lived, however, and new school finance litigation ensued. In 2003 a Kansas judge struck down SDFQPA.[14] Part of the court's reasoning involved student academic performance.[15] In assessing whether student academic performance evidenced "adequacy," the Kansas trial court assessed performance data generated in response to NCLB.[16] Notably, *both* parties pointed to NCLB data as support for their opposing positions.

The plaintiffs introduced into evidence 2002 and 2003 math and reading proficiency scores for fifth-, eighth-, and eleventh-grade students, by racial and ethnic cohort.[17] The student performance data uncovered substantial achievement gaps between and among student cohorts. The court noted that the evidence was both "informative and disturbingly telling."[18] The court then quickly ascribed the students' poor academic performance to inadequate funding.[19]

The defendant school districts also sought (albeit unsuccessfully) legal refuge from student academic performance as defined by NCLB. The defendant districts pointed to their schools' meeting the adequate yearly progress requirements articulated in NCLB as evidence of adequate educational services.[20] The court dismissed this interpretation of the student achievement data, noting that the districts could achieve the required adequate yearly progress even though, for the 2002 and 2003 school years, up to 56 percent of all kindergarteners through eighth graders, and 48 percent of high school students, failed the reading standard.[21] For math performance, adequate yearly performance standards permitted a 53 percent failure rate for kindergarteners through eighth graders and a 70 percent failure rate for high school students.[22] The Kansas experience demonstrates the courts' willingness to treat NCLB student achievement data asymmetrically in the context of adequacy litigation. Although courts, such as the Kansas court, are willing to conclude that a district's failure to achieve adequate yearly progress evidences inadequate education, courts appear reluctant to conclude that a district's achievement of adequate yearly progress evidences adequate education.

Adequacy Litigation and the Dilution of Student Proficiency Standards

Potential financial exposure to school finance adequacy lawsuits (as well as other adverse consequences for states and local school districts flowing from NCLB), fueled partly by a school's inability to achieve adequate yearly progress under NCLB, undoubtedly will prompt some states to dilute their student proficiency standards.[23] State lawmakers will be far more reluctant to establish bold student proficiency standards in an effort to stimulate improvement now that litigants can transform such standards into legal entitlements for additional education resources.

Notwithstanding the federal government's direct and significant involvement with K–12 education through NCLB, primary and secondary education endures as principally a concern of state and local government. Prior to 1989 many states engaged in something resembling a race to the top in terms of developing and implementing rigorous student proficiency standards and goals. The emergence of adequacy litigation, however, now fueled by state standards and assessments and NCLB consequences, risks transforming a race to the top into a race to the bottom, as states respond to the unanticipated consequences of establishing aggressive student proficiency standards.

When many states initiated efforts to articulate desired student academic proficiency in the early- and mid-1980s, they did so without the specter of federal liability under NCLB or exposure to adequacy lawsuits. Today, such liability and exposure disquiet many policymakers and assuredly influence standard setting or tinkering; if nothing else, they generate a dilemma. To be sure, some degree of state pullback from demanding student proficiency standards flows from other factors, including political resistance generated by underperforming districts. States with rigorous proficiency standards, however, are more likely to fail to achieve adequate yearly progress and are more likely to trigger NCLB consequences, increase their exposure to adequacy litigation, and consequently generate potentially costly financial exposure. Conversely, states with comparatively weak proficiency standards stand a better chance of successfully navigating through NCLB requirements and thereby avoid NCLB sanctions and the associated stigma as well as potentially significant financial exposure.

Although NCLB affords states significant latitude in setting their own standards of student performance, it obligates states to participate in a national testing program. NCLB requires a sample of each state's fourth and eighth graders to take the National Assessment of Educational Progress (NAEP) reading and math tests every other year.[24] Until NCLB, state participation in NAEP, the nation's only true metric that facilitates comparisons of student achievement across states and, indeed, across nations, was voluntary. Mandating state participation in NAEP was designed, in part, to establish an external check on student achievement. NCLB proponents suggested that the threat of embarrassment flowing from a state reporting that its students performed exceptionally well on state tests but poorly on NAEP tests would blunt a state's desire to lower its student performance standards dramatically.[25]

Perhaps more important than the specter of public embarrassment, unsatisfactory student achievement results can increase legal liability for states. As a result, many states confront a stark dilemma: maintain high standards of student proficiency at the risk of increasing litigation (and financial) exposure. As state budgets tighten, and in a policymaking world of ever-increasing claimants on state resources, the policy path of least financial resistance becomes even more attractive to many lawmakers. Moreover, in states where suburban districts recoil at the prospect—however remote—of their students not achieving state proficiency standards, or in districts that resent the inevitable circular pull of standardized tests, a decision to dilute academic standards becomes even easier for a state to make.[26] How state standards of student proficiency respond to NCLB exposure and whether NCLB will trigger a race to the bottom regarding student proficiency standards is an empirical question. Early evidence, while far from definitive, is not encouraging.

New York State's Regents Standards

Recent changes in New York illustrate the complexities in assessing whether states are diluting academic standards in response to adequacy litigation. On the one hand, in 1996 the New York State Board of Regents voted to require that satisfactory student achievement on the state's prestigious Regents Standards was necessary for any student desiring a diploma from a New York public high school.[27] In 2003, however, the Board of Regents voted to delay imposing the higher standard.[28] New York retreated on other fronts as well, lowering the threshold for a passing score and the number of proficiency exams required.[29] Indeed, it remains unclear whether, how, or when New York will fully implement its Regents Standards statewide as well as whether the Regents Diploma will ever reflect the standards that existed prior to 1996. What changed since 1996 were the passage and implementation of NCLB.

The successful adequacy lawsuit in New York shows why some states revisit achievement standards. Before 1996, New York State's Regents Standards were among the nation's most rigorous. Their rigor, however, guaranteed a steady stream of students who failed to earn the coveted Regents Diploma. New York City successfully leveraged its students' failure to earn the Regents Diploma as evidence of the state's failure to provide an adequate education. Thus New York's high academic standards contributed to a legal judgment against the state in excess of $14 billion.

In light of the immense financial exposure generated by a successful adequacy lawsuit, it is no surprise to find many states revisiting their commitment to high academic standards. States such as Louisiana, Colorado, and Connecticut, for example, have finessed their system of scoring student performance in ways that increase the number of students deemed proficient for purposes of adequate yearly progress under NCLB.[30]

Successful Adequacy Lawsuits, Political Backlash, and Legal Implementation

Successful adequacy lawsuits often generate political opposition and resistance that impede the implementation of court orders. Sources of political opposition and resistance include the obvious: state lawmakers and policymakers. Many lawmakers and policymakers resent outside (that is, judicial) intrusion into their budgeting process. State budgeting is invariably a high-wire political act during the best of fiscal times. When budgets tighten or contract, the political trade-offs incident to the budgeting process can be especially unpleasant. A court order with potentially dramatic budgetary implications can bother even lawmakers otherwise partial to school finance reform. In the world of public budget making, where delicacy and nuance often rein, a court order raising serious budgetary issues can be an especially blunt instrument of reform.

To be sure, a few lawmakers and policymakers may welcome judicial intrusions into school finance policymaking. In particular, lawmakers who prefer increased education funding but are unwilling to support the necessary tax increases for political reasons might seek opportunities to deflect political responsibility onto less politically accountable judges. Lawmakers motivated to externalize political accountability—however prevalent—strain the traditional allocation of powers. Moreover, such political motivations generate their own set of risks. For example, even if lawmakers can successfully deflect immediate accountability for increased tax burdens, over time taxpayers' willingness to shoulder higher education spending is not without limits. As adequacy litigation continues and judgments mount, taxpayer resistance will continue to stiffen.[31]

Institutional Stress and Recent Hints of Judicial Humility

The institutional stresses imposed by adequacy lawsuits on courts as well as the sometimes vigorous opposition to judicial mandates involving education spending may help to explain emerging hints of increasing judicial humility. Judicial humility in the school finance context comes in three main flavors. First, some state courts simply refuse to participate. For example, state courts in Illinois and Rhode Island, when confronted in the mid-1990s with school finance challenges to their state constitutional requirements, declined jurisdiction and found refuge in the political question doctrine.[32]

Although not textually articulated in the federal or state constitutions, the political question doctrine operates as a check on judicial power by removing certain "political questions" from the scope of judicial review.[33] Within the school finance context, the political question doctrine supplies at least two safe harbors for courts disinclined to resolve school finance disputes. First, a court can "decide not to decide" by concluding that the state constitution possesses a "textually demonstrable constitutional commitment of the issue to a coordinate political department."[34] Such a commitment flows from the state's constitutional text and expressly, implicitly, or structurally directs school finance matters to the legislative branch.

When confronted with a school finance challenge, the Illinois Supreme Court pointed to concerns about trenching into legislative terrain as one reason to decline the plaintiff's invitation to strike down the state's school finance system. The Illinois constitution's education clause guarantees to its citizens an "efficient system of high-quality public educational institutions and services."[35] In *Committee for Educational Rights* v. *Edgar*,[36] although the court cited numerous grounds for upholding a lower-court dismissal of the plaintiff's challenge, the court remarked, "Nor is education a subject within the judiciary's field of expertise, such that a judicial role in giving content to the education guarantee might be warranted. Rather, the question of educational quality is inherently one of policy involving philosophical and practical considerations that call for the exercise of legislative and administrative discretion."[37] To hold otherwise, the court warned, "would largely deprive the members of the general public of a voice in a matter which is close to the hearts of all individuals in Illinois."[38]

Second, even where a court is persuaded that school finance disputes are not committed to other branches of government, under the political question doctrine a court can nonetheless still decline jurisdiction by concluding that it lacks "judicially discoverable and manageable standards" to resolve the conflict.[39] More specifically, some courts have concluded that judicially operationalizing such notions as "equal" and "adequate" in the school finance context resists easy consensus. As the Supreme Court has noted, what constitutes an equal or adequate education "is not likely to be divined for all time even by the scholars who now so earnestly debate the issues."[40] In addition, whether the courts are the best institution to undertake an effort to define what an equal or adequate education means is another critical question. Too many discussions about the judiciary's involvement with school finance disputes focus on what courts *should* do independent of discussion about what courts effectively *can* do.[41]

The Rhode Island Supreme Court noted such concerns in *City of Pawtucket* v. *Sundlum*,[42] when it resisted the plaintiff's desire to engage the court in an effort to recraft Rhode Island's school finance system. The court concluded that it could not identify standards that would assist it in the task of discerning whether "equal" or "adequate" education was provided to the plaintiffs. Moreover, the court declined to undertake the task of judicially crafting such standards, as such an endeavor risked injecting the court into a "morass comparable to the decades-long struggle of the Supreme Court of New Jersey."[43] Indeed, the Rhode Island justices, hinting at comparative institutional disadvantages, characterized the multi-decade New Jersey school finance saga as a "chilling example of the thickets that can entrap a court that takes on the duties of a legislature."[44]

A second form of judicial humility emerges in states where courts recognize jurisdiction, accept the invitation to decide school finance challenges, but, after reviewing the evidence presented in light of the relevant constitutional text, conclude that no violation exists. The Nebraska Supreme Court's decision in *Gould* v. *Orr*[45] illustrates this version of judicial humility. Unlike its counterparts in Illinois and Rhode Island, the Nebraska court did not flinch from granting jurisdiction over a school finance dispute. The court noted that while the plaintiffs—pushing an equity theory—successfully demonstrated funding inequality, the plaintiffs did not successfully demonstrate how such unequal per-pupil funding fell below constitutional requirements. While the *Gould* decision effectively foreclosed an equity challenge to Nebraska's school finance system, it conspicuously left open a question about the efficaciousness of an adequacy challenge. Indeed, such a challenge was launched in subsequent litigation in 2003.[46]

Recent judicial pullback by a few state courts evidences a third genre of judicial humility. This version involves states where courts accept jurisdiction, conclude that school finance systems violate state constitutional requirements, and demand either legislative or executive action consistent with the judicial opinion. Once state lawmakers and executives act, however, follow-up litigation invariably ensues and typically asserts that constitutional violations persist. This follow-up litigation invites the judicial branch not only to reengage but also to assume even broader and deeper roles in reshaping school finance systems.

It is at this precise point where school finance litigation enters a critical stage. On the one hand, such litigation can follow the "New Jersey" path and risk a multi-decade struggle among the executive, legislative, and judicial branches over school finance turf. New Jersey's saga—still ongoing after more than three decades—is well chronicled. New York appears destined to follow its neighbor's path. New York's school finance litigation push—launched in 1978—has persisted for almost three decades and involves intragovernmental fighting. Indeed, despite sustained litigation, numerous court decisions, and appeals, it remains unclear whether New York courts have the legal authority to compel the governor and state lawmakers to direct additional funding to New York City schools.[47]

Experiences in others states differ, however, and hint at a potential trend. During the 1990s school finance reform activists cited state supreme court decisions in Alabama, Ohio, and Massachusetts as evidence of the dominance and efficaciousness of adequacy theory.[48] Subsequent decisions in all three states, however, suggest something of a judicial retreat. In 1993 an Alabama court boldly announced that the state was obligated to provide an adequate education to its citizens.[49] The court order was especially particular in what it meant by an adequate education.[50] More recently, however, and incident to follow-up litigation, the Alabama Supreme Court dismissed further proceedings, pointing to concerns about the separation of powers.[51] Likewise, after protracted litigation in Ohio, the Ohio Supreme Court granted a writ of prohibition in 2003 forbidding the trial court from exercising further jurisdiction over the school finance case.[52]

The Massachusetts Saga

As recent court decisions in Alabama and Ohio illustrate, judicial hesitation emerges even in states where courts had previously found inadequate education. A dramatic turn of events in Massachusetts embodies many of these common themes and warrants close attention.[53] In 1993 Massachusetts's Supreme Judicial Court ruled in *McDuffy* v. *Secretary of the Executive Office of Education*[54] that the state failed to fulfill its constitutional obligation and noted in particular the deleterious consequences of the state's overwhelming reliance on local property tax revenues.[55] The Massachusetts court directed the state's governor and legislature to correct the constitutional defects.[56] Three days after the *McDuffy* opinion was announced, Massachusetts lawmakers passed the Education Reform Act of 1993.[57] The Education Reform Act dramatically restructured education in Massachusetts, especially as it relates to school funding, student goals and performance, and school and school district accountability.[58]

Notwithstanding the *McDuffy* opinion and the Education Reform Act, in 1999 litigants sued anew, claiming that data from four Massachusetts school districts[59] showed that education—at least for those four districts—had not improved since 1993 and, more important, still violated constitutional obligations, including those articulated in the *McDuffy* decision.[60] The trial court judge found that the state's education department lacked adequate resources to meet the requirements of Massachusetts's education clause.[61] Soon thereafter, once again, litigants asked Massachusetts's highest court for help in restructuring the state's education system.

This time, however, the Massachusetts high court pulled back. Specifically, the court rejected the lower-court report's conclusion that the "Commonwealth [state of Massachusetts] is presently neglecting or is likely to neglect its constitutional duties, thus requiring judicial intervention."[62] Pivotal to the supreme court's analysis was the selection of the appropriate constitutional standard. The Massachusetts high court rejected the assertion that adequacy required all Massachusetts school districts to achieve proficiency in the seven different areas outlined in the 1993 *McDuffy* decision.[63] Rather, in *Hancock* v. *Commissioner of Education*,[64] the court concluded that the state had taken reasonable and appropriate steps in a timely manner to address school funding and student achievement disparities.[65] The decision brought to a close twenty-seven years of litigation and twelve years of state court supervision over school finance matters in Massachusetts.

Notably, the Massachusetts justices also feared replicating the experiences of other states. The *Hancock* decision explicitly references parallel adequacy litigation in both New Jersey and New York. The Massachusetts jurists noted that courts in New York and New Jersey stepped in (repeatedly) "after many years of legislative failure or inability to enact education reforms and to commit resources to implement those reforms."[66]

Certainly, the experiences of lengthy and nasty state supreme court entanglements with their legislative and executive counterparts in New York, New Jersey, and elsewhere provided Massachusetts's justices ample reason to pause and reflect. The damage to the state judicial branch owing to legislative and gubernatorial resistance or outright rejection of state judicial decrees is considerable. Moreover, even in states that do not outright resist state school finance decisions, the empirical evidence on the efficacy of court decisions to achieve the goals sought by the prevailing plaintiffs is mixed, at best.

The likelihood of courts ceding jurisdiction over school finance litigation due to concerns about institutional capacity, however, is far from certain. Existing evidence is decidedly split; discernible trends elude. The *Hancock* decision in Massachusetts could signal a potential judicial reluctance to trench too deeply into educational policymaking. At the same time, *Hancock* could just as easily represent a brief diversion of a trend toward increased judicial engagement with school finance issues.

Adequacy Litigation in the Twenty-First Century

The centrality of school finance adequacy litigation in education reform and policy discourse is unlikely to recede anytime soon. If anything, for the immediate future, adequacy litigation is likely to strengthen due to its interactions with NCLB. That NCLB—a federal law—reinforces the salience of school finance adequacy litigation for states, of course, abounds with irony. To be sure, NCLB was not enacted for the benefit of adequacy litigation activists. Unable to forestall any longer an important shift at the policy level from a focus on education resources to a focus on school and student performance—embodied in

NCLB—adequacy litigants turned their collective attention to executing a reversal at the legal level: leveraging disparities in school and student performance into state constitutional claims for increased education resources.

The ability of adequacy litigation to increase education spending pivots on the endurance of two key elements: first, that litigants, judges, and juries collapse educational policy goals and aspirations into legally enforceable minimums and, second, that judges and courts willingly engage—deeply—in complicated, politically perilous, and contentious school finance policy terrain. The long-term stability of both key elements, however, is far from clear. The first element risks conflating policy and law; the second places increasingly enormous stress on traditional understandings of separation of powers.

Although society's unending quest for greater equal educational opportunity implies a robust role for state (and federal) courts, a judicial role in the service of adequacy litigation is not without limits. Judges disinclined to venture too far into legislative terrain due to concerns related to separation of powers impose one internal limit on judicial power's reach. The courts' limited institutional capacity to achieve desired policy changes imposes an external limit on judicial activity, even where concerns regarding separation of powers might not deter judges.

Conscripting emerging efforts to increase accountability, such as NCLB, into school finance adequacy litigation risks not only irony but also consequential policy threats. Although recent decisions in a few states hint at a judicial pullback, continued court engagement sustains uncertainty about the courts' proper role in disputes about education spending. Such uncertainty, in turn, stimulates intergovernmental jockeying over authority for school finance among the legislative, executive, and judicial branches. That public policy discussions about how best to improve public education invariably involve adequacy litigation is not without consequence and raises important and uncomfortable questions for both law and policy.

Notes

1. *Brown v. Board of Education*, 347 U.S. 483 (1954).

2. No Child Left Behind Act of 2001 (NCLB), 20 U.S.C. § 6301 (2002). For a more complete discussion of No Child Left Behind and its specific statutory provisions, see Andrew Rudalevige, "'No Child Left Behind': Forging a Congressional Compromise," in *No Child Left Behind? The Politics and Practice of School Accountability,* edited by Paul E. Peterson and Martin West (Brookings, 2003).

3. For a discussion of the report, see, for example, Diane Ravitch, "The Test of Time," *Education Next* 16 (Spring 2003): 32–38.

4. New York State United Teachers, "Regents Diplomas: More Than Circumstance and Pomp" (March 2004) (www.nysut.org/excellence/evidence_regents.html [November 2005]); while noting progress in the number of Regents Diplomas being awarded each year, the article also shows New York City as lagging behind the rest of New York State.

5. *Campaign for Fiscal Equity, Inc.* v. *State of New York (CFE 1)*, 100 N.Y.2d 893 (2003).

6. *Campaign for Fiscal Equity, Inc.* v. *State of New York*, no. 111070/93 (N.Y. Sup. Ct., March 16, 2005) (order accepting referees' report on clarifying and enforcing remedies); *CFE 1*.

7. *Campaign for Fiscal Equity, Inc.* v. *State of New York*, 2006 WL 724551 (1st Dep't, March 23, 2006), Slip. Op. 02284.

8. See A. 9558-B, 2006 legislature, 228th sess. (N.Y. 2006); S. 6458-C, 2006 legislature, 228th sess. (N.Y. 2006). For a discussion see Danny Hakim and Jennifer Medina, "Deal in Albany on Budget Gives New School Aid," *New York Times*, March 29, 2006, p. A1.

9. Paul E. Peterson and Frederick M. Hess, "Johnny Can Read . . . in Some States: Assessing the Rigor of State Assessment Systems," *Education Next* 3, no. 5 (Summer 2005): 52–53.

10. Kansas Constitution, Article VI, § 6.

11. School District Finance and Quality Performance Act, 1992 Kansas Session Laws, § 280.

12. Charles Berger, "Equity without Adjudication: Kansas School Finance Reform and the 1992 School District and Quality Performance Act," *Journal of Law and Education* 27 (1998): 28.

13. Berger, "Equity without Adjudication," p. 28.

14. *Montoy* v. *State of Kansas*, no. 99-C-1738, 2003 WL 22902963 (Kan. Dist. Ct. December 2, 2003), at 49.

15. Ibid., at 45.

16. Ibid.

17. Ibid., at 47.

18. Ibid.

19. Ibid., at 49.

20. Ibid., at 41.

21. Ibid.

22. Ibid.

23. See, for example, James E. Ryan, "The Perverse Incentives of the No Child Left Behind Act," *New York University Law Review* 79, no. 3 (2004): 946–48.

24. No Child Left Behind Act, § 1111(c)(2).

25. Compare Lynn Olsen, "Want to Confirm State Test Scores? It's Complex, but NAEP Can Do It," *Education Week*, March 13, 2002, p. A1, arguing that states will respond to NAEP pressure, with Diane Ravitch, "Every State Left Behind," *New York Times*, November 7, 2005, p. A23, arguing that national testing is necessary.

26. Paul T. O'Neill, "High Stakes Testing Law and Litigation," *Brigham Young University Education and Law Journal* 2 (2003): 657–60, discussing suburban backlashes against standardized testing.

27. Karen W. Arenson, "Scaling Back Changes on Regents Standards," *New York Times*, October 14, 2003, p. B5.

28. Ibid.

29. Ibid.

30. See Ryan, "The Perverse Incentives of the No Child Left Behind Act," p. 948.

31. For one example, see Douglas S. Reed, *On Equal Terms: The Constitutional Politics of Educational Opportunity* (Princeton University Press, 2001), pp. 99–100.

32. *Committee for Educational Rights v. Edgar*, 174 Ill.2d 1 (Ill., 1996); *City of Pawtucket v. Sundlum*, 662 A.2d 40 (R.I. 1995).

33. For a general discussion, see Rachel E. Barkow, "More Supreme than Court? The Fall of the Political Question Doctrine and the Rise of Judicial Supremacy," *Columbia Law Review* 102, no. 2 (2002): 237–336.

34. *Baker v. Carr*, 369 U.S. 186, 217 (1962).

35. Illinois Constitution, Article X, § 1.

36. *Committee for Education Rights v. Edgar*, at 1.

37. Ibid., at 29.

38. Ibid.

39. Ibid., at 28.

40. *San Antonio Independent School District v. Rodriguez*, 411 U.S. 1, 43 (Tex. 1973).

41. Jonathan Cohen, "Judicial Control of the Purse: School Finance Litigation in State Courts," *Wayne State Law Review* 28 (1982): 1415–16.

42. *City of Pawtucket v. Sundlum*.

43. Ibid., at 59.

44. Ibid.

45. *Gould v. Orr*, 506 N.W.2d 349 (Neb. 1993).

46. Complaint, *Douglas County School District v. Johanns Nebraska District Court*, no. 1028-017 (June 30, 2003) (www.nebraskaschoolstrust.org/images/complaint.pdf). See also David Hoff, "States on Ropes in Finance Suits," *Education Week*, December 8, 2004, p. 23.

47. For a description of various lawmakers' reaction to the most recent New York court order, see Jennifer Medina, "Judges Once Again Order More Money for City Schools," *New York Times,* March 24, 2006, p. B2.

48. Opinion of the Justices, 624 So.2d 107 (Ala. 1993); *McDuffy v. Secretary of the Executive Office of Education*, 615 N.E.2d 516 (Mass. 1993); *DeRolph v. State* (*DeRolph I*), 677 N.E.2d 733 (Ohio 1997).

49. Opinion of the Justices.

50. Ibid., at 165–66 (noting the essential principles of a "liberal system of public schools").

51. *Ex parte James*, 836 So.2d 813, 815 (Ala. 2002). ("It is the legislature, not the courts, from which any further redress should be sought.")

52. *State of Ohio v. Lewis*, 789 N.E.2d 195 (Ohio 2003), cert. denied, 540 U.S. 966 (2003).

53. For a fuller explication of school finance litigation in Massachusetts, see Robert Costrell's chapter in this volume (chapter 12).

54. *McDuffy v. Secretary of the Executive Office of Education*.

55. Ibid., at 552.

56. Ibid., at 555–56.

57. Massachusetts General Laws, Chapter 71 (1993).

58. *Hancock v. Commissioner of Education*, 443 Mass. 822 N.E.2d 1134 (Mass. 2005).

59. Through the litigation, these four districts were referred to as the "focus districts." See *Hancock v. Driscoll*, no. 02-2978, 2004 WL 877984 (Mass. Sup. Ct. April 26, 2004), at 4. The four districts are Brockton, Lowell, Springfield, and Winchendon.

60. Ibid., at 1.
61. Ibid., at 119.
62. *Hancock* v. *Commissioner of Education.*
63. Ibid., at 1153.
64. Ibid., at 1134.
65. Ibid., at 1154.
66. Ibid., at 1153.

12

ROBERT M. COSTRELL

The Winning Defense in Massachusetts

O N FEBRUARY 15, 2005, the Supreme Judicial Court of Massachusetts found in favor of the commonwealth in the *Hancock* school adequacy case.[1] In so doing, the court lifted its 1993 finding of constitutional violation and decisively terminated twenty-seven years of litigation. The court's decision to "dispose of the case in its entirety"[2] was a stunning reversal of the trial judge's conclusion, and it bucked the trend of plaintiff victories in adequacy lawsuits nationwide. It was a case that had been closely watched by leaders of the adequacy movement, who visited the state repeatedly, viewed it as "the advance wave of the second round" of adequacy suits, and were confident of success.[3]

What was it about the *Hancock* case that distinguished Massachusetts from other states? And what insights can we draw from *Hancock* regarding the meaning and utility of the adequacy theory more generally?

The commonwealth's victory was the result of the state's unusually vigorous education reforms since 1993. In a two-pronged program, the state infused

In this chapter, the author draws heavily on his experience as an expert witness for the commonwealth in *Hancock* as well as his experience in Massachusetts education policy in the Massachusetts Executive Office for Administration and Finance from 1999 to 2006. He would like to acknowledge how much he has learned from assistant attorneys general Deirdre Roney and Juliana Rice, with whom he had the privilege of working closely throughout the case. He would also like to thank Roney and David Danning, of the Massachusetts Teachers Association, for their helpful comments as discussants at the Harvard conference where the original version of this chapter was delivered.

massive sums of money into property-poor districts, followed by a rigorous regime of academic standards, graduation exams, and accountability. As a national leader in both finance equity and standards-based reform, with high test scores that continue to rise, the state was undoubtedly better situated than most to withstand another adequacy lawsuit.

There was, however, more to the decision than simply a good set of facts. In crediting these facts, I argue, the court rejected the adequacy theory itself. That theory posits a constitutional standard that not even these facts, strong as they were, could meet. The court, accordingly, rejected the adequacy theory as, at the very least, unrealistic. Specifically, in reaching its decision, the *Hancock* court found that:

—Educational progress counts,

—Equity in spending counts, and

—Factors other than spending count, especially accountability and standards.

Under the adequacy theory, educational progress, equity in spending, and nonfinancial factors are "all basically irrelevant," according to the plaintiffs and national leaders of the adequacy movement.[4] Thus on all three counts the court implicitly or explicitly rejected key tenets of the adequacy theory.

The adequacy theory seeks to establish a *specific policy* on outcomes and inputs as the *constitutional standard*. Consequently, the theory also raises a separation of powers issue. The *Hancock* court identified that issue and chose to apply a much looser constitutional standard: Has the legislature acted in a rational and appropriate fashion to provide education for all? Given the facts of the case, the answer to that question was obvious. The court accordingly found no reason to make "policy choices that are properly the legislature's domain."[5]

To draw out the lessons of *Hancock*, this chapter begins by reviewing the adequacy theory and highlighting the general issues of contention over that theory. Turning to Massachusetts, it summarizes the legal history of *Hancock* and then presents the history of education reform from 1993, which constituted the commonwealth's positive case in *Hancock*. The core of the plaintiffs' adequacy case—its three adequacy studies—as well as defense rebuttal and the trial court's judgment follow. The chapter then turns to the Supreme Judicial Court's reasoning and conclusions. The chapter closes with my speculations on the lessons of *Hancock*, both for litigation in other states and for educational policy.

The Adequacy Theory

The adequacy theory, in its clearest and undiluted form, can be stated simply:

—The constitutional education clause commits the state to ensuring that all students reach a minimum level of educational achievement, and

—The state is required to ensure a level of spending in all districts that is adequate to obtain the required level of educational achievement.

This theory differs from its predecessor, the equity theory, which held that the state was obliged to close spending gaps between rich and poor districts. That is, instead of comparing financial inputs among districts (the spread), the idea is to establish minimum spending (a floor) required for the minimum level of educational output.

There were good reasons for the shift in approach. After all, perfect equity can obtain at zero spending, in which case there surely remains a violation of the constitutional requirement to provide education to all. Conversely, if the richest districts choose to spend heavily, it does not immediately follow that poor districts must spend the same to assure an adequate education. Indeed, one of the notable drawbacks of the equity approach was that court-ordered policies for equalization could *reduce* spending, due either to the perverse incentives of redistributive finance schemes or to outright caps on spending by rich districts. By shifting to adequacy, it was argued, the state could set a floor for spending and leave rich districts free to spend as much as they choose. Finally, the standards-based reform movement provided the basis, according to adequacy advocates, for setting minimal educational outputs to which floor spending could be tied.

The adequacy theory defines the constitutional standard as a very specific policy on educational output and spending. First, the policy sets a specific floor for the level of educational output presumed to satisfy the education clause. Next, it assumes a simple relationship between spending and outputs. Finally, it derives the corresponding spending requirement by various "costing out" methodologies.

Thorny issues arise in setting the required levels of output and spending. These issues, to which we now turn, concern both the workability of such a policy and the propriety of establishing that policy as the constitutional standard.

Setting Minimum Educational Outputs

Should the courts be in the business of setting minimum levels of educational output and, if so, at what level?[6] Adequacy proponents point to Kentucky's *Rose* factors—a list of seven general capabilities issued by that state's high court in 1989—as precedent for doing so. To make this operational, plaintiffs point to a state's educational standards, tied to test scores. In this way, they contend, the courts would not usurp policymaking authority, since they would only be holding the state to standards they have already set, requiring the authorities to provide funds necessary to meet them.

This approach, however, distorts the intent of state standard-setters, who often set an ambitious goal with the aim of stimulating progress toward that goal, even if it may never be fully achieved. No Child Left Behind (NCLB), which sets a goal of 100 percent student proficiency by 2014, is an obvious example. At the state level, Massachusetts also has set ambitious goals, while establishing sanctions only for more modest standards. It has established curriculum frameworks in seven subjects[7] but thus far has phased in graduation exams in math and English only. The tests are rigorous (for the tenth grade, that is), but passing scores have been set, at least temporarily, below the "proficient" level. The state contended that the system has been effective in driving educational progress toward the more ambitious goals. The plaintiffs replied that *progress* is not the constitutional standard: the standard is the *level* of achievement specified as proficient in the state's full set of seven frameworks.[8]

Under the adequacy theory, states would, in effect, be punished for setting high standards strategically as a means toward obtaining educational progress,[9] as adequacy leaders more or less have acknowledged in their more candid moments. For example, Michael Rebell, the adequacy movement's most prominent leader, said in 2004,

> I must admit it's been a very interesting experience being a plaintiff in this area, because we have some qualms about the heavy emphasis on test scores that many states use, that NCLB uses, but I've got to admit to you from a litigating point of view this stuff is dynamite and the more extreme the NCLB gets, the better it is for us plaintiffs. So, we have a lot of differences with President Bush, but he's given us a lot of tools to drive this thing a lot harder than we ever imagined . . . [The 2014 goal of 100 percent proficiency] is an impossible standard, but I can tell you over the next ten years, as long as the federal government leaves that in effect, we're going to continue to be close to 100 percent in winning these cases.[10]

The plaintiffs' strategy raises the question of whether courts will allow a state's high standards to be used against it under the adequacy theory and, if so, whether such rulings infringe on the state's standard-setting strategy.

In Massachusetts, where the plaintiffs based their case on a curriculum that had not yet been fully implemented in any district, one must ask how this could be a constitutional minimum. Since the education clause is predicated on the needs of a functioning republic, the claim must be that no high school graduate in the state is adequately educated for the responsibilities of citizenship. No doubt the governance of our states has yet to reach perfection, but if *no* graduate is minimally prepared for democracy, it is a wonder that our government functions at all.

Financial and Nonfinancial Inputs

Assuming a minimum level of output can be set, adequacy theory then attempts to determine the required spending. A host of difficulties arise.

First, if the minimum output is set higher than any district's current level of performance (as the plaintiffs proposed in *Hancock*), there is simply no empirical basis for determining the required spending. Consequently, plaintiffs put forth more speculative methods, notably the "professional judgment" model, discussed further below.

If the minimum output is set within the observed range, then there are pertinent data. However, it is problematic to infer spending requirements from those data, since educational output is not systematically associated with spending, contrary to the theory's key assumption. There is typically a wide spread of spending for any given level of output. That is because districts may pay different amounts for the same inputs (for example, some negotiate better terms with their unions), they may use different levels of input with no effect on output (for example, smaller class sizes, but no better instruction), or they may differ in a host of nonfinancial inputs (such as the quality of leadership or the flexibility to lead free from bureaucratic and union restraints). For whatever reason, typically there is little or no relationship between spending and output among demographically similar districts.

This is not to say that money does not—or cannot ever—matter. If spending is cut to zero, educational output will disappear, so it is certainly the case that money matters a great deal at very low levels of spending. Beyond a certain level, however, there are diminishing returns; the maximum obtainable output still increases with spending, but at a much lower rate. Moreover, the *actual* output may increase even less, or not at all, with spending, for the reasons discussed above. Conversely, widely varying levels of output are associated with the same spending. By focusing solely on spending, the adequacy theory ignores what may be far more important determinants of performance. There is much more to be gained by improving the practices of high-spending/low-performing districts—whether in management, resource allocation, or the like—than would be gained by providing them with additional funds.

School Inputs, Home Inputs, and Compensatory Finance

To take the best case so far, suppose we have set minimum outcomes within the observed range and have found an efficient cost level to attain that output in districts with demographic advantages. How, then, does adequacy theory assign a minimum spending level to disadvantaged districts? It is often the case that no disadvantaged district performs at the level of advantaged ones. If so, once again, there is no empirical basis for "costing out" these districts. Instead, adequacy studies typically apply arbitrary premiums to the spending levels found in advantaged districts.

Suppose, however, that the premium can be reliably determined, so one can calculate the compensatory finance required to offset fully a deficiency in nonschool inputs. It is then a hugely important *policy question* to determine the extent of compensatory finance to provide. But is it a *constitutional* one, to be determined by the courts? Does the education clause require 100 percent compensatory finance, sufficient to achieve a given outcome for all students regardless of cost? Or does it call for something more modest—for example, to assure a reasonable level of inputs that are under the state's control?[11]

All of these questions on the viability and propriety of the adequacy theory of constitutionally mandated outputs and inputs arose in Massachusetts's *Hancock* case.

Brief Legal History: From McDuffy to Hancock

Prior to 1993, Massachusetts's school system was highly decentralized: funding was overwhelmingly based on local finance (about 70 percent), and there were no state educational standards to speak of. Starting in 1978, plaintiffs filed suit over the finance system. The suits worked their way through the courts, off and on (as state aid and funding reform waxed and waned), and ultimately were consolidated into the *McDuffy* case of 1993. In *McDuffy* the Supreme Judicial Court found that the education clause established "an enforceable duty on the magistrates and legislatures of this commonwealth to provide education in the public schools for the children there enrolled, whether they be rich or poor and without regard to the fiscal capacity of the community or district in which such children live."[12]

In finding, further, that the commonwealth was not meeting its constitutional duty, the court relied heavily on evidence of spending gaps between plaintiff districts and three property-rich "comparison" districts (Brookline, Concord, and Wellesley): "We need not conclude that equal expenditure per pupil is mandated or required, although it is clear that financial disparities exist in regard to education in the various communities . . . The reality is that children in the less affluent communities . . . are not receiving their constitutional entitlement of education."[13]

Thus although *McDuffy* is often considered one of the nation's early adequacy suits, it is actually not so clear on this. The court relied more on evidence of equity than on measures of educational output and explicitly declined to adopt the language of "adequacy."[14]

The court did raise the issue of educational outputs in the course of providing guidance on what constituted the "duty to educate." It did so by citing Kentucky's *Rose* capabilities, such as "sufficient oral and written communication skills to enable students to function in a complex and rapidly changing civilization."[15] However, the concrete meaning of this citation was unclear and would be vigorously debated in *Hancock*.

In short, *McDuffy* was an adequacy decision only loosely, if at all. It was aimed primarily at establishing overall state responsibility for education, in light of the egregious disparities that had arisen in the absence of such a role. The court stopped well short of defining the "duty to educate" in terms resembling the current adequacy theory, nor did it impose a remedy of the sort typically sought by adequacy plaintiffs today.

Indeed, the *McDuffy* court imposed no specific remedy for the violation. It left the matter to "the magistrates and the legislatures," which were in the process of enacting the Massachusetts Education Reform Act (MERA) of 1993. The court reserved the discretion "to determine whether, within a reasonable time, appropriate legislative action has been taken."[16]

No further legal action was taken until a new set of plaintiffs—Julie Hancock et al.—filed for further remedial action at the end of 1999. The Council for Fair School Finance, an umbrella group led by the American Civil Liberties Union of Massachusetts and funded largely by the Massachusetts Teachers Association, organized this effort. By the time of trial, the educational landscape had changed dramatically from 1993, and so had the commonwealth's defense. The defense refused to acquiesce in broad stipulations sought by the plaintiffs, unlike in *McDuffy*. One key expert witness in school finance switched from the plaintiff in *McDuffy* to the defense in *Hancock*. Finally, the commissioner and Department of Education were fully engaged in their defense, more so than in *McDuffy* and quite unlike many other states facing adequacy claims. As Alfred Lindseth has pointed out, state departments of education are often diffident defendants, since it is the legislatures, not the departments, that are responsible for any financial remedy.[17]

The court assigned the case to Superior Court judge Margot Botsford for trial. During pretrial proceedings, Judge Botsford considered arguments over the critical issue of the constitutional standard to be applied during trial. The plaintiffs argued that *McDuffy* had established the seven *Rose* capabilities as the standard of an adequate education and that the Massachusetts legislature (through the Board of Education) had made the standards concrete in the seven curriculum frameworks. These frameworks, it was argued, established the educational outputs to which all students in the commonwealth were constitutionally entitled. The main task of the trial court, according to the plaintiffs, was to determine whether the inputs available to plaintiff districts were adequate to obtain those outputs.

The defense argued that *McDuffy* established a rather different standard, not a standard for educational outputs, but instead a standard for legislative action: "whether, within a reasonable time, appropriate legislative action has been taken" to address the deficiencies found in *McDuffy*. The task of the trial court, according to the defense, was to evaluate the educational progress made since 1993, the narrowing of spending gaps identified in *McDuffy*, and the reasonableness of the state's policy strategy for further educational progress—namely, targeted assistance and accountability.

Judge Botsford sided with the plaintiffs. The trial court would use the educational outputs implied by the seven curriculum frameworks as the constitutional standard for educational adequacy. The defense vigorously objected on both substantive and procedural grounds. Nonetheless, Judge Botsford's order established the framework for the trial, which was held in 2003. Judge Botsford allowed the defense to present its positive case on the progress of education reform, but she indicated that this would not be the standard she would use in her conclusions.

The heart of the plaintiffs' case would be three pieces of finance testimony aimed at demonstrating that spending was inadequate in the plaintiff districts to reach the level of educational achievement defined by the curriculum frameworks. Judge Botsford rejected two of these three studies. Still, based on the remaining evidence and her reading of the constitutional standard, she recommended in April 2004 that the court find for the plaintiffs. The remedy she proposed was similar to the one pursued in New York: the court should order a cost study with a host of specific guidelines to gauge the additional spending required and retain jurisdiction to ensure that the legislature acts on it.

The Supreme Judicial Court heard oral arguments in October 2004 and, in February 2005, ruled 5-2 for the defense. In doing so, the chapter argues, the court rejected the adequacy theory.

Education Reform since 1993: Funding, Accountability, and Educational Progress

At the same time as *McDuffy* was moving toward conclusion, the legislature and the governor were finalizing MERA. The main features of the act were the reform of funding, with the simultaneous establishment of educational standards, followed by accountability for results.[18]

The key components of the finance reform were:

—Establishment of a foundation budget, which set minimum per-pupil spending for all districts, with an add-on of more than 40 percent for low-income children,

—Establishment of a required local contribution, and

—Commitment by the state to fill the gap between foundation budget and required local contribution over seven years (that is, by 2000).

Figures 12-1 and 12-2, which were presented in court, demonstrate how much these steps accomplished. At the outset, two-thirds of the state's students were in districts that spent below foundation, often by a large margin (figure 12-1). By 2000, after a massive increase in state aid, all students were brought up to foundation, thereby eliminating the left tail of the spending distribution (figure 12-2).

In dollar terms, the spending gaps were reversed between districts with the highest and lowest poverty. Average spending in the highest-poverty quartile (that is, districts with the highest rate of students with free and reduced-priced lunch status, educating a quarter of the students) now exceeds that in the quartile with the least poverty. Similarly, by other measures (district income and property wealth) the gaps were much narrowed, although not eliminated. In comparison to other states, Education Trust has consistently found that Massachusetts is at or near the top in the progressivity of its funding system, by measures similar to those discussed here.[19]

Equally as important were the state's accountability reforms:

—Establishment of curriculum frameworks and state assessments,

—Requirement of students to pass tenth-grade English and math assessments for high school graduation, beginning with the class of 2003, and

—Procedures for evaluating districts and schools, ultimately leading to state intervention in failing schools.

The requirement that students pass tenth-grade math and English assessments for high school graduation was a particularly important driver of education reform and was highly contested. The state's largest teacher union, the Massachusetts Teachers Association, led a vigorous effort against the requirement, including a well-funded advertising campaign. A case was filed against the requirement, but the court pointedly rejected the suit. Significantly, that decision was cited repeatedly in the *Hancock* decision.

The exit exams initially seemed to pose a nearly insurmountable hurdle, as the failure rates were very high in the dry runs, before the exams had high stakes attached to them. Once the graduation requirement kicked in, however (in 2001 for the class of 2003), failure rates dropped dramatically (see figure 12-3). After retakes in grades eleven and twelve, the failure rate dropped to about 5 percent. In addition, racial gaps narrowed on the pass rate, and both majority and minority groups registered large gains at the higher levels of performance.

State performance on national exams also improved.[20] Massachusetts now performs at the top nationally on the National Assessment of Educational Progress. The state's SAT performance has improved markedly over the last decade, passing the national average in 1999 and widening its lead since then, despite one of the nation's highest participation rates.

None of these facts was in dispute during the case. Nor was there any dispute that far more progress needs to be made. Significant gaps in performance remain, especially at the level of "proficiency." Some schools are failing, by state and federal criteria. The state has methodically (if slowly) identified these schools as part of its school and district accountability program and has recently begun a program of targeted assistance and intervention.

The defense asserted that the state's reform efforts and educational progress since 1993 not only had demonstrated appropriate action in a reasonable time but had been exemplary. Consequently, the state should be permitted to continue with its plan of targeted assistance and intervention to address the undisputed shortcomings that remain, rather than be placed under court-mandated spending directives.

Judge Botsford acknowledged "that spending gaps between districts based on property wealth have been reduced or even reversed."[21] However, ultimately she agreed with the plaintiffs that "the issue here is not spending equity but educational adequacy," so data on the closing of spending gaps are irrelevant.[22]

With regard to adequacy, the plaintiffs argued that educational *progress* was not the constitutional standard, and Judge Botsford agreed. Instead, the standard was asserted to be the *level* of performance—specifically, whether the students had reached proficiency in all seven subjects of the curriculum frameworks. Given that standard, her finding of a constitutional violation was a foregone conclusion.

All that remained was to determine whether inadequacy of funding was the source of the violation. That was the subject of the plaintiffs' three adequacy studies. Examining these studies brings the underlying difficulties with the adequacy theory concretely into relief.

Figure 12-1. *Net School Spending as a Percent of Foundation Budget in K–12 Districts in Massachusetts, Fiscal 1993*

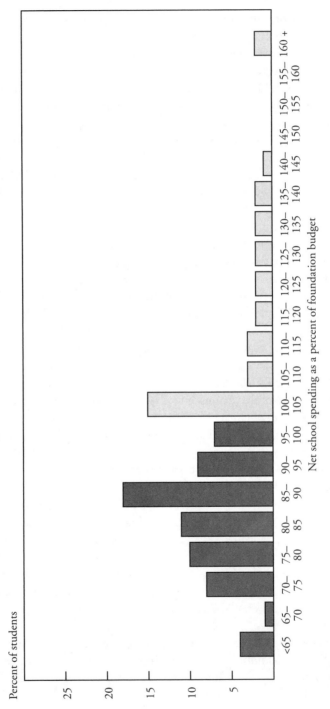

Sources: Massachusetts Executive Office for Administration and Finance; Massachusetts Department of Education.

Figure 12-2. *Net School Spending as a Percent of Foundation Budget in K–12 Districts in Massachusetts, Fiscal 2002*

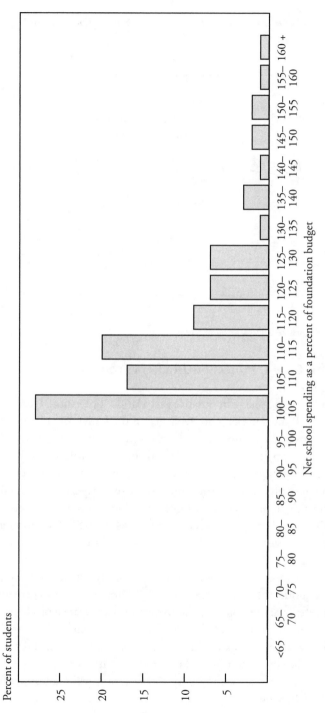

Sources: Massachusetts Executive Office for Administration and Finance; Massachusetts Department of Education.

Figure 12-3. *Failure Rate for First-Time Takers of Tenth-Grade State Exit Exams, 1998–2006*

Percent

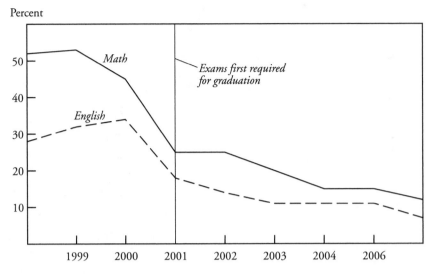

Source: Massachusetts Department of Education.

Plaintiffs' Case I: Professional Judgment Study

The first leg of the plaintiffs' finance case was the professional judgment study prepared by Professor Deborah Verstegen of the University of Virginia.[23] Very simply, a group of educators from the plaintiff districts were presented with the seven curriculum frameworks and asked for their professional judgment regarding the resources, such as class size, teacher aides, and computers, necessary to achieve proficiency in all subjects. Finance experts then assigned dollar amounts to these resources to complete the "costing out." Dr. Verstegen concluded that actual per-pupil expenditures fell $4,100–$8,000 short annually of what was necessary for an adequate education in each of the four plaintiff focus districts.

The key piece of defense testimony on the study extended its findings from the four plaintiff districts to the rest of the state. Using Verstegen's methodology, the defense argued that almost no district in the state had adequate spending, not even the wealthy "comparison" districts chosen by the plaintiffs. More than 80 percent of the state's pupils are in districts that fell short of the Verstegen standard by at least $4,500 per student.[24] Ironically, the only district of any size with adequate spending by this criterion was Cambridge, a notoriously low-achieving district.

The Verstegen study proved too much for the trial judge to swallow. The panelists had been instructed (as is typical for the genre) to be creative in designing programs and not to consider any revenue constraints. As a result, the judge concluded that the study represents "to some extent a wish list."[25] Moreover, the judge wrote, the choice of panelists for a "lawsuit involving funding issues for the very districts in which the panel members teach and work gives one pause about its total objectivity."[26]

The problems with the Verstegen study are common to the professional judgment approach more generally, as discussed by Eric Hanushek in chapter 4 of this volume. One underlying problem that goes to the heart of the adequacy theory is that the level of educational output, on which professional judgment was sought, was chosen to be well above that yet offered by any district. Consequently, there was no data-based approach that *could* be used; there was no alternative but to ask panelists to "be creative."[27] Yet Judge Botsford's dismissal of the Verstegen study did not prevent her from recommending that the court order a cost study of the same type, which almost certainly would suffer from the same defects.

Plaintiffs' Case II: Successful Schools Model

The second adequacy study, conducted by school finance consultant John Myers, was of the "successful schools" variety.[28] The level of output was chosen to be that of the seventy-five highest-scoring districts in the state's math and English assessments. The plaintiffs carefully asserted that this criterion was below the constitutionally required minimum (since it did not cover all seven subjects) but commissioned the study to determine the required expenditures for that more modest goal. The basic idea was to infer from actual expenditures of the "successful" districts what expenditures would be required for the plaintiff districts, after accounting for their demographic disadvantages. The study found that plaintiff districts fell $1,200–$3,500 short in annual per-pupil expenditures.

As with the professional judgment model, the plaintiffs' expert applied the model only to the plaintiff districts. The key piece of defense testimony was to apply the same methodology to the "successful" districts themselves. Two-thirds of these districts were found to spend less than what was determined to be "necessary" for their success. This paradoxical result helped to lead Judge Botsford to reject the model as fatally flawed. Still, because the model she eventually accepted was closely related to the "successful schools" model, it is important to identify the methodology's underlying problems.

Consider figure 12-4, which presents performance on the vertical axis and per-pupil spending on the horizontal axis. The figure identifies districts by poverty level to examine the relationship between spending and performance among demographically similar districts. The bubbles in the top of the diagram represent districts in the lowest-poverty quartile (as measured by free and reduced-price lunch status). These districts correspond closely to the top-scoring districts identified by Myers, since, in practice, the selection of schools in the successful schools model is driven largely by demographics.[29] The diamonds represent districts in the poorest quartile. (Districts in the middle two quartiles are excluded from the diagram, for clarity.)

Stripped to its core, the successful schools model identifies average spending of the high-performing districts (with a few adjustments) as the necessary level of spending for demographically advantaged districts. The model then determines the necessary spending for more disadvantaged districts by applying a premium (50 percent in the Myers study, a figure based on convention rather than scientific evidence) for low-income children, along with similar premiums for other types of disadvantage.

Thus the necessary spending for plaintiff districts, with more low-income children, is determined to be somewhat higher than average spending in the advantaged districts. As shown in figure 12-4, poor districts in Massachusetts already spend a bit more (on average) than low-poverty districts. However, the successful schools model determines that the necessary spending in these districts is higher yet, resulting in the claim of spending shortfalls.

The point here is that this procedure, which purports to be based on the adequacy theory, goes back to the equity approach, but with a twist. By comparing spending in the poor districts with spending in the rich districts, but only after a premium is applied to the rich districts' spending, it establishes an equity-plus standard.

The adequacy rationale for this procedure does not stand up to scrutiny. As figure 12-4 shows, there is a wide range of spending among demographically similar districts and little or no relationship between spending and performance. This contradicts the adequacy theory's assumed relationship between spending and output.

The model ignores this problem and simply defines average spending as the minimum necessary for success in these districts. This is the main source of the paradoxical result cited above: if the *minimum* is defined as the *average*, it is no surprise that half or more of these districts are found to fall short of what is "necessary" for their own success.[30] One must live in Lake Wobegon to pretend that this is an adequacy procedure—that is, a calculation of minimum necessary spending to achieve a given output. It is not. At its core, it is an equity calculation, pure and simple, to set the standard based on average spending of the high-performing, demographically advantaged districts.

Recall that one of the main reasons for the shift from equity to adequacy lawsuits was to set a spending floor that was independent of rich districts' spending, leaving rich districts free to spend as much as they choose. Under the successful schools model, however, *any* level of spending chosen by the rich, high-performing districts can and will be used as the basis to increase the floor in poor districts. Independent of whether this result is good or bad, one thing is certain: it is not what the adequacy theory promised.

Plaintiffs' Case III: Spending as a Percent of Foundation

The third adequacy argument presented, by Robert Berne of New York University (based on exhibits prepared by the Massachusetts Teachers Association), considered spending as a percent of foundation budget rather than as dollars per pupil. Specifically, spending as a percent of foundation in high-scoring, low-poverty districts was compared with that of plaintiff districts. Since, on average, spending exceeded the foundation budget in Myers's seventy-five "successful" districts by about 30 percent, the plaintiffs argued that the foundation budget was inadequate in those districts and must, by extension, be inadequate in poorer districts as well. Consequently, since spending is close to foundation in the plaintiff districts, their spending must be inadequate. Judge Botsford found this argument "rough," but persuasive.[31]

The spending as a percent of foundation argument is essentially a variant of the successful schools model. Figure 12-5 depicts the same spending and performance data as in figure 12-4, except that spending is measured as a percent of foundation instead of as dollars per pupil. Again, this approach begins with the successful, generally low-poverty districts and assumes that the average spending in those districts, as a percent of foundation, is necessary for their success. However, there is a wide spread of spending as a percent of foundation in the high-scoring districts, including several that are close to 100 percent of foundation. Using the *average* spending ratio of 125–130 percent to indicate the *minimum* necessary spending in these districts repeats the Lake Wobegon fallacy and converts a purported adequacy approach into an equity calculation.

Next it is argued that, since many successful districts spend well above foundation, poor districts should, too. Again, this implies that whatever is spent in high-scoring rich districts should be scaled up by a premium for disadvantaged children. That is because the foundation budget in poor districts is set higher than in rich districts. Hence, as shown in the bottom halves of figures 12-4 and

Figure 12-4. *Performance and Per-Pupil Spending among Highest- and Lowest-Poverty Districts, 2001–02 School Year*

Average of math and ELA proficiency index

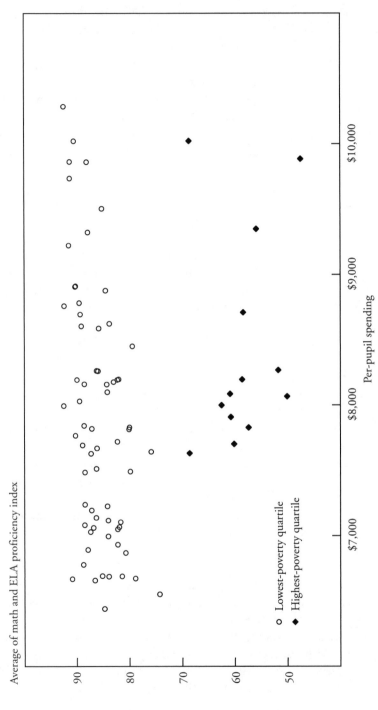

Per-pupil spending

○ Lowest-poverty quartile
◆ Highest-poverty quartile

Sources: Massachusetts Executive Office for Administration and Finance; Massachusetts Department of Education.

Figure 12-5. *Performance and Above-Foundation Spending among Highest- and Lowest-Poverty Districts, 2001–02 School Year*

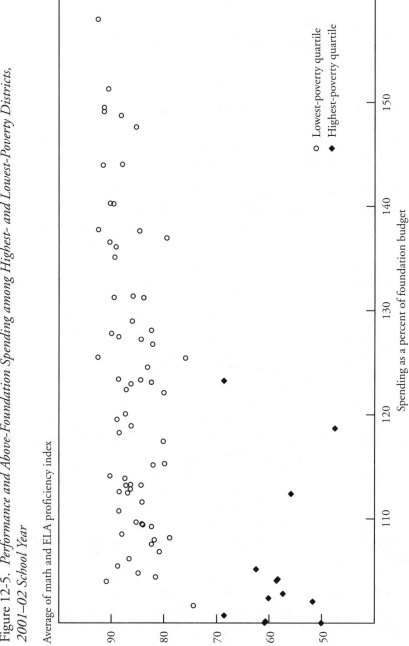

Average of math and ELA proficiency index

Spending as a percent of foundation budget

○ Lowest-poverty quartile
◆ Highest-poverty quartile

Sources: Massachusetts Executive Office for Administration and Finance; Massachusetts Department of Education.

12-5, spending as a percent of foundation is lower in poor districts than in rich ones, even though it is higher in actual dollars. By arguing that spending as a percent of foundation should be raised in the poor districts toward that of the rich ones, this approach implies that the diamonds in figure 12-4 should be moved farther to the right. Once again, a purported adequacy model turns out to be an equity-plus model.

Supreme Judicial Court Rejects the Adequacy Theory

The first two adequacy models were rejected by the trial court, and the third argument—spending as a percent of foundation—fared no better at the Supreme Judicial Court: the court simply ignored it. More important, not only did the high court reject the adequacy models, it also rejected the theory itself. This was made clear both by the standard used in the case as well as by the criteria the court drew on to evaluate the commonwealth's compliance with the standard.

With regard to the constitutional standard, the court wrote, "The plaintiffs read the education clause to mandate that all current public school students demonstrate competency in a specific program of education."[32] The court then rejected this reading of the education clause. In short, the court considered the standard presented by the plaintiffs under the adequacy theory to be a particular policy and ruled that it is not the court's job to set policy.

Instead, the court interpreted *McDuffy* as construing the education clause to be "a statement of general principles and not a specification of details."[33] Consequently, the court's standard was considerably less prescriptive than plaintiffs sought. The court considered the question that *McDuffy* had left open: "whether, within a reasonable time [since 1993], appropriate legislative action ha[d] been taken to provide public school students with the education required under the Massachusetts constitution."[34] The court's answer to that question is indicative of the standard used: "While the plaintiffs have amply shown that many children in the focus districts are not being well served by their school districts, they have not shown that the defendants are acting in an arbitrary, nonresponsive, or irrational way to meet the constitutional mandate."[35]

To find a violation, the court implied, would require the kind of "egregious, statewide abandonment of the constitutional duty" identified in *McDuffy*.[36] Moreover, in finding that the commonwealth had acted appropriately, the court relied on criteria that the adequacy theory explicitly rejects.

Progress Counts

The court's key finding of fact was that, as a result of MERA, "The public education system we review today . . . is not the public education system reviewed in *McDuffy* . . . A system mired in failure has given way to one that, although far from perfect, shows a steady trajectory of progress."[37] The court specifically cited various measures of progress, on inputs and outputs, including the improvement in test scores, both statewide and in the plaintiff districts.

The adequacy theory, by contrast, holds that only the *level* of achievement counts, not *progress*, a point reiterated by plaintiffs throughout the trial. Thus the plaintiffs' brief dismissed "the commonwealth's argument that improvement is enough," arguing instead that "the minimum level of education required by the Massachusetts constitution" was defined by the seven *Rose* factors and given content by the state's seven curriculum frameworks.[38]

Chief Justice Marshall, however, interpreted the *McDuffy* court's citation of *Rose* less prescriptively. It "did not mandate any particular program of public education," nor did the *Rose* capabilities "themselves prescribe a specific curriculum."[39] Indeed, she cites, in apparent agreement, one scholar's comment that "if this standard is taken literally, there is not a public school system in America that meets it."[40] With regard to the seven curriculum frameworks (versus the two subjects required for graduation), the court cited an earlier decision that validated the commonwealth's strategy of "pragmatic gradualism" to achieve educational progress.[41]

Thus the court rejected the first leg of the adequacy theory. The court made it clear that it had no intention of establishing any particular set of educational outcomes as a constitutional minimum. The commonwealth was free to set a *policy* of ambitious goals to drive educational progress, without thereby establishing a *constitutional mandate* that all students demonstrate competency at that level.

Equity in Spending Counts

In evaluating the commonwealth's actions on school finance, the court found, "The [Education Reform] Act eliminated the central problem of public school funding that we identified as unconstitutional in *McDuffy* . . . Specifically, the act eliminated the principal dependence on local tax revenues that consigned students in property-poor districts to schools that were chronically short of resources."[42]

The court gave great weight to the facts that state aid grew rapidly after 1993, especially in the plaintiff districts, and that "spending gaps between districts based on property wealth have been reduced or even reversed."[43] The court cited various equity measures such as those discussed above, which had been declared irrelevant by the plaintiffs and by the trial judge. With regard to finance, the court concluded, "Where the governor and the legislature . . . provide substantial and increasing . . . resources to support public education in a way that minimizes rather than accentuates differences between communities based on property valuations . . . we cannot conclude that they are presently violating the education clause."[44]

The constitutional problem identified here relates to finance disparities based on the property tax. The commonwealth's solution, which achieved at least a rough equity, falls far short of the adequacy theory's standard for financial inputs. As we have seen, some of the key adequacy methods set a standard of *equity-plus* in spending: no matter how much is spent in rich districts, poor districts must spend far more.

In rejecting the adequacy models, and relying instead on equity evidence, the court implicitly declined to adopt the standard of equal outcomes that seems to be embedded in the models or compensatory finance as the means to achieve that goal. That is, it was one thing to find (in 1993) that gross inequities based on property wealth violated the constitutional obligation to provide universal education; but now that at least a rough equity has been achieved, the court saw no need to venture beyond that into the policy debate over compensatory education.

Standards and Accountability Count

In evaluating the commonwealth's actions, the court considered nonfinancial inputs very important, especially standards and accountability: "The [1993] act also established, for the first time in Massachusetts, uniform, objective performance and accountability measures for every public school student, teacher, administrator, school, and district in Massachusetts."[45]

The court went on at some length in praise of these measures, including "world class" curriculum frameworks and graduation exams in core subjects. The court's frequent citation of its previous decision upholding the graduation exams seemed indicative of the importance it attached to them. Indeed, in one of the court's more pointed comments, it concluded that delays in full implementation of education reform owed not to legislative or departmental inaction, but instead to factors such as "protracted litigation over some provisions of education reform," citing again the challenge to the graduation exams.[46]

While all sides agreed that much more progress is required, they differed on the means to achieve that progress. The court accorded great deference and respect to the state's strategy of standards, accountability, targeted assistance, and intervention. By contrast, the adequacy theory focuses almost entirely on district spending. The *Hancock* plaintiffs minced no words: "There is no room for debate in this case about whether accountability is a better solution than increased funding . . . Additional funding is not a policy choice open to debate, but a matter of constitutional necessity."[47]

The court held, to the contrary, that the question of additional funding was very much a policy choice open to debate. Indeed, during oral arguments Chief Justice Marshall seemed to take the other side of that debate: "What . . . comes through to me loud and clear is that there are real problems in these districts that have nothing to do with money."[48] The important question, she said, is why some districts are failing and not others. "We know more money isn't the answer."[49] The written decision, to be sure, did not repeat such openly skeptical comments on the need for more spending, but it did cite "poor leadership and administration" as "a principal cause of poor performance in the focus districts."[50] More important, the court ruled decisively that such policy debates were the province of the legislature.

Separation of Powers

The court recognized that the adequacy theory—specification of required educational outcomes and of the spending needed to achieve them—comprised a specific policy prescription that lay beyond the court's purview. The court particularly stressed the separation of powers for spending decisions: "Because decisions about where scarce public money will do the most good are laden with value judgments, those decisions are best left to our elected representatives."[51]

Thus the court vigorously rejected Judge Botsford's recommended remedy of a court-ordered "cost study," because such a study would be "rife with policy choices that are properly the legislature's domain . . . Each choice embodies a value judgment; each carries a cost, in real, immediate tax dollars; and each choice is fundamentally political. Courts are not well positioned to make such decisions."[52]

The court's conclusion here strikes at the heart of the adequacy strategy. The observation that spending choices involve trade-offs among competing public purposes flatly denies the contention of the adequacy strategists that the education clause places education spending above all other purposes. The court's conclusion that spending choices are "fundamentally political" directly rebuffs the strategy of circumventing the political process to obtain court-ordered spending solutions. As Justice Cowin concluded, in her concurring opinion, "The plaintiffs' remedy, as it always is with political questions, is at the ballot box."[53]

Conclusion: Lessons from Massachusetts?

Massachusetts's Supreme Judicial Court quite fittingly handed down its *Hancock* decision in the newly renovated John Adams Courthouse. It was Adams, of course, who famously wrote the world's first constitutional education clause, to secure the republican experiment he had done so much to launch. As the birthplace of the education clause—and still a national leader in education—perhaps Massachusetts yet has lessons to offer.

The main (and most obvious) lesson is that states that have not already done so may wish to adopt reforms that are strong on equity, standards, and accountability. In this area at least, good policy is the best defense against lawsuits. The reason is that, despite the adequacy theory's flaws, the theory has rightly focused judicial attention on educational outcomes, not just inputs. The *Hancock* court, while rejecting the specific theory, put great stress on progress in educational *outcomes*, and in that respect the adequacy movement has left its mark, even in Massachusetts. States with vigorous reforms like those in Massachusetts stand the best chance of making progress in educational outcomes that courts might credit in the face of an adequacy suit.

The centerpiece of such reforms is the effort to drive educational progress by setting high standards and tying them to high stakes. *Hancock* has now established that the state can set ambitious standards without necessarily having it held against the state, as the adequacy strategists had hoped. Indeed, to the contrary, the court found that high standards and high stakes were key factors in the commonwealth's defense.

To make high stakes successful, the first step in education reform should be to focus on funding.[54] However, a well-constructed funding formula need not—and should not—rely excessively on state revenues. State revenues are typically based on income and sales taxes, which are much more volatile than local property taxes, so a high state share makes education funding more vulnerable in an economic downturn. In addition, local funding of education gives local officials a greater stake in educational success.[55] If state aid is well targeted to supplement local revenues in property-poor districts, a great deal of equalization can take place without a dramatic rise in the state share of funding. In Massachusetts, the state share rose from about 30 to 40 percent in the years following the reforms of 1993. This is still below the national average, and yet the degree of spending progressivity is among the highest in the nation, according to Education Trust. In general, there is no relationship between state share and progressivity.[56]

Many states have already adopted equitable funding policies. According to data from Education Trust and *Education Week*, at least half of the states spend more in their poor districts than in their rich ones.[57] Some of these states are pursuing the second step of the reform formula—high standards with high stakes and accountability for results—and others are poised to follow. The road beyond is still uncharted, as states grapple with the challenge of turning around underperforming schools in the midst of overall progress.

There is now a vibrant debate in Massachusetts over policies such as merit pay, turnaround strategies, reconstitution, and the like. This debate would surely have been short-circuited had *Hancock* turned out differently. The debate would not be over education reform, but over funding formulas and revenue sources—a repeat of the first step of reform, instead of a debate over the next steps. As courts in other states consider whether to drive policy under the adequacy theory's reading of the education clause, one can only hope that they will bear in mind John Adams's other great constitutional principle, arguably far more fundamental to our system of government: "The judicial shall never exercise the legislative and executive powers, or either of them: to the end it may be a government of laws and not men."[58]

Notes

1. *Hancock* v. *Commissioner of Education*, 443 Mass. 428, 822 N.E.2d 1134 (Mass. 2005).

2. Ibid., at 1137.

3. Michael Rebell, Askwith Forum at Harvard Graduate School of Education, November 16, 2004 (video at forum.wgbh.org/wgbh/forum.php?lecture_id=1723 [October 30, 2005]). See Rebell's comments on *Hancock* at approximately 1:05 to 1:10. This forum was held after the trial judge's report was issued, but prior to the Supreme Judicial Court's decision.

4. Ibid., at approximately 1:05. See also citations below to the plaintiffs' briefs.

5. *Hancock* v. *Commissioner of Education*, at 1156.

6. Adequacy advocates claim that the standard does not require specified outcomes, but merely the *opportunity* to achieve those outcomes. If so, this would seem to allow for something fewer than all students achieving the outcome in any given school or district ("how few" is not specified). As argued in court, however, the distinction between results and opportunity is minimal. Thus in *Hancock*, although plaintiffs described the standard as assuring a "reasonable opportunity" to acquire specified capabilities (Plaintiffs-Appellees Brief, 2004 WL 3250225, at 103), they stressed that the districts in question "are not equipping all of their students" with those capabilities, as judged by outcomes (Plaintiffs-Appellees Brief, at 87, and similar language throughout). To the court, the plaintiffs' case seemed to be about outcomes for all students.

7. English language arts (ELA); mathematics; science and technology; history and social science; foreign languages; the arts; and health.

8. Ibid., at 5–6, 96–97.

9. See Alfred A. Lindseth, "Educational Adequacy Lawsuits: The Rest of the Story," PEPG 04-07 (Harvard Program on Educational Policy and Governance, April 2004).

10. Rebell, Askwith Forum, at approximately 1:11. In Massachusetts, the plaintiffs emphasized in court their support for the state standards and assessments (MCAS), but the case was funded largely by the teacher union, which had vigorously opposed the assessments.

11. During oral arguments before the Supreme Judicial Court, the plaintiffs' counsel cited the number of students who dropped out prior to their senior year. Justice Cowin responded pointedly, "What are we supposed to do about that?" The justice's reaction suggests that there are limits to the state's obligation to secure results when inputs such as the student's own effort and commitment are beyond state control.

12. *McDuffy* v. *Secretary of the Executive Office of Education*, 415 Mass. 545, 615 N.E.2d 516 (Mass. 1993). John Adams's famous education clause states: "Wisdom, and knowledge, as well as virtue, diffused generally among the body of the people, being necessary for the preservation of their rights and liberties . . . it shall be the duty of legislatures and magistrates . . . to cherish the interests of literature and the sciences, and all seminaries of them; especially the university at Cambridge, public schools and grammar schools in the towns." Much of the *McDuffy* decision rested on the interpretation of the eighteenth-century meaning of "cherish."

13. Ibid., at 614.

14. Ibid., note 8, as well as the dissenting opinion.

15. Ibid., at 618.

16. Ibid., at 620–21.

17. Lindseth, "Educational Adequacy Lawsuits."

18. For an account of the politics of this act, including the key role of business-backed reform groups, see Robert M. Costrell, "Comment on 'Test-Based Accountability: The Promise and the Perils,'" in *Brookings Papers on Education Policy 2005*, edited by Diane Ravitch (Brookings, 2005) pp. 27–37.

19. Education Trust, *The Funding Gap* (various years).

20. See S. Paul Reville, "High Standards + High Stakes = High Achievement in Massachusetts," *Phi Delta Kappan* (April 2004): 591–97.

21. *Hancock* v. *Commissioner of Education*, 2004 WL 877984 (Mass. Super. Ct., April 26, 2004), at 14.

22. Ibid., note 33, which makes particular reference to equity comparisons with other states.

23. Deborah A. Verstegen, "Calculation of the Cost of an Adequate Education in Massachusetts under the Curriculum Frameworks" (University of Virginia, June 2003).

24. This result was no different from what the head of the plaintiffs' organization had been publicly saying for months prior to the trial—namely that she had evidence that *all* districts in the state were dramatically underfunded. In court, however, the plaintiff lawyers chose not to present this implication of the study.

25. *Hancock* v. *Commissioner of Education*, 2004 WL 877984 (Mass. Super. Ct., April 26, 2004), at 121.

26. Ibid. During the trial, the judge expressed particular surprise at finding among the list of panelists the mother of Jami McDuffy (the original plaintiff), who works in the school system attended by her daughter and also by the subsequent lead plaintiff.

27. Verstegen, "Calculation of the Cost of an Adequate Education," p. 77.

28. For further discussion of the successful schools model, and also for an alternative approach, see James Peyser and Robert Costrell, "No Money Left Behind: Exploring the Costs of Accountability," *Education Next* 4 (Spring 2004): especially pp. 28–29.

29. Of Myers's forty-five top-scoring K–12 districts, thirty-nine are included in the sixty-eight low-poverty districts depicted. (Myers's set of seventy-five districts included districts that are elementary only and high school only, as well as K–12 districts. However, high school costs differ from elementary school costs, so the figure depicts K–12 districts only to facilitate comparisons.)

30. The dynamic implications of this procedure are even more paradoxical. If the minimum is taken to be the average, then every district below average must raise its spending to the average. But, of course, this raises the average further. The process does not end until all districts are brought up to that of the highest-spending district. Thus by setting the average as the minimum, one ultimately ends up with the *maximum* as the minimum. This is not simply an exercise in reductio ad absurdum; it is a recipe for constantly recurring litigation, if the successful schools model is taken as dispositive, since each round's remedy lays the ground for the next round's complaint.

31. For a fuller discussion of this strand of evidence (and the Botsford report more generally), see Robert M. Costrell, "Wrong Answer on School Finances," *CommonWealth* (Fall 2004): 79–87.

32. *Hancock* v. *Commissioner of Education*, at 1153.

33. Ibid., at 1146.

34. Ibid.

35. Ibid., at 1140.

36. Ibid., at 1138.

37. Ibid., at 1139.

38. Plaintiffs-Appellees Brief, at 6, 12.

39. *Hancock* v. *Commissioner of Education*, at 1153.

40. Ibid., at 1154, note 29, citing William E. Thro, "A New Approach to State Constitutional Analysis in School Finance Litigation," *Journal of Law and Politics* 14 (1998): 525, 548. Justice Cowin (writing also for Justice Sosman) distanced herself from *Rose* even more vigorously, on separation of powers grounds. She argued that *McDuffy* did indeed embrace the *Rose* capabilities more prescriptively than Chief Justice Marshall's opinion portrayed. In her view, *McDuffy* was wrongly decided, and the embrace of the *Rose* capabilities was the most egregious aspect of that "overreaching" decision, "a display of stunning judicial imagination." Ibid., at 1160.

41. Ibid., at 1152.

42. Ibid., at 1141.

43. Ibid., at 1147.

44. Ibid., at 1152–53.

45. Ibid., at 1138.

46. Ibid., at 1155.

47. Plaintiffs-Appellees Brief, at 143–44.

48. Quoted in Jonathan Saltzman, "School Woes Not Simple, Say Justices," *Boston Globe*, October 5, 2004.

49. Quoted in Kevin Rothstein, "SJC: Money Alone Won't Boost Education," *Boston Herald*, October 5, 2004.

50. *Hancock* v. *Commissioner of Education*, at 1149 and note 35 at 1157.

51. Ibid., at 1156.

52. Ibid., at 1156–57.

53. Ibid., at 1165.

54. For a fuller discussion of how and why the "grand bargain" sequence (funding first, high stakes second) worked in Massachusetts, see Costrell, "Comment on 'Test-Based Accountability.'"

55. See Caroline M. Hoxby, "Are Efficiency and Equity in School Finance Substitutes or Complements?" *Journal of Economic Perspectives* 10, no. 4 (1996): 51–72.

56. Robert M. Costrell, "Equity v. Equity: Why *Education Week* and the Education Trust Don't Agree," *Education Next* 32 (Summer 2005): 77–81.

57. Ibid., p. 80.

58. Constitution of the Commonwealth of Massachusetts, Part the First: A Declaration of the Rights of the Inhabitants of the Commonwealth of Massachusetts, Article XXX.

PART V

Reflections

13

KENNETH W. STARR

The Uncertain Future of Adequacy Remedies

M ORE THAN A century ago, one of the leading lights of American law
penned these simple words: "The life of the law has been experience,
not logic."[1] That is true especially in the arena of education litigation, and in
particular in the nettlesome question of remedies. My thesis is equally simple,
but not nearly so elegant as Holmes's insight: When responding to adequacy
petitions, the judiciary is well advised to be mindful of the experience of the
last half-century in education litigation. That experience, at the dawn of the
Roberts era in this nation's constitutional law, counsels caution and humility.

The Traditional Role of the Judiciary

Before Oliver Wendell Holmes Jr. tackled the rather large subject of the common law, Mr. Webster came forward with a simple definition of "remedy."[2]
Lawyers, especially in this age of textualism, love definitions. Webster advises
the gentle reader that the preferred definition for the subject that now arrests
our attention is, in effect, medicine for what ails a person.[3] It is a curative, a
response from science to a condition or disease. The purpose is relief, restora-
tion, and elimination of the undesired condition (or ailment).

Judges are superb doctors, at least when the ailment is identifiably reflec-
tive of conditions that have, by tradition, come to the judiciary for diagnosis
and relief. For example, who owns Blackacre? Or, to pose perhaps more of a

307

challenge, can the city of, say, New London take Blackacre for economic rede-velopment purposes? Such questions are familiar grist for the judicial mill.[4] Judges in the English and American traditions welcome such cases, and they apply familiar rules from the judicial counterpart to the Physicians' Desk Reference.[5] One might not like the rule, and judges may not like their own analysis, as seen recently in a remarkable speech by the author of *Kelo* v. *City of New London*, Justice John Paul Stevens.[6] But judges (and justices) feel constrained by those rules (such as precedents) that have been fashioned in the crucible of litigation. Deep respect tends naturally to be displayed by the judges of today (and presumably those of tomorrow) for the accumulated wisdom of what has gone before.[7] Indeed, judges tend to be wary of bold new inventions and imaginative breakthroughs. While the Warren Court is now one for the ages, the fact remains that the judiciary is seen as doing well when it diagnoses the condition, but is well advised to be careful and cautious in administering a proposed cure.[8]

A New Frontier: Will Old Precepts Hold?

The counsel of caution is familiar in education litigation. Before returning to the fount itself (*Brown* v. *Board of Education*), let's briefly examine the culture of judicial humility in the most directly applicable context, namely the early post-*Brown* litigation on educational funding.

Adequacy: The History Lesson

Relying on the strong language in *Brown* and the long record of general discrimination lawsuits, education reformers in pursuit of fiscal equality filed an important post-*Brown* federal lawsuit in the western district of Virginia in 1968.[9] Because state constitutional language required the general assembly to "establish and maintain an efficient system of public free schools throughout the state,"[10] the lawsuit sought to strike down a Virginia school funding statute.[11] A representative group of parents and children from Bath County claimed that the statute created and perpetuated "substantial disparities in the educational opportunities available in the different counties and cities of the State." As a result, the argument went, the statute was "repugnant to the equal protection clause of the Fourteenth Amendment" and failed to meet the mandate set forth by the Virginia Constitution.[12]

The resulting decision in *Burruss* deeply disappointed those inspired by the soaring pro-equality language of *Brown*. A three-judge panel found that the plaintiffs' goal to provide students with the same educational opportunities throughout Virginia was "a worthy aim, commendable beyond measure."[13] However, the panel ultimately determined that the judiciary had "neither the knowledge, nor the means, nor the power to tailor the public moneys to fit the varying needs of these students throughout the State."[14]

Following closely on the heels of *Burruss* was a similar case, *McInnis* v. *Shapiro*, a suit on behalf of public school students in Cook County, Illinois.[15] The gravamen of the Illinois challenge was that state statutes controlling educational disbursements violated equal protection and due process. The statutory regime guaranteed a baseline allocation to each school district of $400 per pupil, but allowed each locality, if it so desired, to supplement the minimum $400 assurance through local taxation.[16] The claim was that the statute was constitutionally infirm because it allowed for wide variations in available education funding between districts.[17] The proposed remedy: to allow each district to set its own tax rate but require the state to capture and redistribute any amount above the $400 baseline minimum.[18]

The *McInnis* panel began its review by emphasizing a key structural principle, namely that "the allocation of public revenues is a basic policy decision more appropriately handled by a legislature than a court."[19] With that principle in mind, the court applied a "reasonableness" standard of review and concluded that under governing Supreme Court standards, the Illinois statute was neither arbitrary nor invidiously discriminatory. In upholding the statute, the court relied on the tried-and-true principles of local choice and local control, explaining that the Illinois general assembly delegated authority to local school districts in order to "allow individual localities to determine their own tax burden according to the importance which they place on public schools."[20] The value of local control was bolstered by the fact that the legislature was "constantly upgrading the quality of education" and already provided for some degree of equalization through the baseline minimum.[21]

That was the easy part. The *McInnis* panel went on to confess that no discoverable and manageable standards existed by which the court could determine the statute's constitutionality.[22] In other words, the controversy was nonjusticiable; it was *not* for the courts to decide. The court reasoned that "local autonomy in education . . . indicates the impracticability of a single, simple formula."[23] It concluded: "[E]ven if there were some guidelines available to the judiciary, the courts simply cannot provide the empirical research and consultation necessary for intelligent educational planning."[24] The intractable problem, in short, was the institutional incapacity of the judiciary to tackle such issues. The basic message was this: no constitutional requirement mandates uniform per-pupil expenditures under the Fourteenth Amendment's equal protection clause.[25]

Both decisions trumpeted the principle of separation of powers and, at least in the absence of invidious discrimination, mandated deference to the state legislature.[26] The eventual ruling (by summary affirmance) suggested the Supreme Court's unwillingness "to go beyond the historically narrow application of the race relations" in education reform.[27]

Judicial Humility: A Return to First Principles

The preceding early examples illuminate the broader judicial culture, which I am suggesting is a tradition of humility in constitutional adjudications. It is a tradition born in response to the now universally condemned exercises of judicial power in the much-maligned "*Lochner* era."[28] *Lochner* stands familiarly for the period when the robust exercise of judicial power gave rise to the great dissents of Harlan and then of Holmes, joined soon by Brandeis. It signifies as a rather ugly era in American law, when judges were riding roughshod over considered judgments of the states and, famously, of early New Deal initiatives.[29] That muscular judicial approach is now widely condemned as profoundly misguided and deeply antidemocratic. The *Lochner* era justices are sharply criticized, especially in law schools, for having displaced thoughtful, or, in any event, democratic judgments of the Progressive Era.

Brown: The Simple Principle of Equality

We return, briefly, to the fount: *Brown* v. *Board of Education*.[30] As Michael Heise has aptly observed, *Brown* "helped animate a movement towards pressing courts into the service of litigated reform."[31] *Brown*, however, at bottom expressed a bedrock principle of limited transferability. Building on a considerable body of precedent and on race-related reforms at the national level, the Supreme Court articulated a powerful vision of legal equality.[32] Schoolchildren could not be singled out for disparately unfavorable treatment on the basis of race.[33] The contrary rule—that of de jure segregation—embodied an enormous evil, depriving individuals of basic human dignity. Little children were dispatched to schools arranged on the basis of apartheid. Community and neighborhood lines were ignored. Topeka, the school system where the *Brown* case had originated, illustrated the point, as black schoolchildren were sent to schools far away from hearth and home. It was racism pure and simple. The de jure system of segregation had nothing to redeem it, such as the principles of "local control" or "decentralized decisionmaking authority."

Could *Brown*'s logic, though, be expanded to include a more expansive vision of equality? The early returns suggested not. The coup de grace—at the federal level—came in the Edgewood school district case.[34] In *San Antonio Independent School District* v. *Rodriguez*,[35] the Court first rejected the concept of wealth as a suspect class,[36] a claim that would have triggered the likely doomsday standard of strict scrutiny. Few government programs have successfully run the "strict scrutiny" gauntlet, and indeed various justices have expressed concerns about the displacement of democratically chosen mechanisms by such extraordinarily powerful standards.[37] In rejecting each of the challengers' claims in the *Edgewood* case, the Court brought down the curtain on the equal protection clause's role as a powerful engine of social change.

Adequacy: The Modern Morass

Some state courts, to be sure, have adopted remedies that trigger first principles–type debate over separation of powers, the nature and extent of judicial power, and the displacement of local control.[38] But two episodes from the federal experience counsel caution.

The Zelman *Child Forges Its Own Path: Moving Away from the Legacy of Brown*

The first episode, and the one to counsel caution most concretely, is the uneasy implementation of *Brown* itself. That story, oft told, is a rather unhappy chapter in American social (and legal) history. Desegregation efforts languished, year after year, eventuating in increasingly far-reaching remedies generously authorized in a sweeping (and unanimous) Supreme Court decision in *Swann* v. *Charlotte-Mecklenburg Board of Education*.[39] Writing for the entire Court, Chief Justice Burger presented a vision of the wise, discerning local district judge, close to the scene, who would know best what to do.[40] Desegregation must be achieved, *Brown* and its progeny demanded, and the wise "Chancellor sitting in equity" would measure and craft the appropriate response fitted to the exigencies of the particular community in question.[41] And thus *Swann* ushered in nationwide programs of forced busing, with vigorous debates (scholarly and otherwise) as to the wisdom and efficacy of such regimes.[42] Fairly viewed from today's more distant vantage point, federal judges were simply seeking, as they saw best, to fulfill this heavy duty as passed down by the High Court. But the storm of criticism directed at socially disruptive remedies was powerful, even spawning violence in major cities.[43] As time went on, the public school systems in major metropolitan efforts fell into disarray and disrepair.[44] Families, by the thousands, left the system.[45]

The judicial denouement came in Kansas City.[46] There, a district judge famously determined that more was better than less, and in the course of a long-lived desegregation effort mandated a tax increase to finance a very bold plan to remediate the schools of Kansas City (and otherwise make them more attractive to families that had long since fled the inner-city system).[47] The Supreme Court said no. *Missouri* v. *Jenkins* was the Supreme Court's yellow light, bringing a strong note of caution to the arena of judicial remediation.

The second episode involved school choice. The better part of educational valor, it seemed, was to grant exit visas to students caught up in underper-forming school districts.[48] The issue was not judicial power per se, but whether the political branches' decision to employ the educational capacity of reli-giously affiliated schools would run afoul of the Supreme Court's controversial establishment clause jurisprudence.[49] *Zelman* answered the question authori-tatively, albeit by a 5-4 margin, and the constitutionality of school choice (in terms of the U.S. Constitution) seems settled.[50] The Rehnquist Court was at peace with school choice, and no reason for instability of that precedent was suggested by the arrival, in 2005, of the new chief justice.

But the more relevant story within the saga of school choice is the reluc-tance of federal judicial authorities to intervene in an aggressive fashion in the public school system itself. When the presiding judge in the Cleveland deseg-regation case eventually threw up his hands in frustration over the lamentable condition of Cleveland schools, the judicial response was to place the entire school system in receivership—but in the hands of the state superintendent of education.[51] Drawing a lesson from judicial experience, the federal district judge sent Cleveland's school system to the state capital for management and direction. Accountability principles loomed large in the selection of the rem-edy, and school choice emerged as an important (if limited) policy response to the scandal of public education in Ohio's largest city.

The End of Grand Remedies

So, too, the *Swann* era itself was destined to end. The conclusion came in an Oklahoma City school case, *Board of Education of Oklahoma City* v. *Dowell.*[52] Overturning the decision of the federal court of appeals in Denver, the Supreme Court ordered termination of federal supervision of local school dis-tricts under the rubric of desegregation remedial efforts.[53] Enough was enough, the High Court said, even though Oklahoma City's public schools remained racially identifiable. Racial identifiability, from aught that appeared, resulted not from state action, but from demographics beyond at least direct state control.[54] In addition, local authority and control was seen as an overridingly important value, especially since the school district's labors toward dismantling the prior de jure system of segregation had been long, arduous, and systematic.[55] As decades of school desegregation efforts came to a close, the idea of semi-permanent judicial receivership was perceived as creating sharp tension with basic principles of self-governance and democratic theory.

The *Dowell* case was an awakening. The Supreme Court, it seemed, had recognized that the "command and control" model utilized in *Swann* had failed. Although the federal judiciary was under an obligation to enforce the societal imperative handed down in *Brown*—that full participation within the system is not to be denied on the basis of race—the elaborate federal court supervision ushered in by *Swann* was inadequate. The problem was one of expertise—or rather, lack thereof. The judiciary was taking on the functions typically left to local school boards, and the courts' efforts yielded schools that may have become desegregated but that had not become truly integrated. As noted in *Zelman*, parents and children responded by leaving the system altogether.

Adequacy litigation faces similar problems, as many adequacy lawsuits are the contemporary embodiment of the "command and control" model. Although they are doing so at the state rather than federal level, judges are asserting aggressive power. That raises profound questions about judicially manageable standards, especially when a single court makes fundamental public policy determinations. The judiciary is fully capable of discerning whether a state is engaged in segregation, but it should not be called on to tell local school districts how to provide an adequate education to their students.

Local Control and Judicial Caution

The articulation of concerns about the separation of powers has not been limited to voices within courthouses. In the field of education litigation, scholars are increasingly attentive to broader questions regarding the judiciary's role in school finance reform (and in the U.S. democratic system more generally).[56] Commentators fall comfortably on both sides of the debate, with some suggesting that it is entirely appropriate for courts to take an active role as overseer of important parts of community life, while others embrace a cautious approach by reason of the traditional principle of separation of powers.[57]

Commentators supporting a more muscular judicial power nevertheless recognize that the courts are hesitant to exceed their traditional limits under the separation of powers principle. For example, one commentator noted that "it is likely that courts will always be reluctant to engage in specific judicial pre-scription as a remedy to education finance distribution problems because courts are bound to respect the separation of powers."[58] Interestingly, the sug-gestion that "courts are poor tools for school finance reform" is then countered with an admonition to plaintiffs not to forsake litigation-based remedies, not-ing that the "power of the courts should never be underestimated; if it were not for litigation, it is absolutely certain that less progress toward fundamental fairness in the financing of public elementary and secondary education would exist today."[59]

On the other side are voices of caution. Michael Heise has suggested one example, namely that the Wyoming Supreme Court's decision in *Campbell County School District* v. *Wyoming*[60] provided the impetus for legislative policy reform that otherwise might not have taken place.[61] Heise raises the possibil-ity that the "judicial excursion" into such territory "risks upsetting the precar-ious and delicate system of checks and balances between and among Wyoming's legislative, executive, and judicial branches."[62]

Separation of powers concerns will likely be paramount as this field of liti-gation evolves. For sound, familiar reasons, the structure of education systems and the allocation of resources have historically been an issue reserved exclu-sively for the legislature.[63] The fundamental importance of honoring the democratic process is too obvious to require extended comment. Suffice it to say that the people are given their strongest voice when they can petition their local representatives, instead of seeking redress from a relatively remote court system.

Local control looms large as a factor in public education.[64] Allowing sweep-ing judicial mandates to control historically local *legislative* issues should be disquieting in a representative democracy. Such a result not only blurs the sep-aration of powers but also (with respect to the federal judiciary) raises issues of federalism. In this doubly sensitive arena, the lack of judicially manageable standards remains an abiding concern.

Even courts purporting to have established manageable standards may find themselves caught up in horribly protracted litigation, with dissatisfied plaintiffs continually appealing to the court as their first means of redress.[65] Yet in the field of educational reform, judicial expertise is obviously limited. To state the obvious: the judiciary deals with a wide range of issues and has neither the time, institutional capacity, nor resources to become fully equipped to formulate, implement, and then manage a system that would ensure "adequate" education.[66] Indeed, even when such a task is delegated to a legislative body, the judiciary may well lack the needed resources to over-see effective implementation.

Can We Learn from Past Mistakes? State Inadequacies

Consider also the ramifications of judicially mandated reform. As courts have shifted from equity-based to adequacy-based remedies, a new wave of education litigation has begun to form. Some scholars have praised the resurgence in education and public law litigation, noting that this movement was the direct result of a change in judicial remedies.[67]

Even if true, that response does not alleviate the concern that such remedies may have unintended and far-reaching consequences for policymaking. As plaintiffs shift from challenging school finance schemes to attacking achievement gaps (as indicators of unequal educational opportunity), a new array of complex variables comes into play. How should schools be organized to ensure that all students achieve at desired levels? How might pedagogical practices need to be changed? These variables "are located deeper inside schools and classrooms, and, as such, further away from the reach of lawsuits and court decisions."[68] They add to the inherent complexity of adequacy lawsuits; moreover, "to an even greater degree than for school desegregation or finance, courts and lawsuits seem ill-equipped to shoulder the task."[69]

While many anticipate that this embryonic litigation strategy will fully develop in due course, others have noted that with respect to already completed adequacy lawsuits, "the issue of equity and adequacy among schools continues to be elusive—even after court-ordered changes."[70] That leaves little promise that the lawsuits of tomorrow will prove effective vehicles for education reform.

An unfolding story from New York tells the tale. The New York City Department of Education has been unable to meet a court order that mandated billions of dollars in additional aid for the public schools.[71] This is an example of a direct clash between lofty judicial ideals and the flinty realities that legislatures face in trying to sustain judicial demands and balance competing budget concerns. Indeed, such a result is common, as legislatures often are unable to meet judicially mandated goals, leading to repeat litigation attempts by education reformers.[72]

Another example comes from Idaho.[73] After the state supreme court ruled Idaho's educational finance system unconstitutional, the apparently miffed legislature reacted by passing a law that authorized judges to impose unlimited property taxes to repair dangerous school facilities.[74] Though it reacted idiosyncratically, the legislature conceivably may have viewed this as its only available course.[75]

While advocates of reforming the education system through litigation praise recent court decisions and proclaim victories, the overwhelming evidence of repeat appeals and follow-up lawsuits suggests that this protracted and complex litigation has not been an unalloyed success.[76] Such a result not only highlights the complex problem of judicially manageable educational standards but also emphasizes the challenge of the judiciary's ability to fully address the complicated problems inherent in education reform. Indeed, a review of the decisions strongly suggests that such reform is appropriately left to a better-informed government body—the legislature.

Pending litigation in California is the direct result of legislatively driven education reform. However, unlike in New York and Idaho, where reform efforts were based on state constitutional directives, in California plaintiffs are invoking the federal No Child Left Behind Act (NCLB)—specifically, its provisions allowing children to transfer out of schools that, on the basis of annual progress reports, are classified as underperforming.[77] The California plaintiffs, in Los Angeles and Compton, are alleging that the school districts have engaged in a systematic campaign to limit that remedy by thwarting the transfer of children to better schools within the state.[78] According to the plaintiffs, the school districts have been "downplaying" the rights of parents to send their children to nonfailing schools. Los Angeles and Compton, they say, have not been explaining the transfer procedures in a "uniform and understandable" manner, and they have been promoting after-school tutoring within a failing school as a substitute for transfer to a nonfailing school.[79]

The advantage of this type of legislatively driven litigation is the manageability of the remedy sought. Unlike *Brown*, which handed the judiciary a broad, unwieldy societal directive to implement, or even the cases of court-ordered spending in New York and Idaho, the pending California litigation provides an opportunity for the courts to do what they do best—that is, settle a case or controversy. There is no need for the California courts to engage in broad rulemaking. Instead, they may simply look to the provisions of NCLB, look to the evidence before them, and decide whether Los Angeles and Compton are in violation of the statute. If the school districts have violated NCLB, the remedy is relatively simple: the school districts must comply. NCLB creates a remedial structure of its own, and the courts are fully capable of deciding whether that legislatively created adequacy remedy is being followed.

Conclusion

In the end, the enduring lesson is the one taught by Holmes: litigation has its limits. At the very least, it should be seen as a rather uncertain method of achieving desired social goals. That, as Holmes would say, is the lesson of experience. Humility, at the end of the day, is the most admirable judicial response to invitations to judges to embark upon education-related adventures.

Notes

1. Oliver Wendell Holmes Jr., *The Common Law* (New York: Courier Dover Publications, 1991), p. 1. *The Common Law* was culled from a series of lectures given by Holmes at the Lowell Institute, which was founded in 1836 by John Lowell Jr., the father of A. Lawrence Lowell, who became president of Harvard College (and for whom Lowell House is named). A. Lawrence Lowell invited Holmes to speak at the Lowell Institute in 1879, and *The Common Law* was first published on March 3, 1881. G. Edward White, *Justice Oliver Wendell Holmes: Law and the Inner Self* (New York: Oxford University Press, 1993), p. 148.

2. The publication of *The Common Law* thrust Holmes into the forefront of legal thought. The book, though dense, is regarded as "one of the classic works in American legal scholarship." White, *Justice Oliver Wendell Holmes*, p. 149.

3. The most current definition of "remedy" is "a medicine, application, or treatment that relieves or cures a disease." See "Merriam-Webster Dictionary Online" (www.m-w.com/dictionary/remedy [August 23, 2006]).

4. *Kelo v. City of New London, Connecticut*, 125 S. Ct. 2655 (2005). For an illuminating discussion of *Kelo*, see Shelly Saxer, "Eminent Domain, Municipalization, and the Dormant Commerce Clause," *U.C. Davis Law Review* 38 (June 2005): 1505.

5. The *Physicians' Desk Reference* is an annual compendium of available prescription drugs. Just as a copy of *Black's Law Dictionary* rests on the bookshelf of nearly every lawyer or judge, the *Physicians' Desk Reference* is one of the most widely used volumes in the medical field.

6. In a speech before the Clark County Bar Association, Justice Stevens criticized his own decision in *Kelo* as "unwise." Justice Stevens also stated that the law compelled him to reach a holding that he "would have opposed" had he been a legislator. Linda Greenhouse, "Justice Weighs Desire v. Duty (Duty Prevails)," *New York Times*, August 25, 2005, p. A1.

7. *Payne v. Tennessee*, 501 U.S. 808 (1991) (Marshall, J., dissenting) ("fidelity to precedent is part and parcel of a conception of the judiciary as a source of impersonal and reasoned judgments . . . this Court can legitimately lay claim to compliance with its directives only if the public understands the Court to be implementing principles . . . founded in the law rather than in the proclivities of individuals").

8. One of the most notable examples of this philosophy was embodied by Justice Holmes during the Court's *Lochner* era. Justice Sandra Day O'Connor described Holmes's philosophy in this way: "[H]is disagreement with his colleagues was not based on any concern for the health of bakers, or for the ability of women to earn a decent wage, or for the rights of workers to join unions . . . Holmes's point was a different one: it was not that the law was properly aimed, but that the state had the power to pass the law regardless of its aim." Sandra Day O'Connor, *The Majesty of the Law: Reflections of a Supreme Court Justice* (New York: Random House, 2003), p. 104. In other words, Justice Holmes recognized that, although the Court may prefer a certain policy, policy choices should be left to the state legislatures. Decades later, Chief Justice Rehnquist warned against the judicial prerogative to "feel that the sky is the limit when it comes to imposing . . . solutions to national problems on the popularly elected branches of the government and on the people." William H. Rehnquist,

The Supreme Court: How It Was, How It Is (New York: William Morrow and Company, Inc., 1987), p. 316.

9. *Burruss* v. *Wilkerson*, 310 F. Supp. 572 (W.D. Va. 1969), *aff'd*, 397 U.S. 44 (1970).

10. Virginia Constitution, art. I, sec. 15, cl. 2. Virginia's Constitution declares that "free government rests, as does all progress, upon the broadest possible diffusion of knowledge, and that the Commonwealth should avail itself of those talents which nature has sown so liberally among its people by assuring the opportunity for their fullest development by an effective system of education throughout the Commonwealth."

11. *Burruss*, 310 F. Supp. at 573–74.

12. Ibid.

13. *Burruss*, 310 F. Supp. at 574.

14. Ibid. See also *Shepheard* v. *Godwin*, 280 F. Supp. 869, 872 (E.D. Va. 1968) (holding that federal funds would no longer be counted against local school districts in determining uniform state apportionment).

15. *McInnis* v. *Shapiro*, 293 F. Supp. 327 (N.D. Ill. 1968).

16. Ibid. at 330.

17. Ibid. at 328–29.

18. Ibid.

19. *McInnis*, 293 F. Supp. at 332. Like *Burruss*, *McInnis* was decided by a three-judge panel. Judge Hastings, from the Seventh Circuit, sat with judges from the eastern district of Illinois

20. Ibid. at 333.

21. Ibid. at 334.

22. *McInnis*, 293 F. Supp. at 335–37.

23. Ibid. at 336.

24. Ibid.

25. Ibid. at 335–36.

26. R. Craig Wood, "Constitutional Challenges to State Education Finance Distribution Formulas: Moving from Equity to Adequacy," *Saint Louis University Public Law Review* 23, 2 (2004): 538–39.

27. Ibid. at 540.

28. In *Lochner*, the Court struck down a New York statute that limited the number of hours that bakers could work each week. The Court justified its decision on the grounds that limiting the number of hours that bakers could work interfered with a worker's substantive due process right to freely enter into labor contracts. *Lochner* v. *New York*, 198 U.S. 45 (1905).

29. From 1935 to 1936 the Court invalidated more than a dozen of FDR's New Deal enactments. Not until FDR's maligned court-packing scheme and the "stitch in time that saved nine" did the Court begin to defer to the president and Congress. Stephen K. Shaw, "Introduction," in *Franklin D. Roosevelt and the Transformation of the Supreme Court*, edited by Stephen K. Shaw, William D. Pederson, and Frank J. Williams (Armonk, N.Y.: M. E. Sharpe, 2004), pp. 1–10.

30. *Brown* v. *Board of Education*, 347 U.S. 483 (1954).

31. Michael Heise, "Litigated Learning and Limits of the Law," *Vanderbilt Law Review* 57 (November 2004): 2446–47.

32. *Brown*, 347 U.S. at 493 (stating that "education is perhaps the most important function of state and local governments. . . . In these days, it is doubtful that any child may rea-

sonably be expected to succeed in life if he is denied the opportunity of an education. Such an opportunity, where the state has undertaken to provide it, is a right which must be made available to all on equal terms.").

33. Ibid. at 495.

34. The Texas Supreme Court has visited the issue of "equal opportunity for education" four times since 1989; see *Edgewood Independent School District* v. *Kirby*, 777 S.W.2d 391, 392 (Tex. 1989). According to J. Steven Farr and Mark Tractenberg, "The *Edgewood* Drama: An Epic Quest for Education Equity," *Yale Law and Policy Review* 17 (1999): 607–09, "After the first three *Edgewood* cases, the Texas Legislature responded with a reformed finance system." However, Texas's quest for education equality was not limited to the journey between its courthouse and the state capitol building.

35. *San Antonio Independent School District* v. *Rodriguez*, 411 U.S. 1 (1973).

36. Ibid. at 17–25.

37. For example, Justice Marshall has noted that "the failure of legislative action to survive strict scrutiny has led some to wonder whether our review of racial classifications has been strict in theory, but fatal in fact." *Fullilove* v. *Klutznick*, 448 U.S. 448, 519 (1980) (Marshall, J., concurring).

38. Perhaps the most sweeping decision was the California Supreme Court's ruling in *Serrano* v. *Priest*, 487 P.2d 1241 (Cal. 1971). *Serrano* is the counterpoint to *Rodriguez*: it categorized wealth as a suspect class, it determined that education is a fundamental right, and it examined California's statutory regime under the strict scrutiny standard. Not surprisingly, *Serrano* held that the challenged statutory scheme violated the Constitution's equal protection clause. The *Serrano* decision had an immediate, far-reaching impact. It brought education finance under the umbrella of equal educational opportunity, and it sparked unprecedented reform of state education funding in several states. Wood, "Constitutional Challenges," p. 546.

39. *Swann* v. *Charlotte-Mecklenburg Board of Education*, 402 U.S. 1 (1971).

40. Ibid. at 22 ("In devising remedies where legally imposed segregation has been established, it is the responsibility of local authorities and district courts to see to it that future school construction and abandonment are not used and do not serve to perpetuate or re-establish the dual system. When necessary, district courts should retain jurisdiction to assure that these responsibilities are carried out.").

41. Ibid. at 15.

42. See, for example, Angela Onwvachi-Willig, "For Whom Does the Bell Toll: The Bell Tolls for Brown?" *Michigan Law Review* 103 (May 2005): 1532–33; Derrick Bell, "How Would Justice Hugo Black Have Written *Brown* v. *Board?*" *Alabama Law Review* 56 (Spring 2005) 856; James T. Patterson, *Brown* v. *Board of Education: A Civil Rights Milestone and Its Troubled Legacy* (New York: Oxford University Press, 2001), p. 87.

43. See Michael J. Kalarman, *From Jim Crow to Civil Rights: The Supreme Court and the Struggle for Racial Equality* (New York, Oxford University Press, 2004), pp. 442, 468 (stating that "[w]ithout *Brown*, negotiation might have continued to produce gradual change without inciting white violence" and that *Brown* led to unnecessary violence by "inspir[ing] southern whites to try to destroy the NAACP").

44. See, for example, *Zelman* v. *Simmons-Harris*, 536 U.S. 639, 643-45 (2002), describing the state of Cleveland's educational system as a "crisis that is perhaps unprecedented in the history of American education."

45. For a detailed description of the effect that *Brown* had on public education, see Michael Heise, "*Brown* v. *Board of Education*, Footnote 11, and Multidisciplinarity," *Cornell Law Review* 90 (January 2005): 279.

46. *Missouri* v. *Jenkins*, 515 U.S. 70 (1995).

47. *Jenkins* v. *Missouri*, 639 F. Supp. 19 (W.D. Mo. 1985).

48. *Zelman*, 536 U.S. at 662-663, holding that Cleveland's school choice and voucher system was a sound remedy for the failings of the public education system even though parents could use the vouchers to attend religiously affiliated schools.

49. Ibid. at 643–44.

50. Ibid. at 662–63, stating that "the Ohio program is entirely neutral with respect to religion. It provides benefits directly to a wide spectrum of individuals, defined only by financial need and residence in a particular school district. It permits such individuals to exercise genuine choice among options public and private, secular and religious. . . . In keeping with an unbroken line of decisions rejecting challenges to similar programs, we hold that the program does not offend the Establishment Clause."

51. On March 3, 1995, District Judge Thomas I. Atkins entered an order that directed "the State Board of Education, by and through its Superintendent of Public Instruction, to assume and exercise the authority and responsibility invested in it by the Ohio Constitution, its duly-enacted statutes, and the Court's various desegregation orders and consent decrees." That order was upheld in February 1996. *Reed* v. *Rhodes*, 934 F. Supp. 1485, 1486 (N.D. Ohio 1996).

52. *Board of Education of Oklahoma City* v. *Dowell*, 498 U.S. 237 (1991).

53. Ibid. at 250–1.

54. Ibid. at 250, n. 2, noting that "present residential segregation in Oklahoma City was the result of private decisionmaking and economics, and that it was too attenuated to be a vestige of former school segregation."

55. Ibid. at 248, stating that it is proper for a court to dissolve "a desegregation decree after the local authorities have operated in compliance with it for a reasonable period of time."

56. Michael Heise, "Schoolhouses, Courthouses, and Statehouses: Educational Finance, Constitutional Structure, and the Separation of Powers Doctrine," *Land and Water Law Review* 33, 1 (1998): 281.

57. Heise, "Litigated Learning," p. 2449, citing Michael Rebell and Arthur Block, *Education Policy-Making and the Courts: An Empirical Study of Judicial Activism* (University of Chicago Press, 1982), p. 210.

58. Wood, "Constitutional Challenges," p. 562.

59. Ibid. at 563.

60. *Campbell County School District* v. *Wyoming*, 907 P.2d 1238 (Wyo. 1995).

61. Heise, "Schoolhouses, Courthouses, and Statehouses," p. 281.

62. Ibid.

63. See Michael D. Blanchard, "The New Judicial Federalism: Deference Masquerading as Discourse and the Tyranny of Locality in State Judicial Review of Education Finance," *University of Pittsburgh Law Review* 60 (Fall 1998), pp. 249–56.

64. See generally *Zelman*, 536 U.S. at 639; *Reed*, 934 F. Supp. at 1485; and Blanchard, "The New Judicial Federalism," p. 231.

65. Heise, "Litigated Learning," p. 2447, stating that "[s]imilar to school desegregation litigation, the school finance litigation effort has encountered numerous difficulties."

66. Stephen Breyer, "Our Democratic Constitution," *New York University Law Review* 77 (May 2002), p. 250.

67. Heise, "Litigated Learning," p. 2450.

68. Ibid. at 2447–48, 2450.

69. Ibid at 2456.

70. Joe Agron, "Raising the Bar," *American School and University* (June 2005), p. 6.

71. *Campaign for Fiscal Equity* v. *New York*, 801 N.E.2d 326 (N.Y. 2005).

72. Mike Kennedy, "Equity and Adequacy," *American School and University* (May 2005), p. 19.

73. *Idaho Schools for Equal Educational Opportunity* v. *Idaho*, 97 P.3d 453 (Id. 2004).

74. Kennedy, "Equity and Adequacy," p. 23.

75. Ibid.

76. For example, Molly Hunter of the Advocacy Center for Children's Educational Success with Standards (ACCESS) has stated that plaintiffs have won twenty of the twenty-six adequacy cases. However, "school finance litigation has occurred in 45 states, and lawsuits are still pending in approximately 22 states." Michael D. Simpson, "The Right to an 'Adequate' Education," *NEA Today* 23 (May 2005).

77. Pub.L. 107-110, Jan. 8, 2002, 115 Stat. 1425, *codified at* 20 U.S.C., sec. 6316 et seq. (2006).

78. *Coalition on Urban Renewal and Education and Alliance for School Choice* v. *Los Angeles Unified School District*, "Complaint for Failure to Provide 'Understandable and Uniform' Notice and Explanation to Parents of their School Choice Rights and for Denying and Discouraging Public School Transfers under the No Child Left Behind Act," filed March 23, 2006; *Coalition on Urban Renewal and Education and Alliance for School Choice* v. *Compton Unified School District*, "Complaint for Failure to Provide 'Understandable and Uniform' Notice and Explanation to Parents of their School Choice Rights and for Denying and Discouraging Public School Transfers under the No Child Left Behind Act," filed March 23, 2006.

79. *Coalition on Urban Renewal and Education and Alliance for School Choice* v. *Los Angeles Unified School District*, p. 7.

14 JOSHUA DUNN
MARTHA DERTHICK

Adequacy Litigation
and the Separation of Powers

A SUBSTANTIVE DISTINCTION BETWEEN equity and adequacy in school finance litigation is often hard to detect. Pure equity cases can occur in the new era of adequacy, as in Vermont in *Brigham* v. *State* (1997). And cases nominally fought on grounds of adequacy—as, for example, in Kansas in *Montoy* v. *State* (2005)—look more and more like equity cases as one plumbs arguments and remedies. Yet we argue that there are important differences between the two and that those differences are essentially political. Adequacy cases have enjoyed greater success in the courts because they mobilize more support and less opposition than equity cases did, and, if only because of their greater success, they are a deeper challenge to the traditional constitutional order.

Adequacy as a Political Success

At first glance it appears ironic that plaintiffs have enjoyed a higher rate of success in adequacy cases than in the earlier cases grounded in equity, because courts would seem to have greater legitimacy and competence in adjudicating the latter. The irony disappears, however, if school finance lawsuits are viewed as essentially political rather than legal events. As political events, equity cases

The authors would like to thank John Dinan for comments.

suffered the handicap of compelling the redistribution of wealth and of spending for education, which incited a strong reaction from the losing parties in property-rich school districts. By contrast, adequacy cases have the political advantage that they aim to enlarge the educational pie. Any interest that benefits from school spending—districts rich and poor or urban and rural, teachers and administrators, equipment suppliers, consultants, building contractors, pension funds, and the advocacy organizations that everywhere push for more school spending—can detect opportunities for gain, at least up to the point at which remedies are specified and the bigger pie begins to be sliced. If the pool of beneficiaries appears to be insufficiently encompassing, it can be broadened, as in 2004–05 when the plaintiffs in a highly controversial New York case, *Campaign for Fiscal Equity (CFE)* v. *State,* prepared legislation to extend statewide the benefits of increased spending that until then had been focused by litigation on New York City alone.

Adequacy suits have gained politically also from their link to the standards-and-accountability movement, which spread nationwide through the 1990s and reached a climax with the passage of the No Child Left Behind Act (NCLB) in 2002. Courts are most confident when they are buttressed by other institutions, and it has helped the adequacy cases to have the support of presidents and of Congress. Michael Rebell, a leader of both the adequacy movement in New York City and the broader movement, has chastised critics for failing "to grasp that the education adequacy lawsuits have become the driving force for achieving the aims of the standards-based reform movement."[1] Implementation of national statutes is always problematic in a federal system and when a national legislature habitually underfunds its promises. The adequacy movement, which is a national movement committed to bringing lawsuits in state courts, conceives of itself as stepping into that breach.

The head litigators in adequacy lawsuits—lawyers in state capitals and other cities around the country who keep in touch with one another and plead the cases in trial and appellate courts—are keenly aware of their role and responsibilities as coalition builders, and they are likely recruited for their political savvy as well as their skill as litigators. For example, Robert Spearman of Parker Poe Adams and Bernstein in Raleigh, who is the lead lawyer in North Carolina's long-running *Leandro* case, has been the state Democratic Party chairman.

Because litigators know that judicial decisions depend on effectuation by the political branches, they are alert to ways in which that might be achieved. At a conference of the adequacy movement that one of us attended in 2005, winning lawyers from North Carolina, Montana, and Kansas constituted a panel devoted to the subject of converting court victories into solid remedies.

Beyond speaking of standard litigating tactics, such as picking plaintiffs, witnesses, and exhibits with due attention to their anticipated effects in court, they spoke also of success at spinning the media, hiring public relations firms, and hiring a lobbying firm to work with the legislature (in Kansas), all standard political tactics. One lawyer hinted at success in having a school board attorney "from one of our [plaintiff] districts" appointed to the state supreme court (again, in Kansas). They spoke of the utility of lawsuits as a tactic of agenda setting—of keeping school spending inescapably before the legislature when otherwise it might slip from view.[2]

The conference did not consist of litigators only. It included community organizers, representatives of teacher organizations, school administrators, school board members, and other advocates of more school spending, as well as officials from the foundations that finance the adequacy litigation movement. Among the speakers were experts on state finance and on how to run ballot initiatives. The keynote speaker was Representative George Miller, a California Democrat and one of the principal authors of NCLB. He told the conference that "you have to continue to litigate. Only through litigation will we capture attention. . . . You can help us realize the goals and live up to the promise of No Child Left Behind."

Shaping the Role of the Courts

Adequacy lawsuits are, then, political events: they allocate things of value; they propel the courts into an institutional sphere normally reserved for the legislature, which has the authority to raise revenue and appropriate funds; and they depend for implementation on action by governors and legislatures.

Because the challenge to separation of powers is so plain, one might expect adequacy lawsuits to have given rise to constitutional debate within the states. State constitutions are much more open to revision than is the federal one, and amendment of state constitutions takes place in periodic conventions or in proposals initiated by or submitted to the electorate. It does not proceed, as interpretation of the U.S. Constitution does, almost entirely through judicial decisions.[3]

Angered legislators have sometimes proposed constitutional amendments in order to defend their prerogatives, as when conservative Republican members of the Kansas legislature in 2005 tried to couple school spending that had been compelled by the courts with a proposed amendment that would have prohibited courts from ordering the legislature to make appropriations. The proposal failed to get the two-thirds majority in the Kansas house that was needed for submission to the electorate.[4] More school spending had support from Democrats and a few Republicans in the legislature, despite the challenge to the institution.

Where legislatures have fought back by statute, courts have struck the statutes down. In Idaho, for example, the supreme court in 2004 invalidated a law that required parents who were seeking safe school buildings through litigation to sue their local district instead of the state, authorized the legislature to sue the local school districts that joined with the parents as plaintiffs, and required Idaho's courts to order property tax increases in school districts if unsafe building conditions were found. The supreme court held that the law was a special one designed to affect one particular lawsuit, contrary to the state constitution, and also that it violated the constitutional separation of powers by assigning the power to tax to the judiciary.[5]

Legislatures per se are not normally defendants in the lawsuits and so cannot mount their own defense in that forum. State officials who are in charge of the defense do not necessarily have strong incentives to conduct it vigorously. No attorney general has yet won a large following as a champion of opposing more spending on schools or supporting the constitutional principle of separation of powers, and state superintendents of instruction, who often have a great deal of influence in shaping the defense, have even less incentive to oppose increased spending on schools.[6]

State electorates are another potential source of constraint, inasmuch as state courts often are elected. Half of state supreme courts are subject to popular election, and another thirteen are subject to retention elections even though initially they are appointed. Elections for state judges have not in general turned into referendums on adequacy lawsuits or on school spending. As of the late 1990s, they typically have raised issues of tort reform and have pitted corporate interests and the medical profession against unions and trial lawyers. But if the main issue were to become the adequacy of school spending or the propriety of the lawsuits, it is not clear where the public would stand. A Hart-Teeter opinion poll on school spending conducted for the Educational Testing Service and published in 2004 produced equivocal results. On one hand, the public favors more spending, but on the other, a majority does not believe that a shortage of money is the schools' main problem, and it lacks confidence that more money would be well spent. The poll found the public to be divided on whether equity or adequacy should be the policymakers' guiding principle. It did not survey attitudes toward the lawsuits per se.[7]

Where judicial elections have specifically influenced adequacy lawsuits, it has not been to the advantage of the plaintiffs. In the notable case of Ohio, a series of supreme court decisions in favor of adequacy plaintiffs in *DeRolph* v. *State* has been thwarted by a change in the composition of the court following an election in which school finance lawsuits and the role of the court were a partisan issue. Also in Alabama, a change in the supreme court's composition after an election caused the court to reverse itself, but unlike in Ohio, school finance was not a leading issue in the election.[8] Electorates have also fought back against spending increases generally with Tabor (Taxpayer Bill of Rights) laws, pioneered by Colorado in the 1990s, which are designed to prevent state spending from increasing faster than the state population plus inflation. But there is nothing to prevent electorates from violating their own rules, as happened in Colorado in 2000, when voters passed an initiative that in effect exempted education spending from their Tabor law, and then again in 2005, when they approved suspending the law for five years.[9]

Given the absence of any widespread constraints imposed on the courts by judicial elections or by legislators' retaliation, it has been up to the courts to work their way through the justiciability issues that the adequacy cases pose. While most courts have elected to advance into legislative terrain, all the while denying that they are doing any such thing, some have stopped short.

Justiciability

Justiciability has forced adequacy advocates to overcome two arguments. One is that because school spending is a political question, judicial action violates the principle of separation of powers. The other is that the language of the state constitution is unclear and therefore provides no justification for regulating the policies of the elected branches. For political rather than constitutional reasons, the political question doctrine is likely to remain a troubling issue while the clarity of constitutional language is not.

The Political Question Doctrine

On the basis of evidence from state courts, where application of the political question doctrine is wildly uneven in remarkably similar cases, the doctrine does not have much force of its own. Courts use it only if they are not predisposed to enter into a controversy, deploying it or ignoring it as they choose.[10] There is nothing in the doctrine to demand that courts restrain themselves. However, one of the standards in the classic formulation of the doctrine is likely to trouble intervening courts for political if not legal reasons.

William Brennan gave the standard formulation of the political question doctrine. In, ironically, *Baker* v. *Carr*, he said that the doctrine is "a function of separation of powers" and applies in cases where there is a textually demonstrable commitment of the issue to a coordinate political department; or a lack of judicially discoverable and manageable standards for resolving it; or the impossibility of deciding without an initial policy determination of a kind clearly for nonjudicial discretion; or the impossibility of a court's undertaking independent resolution without expressing lack of the respect due coordinate branches of government; or an unusual need for unquestioning adherence to a political decision already made; or the potentiality of embarrassment from multifarious pronouncements by various departments on one question.[11]

This definition could potentially justify dismissing education reform litigation for many reasons. But for advocates of judicially imposed reform, "judicially manageable standards" has been a long-standing obstacle. The other components of the definition are left to the courts to determine. But "judicially manageable standards" requires that there actually be a solution; if courts do not think that they have a manageable solution, institutional self-interest may restrain them.

The lack of judicially manageable standards has, in fact, been a continuing source of frustration for education reform. In *San Antonio Independent School District* v. *Rodriguez*, Justice Powell cited that lack as a reason for leaving the issue to elected bodies. "This case," he said, "involves the most persistent and difficult questions of educational policy, another area in which this Court's lack of specialized knowledge and experience counsels against premature interference with the informed judgment made at the state and local levels."[12] The lack of standards continued to plague education reform litigation at the state level until the advent of adequacy. The relatively manageable standard of equal spending proved unattractive to plaintiffs since it provided powerful incentives to simply reduce spending. As a result, justiciability faced a legal and political obstacle. Legally, anything more than equal spending seemed devoid of precise content or guidance. Politically, equal spending risked reducing spending for everyone. In particular, it failed to promise more money for the poor populations of central cities, in which per-pupil expenditures were often relatively high.[13]

The solution to the dilemma came courtesy of the standards movement. According to Rebell, the standards movement "provided the courts with practical tools for developing judicially manageable approaches for implementing effective remedies." All that remained was marrying standards to the idea of adequacy. Instead of reducing spending for everyone, "adequacy offers the possibility of increasing the size of the pie for all."[14] Hence, adequacy solves the legal and political problem of justiciability. Now courts ostensibly know how to improve education and create a stable political coalition supporting judicial intervention.

However, any optimism is unjustified. Despite the claims of adequacy advocates that they have a precise definition of an adequate education, on closer inspection it becomes clear that without evidence of inequity there is no evidence of inadequacy. Courts can evade the problems of justiciability raised by equity for a while by claiming that they have a new standard that bypasses those previous problems. But the evidence from their opinions indicates that all roads eventually lead back to the inequitable distribution of resources. For courts that engage in what Michael Heise has called "passive dialogue," that is not a problem because they are not actually trying to manage a judicially imposed program of reforms.[15] But as courts engage more and more in "active dialogue" and try to oversee reforms, the problem of justiciability is likely to return.

The evidence since 1989, when the adequacy era began, reveals the difficulty in solving this problem. In *Rose* v. *Council for Better Education,* the Kentucky Supreme Court established an "operative definition of adequacy" that other state courts have since "adopted."[16] The court concluded that an adequate education requires among other things "sufficient oral and written communication skills" for functioning "in a complex and rapidly changing civilization," "sufficient knowledge of economic, social and political systems to enable the student to make informed choices," and a "sufficient grounding in the arts to enable each student to appreciate his or her cultural and historical heritage."[17] Since the Kentucky court did not mandate a specific set of reforms, this broad definition is more political rhetoric than a reasonable judicially manageable standard. Leaving aside the inherent ambiguity of terms such as "sufficient," "informed," and "grounding," the court's definition in fact assumes that in a complex and rapidly changing society the skills needed, and therefore constitutionally required, will change as well. Imposing a manageable judicial standard is impossible because the standard must constantly change.

When courts have dismissed adequacy suits, it has most often been on the merits. But on occasion courts have dismissed such claims because they find the issue nonjusticiable. The Pennsylvania Supreme Court explicitly argued that educational requirements are constantly evolving, which meant that it could not impose its own static standards on the state legislature:

The Constitution "makes it impossible for a legislature to set up an educational policy which future legislatures cannot change" because "the very essence of this section is to enable successive legislatures to adopt a changing program to keep abreast of educational advances." It would be no less contrary to the "essence" of the Constitutional provision for this Court to bind future Legislatures and school boards to a present judicial view of a constitutionally required "normal" program of educational services.[18]

For that reason, the court argued that the only "judicially manageable standard" that it "could adopt would be the rigid rule that each pupil must receive the same dollar expenditures," which it ruled is "not the exclusive yardstick of educational quality, or even of educational quantity." The premise of adequacy presumes that as well. Some districts need to provide an adequate education more than others do.

Two prominent and recent adequacy cases—from New York (*CFE* v. *State*) and Kansas (*Montoy* v. *State)*—show that when courts attempt to overcome the problem of justiciability they will either founder while trying to establish what an adequate education actually is or retreat to the legally safe but politically dangerous standard of equity.

In *CFE* v. *State*, Judge Leland DeGrasse ruled that an adequate education included the "foundational skills that students need to become productive citizens capable of civic engagement and sustaining competitive employment," the "intellectual tools to evaluate complex issues, such as campaign finance reform, tax policy, and global warming," and the ability to "determine questions of fact concerning DNA evidence, statistical analyses, and convoluted financial fraud."[19] These requirements are frustratingly vague, a fact that DeGrasse inadvertently demonstrated when arguing that New York City's public schools were inadequate.

When marshaling evidence for inadequacy, DeGrasse looked at what he called the "inputs" and "outputs" of the system. The inputs were "the resources available in public schools" and the outputs were the "measure of student achievement." Both the inputs and outputs, he said, demonstrated the school system's inadequacy. But the evidence for their inadequacy was based solely on equity. For example, New York City teachers were found on a variety of levels to be inferior to their statewide counterparts. However, simply being less qualified does not demonstrate inadequacy; teachers can be less qualified but still manage to impart the "intellectual tools" needed "to evaluate complex issues." The same problem plagues the rest of DeGrasse's evaluation of "inputs" such as facilities, curriculum, and class size.

DeGrasse was also unable to present any independent standards of inadequacy when discussing the outputs of the school system. His evidence is, once again, comparative. New York City public schools have lower graduation rates and test scores than other New York schools. But that is at best a demonstration of unequal "outputs," which might not be caused by the "inputs."

Socioeconomic factors initially seem to offer a way out of this dilemma. It could be that that New York City's educational system is inadequate for the particular needs of its students. But this opening quickly closes on closer analysis. DeGrasse offers a very grim picture of the socioeconomic condition of New York City public school students. They suffer from poverty, homelessness, poor health, teen pregnancy, and frequent changes of residence.[20] With such obstacles it seems implausible that more spending on education is the solution. It also raises the question of whether the lower "outputs" of the school system are the result of inadequate "inputs." DeGrasse seems to make the case that the quality of New York City schools is not to blame. The state's highest court, the Court of Appeals, apparently recognized that possibility even as it approved DeGrasse's ruling. It noted: "Decisions about spending priorities are indeed the Legislature's province, but we have a duty to determine whether the State is providing students with the opportunity for a sound basic education. While it may be that a dollar spent on improving 'dysfunctional homes' would go further than one spent on a decent education, we have no constitutional mandate to weigh these alternatives."[21]

In *Montoy* v. *State* the Kansas Supreme Court blurred the line between equity and adequacy even more. The Kansas legislature allowed a variety of different taxes based on local circumstances, such as high cost of living, low enrollment, and extraordinarily declining enrollment. But the state supreme court struck down all of them because of their "disequalizing effects." Normally such accommodations would be allowed under rational basis scrutiny, but the court objected because they might lead to unequal amounts of spending. The supreme court did say that "once the legislature has provided suitable funding for the state school system, there may be nothing in the constitution that prevents the legislature from allowing school districts to raise additional funds for enhancements to the constitutionally adequate education already provided."[22] However, the court gave no indication at what point some school districts could spend more than others. For the time being the court is demanding only that more spending be authorized to equalize expenditures across school districts.

These cases then indicate that outside of equity, adequacy has little precise content. Without inequity there is no evidence of inadequacy. But the appeal of adequacy is that it is not based on equity.

The adequacy advocates driving the litigation have searched along with the courts for conceptual foundations. Rebell says that a "core constitutional concept" has emerged from recent adequacy lawsuits. That concept, he says, emphasizes that an adequate education must (1) prepare students to be citizens and economic participants in a democratic society; (2) relate to contemporary, not archaic educational needs; (3) be pegged to a "more than minimal" level; and (4) focus on opportunity rather than outcome.[23]

What characterizes these components is that they are hopelessly unclear. For instance, to explain the meaning of "to be citizens and economic participants in a democratic society," he says that "there is widespread agreement that an adequate system of education is one that 'ensures that a child is equipped to participate in political affairs and compete with his or her peers in the labor market.'" As evidence of this agreement, he quotes the Vermont Supreme Court's opinion in its largely equity, rather than adequacy, based decision, which held that the state constitution guarantees "preparation 'to live in today's global marketplace.'" The idea that education should "relate to contemporary, not archaic educational needs" means that as "the level of skills necessary to participate as a citizen and as a wage-earner in society rise, expectations for an adequate education will also necessarily rise."[24] These tautological explanations have no content because tautologies have no content. Defining a generality with more generalities does not make a generality more precise. As a result, adequacy advocates turn to money. The way courts guarantee this core constitutional concept is by ensuring "the availability of essential resources." As *CFE* v. *State* shows, the easiest way to gauge "essential resources" is by comparison with other school districts.

Adequacy advocates then face a dilemma. How can they provide a clear standard that is distinct from equity but does not undermine the political support needed to sustain judicial intervention? Costing out studies, which allegedly give judges a precise measure of how much it costs to educate students adequately, could provide a solution to this dilemma, but they are unlikely to do so for several reasons. If these studies come back with a single figure for all students, then it is nothing more than equity. If they return with different numbers for different districts, it increases the likelihood of political resistance. If they return with an extravagantly high number, as seems invariably to be the case, legislatures and governors are likely to ignore them.[25]

Constitutional Language

The state constitutional education clauses also raise questions based on separation of powers about the appropriateness of judicial intervention. However, while the language raises questions, it is unlikely to undermine the movement the way that the political question doctrine potentially could. Simply put, saying that the constitution requires an "adequate" education is politically popular. It will become unpopular only if voters start connecting higher taxes with the definition. But that the public does not oppose broad interpretations of education clauses does not mean that the interpretation is proper.

The state education clauses are characterized by generality and often by their delegation of authority to the legislature. Scholars have divided the different clauses on the basis of their language. Some clauses simply require free public schools. Others imply a standard of quality such as "thorough and efficient" or "high quality." The strongest give education a special status, calling it "fundamental" or "primary."[26]

While scholars and activists have made much of the difference in constitutional language and sometimes hazarded—incorrect—predictions about the success of reform litigation based on the language, it seems fairly clear that constitutional language has little influence on state courts.[27] One would expect that constitutional language would affect the outcome of adequacy suits, but that has not been the case. Rebell argues that "[s]pecific definitions of education adequacy are, of course, created by particular state constitutional provisions, statutes, and regulation," but in a footnote in the same article, he points out that state constitutional language apparently has little relationship to court decisions.[28] Adequacy suits have failed in states with stronger language, such as Maine and Illinois, but won in states with weaker language, such as North Carolina and New York.

The reason is relatively clear: the distinctions between weak and strong education clauses have been too finely drawn. It is not unfair to call all of them, as one scholar has, "inherently nebulous."[29] Even the most specific clauses are hopelessly general. What for instance does it mean to say that education is a "primary" obligation of a state? How does one know when the state has not made it (or some other constitutionally grounded function such as transportation) a "primary" obligation?

The obvious question is whether it is appropriate for the judiciary to find in these generalities the specific standards that it imposes on legislatures. In states that have rejected adequacy suits, the courts' analyses have hinged on the inherent arbitrariness of finding a specific standard and the unconstitutionality of applying a static interpretation on clauses whose meaning must evolve. In Pennsylvania, the court ruled that the "Constitution 'makes it impossible for a legislature to set up an educational policy which future legislatures cannot change' because 'the very essence of this section [the education clause] is to enable successive legislatures to adopt a changing program to keep abreast of educational advances.'" Thus, it would be unconstitutional to impose "a present judicial view" of what the constitution requires.[30] In Illinois, which has one of the more demanding education clauses, the court also ruled that it would be impossible to divine any meaning from it. The Illinois Constitution says that the state must "provide for an efficient system of high-quality public educational institutions and services." But twice the court held that "[i]t would be a transparent conceit to suggest that whatever standards of quality courts might develop would actually be derived from the constitution in any meaningful sense."[31] Judicial standards then would be hopelessly capricious, composed of nothing but a court's own preferences.

A potential way around this problem is the model adopted by many state courts, finding that the educational system is unconstitutional but leaving it to the legislature to provide a remedy. Much like Justice Stewart in offering his definition of pornography, they simply know inadequate education when they see it. Of course, saying that something is unconstitutional implies that one has some standard of constitutionality. Allowing legislatures to produce a remedy helps ameliorate the danger of violating the principle of separation of powers, but it does little to overcome the arbitrariness of judicial intervention. In fact, this approach exacerbates it because the court does not have to define any meaningful standard of adequacy. The court just strikes down the system because the system strikes the court the wrong way, and it never has to explain precisely why it is inadequate.

Since education clauses provide little textual substance, it is unsurprising that their analysis by courts in successful adequacy suits is sparse. It is occasionally nothing more than a bald assertion obscured by fallacious reasoning. For instance in *Abbeville* v. *State,* in South Carolina, the supreme court simply asserted that the education clause, in spite of its lack of qualitative language, must have a qualitative component. The circuit court had initially dismissed the case on the ground that the state constitution's education clause—"The General Assembly shall provide for the maintenance and support of a system of free public schools open to all children in the state"—did not impose a qualitative standard on the legislature.[32] However, the supreme court said that in refusing to find any qualitative standard, the circuit court had failed "to decide the meaning of the education clause."[33] The supreme court said that the circuit court had a "duty to interpret and declare the meaning" of the clause. In reality, the supreme court was simply saying that the circuit court's interpretation was wrong. But by saying that the circuit court had failed to interpret the clause and neglected its judicial duty, the supreme court was able to smuggle an unstated premise into its interpretation of the clause, which was that if one interprets the clause one must find a qualitative requirement. Thus, the supreme court does not have to justify its interpretation, and it never does: it is simply doing its job. Interpretation means arriving at the court's interpretation.

In New York, also the owner of a sparely worded education clause, Judge De Grasse without apology explained that in the "third wave" of education litigation, courts "are called on to give content to Education Clauses that are composed of terse generalities,"[34] in New York's case the following: "The legislature shall provide for the maintenance and support of a system of free common schools, wherein all the children of this state may be educated."[35] From that clause, De Grasse determined that the New York City schools were unconstitutional in everything from library expenditures to arts courses. The judge had become completely unmoored from the text and was sailing in purely policy waters.

Judicial Competence

When considering the competence of state courts, the analysis must distinguish between courts that order specific remedies and those that find the educational system unconstitutional but let elected branches decide what should be done. When courts are more reticent, the principle of separation of powers is less likely to be offended and concerns about the judicial capacity for policymaking are likely to be more limited. The following analysis concentrates on the problems confronting more aggressive courts, whose number has increased in the era of adequacy. Despite the assurances of adequacy advocates that courts now have the tools necessary for implementing effective reforms, there are historical and institutional reasons for skepticism.

For example, Rebell has argued that evidence "has demonstrated to the courts' satisfaction that educational resources, if effectively utilized, can result in impressive learning gains by at-risk students" but "that these demonstrations have not yet been brought to scale because sufficient resources have never been made available in large urban school districts or other systems with large numbers of at-risk students."[36] Initially it should be noted that even academic supporters of equity and adequacy suits are cautious and tentative about advancing claims that "money matters," a question that is the subject of a growing and contested academic literature.[37] Confidence that money will be effectively utilized is largely confined to political advocates. But more fundamentally, there is in fact historical evidence that bringing resources "to scale" is the most difficult part of educational reform.

In *Missouri* v. *Jenkins*, the long-running (1977–2003) desegregation case that provides the closest federal parallel to the adequacy cases, a district judge ordered massive state expenditures, more than $2 billion in the end, to improve the Kansas City, Missouri, school system. The dual aims of the order were to attract white students from the suburbs and private schools back into the system and to offer a better education to the majority black population already enrolled. A central focus of the remedial plan was the implementation of an "effective schools" program. There was substantial evidence that the program actually worked, but all of the studies looked at implementation in single schools, not at systemwide implementation. The plaintiff's attorney, who called the case an "end run" on *San Antonio* v. *Rodriguez*, said that the problem was that no one "understood the problems of scaling something up to a district wide remedy."[38] Implementing the program across such a large and dysfunctional system proved impossible. The inertia of the system overwhelmed the best efforts of the court, the plaintiff's attorney, and their team of educational experts. Desegregation was not achieved, nor did the money improve the quality of education in Kansas City, judging from evidence such as test scores and graduation rates, which if anything grew worse.[39]

While *Missouri* v. *Jenkins* is only a single case, it should give pause to anyone convinced that a reform program can be "scaled up" in a district as large as New York City's. The court called on the best and brightest minds in urban education; moreover, the Kansas City school system had only around 35,000 students. New York City today has 1.1 million.

Adverse evidence is emerging also from New Jersey, home of one of the most aggressive supreme courts with one of the longest histories of school finance litigation. A recent story in the *New York Times* described the inability of the state government to carry out an $8.6 billion capital improvement program that the supreme court ordered in 1998 to reduce the disparity between suburban and urban facilities. The legislature responded with authorization in 2000, but the special Schools Construction Corporation, which the governor created in 2002, has proved more adept at demolishing homes than constructing new schools, with demoralizing consequences for the cities that are the putative beneficiaries of the court's largesse. Administrative agencies of ordinary capacity falter under the burden of extraordinary responsibilities, even those as relatively simple as the construction of buildings.[40]

There is a well-developed body of literature documenting the institutional difficulties that courts have in creating social change, beginning in 1977 with Donald Horowitz's pioneering book, *The Courts and Social Policy*.[41] This literature grew up around the study of federal courts, which, as *Missouri* v. *Jenkins* illustrates, were not shy about imposing their own policies. To the extent that state courts are beginning to behave like federal courts, much of this literature applies.

Horowitz said that litigation is a poor vehicle for making policy because, among other things, the adversarial format produces unreliable information, leads to unintended consequences, and artificially isolates issues that are connected in the real world. Examples of all of these problems—*inadequate information, unintended consequences,* and *isolated issues*— can be found in the adequacy litigation.

Horowitz argued that generalist judges lack the capacity to assimilate and evaluate the specialized information that policymaking often requires. It is doubtful, however, that state court judges are so bound to the profession of law that they have the trained incapacity that Horowitz feared. State supreme courts, which are physically located in state capitals close to other branches of government and whose members often are elected and subject to mandatory retirement at a certain age, are more fluid and exposed to the social context of their policymaking than are federal courts, whose members are appointed for life. Their members often bring to the bench eclectic experience in civic affairs and public office. We found that as of 1997 more than half of the state supreme courts included one or more members who had served in the state legislature, either as an elected member or as staff. Nevertheless, once on the bench state judges are subject to the constraints and liabilities of their role, which lead them to act as if they know more than they do, often by crediting unreliable expert testimony, because only with the pretense of knowledge can they settle cases and controversies and issue authoritative decrees. Being judges requires them to pretend to a wisdom that in truth no one possesses in the fiercely disputed world of education policy, curriculum design, and school management.

An example of judicial action with inadequate information is found in Kansas, where a willfully blinkered court chose to rely on one study, by the firm of Augenblick and Myers (A&M), in ordering how much the legislature should appropriate. Ironically, the study had been commissioned by the legislature, and to compound the irony, John L. Myers, the firm's co-principal, had served six years (1977–83) in the Kansas legislature, as well as in the executive branch of the state government.

In *Montoy* v. *State*, the Kansas Supreme Court said it would be guided by the A&M study because it was "competent evidence presented at trial"; the legislature "maintained the overall authority to shape the contours of the study"; it was "the only analysis resembling a cost study" before the court; and the state Board of Education and Department of Education had concurred with the results.[42] The implication of this reasoning—other than that legislatures must follow the recommendations of studies that they commission—is that the court was unwilling to seek as much information as possible. The court assumed the reliability of the study and impugned the motives of members of the legislature who disputed its findings. It repeatedly said that it must make its decision "based solely on the record before us," an artificial but convenient standard peculiar to litigation. Despite the court's exaggerated rhetoric claiming that it could not ask "current Kansas students to 'be patient'" and that "[t]he time for their education is now," there was no compelling reason for haste, unless it was that a Shawnee County district court judge in Topeka, the trial judge, was threatening to close the state's schools, a threat subject to the approval of the state supreme court.[43] Making a more informed decision was apparently sacrificed to reach an outcome under circumstances of mounting stress.

A contrasting example of inadequate information is available from the *Abbott* litigation in New Jersey, where the courts have ordered implementation of the well-known Success for All (SFA) reading program of Robert Slavin and Nancy Madden of Johns Hopkins University. Because of their high degree of autonomy, the New Jersey courts resemble federal courts more than those of any other state, but in this case a trial judge followed the advice of the state's education commissioner in ordering the adoption of SFA, perhaps reasoning that this would increase the chances of acceptance by teachers.[44] SFA had been opposed by the Education Law Center of New Jersey, a leading participant in the litigation movement. The judge visited schools in advance of his ruling to watch SFA in action and gathered all the information he could, but many New Jersey teachers nonetheless were resentful and frustrated at having the program thrust upon them. Meanwhile, critical evaluations of SFA from professional experts around the nation proliferated. Peter Schrag concluded that the mixed early results in the *Abbott* districts "were a cautionary signal about the danger of any judicial romance with across-the-board programmatic remedies imposed by even the most thorough judges."[45]

Closely related to the problem of inadequate information is the problem of unintended consequences. Litigation and legislation both produce unintended consequences, but because the remedy in litigation is designed to restore a right or fulfill a government obligation it cannot easily be modified. In *Democracy by Decree*, Ross Sandler and David Schoenbrod explain how court control over special education in New York City created a variety of perverse incentives to place students who were not learning disabled in special education programs. Most important, when a student is placed in special education, that placement increases the amount of money that is supposed to be spent on the child. With a federal court requiring that these resources be made available, it becomes quite tempting for schools to place students in special education, because each special education student means more money for the school. The case *Jose P.* v. *Ambach* led to an explosion of children in special education and of staff needed to comply with the consent decrees. In the end, this litigation strained the school system's budget and starved general education of needed resources.[46] In *CFE* v. *State*, Judge De Grasse observed that reforming the bloated special education program could save "tens of millions of dollars annually" for the school district.[47]

In *Montoy* v. *State*, it appears that the Kansas Supreme Court is on the verge of repeating the mistakes of the federal court in *Jose P.* In Kansas, the state wanted to control the percentage that it reimburses local school districts for special education pupils in order to deter the "over-identifying" that occurred in New York. Normally, that is the sort of justification that easily passes "rational basis" scrutiny. But the court found the argument unpersuasive because the state did not provide evidence that over-identification was occurring.[48] The court did not entertain the possibility that the state's policy, already in place, had been effective because it required local districts to absorb a significant share of the costs of special education. The court has ordered the state to assume a progressively increasing share of the cost of special education.

The final institutional defect is that courts must isolate problems that are connected and demand a comprehensive approach if there is to be any chance of solving them. When courts look at the problems of education, they do so through the narrow lens of the legal process. But education is a broad and complicated area of public policy that is intertwined with other broad and complicated areas of public policy. But because courts can deal only with the issue before them, their approach is inherently piecemeal. For example, in New York, as mentioned, the trial and appeals courts admitted that the problem of educational performance in New York City did not arise solely out of deficiencies in the educational system. Poverty, family structure, crime, and poor health obviously affect whether a child succeeds in school. Improving educational performance would require confronting all of these social problems, a task that a lawsuit is poorly equipped for. As the appeals court, quoted before, stated: "While it may be that a dollar spent on improving 'dysfunctional homes' would go further than one spent on a decent education, we have no constitutional mandate to weigh these alternatives."[49] Weighing these alternatives and considering their opportunity costs would be the mark of a rational approach to public policy. Unless courts are willing to expand the scope of these cases beyond education, they cannot do that. The statement from the appeals court is tantamount to an admission that it is obligated to waste resources.

Even defenders of judicial policymaking, such as Rebell in his academic work, acknowledge that courts will be hampered by many of the same obstacles to successful problem solving that other institutions encounter. In an empirical study that lauded courts for their rationality and distinctive competence in giving voice to principles, Rebell wrote that "the most notable defects in judicial performance, whether they concern interest representation, fact-finding, or remedies, are often caused not by comparative incapacities of the judiciary vis-à-vis other governmental agencies, but by the social, political, and technical characteristics of the particular controversies; or by the limitations of the participants in resources, skill, and motivation, which manifest themselves similarly regardless of whether a given dispute is addressed by a court or by another governmental institution."[50] In devising remedies for what are found to be poorly performing schools, for example, courts appear to be no less inhibited than other actors by the power of teacher unions. In New York, Judge De Grasse cited bountiful evidence that New York City's teachers have lower certification rates, lower scores on certification tests, and a lower-quality undergraduate education than teachers elsewhere in New York State. The New York City school district, he said, has "too many ill-trained and inexperienced teachers to meet the difficult challenges" of the school system.[51] It is arguable that any remedy in New York City should include dismissing those teachers and replacing them with better ones, but that was not a remedy that the judge ordered. Challenging organized teachers could be particularly difficult in an adequacy lawsuit, given the strength that teachers bring to the coalition supporting such suits.

A Radical Revision

The advocates of school finance litigation distrust the political branches, believing that they serve the interests mainly of suburban constituencies, which are both relatively well populated (hence electorally powerful) and relatively wealthy (hence able to finance schools to their own satisfaction). The advocacy movement attempts to unite the poor populations of central cities and rural districts in order to bypass legislatures whose defect, in the wake of *Baker* v. *Carr*[52] and *Reynolds* v. *Sims*,[53] is—ironically—that they are at last correctly apportioned.

Both through the efforts of elected officials—mainly Southern governors, who initiated the late-twentieth-century drive for better financed and more accountable schools—and through the impact, both real and threatened, of equity lawsuits, state spending for elementary and secondary schools rose rapidly in the 1980s and 1990s. A further influence has been the increasing political activity of teachers, who have entered state legislatures as members and whose unions lobby, contribute to state legislative candidates, and participate in referendum campaigns and lawsuits.[54] Between 1980 and 2001, state school revenues more than quadrupled, rising from $45.3 to $199.1 billion, while enrollment in public elementary and secondary schools was rising by a mere 13.3 percent (from 41,651,000 to 47,204,000 students).[55] The state share of school revenue, which surpassed the local share in the late 1970s, rose from 46.8 to 49.7 percent. Recent history suggests both that state elected officials take seriously their constitutional obligation to provide public education and that courts are available to correct flagrant interdistrict inequalities in spending, such as had existed in Texas—although we discern that the precise impact of court-ordered reforms on the interdistrict distribution of spending remains at issue among economists specializing in education finance.[56]

If adequacy lawsuits resulting in active and continuing judicial supervision of school spending were to become institutionalized, the result would be a radical—and unnecessary—revision of a bedrock feature of the American constitutional system, under which elected, representative legislatures have responsibility for raising revenue and appropriating public funds. Instead, judgments of courts in combination with a new industry of costing out consultants would be substituted for the bargaining and mutual adjustment—that is, the politics—of state legislatures. Indeed, this new day has already dawned, according to a presentation that the financial consultant John Myers made to the National Association of State Budget Officers in the summer of 2005. "Historically adequacy was determined politically, using input measures and available resources," he said. "Now adequacy is technically determined and output orientated."[57]

If money—and money alone—were all that is required to educate the nation's children and if courts alone could provide the money, then perhaps one would be willing to entertain, if only for a fleeting moment, this constitutional departure. But then one would recall that other public functions exist, such as health, transportation, and higher education, that make large and urgent claims on the budgets of state governments; that problems other than a lack of money afflict the schools, such as students who arrive unprepared for learning or life in a classroom; and that evidence for the efficacy of money per se is weak and mixed. One might then be less willing to have the core institutions of democratic government cast aside as incapable or biased and to have courts-with-consultants put in their place.

Going Federal

It is a well-established function of American courts to protect individuals from violations of their rights by the other branches of government. It is not a proper or well-established function of the courts to determine the level of expenditures for major public services, even if, in the course of supervising state and local public institutions such as prisons, schools, and mental institutions, federal courts have frequently used equal protection and due process clauses to compel expenditures in an effort to remedy conditions that they found to be unconstitutional. *Missouri* v. *Jenkins* is an example of this practice, from which the federal judiciary in recent years has tended to retreat. Yet state litigation on school finance has sometimes proceeded in tandem with lawsuits filed in federal court under civil rights or disability statutes, as plaintiffs hedge their bets. In Kansas, litigators began in 1999 with one lawsuit that asserted both federal and state causes of action and was filed in a federal court in Wichita. The state's objection to that approach led to the filing of a second suit in a state court in Topeka, which culminated in a victory for the plaintiffs. The federal judge "paused" while he awaited the state outcome.[58]

Fully cognizant of such facts and battle-weary after several decades of litigation in state courts with only mixed progress, the adequacy movement would like to secure a foundation in federal law for its claims, which would then have access to federal courts. That might be done by importing, through amendments to the No Child Left Behind Act, some of the rights language produced by state courts. "We want to see the issue of equity on the national agenda," Arthur E. Levine, president of Teachers College of Columbia University, told an interviewer in 2005. (Michael Rebell has moved to Teachers College to direct its equity campaign.)[59] More or less simultaneously with the reorganized effort based in New York, a West Coast branch of the movement has set up operations as the Earl Warren Institute on Race, Ethnicity, and Diversity at the school of law at the University of California in Berkeley. One of its initial projects in 2004–05 was to convene an interdisciplinary working group entitled "Rethinking *Rodriguez*: Education as a Fundamental Right," which was followed by a national call for papers on the same subject. The aim was not necessarily to overturn the Supreme Court decision, a daunting task if strictly conceived, but to inquire into what would be required to make education a fundamental right—"that is, *a right belonging to all children, protected by an enforceable guarantee of 'adequacy' or 'equality' or both* [emphasis in original]."[60]

The successes of the adequacy movement in state courts thus are to be seen as stepping-stones to the broader arena of national legislation and litigation, in keeping with a common pattern of the development of law and policy in the American federal system. *Rodriguez* may have pushed action down to the states, but action in the states has laid the foundation for a climb back to Washington. If the adequacy-cum-equity advocates succeed in wedding centralization and judicialization in a regime of a federally guaranteed right to education and federally prescribed school spending, transformation of the traditionally local and democratic regime of school governance in the United States, already far advanced, will be complete.

Notes

1. Michael A. Rebell, "Why Adequacy Lawsuits Matter" (www.edweek.org/ew/articles/2004/08/11/44rebell.h23.html [June 2, 2005]).

2. The conference, entitled "Schools for Our Future: Expanding the National Movement for Education Adequacy," took place in Washington, June 13–14, 2005. Derthick attended.

3. G. Alan Tarr, "Introduction," in *Constitutional Politics in the States,* edited by G. Alan Tarr (Greenwood Press, 1996), pp. xiv–xv; John J. Dinan, *The American State Constitutional Tradition* (University Press of Kansas, 2006).

4. David J. Hoff, "Kansas Lawmakers Agree on Spending Plan" (www.edweek.org/ew/articles/2005/07/13/42kansas.h24.html [July 13, 2005]).

5. "Idaho Supreme Court Thwarts Legislature's Attempt to End School Funding Suit" (www.schoolfunding.info/news/litigation/8-30-04idahofacilities.php.3 [July 4, 2005]).

6. Alfred A. Lindseth, "Educational Adequacy Lawsuits: The Rest of the Story," pp. 24–25 (www.ksg.harvard.edu/pepg/PDF/events/BrownConf/PEPG_04-07Lindseth.pdf [September 25, 2006]).

7. Educational Testing Service, *Equity and Adequacy: Americans Speak on Public School Funding* (www.ets.org/Media/Education_Topics/pdf/2004report.pdf [April 19, 2006]).

8. Peter Schrag, *Final Test* (New York: New Press, 2003), pp. 125–55.

9. "America's Next Tax Revolt," editorial, *Wall Street Journal,* June 17, 2005, p. A14; "Tabor's 'Time-Out,'" editorial, *Wall Street Journal,* November 3, 2005, p. A12.

10. See Michael Heise, "Schoolhouses, Courthouses, and Statehouses: Educational Finance, Constitutional Structure, and the Separation of Powers Doctrine," *Land and Water Law Review* 33 (1998): 281–327, and compare, for example, *Marrero v. Commonwealth,* 559 Pa. 14 (Pa. 1999) and *Campaign for Fiscal Equity v. State,* 100 N. Y. 2d 893 (N. Y. 2003).

11. *Baker v. Carr,* 369 U.S. 186, at 217 (1962).

12. *San Antonio Independent School District v. Rodriguez,* 411 U.S. 1, at 42 (1973).

13. Michael Heise, "Educational Jujitsu," *Education Next* 2, no. 3 (2002): 31–35.

14. Michael Rebell, "Educational Adequacy, Democracy, and the Courts," in *Achieving High Educational Standards for All,* edited by Timothy Ready, Christopher Edley Jr., and Catherine E. Snow (Washington: National Academies Press, 2002), pp. 230–31.

15. Michael Heise, "Preliminary Thoughts on the Virtues of Passive Dialogue," *Akron Law Review* 34, no. 1 (2000): 73–106, quoted on p. 73.

16. Rebell, "Educational Adequacy," p. 235.

17. *Rose v. Council for Better Education, Inc.,* 790 S. W. 2d 186, at 212 (Ky. 1989).

18. *Marrero v. Commonwealth,* 559 Pa. 14, at 18 (Pa. 1999).

19. *Campaign for Fiscal Equity v. State,* 719 N. Y. S. 2d 475, at 487 and 485 (NY Sup. Ct. 2001).

20. Ibid. at 490.

21. *Campaign for Fiscal Equity v. State,* 100 N. Y. 2d 893, at 920–921 (N.Y. 2003).

22. *Montoy v. State,* 112 P. 3d 923, June 3, 2005 Supplemental Opinion at 44–45 (Kan. 2005).

23. Rebell, "Educational Adequacy," p. 239.

24. Ibid. at pp. 239, 240, and 242.

25. See William J. Mathis, "Estimating the Costs of Adequacy: Correlations and Observations from Forty-Six Recent State Adequacy Studies," presented at the conference "Schools for Our Future: Expanding the National Movement for Educational Adequacy," June 13–14, 2005 (copies in authors' files).

26. For analyses of state education clauses, see William E. Thro, "To Render Them Safe: The Analysis of State Constitutional Provisions in Public School Finance Reform Litigation," *Virginia Law Review* 75, no. 8 (1989): 1639–79; and Molly McUsic, "The Use of Education Clauses in School Finance Reform Litigation," *Harvard Journal on Legislation* 28, no. 2 (1991): 307–40.

27. See, for example, William E. Thro, "The Role of Language of the State Education Clauses in School Finance Litigation," *Education Law Reporter* 79 (1993): 19–31.

28. Rebell, "Educational Adequacy," p. 230 and p. 257 n. 80.

29. Clayton P. Gillette, "Reconstructing Local Control of School Finance: A Cautionary Note," *Capital University Law Review* 25 (1996): 37–50, quoted on p. 37.

30. *Marrero* v. *Commonwealth*, 559 Pa. 14, at 18 (Pa. 1999).

31. *Lewis* v. *Spagnolo*, 186 Ill. 2d 198, at 803 (Ill. 1999), quoting *Committee for Educational Rights* v. *Edgar*, 174 Ill. 2d 1, at 27 (Ill. 1996).

32. South Carolina Constitution, art. XI, sec. 3.

33. *Abbeville* v. *State*, 335 S. C. 58, at 67 (S. C. 1999).

34. *Campaign for Fiscal Equity* v. *State*, 719 N.Y.S. 2d 475, at 481 (NY Sup Ct 2001).

35. New York Constitution, art. XI, sec. 1.

36. Rebell, "Educational Adequacy," pp. 242–43.

37. See, for example, the introduction to Helen F. Ladd, Rosemary Chalk, and Janet S. Hansen, eds., *Equity and Adequacy in Education Finance: Issues and Perspectives* (National Academy Press, 1999).

38. Dunn's interview with Arthur Benson, Kansas City, Missouri, January 17, 2001. The interview was conducted for a Ph.D. dissertation in political science at the University of Virginia, "Complex Justice: Educational Policy, Desegregation Law, and Judicial Power in *Missouri* v. *Jenkins*," completed 2002.

39. See, for instance, the evidence presented by Judge Arlen Beam in his dissent in *Jenkins* v. *Missouri*, 216 F.3d 720 (2000).

40. Jeffrey Gettleman, "As School-Building Plan Fails, New Jersey Is Left with Slums," *New York Times*, August 26, 2005, p. A1. The Education Law Center in Newark has filed a motion with the state supreme court charging that the state is in default of the court's orders and asking it to order the construction agency to obtain additional funding from the legislature. See "Education Law Center Files Motion for School Construction Funding" (www.schoolfunding.info/news/litigation/8-23-05elcfacilitiesmotion.php3 [September 14, 2005]).

41. Donald L. Horowitz, *The Courts and Social Policy* (Brookings, 1977); Gerald N. Rosenberg, *The Hollow Hope: Can Courts Bring About Social Change?* (University of Chicago Press, 1991); Ross Sandler and David Schoenbrod, *Democracy by Decree* (Yale University Press, 2003).

42. *Montoy* v. *State*, 112 P.3d 923, June 3, 2005 Supplemental Opinion at 26–27 (Kan. 2005).

43. Ibid. at 55.

44. For an extended analysis of New Jersey's Supreme Court, see G. Alan Tarr and Mary Cornelia Aldis Porter, *State Supreme Courts in State and Nation* (Yale University Press, 1988), chapter 5.

45. Schrag, *Final Test*, p. 120.

46. See chapter 3 of *Democracy by Decree* for a comprehensive analysis of *Jose P.* v. *Ambach*, No. 79 Civ. 270 (E.D.N.Y. Feb. 1979).

47. *Campaign for Fiscal Equity* v. *State*, 719 N.Y.S. 2d 475, at 539 (NY Sup. Ct. 2001).

48. *Montoy* v. *State*, 112 P.3d 923, June 3, 2005 Supplemental Opinion at 32–33 (Kan. 2005).

49. *Campaign for Fiscal Equity* v. *State*, 100 N. Y. 2d 893, at 920–921 (N. Y. 2003).

50. Michael A. Rebell and Arthur A. Block, *Educational Policy Making and the Courts: An Empirical Study of Judicial Activism* (University of Chicago Press, 1982), p. 215.

51. *Campaign for Fiscal Equity* v. *State*, 719 N.Y.S. 2d 475, at 492 (NY Sup. Ct. 2001).

52. *Baker* v. *Carr*, 369 U.S. 186 (1962).

53. *Reynolds* v. *Sims,* 377 U.S. 533 (1964).

54. Alan Ehrenhalt, *The United States of Ambition* (New York: Times Books, 1991), chapter 9; Myron Lieberman, *The Teacher Unions* (New York: Free Press, 1997), chapter 6; Dante Chinni, "Teacher's Pets," *Washington Monthly* 29 (January–February 1997), p. 22; Niki Kelly and Krista Stockman, "Teachers Sue State, Alleging Inequality," *Fort Wayne Journal Gazette*, April 21, 2006 (www.fortwayne.com/mld/fortwayne/14395947,htm [April 29, 2006]).

55. U.S. Department of Education, National Center for Education Statistics, *Digest of Education Statistics* (http://nces.ed.gov/programs/digest [August 29, 2005]).

56. William N. Evans, Sheila E. Murray, and Robert M. Schwab, "The Impact of Court-Mandated School Finance Reform," in *Equity and Adequacy in Education Finance*, edited by Ladd, Chalk, and Hansen, pp. 72–98; Douglas S. Reed, *On Equal Terms: The Constitutional Politics of Educational Opportunity* (Princeton University Press, 2001), chapter 2; Matthew H. Bosworth, *Courts as Catalysts: State Supreme Courts and Public School Finance Equity* (State University of New York Press, 2001); John Dinan, "Can State Courts Produce Social Reform? School Finance Equalization in Kentucky, Texas, and New Jersey," *Southeastern Political Review* 24 (September 1996): 433–49.

57. "School Finance Litigation," a presentation by John L. Myers of Augenblick, Palaich, and Associates to the National Association of State Budget Officers, Denver, Colorado, July 20, 2005. We thank the Rockefeller Institute of Government in Albany for sending this source to us.

58. John S. Robb and Alan L. Rupe, "Kansas School Finance Litigation Chronology," in Derthick's files.

59. Karla Scoon Reid, "Campaign for Equity to Push beyond Dollars" (www.edweek.org/ew/articles/2005/06/15/40equity.h24.html [June 15, 2005]). Our observations are based also on Rebell's remarks at the June 2005 conference of the Movement for Education Adequacy.

60. "Rethinking *Rodriguez*: Education as a Fundamental Right, A Call for Paper Proposals," no date, but the deadline for proposals was September 6, 2005. This document is in Derthick's files. We thank Gareth Davies for giving us a copy.

APPENDIX

Significant School Finance Judgments, 1971–2005

THE TABLE FOLLOWING lists significant state court decisions on school finance by state from 1971 through 2005. It includes only decisions made by the state court of last resort and lower court decisions that were not contested. Withdrawn or settled cases are included only if there is evidence that they induced substantial reforms. We also have included litigation that, to the best of our knowledge, was pending as of December 2005.

School finance cases do not fall neatly into "equity" or "adequacy" boxes. We define equity cases as those in which plaintiffs challenged the constitutionality of the school finance system based on the state constitution's general equal protection clause or on language in its education clause that emphasizes equity considerations. Adequacy cases are those that claim relief on the grounds that the state's education clause guarantees a right to a minimum quality of education, regardless of whether the complaint also includes an equity complaint. In making these determinations we relied on the courts' written opinions and, when available, the complaints. The line between the two types of cases is far from clear, however, and we acknowledge that other scholars may reach and have reached different conclusions.

Case	Type[a]	Court	Year	Outcome
Alabama				
Opinion of the Justices	Adequacy	Highest	1993	Upheld lower court liability order.
Ex parte James[b]	Adequacy	Highest	1997	Vacated lower court remedy order.
Ex parte James	Adequacy	Highest	2002	Dismissed case.
Alaska				
Matanuska-Susitna Borough School District v. *State*	Equity	Highest	1997	Upheld school finance system.
Kasayulie v. *Alaska*	Adequacy	Trial	1999	Granted plaintiff's motion for partial summary judgment that system for funding school facilities was unconstitutional.
Moore v. *Alaska*	Adequacy	Trial		Pending.
Arizona				
Shofstall v. *Hollins*	Equity	Highest	1973	Upheld system, reversing lower court summary judgment in favor of plaintiff.
Roosevelt Elementary School District 66 v. *Bishop*	Adequacy	Highest	1994	Required reform of capital funding system.
Hull v. *Albrecht (Roosevelt ESD II)*	Adequacy	Highest	1997	Required further reform of capital funding system.
Hull v. *Albrecht (Roosevelt ESD III)*	Adequacy	Highest	1998	Required further reform of capital funding system.
Hull v. *Albrecht (Roosevelt ESD IV)*	Adequacy	Highest	1998	Upheld reform legislation.
Roosevelt Elementary School District 66 v. *Hull (Roosevelt ESD V)*	Adequacy	Trial		Pending. In 2003, the intermediate court of appeals reversed a trial court decision requiring the state to restore funds to the state's building renewal fund but remanded the case for further proceedings.
Crane Elementary School District v. *Arizona*	Adequacy	Intermediate appellate		Pending. Appeal of 2003 trial court dismissal.

Case	Type[a]	Court	Year	Outcome
Arkansas				
DuPree v. *Alma School District No. 30*	Equity	Highest	1983	Required reform.
Lake View School District No. 25 v. Huckabee, cert. denied, sub nom. Wilson v. *Huckabee*	Adequacy	Highest	2002, 2003, 2004	Required reform, affirming lower court decision.
Lake View School District No. 25 v. Huckabee	Adequacy	Highest	2005	Required reform.
California				
Serrano v. *Priest*	Equity	Highest	1971	Reversed lower court decision against plaintiff and remanded for further proceedings.
Serrano v. *Priest*	Equity	Highest	1976	Required reform.
Serrano v. *Priest*	Equity	Intermediate appellate	1986	Upheld reform legislation.
Williams v. *California*	Adequacy	Trial	2004	Settled with reform.
Colorado				
Lujan v. *Colorado State Board of Education*	Equity	Highest	1982	Upheld existing system, reversing trial court's decision.
Haley v. *Colorado Department of Education*	Adequacy	Trial		Pending case on funding for disabled students.
Connecticut				
Horton v. *Meskill*	Equity	Highest	1977	Required reform.
Horton v. *Meskill*	Equity	Highest	1985	Upheld reform legislation in part; reversed trial court finding of unconstitutionality; remanded case for further review based on new standard.
Sheff v. *O'Neill*	Adequacy	Highest	1996	Required reform.
Sheff v. *O'Neill*	Adequacy	Trial	2003	Settled with reform.
Connecticut Coalition for Justice in Education Funding (CCJEF) v. *Rell*	Adequacy	Trial		Pending.

Case	Type[a]	Court	Year	Outcome
Delaware				No lawsuit.
Florida				
Coalition for Adequacy and Fairness in School Funding v. Chiles	Adequacy	Highest	1996	Upheld existing system, affirming lower court decision.
Georgia				
McDaniel v. Thomas	Adequacy	Highest	1981	Upheld existing system, reversing lower court decision.
Consortium for Adequate School Funding in Georgia v. State of Georgia	Adequacy	Trial		Pending. In 2005, a superior court dismissed plaintiff's equal protection claim but denied motion to dismiss plaintiff's adequacy claim.
Hawaii				No lawsuit.
Idaho				
Thompson v. Engelking	Equity	Highest	1975	Upheld existing system.
Idaho Schools for Equal Educational Opportunity v. Evans	Adequacy	Highest	1993	Required reform, reversing lower court dismissal of plaintiff's claim.
Idaho Schools for Equal Educational Opportunity v. Idaho State Board of Education	Adequacy	Highest	1996	Reversed trial court's dismissal of plaintiff's claim and remanded for further proceedings.
Idaho Schools for Equal Educational Opportunity v. Idaho	Adequacy	Highest	1998	Reversed trial court summary judgment against plaintiff in part and remanded for further proceedings.
Idaho Schools for Equal Educational Opportunity v. Idaho	Adequacy	Highest	2005	Required reform to facilities funding system.
Illinois				
Committee for Educational Rights v. Edgar	Adequacy	Highest	1996	Upheld existing system (issue nonjusticiable).
Lewis v. Spagnolo	Adequacy	Highest	1999	Upheld existing system (issue nonjusticiable).

Case	Type[a]	Court	Year	Outcome
Indiana				
Lake Central v. *Indiana*	Equity	Trial	1987	Withdrawn after state revised funding system.
Iowa				
Coalition for a Common Cents Solution v. *Iowa*	Adequacy	Trial	2004	Settled with reform.
Kansas				
Caldwell v. *Kansas*	Equity	Trial	1972	Required reform.
Mock v. *Kansas*	Adequacy	Trial		Settled with reform in 1991.
Unified School District No. 229 v. *Kansas*	Adequacy	Highest	1994	Upheld reform legislation.
Montoy v. *Kansas*	Adequacy	Highest	2003	Reversed trial court judgment against plaintiff and remanded for further proceedings.
Montoy v. *Kansas*	Adequacy	Highest	2005	Ruled in favor of plaintiff's claims on adequacy grounds but against plaintiff on equity grounds.
Kentucky				
Rose v. *Council for Better Education*	Adequacy	Highest	1989	Required reform.
Young v. *Williams*	Adequacy	Trial		Pending.
Louisiana				
Charlet v. *Legislature*	Adequacy	Intermediate appellate	1998	Upheld existing system. The court of appeal granted defendant's motion for summary judgment, and the state supreme court denied plaintiff's writ for review.
Jones v. *Board of Elementary and Secondary Education (BESE)*	Adequacy	Trial		Pending.

Case	Type[a]	Court	Year	Outcome
Maine				
School Administrative District No. 1 v. Commissioner	Equity	Highest	1995	Upheld method of implementing funding reduction.
Maryland				
Hornbeck v. Somerset County Board of Education	Equity	Highest	1983	Upheld existing system and endorsed adequacy standard.
Bradford v. Maryland State Board of Education	Adequacy	Trial	2000	Required reform.
Massachusetts				
McDuffy v. Secretary	Adequacy	Highest	1993	Required reform.
Hancock v. Driscoll	Adequacy	Highest	2005	Upheld existing system, reversing lower court decision.
Michigan				
Milliken v. Green, vacating	Equity	Highest	1973, 1972	Vacated initial opinion and dismissed case.
East Jackson Public Schools v. State of Michigan	Equity	Intermediate appellate	1984	Dismissed for lack of standing.
Durant v. Michigan	Adequacy	Highest	1997	Required reform of special education services.
Minnesota				
Skeen v. Minnesota	Equity	Highest	1993	Upheld existing system, reversing lower court decision.
Minnesota NAACP v. Minnesota	Adequacy	Trial	2000	Settled with reform.
Mississippi				No lawsuit.
Missouri				
Committee for Educational Equality v. Missouri	Adequacy	Trial	1993	Required reform. In 1994, the state supreme court dismissed the appeal for lack of jurisdiction.
Committee for Educational Equality v. Missouri	Adequacy	Highest	1998	Upheld reform legislation.

Case	Type[a]	Court	Year	Outcome
Committee for Educational Equality v. Missouri	Adequacy	Trial		Pending.
Montana				
Helena Elementary School District No. 1 v. Montana, as modified	Equity	Highest	1989, 1990	Required reform.
Columbia Falls Elementary School District No. 6 v. Montana	Adequacy	Highest	2005	Required reform. Affirmed lower court ruling in favor of plaintiff on adequacy grounds and vacated lower court ruling in favor of plaintiff on equity grounds.
Nebraska				
Gould v. Orr	Adequacy	Highest	1993	Upheld grant of sumary judgment against plaintiff, ruling that the petition failed to allege that unequal funding of schools affected the quality of the education that students were receiving.
Nebraska Coalition for Educational Equity and Adequacy (NCEEA) v. Johanns	Adequacy	Trial	2005	Upheld system.
Douglas County v. Johanns	Adequacy	Trial		Pending. In 2004 lower court decided that claims based on the education clause were nonjusticiable; however, the case is going forward on plaintiff's claims under the state equal protection and due process clauses.
Nevada				No lawsuit.

Case	Type[a]	Court	Year	Outcome
New Hampshire				
Claremont School District v. Governor	Adequacy	Highest	1993	Reversed trial court dismissal of plaintiff's claims and remanded for further proceedings.
Claremont School District v. Governor	Adequacy	Highest	1997	Required reform. Held that current finance system violates constitutional provision requiring taxes to be proportionate and reasonable.
Claremont School District v. Governor	Adequacy	Highest	1999	Required reform. Held that phase-in provision of reform legislation violates constitutional requirement that taxes be proportionate and reasonable.
Claremont School District v. Governor	Adequacy	Highest	2002	Required further reform.
Londonderry School District SAU v. State[b]	Adequacy	Trial		Pending in December 2005. (In 2006, the trial court granted the plaintiff's motion for summary judgment and declared the school funding system unconstitutional.)
New Jersey				
Robinson v. Cahill, cert. denied sub nom. Dickey v. Robinson	Equity	Highest	1973	Required reform.
Robinson v. Cahill	Equity	Highest	1976	Upheld reform legislation and required the legislature to fund it fully.
Abbot v. Burke	Adequacy	Highest	1990	Required reform.
Abbot v. Burke	Adequacy	Highest	1994	Required further reform.
Abbot v. Burke	Adequacy	Highest	1997	Required further reform.
Abbot v. Burke	Adequacy	Highest	1998	Required implementation of specific reforms and remedial measures.
Abbot v. Burke[b]	Adequacy	Highest	2000	Clarified required reforms regarding preschool education.

Case	Type[a]	Court	Year	Outcome
Abbot v. *Burke*[b]	Adequacy	Highest	2000	Clarified required reforms regarding capital financing.
Abbot v. *Burke*[b]	Adequacy	Highest	2002	Granted in part and denied in part state's request for delay in implementing remedial measures.
Abbot v. *Burke*[b]	Adequacy	Highest	2003	Ordered parties to mediation.
Board of Education of City of Millville v. *N.J. Department of Education*	Adequacy	Highest	2005	Reaffirmed the state's duty to ensure full funding for the Abbott preschool program.
Abbot v. *Burke*	Adequacy	Trial		Pending.
New Mexico				
Alamagordo v. *Morgan*	Equity	Trial	1974	Settled with reform.
Zuni School District v. *New Mexico*	Adequacy	Trial	1999	Granted partial summary judgment on plaintiff's claims on facilities funding.
New York				
Board of Education, Levittown Union Free School District v. *Nyquist*	Equity	Highest	1982	Upheld existing system.
Reform Educational Financing Inequities Today v. *Cuomo*	Equity	Highest	1995	Upheld dismissal of plaintiff's claims.
Campaign for Fiscal Equity, Inc. v. *New York*	Adequacy	Highest	1995	Reversed dismissal of plaintiff's claims and remanded for further proceedings.
Campaign for Fiscal Equity, Inc. v. *New York*	Adequacy	Highest	2003	Required reform. (The intermediate appellate court upheld the remedy order in March 2006.)
North Carolina				
Britt v. *North Carolina State Board of Education*	Equity	Highest	1987	Dismissed plaintiff's claims.

Case	Type[a]	Court	Year	Outcome
Leandro v. *North Carolina*	Adequacy	Highest	1997	Reversed dismissal of plaintiff's claim and remanded for further proceedings.
Hoke County Board of Education v. *North Carolina* (*Leandro II*)	Adequacy	Highest	2004	Required reform, affirming lower court decision.
North Dakota				
Bismarck Pubic School District No. 1 v. *North Dakota*	Equity	Highest	1994	Upheld system.
Williston Public School District v. *North Dakota*	Adequacy	Trial		Pending.
Ohio				
Board of Education of Cincinnati v. *Walter*	Equity	Highest	1976	Upheld system.
DeRolph v. *Ohio, as clarified*	Adequacy	Highest	1997	Required reform.
DeRolph v. *Ohio*	Adequacy	Highest	2000	Required further reform.
DeRolph v. *Ohio*	Adequacy	Highest	2002	Held system unconstitutional but vacated prior remand and ended court's jurisdiction over case.
Ohio v. *Lewis*	Adequacy	Highest	2003	Prevented trial court from holding compliance conference or supervising state's compliance with *DeRolph* orders.
Oklahoma				
Fair School Finance Council v. *Oklahoma*	Equity	Highest	1987	Upheld system.
Oregon				
Olsen v. *Oregon*	Equity	Highest	1976	Upheld system.
Coalition for Equitable School Funding Inc. v. *Oregon*	Adequacy	Highest	1991	Upheld system.

Case	Type[a]	Court	Year	Outcome
Withers v. *Oregon*	Equity	Intermediate appellate	1995	Upheld system.
Withers v. *Oregon*	Equity	Intermediate appellate	1999	Upheld system.
Pennsylvania				
Danson v. *Casey*	Adequacy	Highest	1979	Dismissed case.
Marrero v. *Commonwealth*	Adequacy	Trial court	1998	Dismissed case.
Pennsylvania Association of Rural and Small Schools v. *Ridge*	Equity	Highest	1999	Upheld system.
Rhode Island				
City of Pawtucket v. *Sundlun*	Adequacy	Highest	1995	Upheld system.
Town of Exeter v. *Rhode Island*	Adequacy	Highest	2000	Granted defendant's motion to dismiss without issuing an opinion.
South Carolina				
Richland County v. *Campbell*	Equity	Highest	1988	Upheld system.
Abbeville County School District v. *South Carolina*	Adequacy	Highest	1999	Reversed dismissal of plaintiff's claim and remanded for further proceedings.
Abbeville County School District v. *South Carolina*	Adequacy	Trial	2005	Required reform.
South Dakota				
Bezdichek v. *South Dakota*	Adequacy	Trial	1994	Upheld system.
Tennessee				
Tennessee Small School Systems v. *McWherter*	Equity	Highest	1993	Required reform. Having found the school system unconstitutional on equal protection grounds, the court did not analyze an adequacy complaint.

Case	Type[a]	Court	Year	Outcome
Tennessee Small School Systems v. *McWherter*	Adequacy	Highest	1995	Required further reform on teacher salaries.
Tennessee Small School Systems v. *McWherter*	Adequacy	Highest	2002	Required further reform on teacher salaries.
Texas				
Edgewood Independent School District v. *Kirby*	Equity	Highest	1989	Required reform.
Edgewood Independent School District v. *Kirby*	Equity	Highest	1991	Required further reform.
Carrolton-Farmers Branch Independent School District v. *Edgewood Independent School District*[b]	Equity	Highest	1992	Struck down reform legislation in response to a challenge brought by wealthy districts.
Edgewood Independent School District v. *Meno*	Equity	Highest	1995	Upheld reform legislation.
West Orange-Cove Consolidated Independent School District v. *Alanis*[b]	Adequacy	Highest	2003	Reversed trial court dismissal of a challenge of reform legislation brought by wealthy districts and remanded for further proceedings.
Neeley v. *West Orange-Cove Consolidated Independent School District*	Adequacy	Highest	2005	Ruled statewide property tax unconstitutional but upheld the school funding system on adequacy and equity grounds (reversing trial court's decision).
Utah				No lawsuit.
Vermont				
Brigham v. *Vermont*	Equity	Highest	1997	Required reform.
Brigham v. *Vermont*	Equity	Highest	2005	Reversed lower court dismissal of plaintiff's claims and remanded for further proceedings.

Case	Type[a]	Court	Year	Outcome
Virginia				
Scott v. Common-wealth of Virginia	Equity	Highest	1994	Upheld system.
Washington				
North Shore School District No. 416 v. Kinnea	Equity	Highest	1974	Upheld system.
Seattle School District No. 1 v. Washington	Adequacy	Highest	1978	Required reform.
Seattle School District No. 1 v. Washington	Equity	Trial	1982	Required reform.
West Virginia				
Pauley v. Kelly	Adequacy	Highest	1979	Reversed judgment against plaintiff and remanded for further proceedings.
Pauley v. Bailey	Adequacy	Highest	1984	Ordered implementation of "master plan" developed in response to trial court order.
Tomblin v. Gainer	Adequacy	Trial	1995	Required reform.
Tomblin v. West Virginia Board of Education	Adequacy	Trial	2003	Declared reformed system constitutional and ended jurisdiction.
Wisconsin				
Buse v. Smith	Equity	Highest	1976	Ruled that the negative-aid provisions of school district financing violated the constitutional rule requiring uniform taxation.
Kukor v. Grover	Equity	Highest	1989	Upheld system.
Vincent v. Voight	Equity	Highest	2000	Upheld system.
Wyoming				
Washakie County School District No. 1 v. Herschler, cert. denied	Equity	Highest	1980	Required reform.
Campbell County School District v. Wyoming	Adequacy	Highest	1995	Required reform.

Case	Type[a]	Court	Year	Outcome
Campbell County School District v. *Wyoming*	Adequacy	Highest	2001	Required further reform.
Campbell County School District v. *Wyoming*	Adequacy	Trial		Pending.

Sources: John Yinger, ed., *Helping Children Left Behind: State Aid and the Pursuit of Educational Equity* (MIT Press, 2004), table A.2, pp. 320–29; Matthew Springer, Keke Liu, and James W. Guthrie, "The Impact of Education Finance Litigation Reform on Resource Distribution: Is There Anything Special About Adequacy?" Vanderbilt University, 2005, table 1, pp. 38–39; www.schoolfunding.info/; http://www.nsba.org/; and various online databases.

a. Adequacy cases include cases that were decided on adequacy grounds only or on both adequacy and equity grounds.

b. Atypical cases not included in figures 1-1 and 1-2.

Contributors

Christopher Berry
University of Chicago

Richard Briffault
Columbia University School of Law

Robert M. Costrell
University of Arkansas

Martha Derthick
University of Virginia

Joshua Dunn
University of Colorado–Colorado Springs

John C. Eastman
Chapman University School of Law

James W. Guthrie
Vanderbilt University

Eric A. Hanushek
Hoover Institution, Stanford University

Michael Heise
Cornell Law School

Frederick M. Hess
American Enterprise Institute

Paul Peterson
Harvard University

Michael Podgursky
University of Missouri–Columbia

Andrew Rudalevige
Dickinson College

Matthew G. Springer
Vanderbilt University

Kenneth W. Starr
Pepperdine University School of Law

Martin R. West
Brown University

Joe Williams
Education Sector

Index